W9-ANN-530

P. 140

Urban politics
and public policy

Urban politics and

Second edition

public policy

Robert L. Lineberry
University of Texas, Austin

Ira Sharkansky
University of Wisconsin

Harper & Row, Publishers
New York, Evanston, San Francisco, London

Sponsoring Editor: *Ron Taylor*
Project Editor: *Elizabeth Dilernia*
Designer: *Frances Torbert Tilley*
Production Supervisor: *George Buckman*

URBAN POLITICS AND PUBLIC POLICY, Second Edition

Library of Congress Cataloging in Publication Data

Lineberry, Robert L
Urban politics and public policy.

   Includes bibliographical references.
   1. Metropolitan government—United States.
2. Metropolitan areas—United States.   I. Sharkansky,
Ira, joint author.   II.   Title.
JS422.L54 1974   301.36'4   73–15418
ISBN 0–06–044003–1

For our wives

Nita Lineberry
Ina G. Sharkansky

contents

preface

While we were at work on the second edition of this book, President Nixon announced that the "urban crisis" was over. We hope very much that the worst manifestations of the urban troubles are a matter of history. But, even if the President's view is correct, the rationale and relevance of inquiry into urban politics and public policy are not diminished. The need for information about urban problems, policy making, and policies remains critical in an urban society. In fact, the study of urban political life may be changing as rapidly as the urban scene itself. As in the first edition, we have tried here to incorporate the best and the most recent research. Developments like revenue sharing, the increasing fiscal incapacity of some local governments, a growing concern for energy and environmental issues, a renewed attention to the learning process and to school finance, as well as other crucial issues should maintain interest in urban governance.

This edition reflects our conviction that the process of urban decision making has changed less than the problems that decision makers confront. We have responded to suggestions of colleagues and students to expand the policy materials, particularly in the areas of education, law enforcement, environment, and transportation. We have strengthened, we think, our concern for a political economy perspective, emphasizing the necessity for choice among alternative policy options. Throughout, we have updated our evidence wherever possible.

For critical reviews of the first edition, we are indebted to Robert E. Welch, Jr., University of Missouri, St. Louis; Robert E. O'Connor, Pennsylvania State University; Clifford Kaufman, Wayne State University; Henry J. Pratt, Wayne State University; John M. Orbell, University of Oregon; and Neil Snortland, Wichita State University. Janet Boles aided us not only by a persistent effort to update our information but also by a careful reading of the manuscript. None of these people need fear being held responsible for our errors, as coauthors can always blame these on each other.

R. L. L.

I. S.

Urban politics
and public policy

prologue

The urban setting

The 1920 Census revealed that a majority of Americans lived in urban areas; the 1970 Census demonstrated that a majority of Americans are becoming suburbanites as well. Louis Wirth wrote the classic definition of urbanism in 1938: "On the basis of three variables, number, density of settlement, and heterogeneity of the urban population, it appears possible to explain the characteristics of urban life and to account for the differences between cities of various types and sizes."[1]

In terms of *size*, cities range from the community of 2500 people to a metropolis the size of New York City, with 8 million people. In actuality, the legal entity called a *municipality* is hardly ever coterminous with the social and economic city. In large urban complexes, the borders between one city and a neighboring city are imperceptible, and only signs separate one municipality from another. A *standard metropolitan statistical area* (SMSA)—defined by the Census Bureau as consisting of a central city or contiguous twin cities with a population of at least 50,000, together with its county and contiguous counties of a metropolitan character—contains a multiplicity of local governments.[2] Usually an SMSA includes a dominant central city (CC) plus a number of suburban governments, special districts, and school districts. The area described by the Census Bureau as the "New York–Northeastern New Jersey Standard Consolidated Area" is not governmentally

1

consolidated at all and contains twice as many people as does New York City itself.

Density also varies between and within cities, ranging from the single-family dwelling units of suburbia to the tightly packed tenements of the central city. The number of persons per square mile (a common measure of density) in the suburban city of New Rochelle, New York, is 7500. On the other hand, the population density of Harlem's densest blocks, only a few miles south of New Rochelle, is so high that the United States Civil Rights Commission estimates that, if densities in the rest of the city were comparable, the entire American population could live in three of the city's five boroughs.

Heterogeneity is the third dimension of urbanism. Heterogeneity of class, occupational, religious, and ethnic interests generates conflicts that spill over into politics, and the spatial proximity arising from higher population densities exacerbates the conflicts that reflect these diverse interests.

Technically, about three-fourths of the American population now lives in areas the Census Bureau defines as "urban." It is easy to argue, as Senator Abraham Ribicoff has done, that because "seventy percent of all Americans now live in or close to cities . . . the fate of the city and the future of our country are one and the same thing."[3] There is something to be said for this line of reasoning, but it can also be seriously misleading. In the first place, the United States is not so overwhelmingly urban as Census Bureau figures imply. Figures depicting three-quarters of the population as urban are a statistical artifact of the Census Bureau standard—first adopted in 1790—that designates all places of 2500 or more persons urban. Unless we want to think of Tyler, Texas, and Pekin, Illinois, as urban in the same way that St. Louis and Boston are urban, then we shall want to take all claims that urbanization is nearly complete with considerable skepticism. In fact, the 1970 Census revealed that only about 10 percent of the American population lived in cities with populations of 1 million or more and only a third lived in cities with populations of 50,000 or more. Many more lived in metropolitan areas, but in smaller communities, which guarded jealously their own autonomy against encroachment of urban giants. Air travelers flying over megalopolis see both forest and farmland between the cities.[4] A balanced view of urbanization recognizes that, although most Americans *are* urbanites, there are many kinds of urban places.

In the second place, Americans have never been characterized by the psychological and philosophical traits of an urban people. Even contemporary Americans share much of Thomas Jefferson's aversion to urbanism. A recent survey revealed that only 18 percent of the population preferred to live in cities, 22 percent wanted to live in suburbia, 19 percent preferred towns, and a plurality, 38 percent, preferred rural areas.[5] Americans may be urbanites, but their clear preference is for smaller, rather than larger, communities.

Recently a profusion of books and articles with ominous titles have decried the state of urban life. *Sick Cities, Cities in a Race with Time, The Death and Life of Great American Cities,* and *The Metropolitan Enigma* suggest the widely held view that life in the city is increasingly inhospitable.[6] Some observers, however, take a more optimistic view and argue that life in the city today is better than it ever has been.[7] They see a fallacy in lumping together everything from automotive fumes to gouging by ghetto merchants in a single overarching *urban crisis.* Our book is not about the urban crisis and its components. Our subject is urban politics and the policy choices of urban governments, and our discussion bears upon such urban ills as pollution, crime, racial strife, poverty, the transportation problem, and fiscal inequities only insofar as they confront policy makers and only insofar as their existence is recognized by demands for public policies designed to deal with them.

By narrowing our focus to urban politics and public policy, we shall be dealing with an important range of questions, but we shall not feel obliged to explore the whole gamut of problems shaping the future of the city. Although not all the problems of the city are political ones, many of them come into sharper focus when they are viewed in relation to the public policies designed to cope with them. Still, in the final analysis, there may be no more important issue in the future of the city than the capacity of public authority to transform the urban condition.

Even though we narrow our focus to urban politics and public policy, rather than investigating every possible ill of the urban milieu, we shall have our hands full. This book covers a multitude of topics, but tries to emphasize their political and policy dimensions. In Chapter 1, we spell out a simple model of the urban political system which will guide our later inquiries. In Chapters 2 and 3, we examine the economic and political aspects of the policy environment. In Chapters 4 and 5, we focus on the decision-making activities of the urban elites, both formal office holders and informal power structures. Chapter 6 introduces the concept of public policy as an important subject of inquiry, and the remaining chapters focus on particular policy problems in the urban political system. Needless to say, the book can only provide an introduction to its subject matter, and the serious student will want to undertake additional investigation of subjects which seem most crucial to him. This book, we hasten to emphasize, is an overview and an introduction. It will have served its purpose if it demonstrates that urban problems are intimately related to the politics and the policy choices of urban governments.

Notes

1. Louis Wirth, "Urbanism as a Way of Life," *American Journal of Sociology*, 44 (July 1938), 18.
2. According to the latest (1967) Census of Governments, there are 227 SMSAs in the United States, containing within them 20,703 units of local government.
3. Statement before the Subcommittee on Executive Reorganization of the Committee on Government Operations, United States Senate, *Federal Role in Urban Affairs* (Washington, D.C.: Government Printing Office, 1966), pt. 1, p. 1.
4. In *Megalopolis*, Jean Gottman's exhaustive study of the urbanized Eastern Seaboard from Boston to Washington, D.C., two chapters are devoted to agriculture and natural resources. (New York: Twentieth Century Fund, 1961), chaps. 6–7.
5. William Watts and Lloyd A. Free, *The State of the Nation* (New York: Universe Books, 1973), p. 81.
6. Mitchell Gorden, *Sick Cities* (Baltimore: Penguin, 1963); Jeanne Lowe, *Cities in a Race with Time* (New York: Random House, 1967); Jane Jacobs, *The Death and Life of Great American Cities* (New York: Random House, 1961); and James Q. Wilson, ed., *The Metropolitan Enigma* (Cambridge, Mass.: Harvard University Press, 1969).
7. Edward C. Banfield, *The Unheavenly City* (Boston: Little, Brown, 1970).

chapter 1

The urban political system

The complexity and variety of governmental structures, political alignments, social problems, and economic resources that occur in American cities are as complicated to the teacher and student as they are to the urban resident and official. How can we organize and view this material in order to reveal its most important parts, and to show how some parts have implications for others?

Some would answer this question by focusing only on urban government and politics: the formal procedures of elections, councils, chief executives and administrative departments, plus the groups that seek to occupy or influence these institutions. This would be a strictly political approach to urban affairs; it might show how the machinery worked, but would not show the meaning of the machinery for the lives of urban residents. A contrary approach would emphasize the problems of urban life (e.g., crime, racial tension, poverty, pollution, unequal opportunities, the high cost of government), and assess various interpretations of the problems and likely remedies. Yet the problem approach alone does not suggest how problems are—or are not—resolved.

Our answer to the question of organization is to incorporate the structures and procedures of urban politics into a discussion of major problems of the city. There are clear links between urban problems and urban politics. The city's problems monopolize the time of decision makers, and they often find their careers being shaped by their reputations for dealing with—or failing to deal with—certain problems. Indeed, the problems often overcome promising politicians and make the big-city mayor a poor bet for further success on the national political scene.

An Urban Political System

This book highlights the relationships between politics and the social and economic features of urban life. Fortunately, other political scientists have worked on this issue of uniting politics with its surroundings. David Easton describes a model of the "political system" that we can modify to suit our purposes.[1] Our model describes various political, economic, and social elements, and the linkages between them: an *environment* that includes the economic and social characteristics of a community that impinge on the local government, as well as the relevant activities of national and state governments; *inputs* that transmit stimuli from the environment; a *conversion* process made up of individuals and agencies that respond to the inputs; the *outputs*, or policies formulated by decision makers in the conversion process; the *impact* of policies on the environment; and the *feedback* of subsequent inputs to decision makers in response to policy impacts. An overview of this model of an urban political system is presented in Figure 1.1.

Inputs

Inputs include demands or commitments of resources by individuals or groups that are intended to influence the choices of decision makers and thereby to alter public policies. In a very simple political system, such as a very small town, the input process is informal and interpersonal.[2] The only political resources needed are friendship and a little time. In larger political systems, the input process is impersonal and institutional. Political parties, elections, interest groups, and even mass demonstrations dominate the process.

Conversion

Decision makers convert inputs into *outputs*. Urban decision makers may be limited to elected and appointed officials and bureaucrats, or they may include members of a relatively concealed power structure of private citizens. They take the raw materials presented to them in the form of demands and resources and use them to determine public policy. Decision makers, however, are not neutral computers, automatically summing up resources and constraints. Rather, they are human beings who set limitations on their decisions and feel additional limits from the institutions in which they operate.

Figure 1.1 The Urban Political System

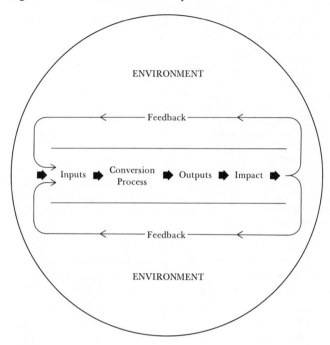

Outputs and impact

As Richard E. Dawson and James A. Robinson have pointed out, many political scientists view public policy as "the major dependent variable which political science seeks to explain. The task of political science, then, is to find and explain the independent and intervening variables which account for policy differences."[3] We concur in this statement of objectives, because we know that different urban political systems pursue different policies, spend more or less money, and tax more or less heavily. A major goal of this book, then, is to explain and understand such variations. But we must also understand the *impact* of policies upon urban populations.

It is tempting to view policies as the end-product of the urban political system, insofar as they are the culmination of the inputs that are processed by the decision makers. But politics does not really end with the enunciation and implementation of policies. Policies have impacts, sometimes intended, sometimes unintended. They may accomplish precisely what decision makers desire, no more and no less, but more commonly there is slippage between the goals of a policy and its actual impact. Moreover, policies generally have side effects or unintended consequences. The impact of, and feedback from, a particular policy can be positive or negative, depending upon the announced goals of the policy and one's own views of the announced goals.

Along these lines, Edward C. Banfield has identified a series of research goals for the student of urban politics:

> One would like to be able to show how particular causes produce particular effects. If one could trace out several links in a causal sequence, that would be especially satisfying. Thus, one might begin by showing how certain "starting place" [environmental] characteristics of a city, such as its size, rate of growth, economic function, rate of home ownership, or the class or ethnic composition of its population exert a causal influence on the form and style of its government. (By "form and style" is meant whether the electoral system is partisan or nonpartisan, whether the office of mayor is strong or weak, whether the city council is elected on a ward basis or at large, whether the system is centralized or decentralized, and so on.) A second link might be established by showing the causal connections between form and style on the one hand and the content of the city government's policy on the other. . . . A third link might be established by showing a causal connection between the content of city government policy and the quality of life in the city.[4]

Banfield's formulation would link the analysis of urban politics and policy with the "quality of life in the city." In the most complete sense, however, this goal is unattainable, because there is neither wide agreement upon, nor any reliable measure of, the quality of urban life. We have, at best, an idea of some things that are not desirable: pollution, poverty, crime, and the like. But neither policy makers nor political scientists are fully able to design policies to rid society of its unwanted urban problems—and guarantee their success.

Feedback

The feedback that comes to decision makers in response to the impacts of earlier policies is an imperfect guide to future policy. There are two broad kinds of feedback, one a "when-the-shoe-pinches" feedback and the other a feedback from technical research on policy impact. The when-the-shoe-pinches type most often takes the form of public complaints. Elected officials are particularly sensitive to this kind of feedback, especially if it comes from groups whose votes they need. Feedback from technical research into policy questions is relatively new. If technical analysis of policy impacts becomes more common, it may be possible to evaluate them in a systematic and continuous way, without having to wait for grievances to build to a boiling point.

Perspectives on the Urban Political System

The components of the urban political system guide us in arranging the features of urban politics and public policy. We have separate sections dealing with the environment, the conversion process, and policies. We try to show how each component of the system helps to shape—and feels the effects of—other components. This approach allows us to include different perspectives and interpretations in a common framework that also shows the linkages in the urban setting. One such perspective focuses on the role of economics in the urban political system.

The argument that economic factors are the primary motivating forces in human behavior unites such otherwise diverse figures as Karl Marx and James Madison. Although their political theories diverge sharply, each begins with an assumption that the seeds of political conflict are sown in the economic differences among men and among classes. Twentieth-century thinkers, realizing that psychological, social, and political phenomena cannot be fully explained by economic differences, have challenged the philosophical underpinnings of such *economic determinism*. Indeed, today it seems clear that no single principle like economic determinism could explain such complex phenomena as racial prejudice, poverty, and criminality. Granted, then, that the economic perspective is only one of several alternative (and not altogether mutually exclusive) ways of viewing the urban political system, we nonetheless believe that certain economic categories are essential to our understanding of this system. We emphasize four particular economic concepts: resources, constraints, interests, and stakes.

Economic resources and constraints

Urban politics is in many respects a politics of economics. The policies of cities depend upon their economic resources to a far greater extent than those of the states or the federal government.[5] This dependence is greater because most communities depend upon the relatively narrow economic bases that lie within their borders.

The economic resources of some communities reflect the continuance of federal programs. Charleston, San Antonio, and El Paso, for example, depend heavily for their existence on the presence of large military bases. Cities also are vulnerable to location choices made in the private sector, over which they have little control. Although location choices are based upon numerous grounds, many city governments mount expensive campaigns to attract or retain industries by offering lower taxes, free or cheap land, zoning manipulations, relocation assistance, and free training of industrial workers. Although larger and more diverse communities are less affected by location decisions, many of the largest cities have lost residents and tax bases because of industrial out-migration.

American cities have enormous resources theoretically available to them, but much of this wealth is locked away from their decision makers by private and public constraints (see Chapter 2). Urban policy making can be seen as the search for strategies to overcome the constraints upon resource use. Policies of attracting industry and the continued search for intergovernmental aids are two devices used by policy makers to cope with limitations on their access to resources. The pursuit of these strategies, however, imposes its own set of constraints. The need to attract industry may make a community wary of industrial taxes, and the existence of intergovernmental grants for specific programs forecloses options in other areas.

While an economist uses the term *resource* for money or things readily convertible into money, a political scientist uses the term *political resource* in a somewhat broader sense. Robert A. Dahl uses the term to mean "anything which can be utilized to sway the specific choice or strategies of another individual." Political resources, Dahl goes on, "might include an individual's own time; access to money, credit, or wealth; control over jobs; control over information; esteem or social standing; the possession of charisma, popularity, legitimacy, or legality . . . the rights pertaining to public office . . . solidarity . . . the right to vote, intelligence, education, and perhaps even one's energy level."[6]

The typical condition of resource use is "slack," rather than "tight," to use Dahl's terminology again.[7] Resources are slack when less than the full supply of an individual's or community's political resources is actually employed. We have already noted, and shall explore more fully in Chapter 2, that communities use only a fraction of the economic resources potentially available to them. The same is true of the political resources available to individuals and groups. Very low levels of political participation and electoral turnout, for instance, indicate slack in voters' resource application.

Every resource is to some degree substitutable for others. Communities short on economic resources can attempt to pirate industry from other communities or can rely upon federal grants. Money can purchase information, time, and political organization for individuals and groups. But even groups without money are not completely without resources: The rich may have money, but the poor have both the franchise and strength in numbers. Groups that have low financial resources can sometimes rely on other resources like protests, charisma, ethnic solidarity, and the manipulation of political symbols. Not all are equally endowed with political resources, but each has slack in some kind of resource. The trick is often to generate the motivation needed to apply available resources. The importance of resources lies less in their potential availability than in the actual extent of their application and in the skills with which they are applied.

Interests and stakes

We also see the overlap between economic and political perspectives in the concepts of *interests* and *stakes*. Political man (like his close cousin the rational economic man) operates to maximize his own self-interest. No economist, of course, wants to be taken literally when he uses a model of human beings as essentially rational (identifying a hierarchy of goals and seeking the most efficient way to attain them) and self-interested (acting only to increase their incomes). In fact, both economists and political scientists emphasize that some people behave, at least part of the time, in a "public-regarding" fashion, setting aside their own interests to further those of the community as a whole. Wilson and Banfield, for example, find that some voters, particularly higher-income WASPs and Jews, vote against their own "self-interest narrowly conceived" and support referenda that cost them higher taxes to benefit other social groups.[8] Indeed, it would be difficult to explain the behavior of high-income groups in supporting all kinds of municipal referenda without introducing a concept like "public-regardingness."[9]

The stakes in local politics are the perceived gains and losses from the political system that may affect one's interests. Sayre and Kaufman list four main kinds of "stakes and prizes" in city politics: (1) public office or public employment, (2) money, (3) governmental services and policies, and (4) ideological and intangible rewards.[10] We expect that persons who perceive high stakes in urban political life will participate heavily, commit their resources to political ends, and be conscious of policy impacts. There is some evidence, for example, that labor unions—active participants in state and national politics—see fewer stakes in local politics and therefore participate less actively at that level (see pp. 70–72). Although both home owners and renters pay local property taxes (renters pay them through rents high enough to cover their share of the taxes), the home owners ordinarily perceive higher stakes in city tax policies, probably because the actual payments are more visible to them. Each may have a corresponding interest in lower taxes, but the home owner sees the stakes more clearly.

Macroanalysis and Microanalysis

The model of the urban political system will accommodate the distinction between macro- and microanalysis. This distinction helps to explain the behavior of whole communities (macro) as well as such subcommunity units as neighborhoods, groups, or individuals (micro).[11]

Macroanalysis deals with the behavior or properties of communities. When we explain variations in the level of public expenditures or segregation in housing, we are explaining differences between communities. When we discuss why municipalities within a metropolis have or have not coalesced into a metropolitan government, we are explaining the interactions of communities. We also use macroanalysis when we generalize about the governmental structures of a community, and refer to them as centralized or decentralized, reformed or unreformed.

Microanalysis examines the behaviors and interactions of individuals and other subcommunity units, like groups, parties, councils, or administrative agencies. To explain who participates in riots, how budgetary decisions are arrived at, and what social and psychological traits affect individual participation in municipal elections is to utilize microanalysis.

The macro-micro distinction enables us to examine any particular behavior from either or both perspectives. Political participation, for example, may vary both from city to city and from individual to individual. Quite often, some additional insights can be gained by examining political participation as a function of both macro (community-level) and micro (individual-level) attributes.[12]

For example, one of the most common characteristics of participation in politics is its strong relationship to indicators of social status. Individuals with higher levels of income and education are more likely than the average to vote and otherwise to participate. Interestingly, however, when we take a macro perspective and examine the levels of turnout from community to community, we find that one measure of social status, education, is actually negatively related to the turnout rates.[13] This finding is puzzling unless we use macroanalysis to explore how a community and its social structure can influence individual voters. Then we discover that the communities with generally high educational attainments are often culturally homogeneous—as in the prototypical dormitory suburb, for example—and have fewer bases of social conflict. Homogeneous communities generate fewer of the political issues that impel people to vote. It is the mixture of social and economic traits in a community that produces political conflict. In local elections citizens in well-educated communities may thus simply have fewer incentives to participate. Many political phenomena other than political participation can also best be understood by examining both their micro and macro dimensions.

The combined use of macro- and microanalysis also directs our attention to the *discrete* (individual) and *contextual* (environmental) factors in political behavior. Microanalysis without attention to macro-level properties may produce serious distortions by leading to a personalistic and voluntaristic view of local politics. Such a perspective, for instance, might attribute policy making to the values of the policy makers without taking account of the environmental constraints upon their behavior. We emphasize throughout this book the myriad ways in which the environment impinges upon and constrains individual choices. For example, the economic base of a community is particularly important in determining the availability of resources. In deciding upon spending and taxing levels, city officials are not free to choose any level of spending they desire, because numerous community factors, not the least of which is the availability of resources, place limits on their discretion. Indeed, a major theme of this book (and of Chapter 2 in particular) is the stringent limitations imposed on urban decision makers by factors outside their control.

On the other hand, macroanalysis, without the corrective provided by microanalysis, may promote a deterministic view of local politics. To view economic forces, social structures, and other macro properties as the only explanations for social change implies that "forces" and "processes," rather than men, are the prime movers in such change. In sum, balanced assessment of urban politics emphasizes both macroscopic and microscopic explanations.

A Model of the Urban Political System

If we combine the elements in the system model with the micro-macro distinction, we can construct the more elaborate model of an urban political system shown in Figure 1.2. Each element in the political system—inputs, conversion process, outputs, impact, and feedback—can be identified at the macro (community) level, and each has an analogue at the micro (subcommunity) level.

Figure 1.2 emphasizes the environment as the source of *resources* and *constraints*. Availability of resources to individuals and groups depends in part, though not entirely, upon the magnitude of community resources. The availability of micro-level resources will enable individuals and groups to make demands on decision makers, and the availability of macro-level resources will enable decision makers to respond to these demands.[14]

Figure 1.2 Micro and Macro Elements of the Urban Political System

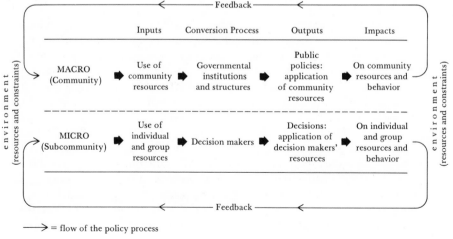

---> = flow of the policy process

FIG. 1-2

The conversion process also has macro and micro aspects. Decision makers, whether they are lower-level bureaucrats or elected city officials, operate within the context of governmental institutions. It is obvious that the attitudes, roles, and preferences of individual policy makers have some effects on policy. If a liberal mayor ousts a conservative, then policies will probably change in the direction of more spending. But governmental institutions also affect the degree of change. For example, change from a conservative to a liberal mayor should produce more genuine difference in the strong-mayor form of government than in the council-manager form, in which the mayor's powers are minimal. Other characteristics of governmental institutions—the structure and rules of the budgetary process, rules and regulations of state and federal governments, the degree of centralization of power—impose their own constraints upon policy makers.

At the micro level, the outputs of individual decision makers are *decisions*. At the macro level, the outputs of governmental institutions are *policies*. Outputs apply the resources of the political system as a whole or the individual decision makers in it to produce certain changes in the urban environment. Any specific policy may be analyzed in terms of its impact upon the community and upon subcommunity units. Education, for example, performs both macro and micro functions. On the micro level, it may increase an individual's earning power and expand his respect for cultural affairs. On the macro level, the educational system may increase the community's attractiveness to industry and thereby alter its economic and tax base.

It is possible that the impact of a policy may be beneficial at one level yet detrimental at another. For example, critics of urban renewal allege that it has benefited communities by increasing tax bases of cities and slowing urban decay but that it has imposed micro-level costs on individuals with lower incomes who have been forced to relocate (see pp. 308–319).

Our model of the urban political system is not a precise theory of local politics or a concrete mold into which all of our analysis must fit. It is designed only to guide ourselves and our readers. As yet, we do not know enough about urban affairs to account for all the manifestations we shall describe, much less to predict what will happen under a given set of circumstances. We propose this model only as a framework for coding information.

The systems model guides us to an appreciation of the relations among phenomena. It emphasizes that politics does not occur in a vacuum. By focusing on policy, we hope to convey some notions about political relations that will help our readers as political scientists and as citizens. Although our model cannot—and does not claim to—account for all that is relevant in the urban scene, it does, we think, combine relevance with rigor. A model should not obscure the real people, their real problems, and the constraints upon their behavior within the urban system. It should, rather, make it possible to organize the fragments of available information so that we get a complete and very *real* picture of the urban scene.

Within each chapter we deal with many issues that are not directly related to the components of the model. This does not mean that we abandon the model. It means, rather, that it is more a framework for assembling information than a rigorous theory. Models are necessarily abstract and deliberately simplified. Their utility lies in their capacity to organize disparate bits of data into some pattern. Indeed, by using one model to the exclusion of others, we may distort research findings that were formulated from different intellectual perspectives. Sometimes we are prepared to pay this cost; sometimes we prefer to break with our model and examine a question of interest to us on its own terms. Our model guides our discussion of diverse subjects, but it does not commit us to mental rigidity. And, although it guides, it does not always govern our treatment of urban politics and public policy.

Summary

We have outlined in this chapter some perspectives useful for understanding the rest of the book. We use the model of a political system to analyze urban politics and public policy. The political system is embedded in its environment, which is the source of both resources and constraints. The task of urban decision makers is to convert inputs from the environment into public policies designed to have an impact upon problems of the environment. Feedback from that policy impact affects future inputs and shapes new demands upon the political system.

By combining the systems model with macro and micro perspectives, we can gain a fuller understanding of the urban political process. The macro level of analysis helps to provide the big picture, and micro analysis enables us to sketch in some of the details. Any particular activity—participation, budget making, the impact of urban renewal— may be seen from either perspective.

In our analysis of the political system and its outputs, we do not pretend to have the final answers to most of the issues; in some cases, we have only hypotheses. But on the basis of the arguments in this chapter, we hope that the reader will have the tools to follow our analysis and to challenge us when our arguments do not fit the realities of urban political life.

Notes

1. David Easton, "An Approach to the Analysis of Political Systems," *World Politics, 9* (April 1957), 384.

2. Arthur Vidich and Joseph Bensman, *Small Town in Mass Society* (Princeton, N.J.: Princeton University Press, 1958).

3. Richard E. Dawson and James A. Robinson, "Inter-Party Competition, Economic Variables, and Welfare Policies in the American States," *Journal of Politics*, 25 (May 1963), 266.

4. Edward C. Banfield, *Big City Politics* (New York: Random House, 1965), p. 7.

5. Ira Sharkansky, *The Politics of Taxing and Spending* (Indianapolis: Bobbs-Merrill, 1969), chaps. 4–5.

6. Robert A. Dahl, *Who Governs?* (New Haven, Conn.: Yale University Press, 1961), p. 225.

7. *Ibid.*, chap. 25; and Roscoe C. Martin et al., *Decisions in Syracuse* (Garden City, N.Y.: Doubleday, 1965), pp. 8–10.

8. James Q. Wilson and Edward C. Banfield, "Public Regardingness as a Value Premise in Voting Behavior," *American Political Science Review*, 58 (December 1964), 876–887.

9. *Ibid.*; see also Eugene S. Uyeki, "Patterns of Voting in a Metropolitan Area: 1938–1962," *Urban Affairs Quarterly*, 1 (June 1966), 65–77; and Alvin Boskoff and Harmon Zeigler, *Voting Patterns in Local Election* (Philadelphia: Lippincott, 1964), chap. 3.

10. Wallace S. Sayre and Herbert Kaufman, *Governing New York City* (New York: Russell Sage, 1960), chap. 2.

11. An abstract, but provocative, treatment of the macro-micro distinction is contained in Amitai Etzioni, *The Active Society* (New York: Free Press, 1968), pp. 43–56.

12. See Robert L. Lineberry, "Approaches to the Study of Community Politics," in Charles M. Bonjean et al., eds., *Community Politics: A Behavioral Approach* (New York: Free Press, 1971), chap. 2.

13. See Robert R. Alford and Eugene C. Lee, "Voting Turnout in American Cities," *American Political Science Review*, 62 (September 1968), 796–813.

14. The term *demand* is used so commonly by political scientists who follow Easton that it is worth noting that it need not imply table pounding. A demand may be articulated as forcibly as rioting in the streets or as subtly as diplomatic discourse.

part one

The environment of urban policy

Environment is our term for the major features that underlie urban policy making. These features produce both the resources and the constraints, as well as the human and economic energies that face the urban decision maker. In keeping with our model of the urban political system, we consider in Part One both macro- and microscopic views of the urban environment: the characteristics and resources of whole communities and those of individuals and groups.

In Chapter 2, "The Socioeconomic Context," we discuss the *irony of urban wealth:* that the vast economic resources of urban America are, for many reasons, virtually inaccessible to urban governments. Factors of distribution, as well as social, political, and legal features of the urban system, keep that wealth from meeting the policy demands of urbanites. In Chapter 3, "The Political Context," we move to a microanalytic perspective, dealing with inputs from individuals and groups. Beginning with the proposition that all political systems must discover something about the interests and needs of their citizens, we examine participation, interest groups, parties, and elections as devices to facilitate the transmission of citizens' demands. We devote particular attention to the timely and multifaceted topic of black politics. Our theme in that chapter is the imperfection of the input process, which makes obtaining information about citizens' needs very costly for decision makers.

chapter 2

The socioeconomic context

The irony of urban wealth is that the tremendous human and economic capital in our cities lies tantalizingly just beyond the reach of urban policy makers. Observers differ in their estimates of our cities' future, but there is wide agreement about the current situation of urban areas—especially about the congestion, pollution, and tensions of the cities and about the inability of local politicians to alleviate these problems because they do not command enough resources to do so. We discuss in this chapter three key aspects of the policy environment of the urban political system: (1) the great economic and human resources of urban areas, (2) the distribution of those resources within the metropolitan area, and (3) the impediments to the use of those resources by urban governments.

It is difficult for urban governments to use these resources because of the distribution of wealth within the metropolis (and the corresponding distribution of problems) and because of legal, political, and economic barriers. In Greek mythology, Tantalus, from whose name the verb "tantalize" is derived, is condemned to have fruit and water recede beyond his reach whenever he tries to grasp them. The irony of urban wealth is not that simple, but the inability of cities to use what lies just beyond their reach is at the core of the American urban crisis.

The Wealth of Cities

Cities are the major producers of wealth in the contemporary United States, primarily because they have the personnel and facilities that process the raw materials of the fields and mines into finished commodities. Almost as important, cities have those specialists in medicine, law, theater, the arts, fashion, and entertainment whose work is highly prized in a culture of increasingly sophisticated tastes. Money flows to the cities to pay for the services of these specialists, and prospective specialists flow to the cities to complete their own training and to compete for employment.

According to Jane Jacobs, cities have always led the way in economic development.[1] She argues against the traditional view that cities grew upon a rural base. Her evidence shows that settled agriculture began in cities, and that historic as well as contemporary cities provided the basic opportunities and technologies for rural development: for example, the markets, hybrid seeds, pesticides, and sophisticated fertilizers that have spurred production; the capital for irrigation; and the financial and commercial mechanisms that have linked growers with consumers. In such a view, human society as we know it is urban, and the large cities of today stand as the latest examples of the sources for economic growth.

The population growth of urban areas is one sign of economic power. Yet this growth is also a source of problems for urban authorities. Prosperity also attracts many untrained segments of the population who want better opportunities for themselves and their families. The cost to the city of providing some newcomers with services is substantially greater than the value of these newcomers' skills to the city's economy. Urban slums, to which many of these immigrants flock, represent a combination of the attractions of the city for poor people and the inability of many immigrants to succeed in the urban environment. Here, again, is an irony of the urban economy: an abundance of wealth that begets poverty even while it reproduces itself, and local authorities who do not have adequate access to the resources to satisfy the intense demands made upon them.

Indicators of urban wealth

Although the economic resources of urban areas are many, ranging from industrial capital, commercial facilities, transportation arteries, and financial institutions to the human capital of citizens' training and skills, state constitutions and statutes generally limit local governments to one main source of revenue: taxes on real property. Local governments determine the value of each taxpayer's property.

Because of wide divergence in assessment standards, market conditions in each community, and the location of one piece of property in relation to others of greater or lesser value, no compilation of property values has the same meaning from one city to another. Therefore, to

ascertain the relative levels of wealth in various kinds of local governmental jurisdictions, we must use indirect measures of the kind of
wealth that is subject to taxation.

We shall use population growth, income levels, and education as our
indicators of the wealth of urban areas,[2] because these features help us
to distinguish urban and rural residents and give us some ideas about
the kinds of urban areas that are most likely to be wealthy. We assume
that population growth signals a dynamic economy that is expanding
rapidly enough to attract immigrants in search of improved living conditions. Levels of personal income indicate the amounts of resources
available to "average" families and should affect the revenues available
from residential property taxes. Similarly, levels of education indicate
the kinds of people who live in various communities—in terms of both
their demands for services and their likely contributions to local taxes.
Urban areas tend to score higher than do rural areas on all these
measures of wealth, and larger urban areas tend to score higher than do
smaller urban areas.

POPULATION GROWTH   The patterns of urban growth indicate the concentration of economic opportunities in urban, as opposed to rural,

Figure 2.1   The Growth of U.S. Population, 1900–1975

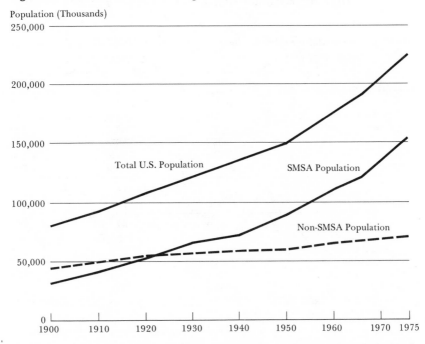

SOURCE: Advisory Commission on Intergovernmental Relations, *Fiscal Balance in the American Federal System,* vol. 2 (Washington, D.C.: Government Printing Office, 1967), p. 29.

areas. Figure 2.1 depicts the population growth in the twentieth century of the United States as a whole, together with the growth in Standard Metropolitan Statistical Areas (SMSAs) and non-SMSAs. In 1900 approximately 42 percent of the American population resided in SMSAs, a proportion that will increase to an estimated 69 percent by 1975. Table 2.1 shows population growth in urban and rural areas between 1950 and 1970.

Rural areas lost population in absolute as well as in percentage terms during this period: from approximately 54.5 million to 53.9 million. The number of Americans actually living on farms plummeted from 15 to 10 million in the short period of 10 years (1960–1970). Most of the population growth in metropolitan areas is accounted for by the natural increase of the population. Indeed, the population explosion is a reality in metropolitan areas; three-quarters of the population increase there has resulted from the propensity to reproduce rather than the propensity to migrate. Rural areas, on the other hand, do not produce enough offspring to replace the migrants to cities.

INCOME AND EDUCATION Median family incomes are consistently higher in metropolitan than in nonmetropolitan areas, as Table 2.2 indicates. Indeed, rural farm residents who live on the fringes of metropolitan areas often find it profitable to commute to jobs in the city, or they profit from truck farming that serves the big-city market.

Table 2.1 *Population Growth, by Type of Area, 1950–1970*

	Population (in thousands)		
	1950	1960	1970
Urban[a]	96,847	125,269	149,325
Urbanized areas[b]	69,249	95,848	118,447
Central cities	48,377	57,975	63,922
Urban fringe	20,872	37,873	54,525
Other	27,598	29,420	30,878
Rural[c]	54,479	54,054	53,877

	Percentage of total population		
	1950	1960	1970
Urban	64.0	69.9	73.5
Urbanized areas	45.8	53.5	58.3
Central cities	32.0	32.2	31.5
Urban fringe	13.8	21.1	26.8
Other	18.2	16.4	15.2
Rural	36.0	30.1	26.5

[a]Communities of at least 2500 population.
[b]At least one city of 50,000 (central city) plus contiguous closely settled areas (urban fringe).
[c]Communities of less than 2500 population and the countryside.

SOURCE: U.S. Bureau of the Census, *Statistical Abstract of the United States, 1972* (Washington, D.C.: Government Printing Office, 1972).

Table 2.2 *Median White Family Income
in Metropolitan and Nonmetropolitan Areas, 1970*

	SMSA[a]	Non-SMSA
Central city	$10,385	—
Outside central city	11,701	—
Nonfarm	—	$8,871
Farm	—	6,819

[a]Standard Metropolitan Statistical Area.

SOURCE: *Statistical Abstract of the United States, 1972* (Washington, D.C.: Government Printing Office, 1972). Data for Blacks are lower, but parallel with respect to SMSA–Non-SMSA differentials.

The distribution of educational attainments shown in Table 2.3 mirrors the distribution of personal wealth and population growth. The urbanite is generally better educated than is his rural cousin, indicating that cities possess greater reservoirs of skills and human resources on which to draw.

In short, the great economic and human energies of the United States are concentrated in its metropolitan areas. Metropolitan areas, containing two-thirds of the nation's population, also account for:

1. More than four-fifths of savings-and-loan deposits;
2. Four-fifths of all bank deposits;
3. More than three-fourths of value added by manufacturing;
4. Three-fourths of the nation's personal income;
5. More than seven-tenths of all retail sales;
6. Seven-tenths of assessed property value.

The Distribution of People, Production, and Problems

Double migration

Two simultaneous migrations—of the poor to the central cities and of the well-to-do to the suburbs—have characterized metropolitan growth

Table 2.3 *Distribution of Educational Attainments in Urban and Rural Areas*

Educational characteristic	SMSA	Non-SMSA
Median school years completed	12.2	11.4
Percentage completing fewer than 5 years of school	4.8	7.0
Percentage completing 4 years of college or more	12.0	7.7

SOURCE: U.S. Bureau of the Census, *U.S. Census of Population, 1970, General Social and Economic Characteristics: Final Report* (Washington, D.C.: Government Printing Office, 1971).

in the twentieth century. These migrations are not yet completed, but they have progressed to the point where now the vast majority of urban population results more from natural increases rather than from the continuing movement of people to and within the metropolis. Metropolitan areas include the greatest concentrations of human and economic wealth in our society. As we see in this section, however, these resources are not distributed evenly within metropolitan areas.

The fundamental distinction in this section is between the *central city* (CC) and the areas *outside central city* (OCC). A metropolitan area is a combination of one large central city and an outer area, sometimes also called the "urban fringe" or "suburbia."

The most prominent political characteristic of the metropolitan area is the fragmentation of its governments. If a cartographer were to color every municipality in each metropolitan area a different color, he would need 474 different colors for the St. Louis SMSA, 268 for the Seattle SMSA, and 191 for the Syracuse SMSA. The enormously fragmented St. Louis area, shown in Figure 2.2, is not atypical. As a matter of comparison, there are approximately four times as many local governments in the St. Louis area alone as there are nation-states in the world. The consequences of this fragmentation of urban governments are discussed in this chapter and again in Chapter 4.

CCs have attracted and held particular kinds of persons and production. The migration to the CC has included disproportionate numbers of Blacks, Puerto Ricans, Cubans, Mexican-Americans, and poor Whites. From 1940 to 1970 over 3.5 million Blacks left the South, mostly for the CCs of the North. Fifty-six percent of all American Blacks now live in the CCs of metropolitan areas, North and South, whereas only twenty-five percent of white Americans live in CCs. In Florida, Cuban refugees populate the CCs; in the Southwest, Mexican-Americans and a small population of American Indians are concentrated in CCs. By far the largest proportion of growth in CCs is accounted for by increases in minority-group populations. The white population in CCs of all SMSAs rose only 5 percent between 1950 and 1960 and remained constant between 1960 and 1970. The black population, on the other hand, grew 50 percent between 1950 and 1960 and another 31 percent between 1960 and 1970. In the five largest metropolitan areas, the white population of CCs actually declined by 13 percent between 1960 and 1970, and nonwhite population increased 44 percent. Especially in the larger urban areas, but to a lesser degree in other SMSAs, the pattern of Blacks in the core and Whites in the periphery is sharply apparent. In fact, the 1970 Census showed that the cities of Atlanta, Washington, and Newark had majorities of non-Whites, while Baltimore, Detroit, and St. Louis showed a more than 40 percent nonwhite population.

A parallel migration, the effects of which are equally significant, has been the movement from CCs. Today *almost all the population growth of the*

	1970 Population	Land area
St. Louis City	622,236	61
Urbanized area	1,882,944	460.6
SMSA	2,363,017	4,119

Figure 2.2 The St. Louis Urbanized Area, One Example of the "Governmentally Crowded" Modern Metropolis

SOURCE: Advisory Commission on Intergovernmental Relations, *Urban America and the Federal System* (Washington, D.C.: Government Printing Office, 1969), p. 85.

KEY TO PLACES
1. FLORDELL HILLS
2. COUNTRY CLUB HILLS
3. NORWOOD COURT
4. BERDELL HILLS
5. NORMANDY
6. COOL VALLEY
7. BEL-RIDGE
8. ELMDALE
9. EDMUNDSON
10. MARY RIDGE
11. SCHUERMANN HEIGHTS
12. MARTIN TERRACE
13. SYCAMORE HILLS
14. CHARLACK
15. MARGONA
16. BEL-NOR
17. BELLERIVE
18. PASADENA PARK
19. PASADENA HILLS
20. NORTHWOODS
21. GOODFELLOW TERRACE
22. PINE LAWN
23. UPLANDS PARK
24. ARBOR TERRACE
25. BEVERLY HILLS
26. VELDA VILLAGE HILLS
27. VELDA
28. GLEN ECHO PARK
29. GREENDALE
30. VINITA TERRACE
31. HANLEY HILLS
32. HILLSDALE

Figure 2.3 The Trend in Distribution of SMSA Population Between Central Cities and Outside, 1900–1975

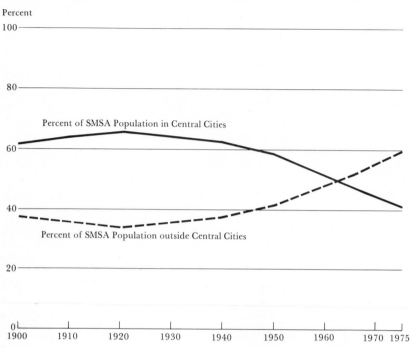

SOURCE: Advisory Commission on Intergovernmental Relations, *Fiscal Balance in the American Federal System*, vol. 2 (Washington, D.C.: Government Printing Office, 1967), p. 30.

United States is concentrated in the OCCs of the metropolis. The populations of rural areas, small towns, and CCs are virtually stagnant. The population advantage of OCC areas, compared with CC areas, is shown in Figure 2.3. In the 1960 Census there was near equality in populations of CCs and OCCs. Since then growth has been concentrated in the OCCs, and projections indicate that this trend will continue. By the 1970 Census, OCC population growth outstripped CC population, with 54.2 percent of metropolitan area residents living in the OCC area. Such growth does not result from larger families in OCCs; it reflects the net balance of out-migration from CCs by those who can afford it and in-migration into the CCs by the less well-to-do. Between 1950 and 1970 the population in each of the 15 largest CCs declined as a percentage of their total metropolitan population. Baltimore's percentage of its SMSA population went from 67.6 to 43.8; Chicago's from 70.0 to 48.2; Milwaukee's from 73.1 to 51.0; and Washington, D.C.'s from 54.8 to 26.9. While the largest SMSAs were growing in population from 1950 to 1970, most of the largest cities lost residents to their suburbs. Among the fifteen largest cities, only Houston, Los Angeles, and Milwaukee increased in population, but even they grew less than their suburbs.[3]

The migration of production

Production has also been moving to the OCCs. The movement of industries and commercial establishments has both followed and encouraged the movement of families, and most economic growth is now concentrated in OCCs. The flight of industry and commerce from the CCs exacerbates the already high unemployment rates in those areas. As for families, there are many explanations for industrial movement. Hoover and Vernon identify five major reasons for choosing to relocate within the metropolis: (1) the search for space, (2) changes in transportation technology, (3) movement of labor, (4) the availability of external economies, and (5) the flight from taxes.[4] Perhaps the paramount reason for both family and business movement is the sheer need for space. The cost of relocating a growing plant in the CC is many times more than that of moving it to the suburbs. Moreover, plants now located in areas zoned for residential purposes often cannot obtain permission to expand.

As rails displace waterways and roads displace rails, there is less reason to concentrate production in small core areas. Indeed, inter-metropolitan movement is facilitated by location outside the congested downtown areas, as are a firm's chances of obtaining a labor supply. The majority of skilled personnel now live in OCCs, and three-quarters of union members under age forty live in the suburbs.

What Hoover and Vernon mean by *external economies* is the input factors and the tertiary services necessary to produce commodities. These elements are more essential to smaller than to larger and more autonomous firms, which have found it relatively easy to locate outside the CC. The smaller (and often less profitable) operations are left in the CC, where they benefit from close contact with suppliers and distributors. The small garment manufacturer is typical of the kind of firm that still benefits from a CC location. Equally typical, unfortunately, are the low wages and unpromising futures that the garment industry offers its employees.

The pursuit of low taxes, though often exaggerated by businessmen and families seeking new locations, has been a determining force in some movement to OCC. We discuss the attractions—and problems—of CC and OCC taxes below.

Disparities between CCs and OCCs

The result of the dual migrations is a series of socioeconomic disparities between CCs and OCCs, reinforced by the fragmentation of metropolitan government. These disparities are illustrated by the personal-income data in Table 2.4. Incomes reflect both demand and supply aspects of the urban political economy. Viewed as reflecting demand, they indicate certain needs associated with poor housing, inadequate health care, and other aspects of poverty, plus the various demands that are made by middle- and upper-income taxpayers; viewed as reflecting supply, they indicate the resources potentially available to policy makers. To be sure, income levels are only imperfect measures of supply and demand, and anyway urban governments rely not on income taxes but on property taxes. The income figures in Table 2.4 must therefore stand as a rough approximation of the disparities in needs and resources within the metropolis. As we can see from those figures, CCs have a larger share— though by no means a monopoly—of poor people, while the suburbs contain a larger proportion of the well-to-do. The ratio of well-to-do (those with incomes in excess of $10,000) to poor (those with incomes below $3,000) people is 0.939 in CCs and 1.694 in OCCs. That is, in CCs the poor outnumber the well-to-do, whereas OCCs have more than half again as many well-to-do as poor persons. To the extent that the poor have more need for government services and the affluent have more ability to pay, it is clear that CCs have a disproportionate share of problems and that suburbs have a considerable advantage in resources. In the words of the Advisory Commission on Intergovernmental Relations, "one set of jurisdictions (usually the central city) has the problems and the other set of jurisdictions (usually the suburbs) has the resources."[5] The most important qualification to this generalization, as indicated by Table 2.4, is related to the size of the metropolitan area. The

Table 2.4 *The Ratio of Number of Families with Incomes over $10,000 to Those with Incomes under $3,000, by SMSA Size, 1959*

Population of SMSA	Entire SMSA	Central city (CC)	Outside central city (OCC)	Difference in ratio (OCC-CC)
United States	1.242	0.939	1.694	0.755
Over 3,000,000	1.830	1.267	3.115	1.848
1,000,000 to 3,000,000	1.605	0.973	2.389	1.416
500,000 to 1,000,000	0.956	0.738	1.293	0.555
250,000 to 500,000	0.828	0.786	0.874	0.088
100,000 to 250,000	0.703	0.731	0.666	0.065
Less than 100,000	0.670	0.763	0.440	0.323

SOURCE: U.S. Bureau of the Census, *U.S. Census of Population, 1960. Selected Area Reports: Standard Metropolitan Statistical Areas.* Fund Report PC(3)–1D, reprinted from Alan Campbell and Seymour Sacks, *Metropolitan America: Fiscal Patterns and Governmental Systems* (New York: Free Press, 1967), p. 23.

larger the metropolitan area, the sharper the resource gap favoring the suburbs. In the smaller SMSAs, the pattern of suburban affluence and CC poverty reverses itself: The CCs contain more affluent populations in metropolitan areas with populations of fewer than 250,000.

In the larger metropolitan areas, therefore, the CC bears a disproportionate number of problems necessitating government action, whereas the suburbs have a disproportionate share of the resources. The CC, for example, contains:

1. More crime, necessitating heavier expenditures on law enforcement;
2. Older buildings and housing, necessitating more costly fire protection;
3. More poverty and more unemployment, necessitating higher welfare expenditures;
4. More aged persons, necessitating greater public assistance to the aged;
5. More substandard housing units, necessitating more public housing;
6. Higher traffic counts, necessitating more highway expenditures and traffic control;
7. More students from culturally disadvantaged backgrounds, necessitating more compensatory-education programs in schools.

The principal disparity that tends to produce certain higher public expenditures in the suburbs is the larger incidence of school-age children there and the larger proportion who actually attend public schools. The economic resources represented by well-educated adults also translated themselves into demands for expensive children's schooling. Suburbs also have one additional characteristic that strains their political economy: high growth rates. CCs are called upon to provide programs to compensate for a decline in their private sectors, but suburban governments must serve the demands resulting from their own growth.

The socioeconomic disparities between CCs and OCCs are reflected in the public expenditures and taxation patterns of urban governments (for further discussion of spending and taxation, see Chapter 7). OCC residents are able to escape not only many problems but also much of the tax burden of CC residents. The average suburbanite pays local taxes amounting to about 5.4 percent of his income, whereas the average CC resident contributes about 7 percent of his income to municipal coffers. Figure 2.4 illustrates that CCs in the largest SMSAs spend much more per capita on such noneducational functions as police, fire protection, urban renewal, public housing, streets and roads, public health, and welfare than do the suburbs. Suburban areas spend a great deal more money on education than CCs do. In thirty-two of the thirty-six largest SMSAs, suburban educational expenditures were

Figure 2.4 Per-Capita Local Educational and Noneducational Expenditures in the Thirty-Six Largest SMSAs and the Remainder of the Nation, 1965

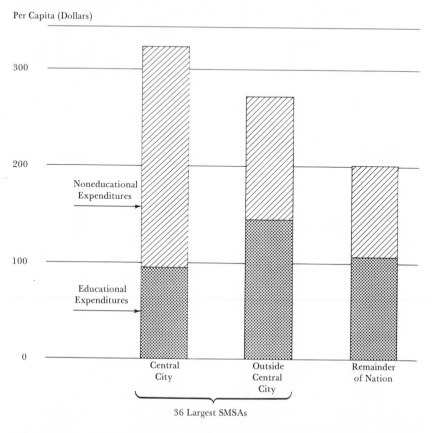

SOURCE: Advisory Commission on Intergovernmental Relations, *Fiscal Balance in the American Federal System*, vol. 2 (Washington, D.C.: Government Printing Office, 1967), p. 72.

larger than CC school spending, often by as much as $100 per capita.[6] It is not surprising, in light of these findings, that the most common explanations for a move to the suburbs include "lower taxes" and "better schools."

This analysis suggests that the judgment that the CC has the problems and the suburbs the resources, though oversimplified, is not unreasonable. The CCs have a concentration of "high-cost citizens" and enterprises, whereas OCCs have the advantage of resources. CCs, like the Red Queen in *Through the Looking Glass*, must run very fast just to stay in the same place. Still, extreme images of either CCs or suburbs should be avoided. Any depiction of CCs as composed exclusively of huddled and starving masses is misleading. Equally, any image of suburbia as composed exclusively of doctors, bankers, and junior executives is, as we shall see in the next section, seriously in error. What we can see from our analysis is the broad pattern common to most metropolitan areas, especially the larger ones.

Suburbia

Suburbanization became a massive social phenomenon in the years after World War II. It has been a response to some of the major social tensions in urban areas and is itself responsible for several of the major issues of urban public policy. The suburbs have also spawned myths, and to understand urban problems and policies it is necessary to examine these myths to see what truth there may be in them.[7]

In suburbia, according to myth, one will find a home of one's own, a small piece of real estate on which to practice yeoman's skills, good schools, plenty of land for recreation, clean and traffic-free neighborhoods, a small-town atmosphere, a local government with whose members one is on first-name terms, low taxes, Christmas lights, a Fourth of July parade, a homogeneous community without social tension, young neighbors, and an open leadership unstratified by age or social class. In many suburban areas, this myth is a reality. When compared to those of metropolitan central cities, suburban homes are far less often judged "dilapidated" or "crowded" by the Census Bureau. Many suburbs also tend to show higher levels of family income and adult education, spend proportionately more of the local budgets on education, and have younger and almost entirely white populations.

These features make the suburbs attractive to many young families, who choose to move there also because of crowding and the lack of suitable dwellings within their financial means in the CC; easy commuting from the suburbs to work or shopping; increasing availability of jobs, shopping, and service facilities in the suburbs themselves; aesthetic appeal of middle-class neighborhoods with private homes and yards; the fear of central-city crime; and reluctance to send their children to central-city schools. Increasingly, young families do not have to face the question of *moving* from the CC to the suburbs. The "war babies" of the 1940s who have now advanced into parenthood have the simpler decision to remain in the type of community they have known since birth.

Not all the elements of the suburban myth are true. Some appear to be rather gross distortions, whereas others are oversimplifications that hide significant exceptions. For one thing, the surplus land in a new suburb is characteristically taken up by private home sites and commercial developments, with the result that there is often a smaller proportion of park land in a mature suburb than in the CC. Suburbs may grow more rapidly than their leaders' taste for—or skill in—controlling land use. One frequent result is a proliferation of filling stations and tawdry drive-ins along a main road that had been tree-lined and free of litter; another may be failure to control unsanitary alignments of private wells and septic tanks. Taxes may be low when the first new families migrate to an established small town, but when the migration increases to flood proportions the demand for more schools and teachers produces a sudden bulge in the local budget that may send property taxes above their levels in the CC. The social homogeneity of many suburbs may be attractive to members of the local "tribe," but, if it is uniformly of the working class and if there is no large tax revenue from industry or shopping centers, it may be impossible to support a level of education that is better than or even as good as that in the city.

The myth also emphasizes high participation in and personal familiarity with suburban government, but studies indicate that the rates of organizational participation are no higher in the suburbs than in central-city neighborhoods of comparable class levels, and voting turn-outs in suburban local elections are frequently lower.[8] Finally, although conflicts in the suburbs may not have their origins in class or ethnic tensions, there are antagonisms. Old-timers and newcomers, Main Street merchants and commuters tend to clash.

TYPES OF SUBURBS   Leo F. Schnore, a specialist in demography and urban growth patterns, has made a useful distinction between two basic suburban types, *employing* suburbs and *residential* suburbs; there is also an *intermediate* type.[9] An employing (or satellite) suburb is characterized by a net excess of daytime over nighttime population. It is a manu-facturing or wholesale- or retail-trade center, producing goods and services for a larger area within the metropolis. Whereas large numbers of suburbanites commute to jobs in the CC, even larger numbers commute from all over the metropolis to jobs in the employing suburbs.[10] A residential (or dormitory) suburb, on the other hand, has a net excess of nighttime over daytime population. Functionally it is a consumer of commodities and a supplier of labor. The economic enterprises found in such a suburb are almost entirely in retail trade.

Table 2.5 shows the population characteristics of residential, employ-ing, and intermediate suburbs in 1960. Residents of dormitory suburbs are considerably more affluent than are residents of employing suburbs. The growth rates of the two polar suburban types also show wide disparities. Employing suburbs experienced a much slower population growth than did the United States as a whole between 1950 and 1960, while residential suburbs grew faster than did the nation as a whole; the 1970 Census confirms these trends.

SOME CONSEQUENCES OF SUBURBANIZATION   Suburbanization produces governmental fragmentation in the metropolitan area. Indeed, sub-

Table 2.5 *Population Characteristics of 300 Employing, Intermediate, and Residential Suburbs of the 25 Largest Metropolitan Areas, 1960*

	Employing	Intermediate	Residential
Percentage of foreign-born	10.5%	8.5%	7.7%
Percentage of nonwhite	7.0%	6.2%	2.4%
Percentage of white-collar occupations	44.6%	49.8%	58.8%
Median family income	$6,869	$7,510	$8,210
Percentage of owner occupancy	57.7%	63.1%	71.4%
Growth rate, 1950–1960	6.0%	18.1%	26.9%

SOURCE: Leo F. Schnore, *The Urban Scene* (New York: Free Press, 1965), p. 178. Copyright © by The Free Press, a Division of Macmillan Publishing Co., Inc.

urbanites claim that such fragmentation is a virtue. By leaving the CC, a young family can escape a political system in which its taxes and its children's education are subject to influence by alien forces. Yet fragmentation also precludes coordination of policies that affect a whole region.

In the suburbs, resources are frequently isolated from need. One suburb may enjoy the tax payments of a shopping center or a major industry, but others must exist solely on the property taxes of home owners. The separation of service demands and economic resources by legal boundaries between the CC and each of its suburbs complicates the translation of private wealth in the urban area into fiscal resources for needed public services. The distinctions between city and suburbs also generate cleavages in the state legislature that may work against the interest of the entire metropolis. If metropolitan legislators were unified, they could more effectively influence the formulas used to apportion state aid. But with city set against suburb, there may be a stalemate of efforts to use the state's taxing powers to overcome local revenue shortages.

It is not true that the suburbs have destroyed the CC. Antisuburbanites have also produced myths. They claim that suburbanites weaken the CC by withdrawing their full contributions as citizens and taxpayers, but it is difficult to evaluate to what extent the suburbs actually deprive the city's policy-making process of needed talent or resources. Commuters can serve the CC as employees of its government or business agencies and even as members of its civic commissions. Moreover, it is not clear that a more heavily middle-class electorate would alter the kinds of policies made by central-city councils or executives. The problems of congestion, social tension, and high crime rates result from persistent social and economic factors, and not solely from the removal of a segment of the population to the suburbs.

The revenue problem in the CC, which deprives local governments of sufficient funds to meet the demands for service, is also composed of numerous elements, including state constitutions that inhibit reliance on anything but local property taxes; state redistribution of aid funds paid by central cities to the suburbs and rural areas; local government boundaries within the metropolis that permit industrial and commercial properties to enjoy the low rates of "tax islands"; high land prices in the central city that prohibit the construction of low-cost single-family homes; and the physical and aesthetic deterioration of the central city. These elements are not easily changed, and it would take more than a greater sense of urban commitment among the suburban middle class to tip the fiscal balance in favor of CCs.

The underside of the urban economy: poverty amid plenty

Completing the irony of the urban economy are the unskilled migrants from rural areas who have come to the city for a better life. Today this migration comes largely from the black-belt counties of the South, from the all-white counties of the southern Appalachians and the Ozarks, from Puerto Rico and other Caribbean islands, from Mexico, and to some extent from Indian reservations.

At the present time, cities all over the country are attracting these unskilled rural folk. New York, Newark, Washington, D.C., Detroit, Chicago, and Los Angeles have received the most attention from the popular media, but there are also streams of migrants to Atlanta, Jacksonville, Miami, Birmingham, Memphis, Denver, and other places. The common attraction is the city's dynamic economy. The migrants no longer anticipate streets paved with gold, but they still come in order to share in the city's wealth, and they look forward to better opportunities than they have had at home.

Today's unskilled migrants encounter frustrations unknown to their predecessors.[11] The urban economy once had plenty of jobs for unskilled workers. Factories and construction were more dependent upon hand labor than they are today, and the municipal government employed large numbers of menial laborers. There are still many such opportunities, but their proportion of the urban economy has diminished markedly. Literacy is increasingly required for even the lowest-paid and least permanent jobs. The spread of the labor movement and union control of apprenticeship programs mean that today's ethnic newcomers suffer from institutionalized discrimination by fellow workers as well as by prospective employers.

GHETTO PROBLEMS Economists often describe themselves as practitioners of the "dismal science" because they focus on problems resulting from scarce resources. When Professor Frank G. Davis writes about the economics of urban black communities, he is even more dismal than is customary for his discipline. He identifies five traits in the economies of urban ghettos:

1. Nonwhite workers' salaries are approximately 58 percent of whites'. Even after adjusting for white–nonwhite differences in education, age, region, and size of city, the income of nonwhite urban males is only 81 to 87 percent of their white counterparts'. This differential of 13 to 19 percent represents the elements that discriminate against non-Whites in the urban setting.
2. There is a net *outflow* of capital resources from the ghetto. This reflects: purchases made by black businesses (mainly small retail and food shops) from outside the ghetto; imports of goods and exports of profits by white-owned businesses; and the export of black labor to employers outside the ghetto.
3. The high concentration of low-income residences attracts small-scale, low-profit retail activities, but excludes manufacturing opportunities due to land scarcity and high land values.
4. Black-owned businesses tend to be smaller and financially more precarious than the "white-enclave" businesses, thus minimizing any hopes for a burgeoning of black capitalism.
5. Industries locate in the low land-value suburban areas, imposing transportation costs on black laborers that make the wages for unskilled labor uneconomic for ghetto Blacks. "The result is the simultaneous existence of job vacancies and unemployed black labor."[12]

Several additional traits mark the larger economy in which the ghetto exists, and have striking consequences for ghetto residents:

1. Investments in industry emphasize technological changes that reduce the need for unskilled labor.
2. Economic growth for industry in the larger society makes black laborers redundant in high-productivity, high-paying manufacturing jobs, and forces them to compete for jobs in low-productivity, low-paying service industries where Blacks are already concentrated. The result of this growth sequence is an inflation in the prices that Blacks must pay for consumer goods, along with a lag in the incomes of unskilled workers.

Professor Davis examines the promise of black capitalism for the ghetto, but remains pessimistic. The structure of black enterprise does not seem likely to generate a large volume of business or high rates of employment. There remains the problem of residential land values that prohibit large-scale industrialization in the ghetto. Davis finds that manpower training programs have not reached the mass of unemployed Blacks: over a 6-year period on-the-job trainees have included only 1.4 percent the estimated number of black unemployed.

Some programs may increase the number or the wealth of black entrepreneurs, but leave untouched the major forces producing black poverty. "Mere substitution of black capitalists for white capitalists under present conditions of resource use is far from an optimum economic condition of ghetto development and growth and could have only minimal effects."[13] Davis' own prescription emphasizes the community ownership of ghetto resources. He would have the sectors of manufacturing and distribution controlled by the community, with the retention of profits as well as labor wages in the community. This is not the place to provide a detailed criticism of Davis' proposals. However, we would be remiss as political scientists if we did not point to the likely opposition from aspiring black capitalists, as well as from the white politicians who would be asked to authorize grants of capital and the regulatory actions needed to establish such ventures.[14]

It is not only jobs, wages, and profits that set the style of life in black ghettos. The widely quoted *Report* of the National Advisory Committee on Civil Disorders reminds us of other features that exist in that economic milieu:

> The culture of poverty that results from unemployment and family breakup generates a system of ruthless, exploitative relationships within the ghetto. Prostitution, dope addiction, and crime create an environmental "jungle" characterized by personal insecurity and tension. Children growing up under such conditions are likely participants in civil disorder.
>
> A striking difference in environment from that of white, middle-class Americans profoundly influences the lives of residents of the ghetto.
>
> Crime rates, consistently higher than in other areas, create a pronounced sense of insecurity. For example, in one city one low-income Negro district had 35 times as many serious crimes against persons as a high-income white district. Unless drastic steps are taken, the crime problems in poverty areas are likely to continue to multiply as the growing youth and rapid urbanization of the population outstrip police resources.
>
> Poor health and sanitation conditions in the ghetto result in higher mortality rates, a higher incidence of major diseases, and lower availability and utilization of medical services. The infant mortality rate for nonwhite babies under the age of one month is 58 percent higher than for whites; for one to 12 months it is almost three times as high. The level of sanitation in the ghetto is far below that in high-income areas. Garbage collection is often inadequate. Of an estimated 14,000 cases of rat bite in the United States in 1965, most were in ghetto neighborhoods.
>
> Ghetto residents believe they are exploited by local merchants; and evidence substantiates some of these beliefs. A study conducted in one city by the Federal Trade Commission showed that higher prices were charged for goods sold in ghetto stores than in other areas.
>
> Lack of knowledge regarding credit purchasing creates special pitfalls for the disadvantaged. In many states garnishment practices compound these difficulties by allowing creditors to deprive individuals of their wages without hearing or trial.[15]

GHETTOS AND GOVERNMENTS The poverty in CCs makes their plight worse than that of other communities within metropolitan areas. It provokes the exodus of middle- and upper-middle-class residents, as well as of merchants, industry, and office buildings to the suburbs, and this exodus reduces the tax bases and leaves the CCs with high concentrations of costly social problems. Local governments, formerly called upon to supply traditional services of public education, welfare, and health, are now asked to support massive programs—including new ventures in adult and preschool education, counseling, job training, housing, and community control of local services—to alleviate the distress of the poor and to attack the basic social problems underlying poverty.

The dissatisfaction the urban poor express at the nature of their public services seems justified when it is viewed in relation to the high level of taxes that they pay to local and state governments. The major state and local taxes (on retail sales and real property) are regressive: They take larger percentages from the incomes of low-income groups than from those of high-income groups. A 1965 study found that sales and excise taxes took 6.1 percent of the annual income from families earning less than $2,000 but only 2.6 percent from families earning more than $15,000; property taxes were even more sharply regressive, taking 6.9 percent from the lowest income group and 2.4 percent from the highest.[16]

These findings may seem odd at first glance, for sales taxes are charged at the same rate on everyone's purchases, and there is no overt discrimination against low-income groups. By the same token, property taxes are not levied directly against the urban poor; they are charged to home owners, not renters. Yet some not-so-subtle economic mechanisms work to the disadvantage of low-income taxpayers. First, the poor must spend most of their current income on retail purchases, even dipping into whatever savings they have or going into debt to make further retail purchases, all of which are, of course, taxable. Higher-income taxpayers, in contrast, use much of their income for investments or other purposes that are not subject to sales taxes. The result is that a relatively large portion of the resources of the poor are subject to sales taxes each year.

A similar principle operates with property taxes. The poor do not pay them directly, but they pay them indirectly as part of their rent. There is little in the ethos of the slum landlord to suggest that he pays his property taxes out of his own profits; rather, he passes the tax on to the tenants, and each increase in the tax rate produces a proportionate increase in rents. Again, the poor pay larger portions of their incomes in property taxes than do the wealthy because they spend a higher portion of their income for housing.

The poor recognize the disadvantages in the local tax system. A survey taken during a gubernatorial campaign in Wisconsin revealed a high degree of awareness among low-income residents that sales and property taxes operate to their disadvantage. They were most in favor of increases in the state income tax, which was progressive and would take the greatest percentage from higher-income families.[17] Other surveys find that low-income urban residents with little education are most resentful about local taxes, whereas the upper-income and professional-managerial-proprietor classes show the most acceptance of current local taxes.[18] Still other studies find that low-income residents express the "illogical" views that welfare, health, and educational services should be improved but that taxes should be reduced.[19] These views are illogical only to the person who pays his fair share of taxes and no more. To the low-income person who needs improved services but who also pays a disproportionately high share of taxes, they make a great deal of sense.

Other service demands growing out of the urban economy

It is not only the urban poor who perceive a need for public policies. Commercial, industrial, and financial groups demand of local governments that public investments be made to enhance their own private investments. Often they justify these demands in terms of micro- and macroeconomics: claiming that what is good for their private investments will spill over to benefit the public sector. If they prosper, so will other residents.

Each kind of economic interest has its own special demands, and the result is competition over urban public policies. Downtown merchants typically fear the competition of suburban shopping centers. They want publicly subsidized mass transportation, traffic control, expressways, and parking facilities that permit convenient access to their stores. They consider the central business district the heart of the community, the single most important feature distinguishing an important city from a rural crossroads. Merchants ally themselves with other occupants of the central business district—the owners of office buildings, theaters, and restaurants—who want to maintain the commercial value of their high-priced and highly taxed properties. Professional, service, and industrial interests value the close interaction possible in a central location, and law firms, accountants, investment counselors, publishers, and advertising agencies share with the operators of manufacturing plants a desire to preserve the appeal of the central area.

Local officials must often cope with the conflicting demands of these various industrial and commercial interests, each of which claims special privileges because of its present—or potential—contributions to the local economy. Those downtown merchants who are not inclined to open branches in the suburbs oppose zoning variations that will permit large tracts of land to be turned into new shopping plazas; the owners of existing apartment houses oppose zoning variations that will permit massive new apartment developments, especially when they are already having some trouble keeping their own units filled to capacity; the operators of a suburban shopping center may oppose a zoning variation for a nearby industrial development if they fear that a smoky or unsightly manufacturing plant will deter shoppers.

An urban-renewal program raises a whole series of economic opportunities and problems for the makers of public policy, for there is frequently sharp antagonism between those who want prime land for development and those who speak for the present occupants of the land. The occupants are typically the poorest residents of the community and often members of an ethnic minority. It is frequently alleged —with some accuracy—that they are to be moved for the benefit of well-to-do businessmen or the prospective occupants of the new middle- and upper-class dwellings.[20] Spokesmen for the poor charge that they are being shunted to other depressed neighborhoods and forced to break whatever community ties they have established in their present locale. To exacerbate matters, the residents of the neighborhoods destined to receive the displaced families often charge that this move will bring the slums to them and expose them to the problems of poor schools, crime, and general social decay.

Public policy makers must also deal with those issues of code enforcement related to housing and urban renewal. Housing codes specify the kinds of features to be provided in each dwelling unit, like the number and types of entrances and exits, plumbing, heat and hot water, fire escapes, trash removal, and general upkeep. If these provisions are enforced rigorously, the problems of physical decay and intense overcrowding that generate slums are not likely to develop. It is the policy makers' task, however, to remind those who want tight enforcement of housing codes that some people need cheap housing. A large and dynamic urban area may need its slums to provide homes for the poor, unskilled immigrants who are attracted by the better life that they believe the city offers or who have been born in the city but lack the training and the good fortune necessary to live outside the slums. In Chapter 12 we shall turn to a more detailed examination of housing and urban renewal.

Local governments are often faced with demands from industrial and commercial interests for concessions. Businessmen insist that they are willing to pay their share, but they object to being the principal source of support for such services as education, health care, and recreation. Some firms—particularly those that can choose freely where they will locate within a metropolitan area—seek special tax concessions in exchange for settling in a specific community. Not all members of the community favor this kind of deal. Industries already located there, for example, object to concessions to competitors that are not matched for themselves. Others object on the principle of equity, claiming that no taxpayer should receive concessions not given equally to all. Such debates are clouded further by ambiguities inherent in the standards of value applied in assessing different categories of land, buildings, and other facilities. We shall see in the discussion of urban taxing and spending in Chapter 7 that tax equity is a subject of great dispute among experts.

Besides tax concessions some firms are interested in service improvements and use their tax payments, payrolls, and local purchases to bargain for higher levels of local services. They want schools and recreational facilities to make the community attractive to their own managers and executives, and they want shipping facilities, electric power, and clean water sufficient for plant needs. They also expect local governments to help them obtain benefits from other authorities. Local shippers seek favorable decisions on transportation rates from the Interstate Commerce Commission and ask political support from municipal officials. Industries seek location of new highways and interchanges convenient to their plants and ask for the support of local authorities in their petitions to state or federal highway officials. When management is caught up in intense negotiations with labor unions, it may ask local officials to urge rapid settlement upon the unions. Companies located in a low-wage area sometimes pressure local authorities to maintain the wage structure by indicating that any major change may force them to relocate.

In this section we have examined a number of key demands on government that arise from the urban environment. Many, though by no means all, are products of conflict of economic interests. Some emerge from conflict among the already well-to-do, others from conflicts between the latter and those who want larger shares of the community's wealth. It is the responsibility of the decision makers to take these problems and apply resources to their solution. Yet the resources at their disposal are not unlimited. One of the most serious constraints on officials' efforts to meet demands is the inaccessibility of urban wealth.

The Access of Urban Officials to Urban Wealth

The inaccessibility of urban wealth to urban policy makers is a function of several problems: (1) an unequal distribution of needs and resources throughout urban areas; (2) legal limits on the kinds and amounts of revenue that local authorities may collect; (3) the "monopoly" of income taxes and sales taxes by federal and state governments; and (4) the failure of local officials to tax or borrow up to the legal limits.

The unequal distribution of needs and resources

The unequal distribution of needs and resources results from what Anthony Downs calls the "Law of Cultural Dominance," and the fragmentation of governments throughout metropolitan areas. Downs believes that most middle-class families want their own values to dominate the home environment, so that "everyday life should be primarily a *value-reinforcing* experience for both adults and children, rather than a *value-altering* one."[21]

Local governments vary greatly in the resources that their residents provide, as well as in the residents' demands for public services. The suburb that is thick with industrial and commercial properties has high tax revenues for its local government but minimal demands for schools and other social services. The purely residential suburb, however, faces high demands for school expenditures but has no source of revenue except private home owners. If the incomes of home owners are high, they can devote ample resources to their children's schooling. Yet residential suburbs that are predominantly working class in composition are often characterized by many children and low incomes and property values. When such communities are new and rapidly growing, they must bear the burden of adding new school buildings and facilities, as well as the operating costs of established programs. Some working-class communities adjoin municipalities with a high incidence of industrial or commercial properties. The industrial complex is likely to draw its labor force from the working-class town, yet the industries' property taxes support only the schools that lie within their own municipality.

In jurisdictions that have more resources than their services demand, some remain untapped. In fact, because metropolitan areas are not governed by integrated institutions, abundant resources lie unused within short distances of unmet service needs.[22]

Legal limits on kinds and amounts of taxation and indebtedness

State constitutions and statutes restrict local authorities to certain kinds of revenues and to certain levels of taxation and indebtedness. Local governments in most states are restricted to taxes on property; charges for city-operated services like water, trash removal, sewage, gas, and electricity; and limited borrowing for capital improvements (for example, construction of buildings and highways or the purchase of major equipment). In several states, local governments also tax their residents' incomes, the retail sales of local merchants, or both. But these taxes are typically low: 1 percent is a common upper limit on local income and sales taxes. Some cities also collect revenues from local "wheel taxes" (on automobiles) or levies on motel and hotel rooms. These taxes, too, typically make only small total contributions to local government resources. The property tax is the single major source of support.

Property taxes may apply to *real* property (land and buildings); *personal* property (clothes, furniture, and other such possessions); and *intangible* property (stocks, bonds, bank accounts). The reluctance of both citizens and officials to reveal their resources in full detail precludes thorough assessment of personal and intangible property, however, and these taxes are widely evaded. It is common for the amount of a local government's debt and the level of its property taxes to be limited to a certain proportion of the assessed value of the real property in the jurisdiction. "Assessed value" is flexible, however, and can be increased to permit more revenues either from taxation or borrowing when the need arises. Nevertheless, legal limits are important in the minds of many officials and citizens, who may keep city budgets low when the limits are approached, even if there are still some options to increase total valuation.

The set of taxes that is legally available to a local government may not be adequate for its revenue potential. Some resort communities could raise significant funds through local amusement or restaurant taxes, and some jurisdictions with large upper-income populations might benefit significantly from local progressive income taxes. The state legislatures, however, decide which taxes can be raised by local authorities, and the individual communities are often left with revenue possibilities not suited to their resources.

The monopoly of income and sales taxes by federal and state governments

One reason for the restrictions on local governments' use of income and sales taxes is the heavy use of these same taxes by federal and state governments. It is said that the latter governments use up almost all the revenues that are potentially available from these sources. Although this allegation is neither clear nor even established as fact, a number of authorities do believe that two levels of government cannot make simultaneous heavy use of the same form of taxation.

Through a series of tacit understandings—as well as through the legal restrictions that state governments have imposed on their municipalities —the federal government has become the chief user of the personal and corporate income taxes, state governments rely heavily on sales taxes, and local governments are left with the tax on real property. In 1970–1971, personal and corporate income taxes accounted for 56 percent of federal revenue, sales taxes accounted for 40 percent of revenues collected by state governments, and property taxes accounted for 55 percent of revenues collected by municipalities.

It has not always been so. Tax *specialization* came after the Depression of the 1930s and may reflect the overall increase in taxes that characterized this period. Before the Depression both state and local governments were major users of the property tax, but the states left that revenue source to municipalities during the 1930s, and they themselves became increasingly dependent upon retail sales taxes. State governments earned almost 45 percent of their revenues from property taxes in 1902. By 1940, however, this had dropped to only 5 percent, and by 1970–1971 it was only 1.5 percent.

As most local governments are left without a major source of tax revenue other than real-property taxes, they find themselves unable to tap large segments of the local economy for support. Much of the wealth in the local community takes the form of profits from retail sales and personal and corporate incomes, but in most places this wealth is not subject to local taxation. Moreover, many earners and retail spenders live outside the community in which they earn or spend their incomes, and their property taxes are paid to their communities of residence. The burden lies especially heavily on central cities. As noted, it is the city that faces heavy demands for social services, transportation, fire and police protection, and housing, yet the incomes of its wealthiest business and professional people are not (in most cases) subject to local taxation, and the purchases made in the central business district are (in most cases) taxed only by the state government. The tax options of most CCs do not match their economic resources, and so there may be starvation of public services in the presence of enormous private resources. We note in Chapter 4 that some state governments have loosened the controls on localities' use of nonproperty taxes. Yet the general picture is still one of constraint, with most local governments relying on the unpopular and regressive levy on real property as their major taxing device.

The failure of local governments to tax or borrow to the legal limits

Governments in some communities do not tax or borrow to their legal limits, yet they fail to satisfy some prominent demands for service. Also some officials compete with other jurisdictions for the location of industrial or commercial establishments by offering the incentive of low taxes. The reason given is that high taxes will discourage a firm from locating in a jurisdiction or even prompt an established firm to move elsewhere. Actually, the availability of manpower, transportation facilities, electric power, and clean water—plus recreational and educational opportunities for the staff—often have more to do with management's decision about location than does the simple factor of the tax rate. Yet local authorities are tempted to compete for industries by means of their tax rates. When different communities in the same urban area do compete over tax rates, an occasional firm may be induced to choose a low-rate community or even to leave a community whose taxes rise significantly above those in a neighboring jurisdiction. In this case, the firm can still recruit its labor force from the surrounding towns, and its officers can live in those surrounding communities with the most attractive amenities. Also if a large firm is persuaded to settle—or stay—in a community because of a low tax rate, the taxes from that firm alone may nevertheless be sufficient in their total magnitude to permit a low tax rate for the community's home owners.

The failure of local governments to tax or borrow up to their legal limits does not result solely from the preferences of municipal officials. Sometimes community leaders may urge tax increases or bond issues to pay for needed services, only to run up against intense popular opposition. Forty-two of the fifty states require that local governments obtain the consent of their citizens in referenda before issuing bonds for improvements in streets, sewers, schools, and other public facilities. Twelve states require consent by extraordinarily high majorities, ranging from 55 percent to two-thirds of the electorate, before capital investments may be undertaken. The proportion of referenda in which local electorates reject such investments has increased in recent years. The voters of Youngstown, Ohio, may hold the record for negative referenda. They defeated proposals for school taxes on six consecutive occasions before the fall of 1968, when the schools ran out of money and shut down for most of the term. In 1971, a majority of school bond proposals were defeated in American cities.

The auxiliary devices of intergovernmental aid and special districts
Although officials face severe problems arising from the inaccessibility of urban wealth, two major devices, the *special district* and *intergovernmental grants and loans*, offer partial solutions to their problems.

THE SPECIAL DISTRICT   The special district broadens the tax base that can be used to support public services in an urban area by joining together an extensive area for the purpose of providing a particular service. Special districts are—as the name implies—created for special purposes. They do not provide the full range of local services. Rather, each provides one basic service or a group of closely related services.[23] The most common special districts are school districts; others include districts for water, sewage, or both; trash collection; police, fire protection, or both; parks; libraries; hospitals; and transportation, bridges, and port facilities.

Most metropolitan areas have several of these districts. The largest and best known is the Port of New York Authority. Each district may have its own borders, not necessarily coterminous with the borders of others. A school district, for example, may include one set of municipalities (or some whole municipalities and parts of others) and may partly, but not entirely, overlap a water-and-sewer district that covers a different part of the metropolitan region. Where special districts have proliferated in this manner, they can provide individual services on the basis of the resources that lie within their extensive boundaries. They appeal to those who prefer that financial support for services be tied directly to the receipt of those services.[24]

Because of the confusion that arises from a variety of separate jurisdictions, however, citizens cannot easily determine which districts provide which services to their homes, much less how they may influence the policies made by the authorities of each district. The governing bodies of many special districts are boards appointed jointly by the councils or mayors of several municipalities, by the state governor, or both, and the indirect lines of responsibility, as well as the confused geographical boundaries, help to isolate special districts from voter control.

INTERGOVERNMENTAL AID Intergovernmental aid permits urban governments to receive some of the revenues raised within their jurisdictions by the income and sales taxes of the federal and state governments.[25] One of the advantages of this scheme is that federal and state authorities can raise revenues from urban areas without imposing differential tax rates that might drive away industry from these jurisdictions. Since they are not troubled by the unequal distribution of needs and resources throughout a metropolitan area, they can use a wider variety of taxing and borrowing mechanisms than can local authorities. Admittedly, only a portion of the revenues raised from an urban area is returned to that area by state and federal governments, because much of this wealth must be used to support a variety of federal and state programs, including national defense and financial aid to small-town and rural citizens.

Until 1972, all federal aid for state and local governments came as funds for particular programs. Now, with the passage of the Revenue Sharing Act, the federal government has committed approximately $5.3 billion per year to state and local governments for purposes selected by the recipients within the broad terms of the legislation. Local governments are assured of two-thirds the annual allotments, with the funds for individual localities coming on the basis of population, the per-capita income of local residents, and the level of local taxes. Communities with *large* populations, *low* income, and *high* local tax effort benefit from the formula. Along with revenue sharing, there remain over 400 separate federal aid programs that help to fund specific activities. Some of these (e.g., public housing, urban renewal, crime control) channel money directly from Washington to municipal authorities. Most other programs provide aid to state governments, which in turn offer some of the funds to municipalities, urban school districts, and other urban units. The nature of these aids varies considerably from one program to another.[26] Some programs are designed to redistribute resources from "have" to "have not" areas; others substitute the resources raised by superordinate governments for those raised locally; others are provided with only portions of the funds needed and are designed to stimulate local authorities to put more effort into raising money through their own taxes or service charges; and others are meant to add resources to those that the municipalities have raised for certain programs from their own resources.

There are systematic variations in state-to-local intergovernmental aids among states. Some state governments assume a large part of the responsibility for financing public services and use aids to municipalities in order to accomplish their objectives.[27] Others provide only minimal state aids, and leave to the local communities the task of supporting whatever services their citizens desire. Not all local officials, however, feel that the disbursement of state money is equitable, even in the former case.

One of the most common complaints of central-city officials is that state and federal aids have failed to equalize the resource disparities between CCs and OCCs. Central-city officials claim that the suburbs have more wealth and fewer problems than do the CCs. As of 1965, however, total per-capita aid to CCs and OCCs was nearly identical ($78 per capita).[28] Federal grants-in-aid support programs that are used more by CCs than by suburbs (e.g., public housing and urban renewal), and state-aid support programs, especially education, that are more important to suburbs than to CCs. The central-city orientation of federal aid is just enough to counterbalance the suburban orientation of state aid. Over the decade of the 1960s, however, state aid changed in the direction of greater generosity for large cities. Between 1960 and 1970–1971 cities with over 1 million people enjoyed a 450 percent increase in per-capita state aid, and cities in the population range of 500 thousand to 1 million enjoyed a 179 percent increase; those cities in the 25- to 50-thousand range merely doubled.

Toward flexibility

Although special districts and intergovernmental aid are important sources of revenue for local governments, they are not the only tools available. Successful officials can demonstrate creative use of the various resources at their disposal and perhaps invent some new ones. Although some local authorities see their property taxes as already at the uppermost feasible limit, for others such taxes are not exhausted as a source of funds. If the statutes or constitution of the state place an upper limit on the tax rate (the proportion of assessed value that an owner can be taxed in one year), local officials might increase the assessments. By increasing such assessments across the board they can spread the tax increase to all kinds of property owners; they can also increase assessments selectively—on those kinds of properties least likely to react negatively to the increase or on those that have enjoyed several years of inordinately low assessments.[29]

In some municipalities officials actively solicit business investments in industrial or commercial developments, because they add to the value of real property and tax revenues. Such campaigns are, of course, likely to be more effective in some communities than in others, for geographical location in relation to the sources of supply and labor and to markets is important to industrialists, as is the availability of water, electric power, and transportation facilities. In many cases these tangible needs of a prospective investor outweigh any arguments—or even temporary tax concessions—that local authorities can provide.

Local authorities are not prohibited from trying to alter provisions of the state constitution or statutes that keep their fiscal position weak. Debt and tax limitations, for example, as well as the formulas for distributing state aid, are subject to change. Recent increases in the representation of urban areas in state legislatures may also aid the city's efforts to reduce its fiscal impediments. Yet in some states reapportionment has only heightened city-suburb conflicts in the legislatures; it may even have ousted certain rural legislators who were allies of the cities. The process of reapportionment is complex and cannot be said to have uniform influence on city-state relations across the country.[30]

It is dangerous to oversimplify our notions of the economic problems and opportunities that face urban governments. Economic and political features vary from one state to another, and within certain states they vary from one metropolis to another. The fortunes of a city may be shaped by something as intangible as a tacit agreement between its representatives and other members of the state legislature. There is plenty of opportunity for the creative local official, and he should not be discouraged by a pessimistic general evaluation of the plight of cities in the 1970s.

Summary

In this chapter we have described part of the context in which urban governments formulate their policies, focusing on economic and social conditions in urban areas. These conditions determine the resources and demands that in turn shape the services provided by local governments.

America's cities have most of our material wealth: most of our industry, professional and technical skills, financial and commercial activity. On three indirect measures of this wealth—population growth, personal income, and education—the large urban areas demonstrate consistently higher scores than do rural and small-town areas. Metropolitan areas are not homogeneous in the internal distribution of their wealth, however, and their populations are diverse and distributed unequally among various neighborhoods and legally autonomous jurisdictions. The resulting unequal distribution of economic needs and resources presents some of the most complex policy problems facing local officials.

Demands on local governments include help in maintaining or enhancing the economic positions of commerce and industry, as well as social service for people attracted to cities but unable to benefit fully from their economic opportunities. Many services that local governments provide are new since the Depression of the 1930s, and some are new since the surge of welfare legislation in the mid-1960s. Now there are programs for housing, slum clearance and urban renewal, welfare payments, job training, personal and family counseling, and mass transportation. Other services lie within the traditional responsibilities of local governments: education, streets, traffic control, zoning, police and fire protection, public health, and sanitation. Even in these fields, however, the nature of policies is shaped by recent escalations in the demands of clients and innovations in social technologies.

With all these demands for economic and social services, there are also demands by individuals and corporations for tax stability or concessions. There is also a host of legal and political impediments that keep local authorities from taking full advantage of the economic resources that lie within their boundaries. These barriers include the unequal distribution of needs and resources throughout extensive urban areas, the failure of local authorities to tax or borrow up to the limits permitted by state constitutions or statutes, limitations on the kinds or amounts of local government taxation or indebtedness, and the control of lucrative income and sales taxes by federal and state governments. Auxiliary devices help local authorities to maximize their economic opportunities. Special districts broaden both the geographic and economic bases of units providing certain kinds of public services, and federal and state aid funnels some of the money raised in urban areas by those governments back to local officials. Creative local officials have numerous opportunities to provide leadership that may allow their municipalities to make the most of their fiscal opportunities, even though their prospects may often appear bleak.

Notes

1. Jane Jacobs, *The Economy of Cities* (New York: Vintage, 1970).
2. For a discussion of the usefulness of various measures of economic resources, see Harvey S. Perloff et al., *Regions, Resources, and Economic Growth* (Baltimore: Johns Hopkins, 1960).
3. See William B. Neenan, *Political Economy of Urban Areas* (Chicago: Markham, 1972), p. 6.

4. Edgar M. Hoover and Raymond Vernon, *Anatomy of a Metropolis* (Garden City, N.Y.: Doubleday, 1962), chap. 2.
5. Advisory Commission on Intergovernmental Relations, *Fiscal Balance in the American Federal System*, vol. 2 (Washington, D.C.: Government Printing Office, 1967), p. 6.
6. *Ibid.*, p. 65.
7. Suburban myths have been explored in a number of careful studies, including Robert C. Wood, *Suburbia* (Boston: Houghton Mifflin, 1959); Bennett Berger, *Working Class Suburb* (Berkeley: University of California Press, 1960); William Dobriner, *Class in Suburbia* (Englewood Cliffs, N.J.: Prentice-Hall, 1963); and Herbert Gans, *The Levittowners* (New York: Basic Books, 1967).
8. John C. Bollens et al., *Exploring the Metropolitan Community* (Berkeley: University of California Press, 1961), pp. 87–88.
9. Leo F. Schnore, *The Urban Scene* (New York: Free Press, 1965), chaps. 7–9.
10. Hoover and Vernon, p. 139, divide the New York metropolitan region into three zones, the *core*, the *inner ring*, and the *outer ring*. More than 80 percent of the metropolitan work force lives and works in single zones. Only 14 percent lives in the inner or outer ring and commutes to the core.
11. A classic work on European immigrants in American cities is Oscar Handlin, *The Uprooted* (Boston: Little, Brown, 1951).
12. Frank G. Davis, *The Economics of Black Community Development: Analysis and Program for Autonomous Community Development* (Chicago: Markham, 1972), p. 104.
13. *Ibid.*, p. 114.
14. On the economics of the urban poor, see also Carolyn Shaw Bell, *The Economics of the Ghetto* (New York: Norton, 1972).
15. National Advisory Commission on Civil Disorders, *Report* (Washington, D.C.: Government Printing Office, 1967), pp. 6–7.
16. *Allocating Tax Burdens and Government Benefits by Income Class* (New York: Tax Foundation, Inc., 1967), p. 7.
17. Ira Sharkansky, *The Politics of Taxing and Spending* (New York: Bobbs-Merrill, 1969), pp. 17–19.
18. Bollens et al., p. 277.
19. V. O. Key, Jr., *Public Opinion and American Democracy* (New York: Knopf, 1961), p. 167.
20. See Herbert Gans, "The Failure of Urban Renewal: A Critique and Some Proposals," *Commentary* (April 1965), 29–37. See also our discussion of urban renewal in Chapter 12.
21. Anthony Downs, *Urban Problems and Prospects* (Chicago: Markham, 1970), p. 34.
22. Many of the arguments in this section are explored more fully in Robert C. Wood, *1400 Governments* (Garden City, N.Y.: Doubleday, 1964).
23. John C. Bollens, *Special District Governments in the United States* (Berkeley: University of California Press, 1957).
24. *Ibid.*, p. 81.
25. See Deil S. Wright, *Federal Grants-in-Aid: Perspectives and Alternatives* (Washington, D.C.: American Enterprise Institute for Public Policy Research, 1968).
26. See, for example, Richard A. Musgrave, *Essays in Fiscal Federalism* (Washington, D.C.: Brookings Institution, 1965).
27. Sharkansky, chap. 4.
28. Advisory Commission on Intergovernmental Relations, p. 84.
29. Wood, *1400 Governments*, pp. 76ff.
30. See Ira Sharkansky, "Reapportionment and Roll Call Voting: The Case of the Georgia Legislature," *Social Science Quarterly*, 51 (June 1970), 129–137 and the references cited.

chapter 3

The political context

Every political system provides channels—more or less imperfect—through which individual and group interests enter as *input* into the political system. In Iran, which is characterized by a "politics of informality," groups as we know them do not play very significant political roles, but there are other ways of expressing political preferences. One observer described a visit by the provincial governor to a small village: Residents' petitions were given to the governor's driver, butler, secretary, and guests in hopes that they would be transmitted to the governor himself. A more direct way to secure community improvements was apparent when the governor's entourage drove through a small village on an inspection tour, for which local crowds were duly assembled to shout: "Long live the Shah! Hurrah! Long live the Governor! Hurrah! We need another doctor in this town! Hurrah!"[1]

In American cities, resources are applied to affect public policy when voters troop to the polls, when rioters "trash," when interest groups talk to councilmen, when parties tout their candidates. The input process encompasses all activities in which individuals and groups use time, information, money, skills, votes, and other resources to secure favorable policy outcomes. The process in American cities in particular is the subject of this chapter.

Here we focus on mass politics, as distinguished from elite politics. Four principal avenues can be used to link mass opinions with elite decisions. The electoral system, the political party, the interest group, and protest have all functioned to give masses *some* influence over community decisions made by elites. How effective these linkages are, how well they communicate mass sentiments and control elite behavior, is a matter of much dispute. But before we attempt to evaluate them, it will be useful to understand them in operation. We also address in this chapter the unique aspects of black politics.[2] The elites themselves, and the decision-making process they dominate, will be discussed in Chapter 5.

Participation in Urban Politics

"You can't fight city hall" is a hallowed cliché in American politics. But judging by the available evidence, relatively few urbanites take advantage of routine opportunities to change things at city hall. Participation in local voting rites is much lower than in either state or national election contests. In 1972, about 55 percent of the adult population voted for its presidential favorite; in the typical state election, about 50 percent of the eligible electorate turns out to vote. In city elections that are not held concurrently with state or national contests, however, only about a third of the adult population appears at the polls.

To be sure, voting is not the only device through which people participate in politics. Participation also includes a variety of such activities as discussing politics, campaigning for candidates, running for office, and contributing money to political causes or candidates. Still, for most Americans, voting is the most vigorous participation they are likely to undertake, and the level of apathy in local politics is quite high relative to interest in state and national politics in the United States.

Participation in community politics may be seen as a function of both *macro* (community) and *micro* (individual or subcommunity) factors. The probability of participation will vary both from individual to individual and from community to community. Unless participation is viewed from both perspectives, a one-sided picture results. Even if two people resemble each other in social characteristics, they may participate differently, depending upon whether factors in the political environment operate to facilitate or to hinder political activism.

The aggregate level of participation in any given community is a product both of the kinds of individuals found in the community and of the characteristics of the community and its socioeconomic and governmental systems. A listing of some of the more significant correlates of participation in community politics, divided into macro and micro categories, appears in Table 3.1. It is important to note that this list conceals the interaction and interrelations among the various factors. It is difficult to isolate the effect of any one of these elements from the

Table 3.1 *Correlates of Participation in Community Politics*[a]

Macro factors		Micro factors	
1. Form of government		1. Social class	
Mayor-council or commission	+	Higher	+
Manager	−	Lower	−
2. Form of election		2. Stakes in policies	
Partisan	+	High	+
Nonpartisan	−	Low	−
3. Type of constituency		3. Ethnicity	
Ward	+	Ethnic	+
At large	−	Nonethnic	−
4. Party system		4. Mobility	
Strong	+	High	−
Weak	−	Low	+
5. Community stability			
Stable	+		
Unstable	−		
6. Intensity of conflict			
High	+		
Low	−		

[a] A + sign indicates that the characteristic identified is usually associated with higher participation rates; a − sign indicates that the characteristic is ordinarily associated with lower participation in community politics.

others, and it is the sum of various factors that produces a higher or lower level of participation, rather than any one factor taken independently.

Macro variables and participation

Robert R. Alford and Eugene C. Lee have gathered the most complete data ever assembled on electoral turnouts in American cities.[3] Drawing upon the resources of the International City Management Association, they conducted a survey of city clerks in all American cities whose populations in 1960 were greater than 25,000 and collected data on the turnouts for the city elections immediately preceding their questionnaire in 1962. Table 3.2 reports correlations between four categories of characteristics and the levels of community turnout. These categories are political structure, social structure, community stability and continuity, and regional location.

The variables categorized under *political structure* indicate that voting in cities with "reformed" institutions is lower than that in cities with "unreformed" institutions. Council-manager governments and nonpartisan elections (and, by implication, elections at large) are found in cities with lower turnouts; mayor-council governments and partisan elections (and, by implication, ward elections) are found in cities with

Table 3.2 *Correlates of Local Voting Turnouts in American Cities with Nonconcurrent Elections, 1961–1962 (N=294)[a]*

Characteristic	Correlation with percentage of adults voting
Political structure	
Council-manager versus *noncouncil-manager*	.50
Partisan versus nonpartisan elections	.29
Social structure	
Ethnicity (percentage of population of foreign birth or foreign or mixed parentage, 1960)	.51
Education (percentage of those 25 or more years old who had completed 4 years of high school, 1960)	−.15
Community stability and continuity	
Mobility (percentage migrant from different counties, 1955–1960)	−.40
Age of city (decade in which the city had reached 25,000 population)	.28
Regional location	
East	.45
Midwest	.21
South	−.44
Far West	−.10

[a]Each entry is a product-moment correlation of the actual percentage of eligible adults voting in the last local election held in the given city. The data were derived from Alford and Lee's study of municipal elections, undertaken with the cooperation of the International City Management Association.

The italicized characteristics indicate the directions of the correlations. For example, we may say that the correlation between a noncouncil-manager form of city government and its turnout is 0.50; that is, noncouncil-manager governments are relatively strongly and positively associated with higher turnouts. Similarly, the "easternness" of a city is also rather strongly and positively associated with its turnout, whereas the opposite is true of the "southernness" of a city, which is strongly and negatively associated with its turnout.

SOURCE: Robert R. Alford and Eugene C. Lee, "Voting Turnout in American Cities," *American Political Science Review*, 62 (September 1968), 803, Table I.

higher turnouts. Even when other factors related to social and economic characteristics are taken into account, the presence of "reformed" institutions was still significantly associated with lower voting rates. (Chapter 4 provides a more extensive discussion of "reformed" and "unreformed" government structures and their political consequences.)

What features of "reformed" and "unreformed" political institutions are responsible for this relationship? "Reformed" institutions, to borrow a medical analogy, operate to make the local political system more sterile and antiseptic. In a "reformed" city the mayoral office, once the center of political controversy and contention, is largely a ceremonial position, chiefly involved in ribbon clipping and Rotary luncheons. Nonpartisanship weakens political parties and removes party identification as a valuable voters' guide to candidates and issues. Elections at large have eliminated "personalized," neighborhood ward leaders and have produced incumbents who enjoy little personal contact with voters. The "reform" movement emphasizes professional management rather than the kind of political accountability that arises out of hotly contested political campaigns.

In terms of the *social structure* of the community, Alford and Lee have shown that turnout decreases when there are larger proportions of well-educated people in the community. In terms of *community stability* and *continuity*, turnouts are lower in cities with high mobility, partly because mobile individuals are disfranchised in the American electoral system; communities whose institutions have long continuity also have more active electorates. Communities with little residential mobility and with long-standing institutions are characterized by regular channels of communications between leaders and public, political patterns familiar to the electorate, and readily obtainable information about local affairs. The electorates of unstable communities, in contrast, find information less readily obtainable and have fewer ties with established community leaders and groups. There are also sharp regional differences in turnout; eastern and southern cities show the most and the least voting participation respectively. Eastern cities show the traits of stability, continuity, and European ethnicity that contribute to turnout. The low turnout in southern cities reflects the features that have long tended to depress political participation in that region. Cities in the West and Midwest have a mixture of traits, especially of stability and continuity, that makes them indistinctive as regions for political participation.

Other macro characteristics of communities may affect participation but are difficult to assess. One is the nature of the party system. A few cities possess vigorous party organizations, whereas others are non-partisan in fact as well as in name. A strong party need not "vote head-stones" in order to increase political participation. Parties can frame issues, engage in personal contact, and link candidates with voters through the medium of party identification. Katz and Eldersfeld found that an active party can produce up to a 10 percent change in the division of the vote—certainly enough to capture a close election.[4] In American politics, as a general rule, competition between parties increases participation in elections. The competitiveness of local parties can add significantly to the size of the electorate.

The level and intensity of social conflict should also affect local political activity. Political conflict reflects racial, ethnic, class, and cultural differences among urbanites. A homogeneous community, whether it is composed of white-collar junior executives or of blue-collar union members, generates fewer political conflicts and thus fewer incentives to participate in politics. Superficial homogeneity may, of course, conceal important conflict. The Hatfields and the McCoys, the famed feuding

West Virginia hillbillies, would look pretty much alike to a casual observer.

Micro variables and participation

Lester Milbrath divided the American public into four groups with respect to political participation: *apathetics, spectators, transitionals,* and *gladiators.*[5] Apathetics engage in no political activities, scarcely opening their awarenesses to political stimuli. One example is a woman who responded to a Survey Research Center interviewer during the 1956 election campaign:

(Is there anything you like about the Democratic party?) *I'm a Democrat.*
(Is there anything you like about the Democratic party?) *I don't know.*
(Is there anything you dislike about the Democrats?) *I'm a Democrat, that's all I know. My husband's dead now—he was a Democrat.* (Is there anything you don't like about the party?) *I don't know.*
(Is there anything you like about the Republicans?) *I don't know.*
(Is there anything you dislike about the Republicans?) *I don't know.*
(Anything you like about Mr. Stevenson?) *Stevenson is a good Democrat.* (Is there anything about him that might make you want to vote for him?) *No, nothing.* (Is there anything you dislike about Mr. Stevenson?) *I don't know.* (Is there anything about him that might make you want to vote against him?) *No.*[6]

Spectators constitute a majority of the American population. They engage in political conversation from time to time and usually vote (though less often in local than in national elections). Transitionals sometimes proselytize for particular candidates or issues but fall short of the political activity exhibited by gladiators, a group for whom politics is a vocation or at least a major activity. Gladiators contribute heavily in time and money, they campaign for candidates and issues, they may seek office themselves, and they provide the political leadership cadres of their communities.

The precise proportions of the public found in these four categories vary from election to election, from one level of government to another, and from community to community. Milbrath estimates that "about one-third of the American adult population can be characterized as politically apathetic or passive; in most cases, they are unaware, literally, of the political part of the world around them. Another 60 percent play largely spectator roles in the political process."[7] Approximately 5 percent consists of transitionals and an estimated 1–2 percent of gladiators. When we consider the very low overall rate of participation in local elections, it is likely that the proportion of apathetics may be even larger in local than in national politics.

What factors are associated with an individual's position on this continuum of participation? One of the most universally identified observations about political participation is the strong positive correlation between social class and political participation. People with higher class positions are generally more likely to participate in politics. (For an explanation of the apparent contradiction between Alford and Lee's finding that voter turnout is lower in communities of well-educated people and the micro-level finding that well-to-do people participate more heavily, see the discussion on pages 11–13 in Chapter 1.) One study of local political involvement, using data from four Wisconsin cities, revealed that two measures of social class (educational attainment and occupation) were among the three most important factors associated with political activity, and Robert A. Dahl's study of New Haven found a 34 percent difference in the proportions of high- and low-income people who were "highly active" in local politics.[8] A study of voting on bond referenda in Atlanta revealed a positive, but not very strong, relationship between indicators of socioeconomic status and turnout, and investigators of the St. Louis metropolitan area did not find class significant in differentiating between high and low participators. In Toledo, a powerful correlation between class and participation was noted.[9] At the urban level there is thus some variability in the relationship between class and voting turnout. Variations may reflect peculiarities of election campaigns, the community itself, or the measurements of both class and participation used.

The stakes perceived in local public policies are another factor that seems to affect participation. By *stakes*, we mean the material or ideological gains and losses that the voter perceives as likely to result from the activities of local government. The fact is that for most Americans city hall is more distant, politically speaking, than is Washington, D.C., despite American rhetoric about "government close to the people." But for some urbanites local public policy can be calculated in a profit-and-loss column. Businessmen, realtors, contractors, developers, and municipal employees are far more likely than is the average person to see local politics as relevant to their pocketbooks. Developers, realtors, and landowners are affected by decisions about urban renewal, zoning, and economic development. Contractors and suppliers are affected by nearly every capital-outlay decision, and municipal employees have obvious economic interests in municipal decisions. As most local taxes are tied to property values, home owners may see greater stakes in local politics than others do (though they probably see lower stakes than street contractors do). Alford and Scoble have noted that "home ownership is apparently a form of politically-relevant group membership, vesting the individual with tangible interests perceived as impinged upon by local politics quite apart from more conventional interests of high social status."[10]

Mobility, race, and ethnic affiliation also relate to local participation. Mobile people are less active participants for two principal reasons. First, legal residence qualifications for voting in most American elections disenfranchise people who have recently moved. Second, highly mobile people also have fewer roots in the community, fewer social ties, and less information about local political affairs.

The ethnic affiliation, or identification, of an individual seems also to be indicative of his political activism. *Ethnics* (an ethnic, for our purposes, means either an immigrant or, more commonly nowadays, the son or daughter of immigrants) are more likely to participate than are native Americans. A study of St. Louis found that 77 percent of the German community in the city and 80 percent of residents of southern and eastern European ancestry had voted at least once in municipal elections, whereas only 61 percent of "old stock" Americans and 62 percent of Blacks reported having ever voted in such an election.[11] Robert E. Lane, in discussing the "way of the ethnic in politics," has noted:

> In a real sense, the seat of ethnic politics is the local community, not the national capital. This is evidenced by the fact that although ethnic groups often vote no more frequently than native white Protestants in national elections (with the Jews excepted) and sometimes less frequently, they usually vote more frequently in local elections.[12]

In the heydey of the political machine, ethnic groups were crucial elements in the party leaders' victory package. "Ticket balancing" still occurs in cities with large ethnic populations, and politicians often woo ethnic voters with promises of symbolic group-related rewards.

Government close to the people?

American political rhetoric waxes eloquent about "government close to the people" at the local level. But the most obvious characteristic of participation in local politics is how little there is of it. Voting—which is the most vigorous act of participation undertaken by most Americans— typically involves no more than a third of the eligible local electorate. Turnouts of 5 to 10 percent of the adult population are common in referenda, in special-district elections, in county and other local elections, and in some cities. In terms of participation beyond voting— talking to councilmen, campaigning, pressing for specific policies, and so on—the proportion of participants borders on the miniscule. Robert Dahl once observed that politics is only a "sideshow on the great circus of life." This is doubly true at the local level. We shall have more to say shortly on the consequences of low participation for the representation of mass interests.

Political Parties and Elections

The Nineteenth Ward

In the 1890s, Chicago's Nineteenth Ward, where Jane Addams and her associates established the famed Hull House, contained 50,000 people of twenty different nationalities, crammed together in a few square miles of dingy tenements.[13] Most were immigrants, and, because of universal manhood suffrage, most of the men were voters.

The political boss of the Nineteenth Ward was Johnny Powers, a short, stocky Irishman and one of the most powerful figures in Chicago city politics. He was chairman of the finance committee of the Chicago City Council and used his position to manipulate public-utility franchises and the jobs of thousands of city employees. Powers ran for office on a year-round basis: bailing a son or husband out of jail, fixing matters with a judge, buying funerals through his standing account at the undertaker's, buying turkeys at Christmas, and keeping 2600 residents of the ward on the city payroll. Public policy under the Powers machine was "personalized." There was no commitment to alter the conditions that had produced the need for his patronage and favors and little concern for the niceties of honest and efficient municipal government.

This whole system was disturbing to the women of Hull House. They tried to defeat Powers in the elections of 1895, 1896, and 1898. But Powers and his associates survived every challenge from Hull House and its reformist allies. Following the second unsuccessful attempt in 1896, Powers gave a municipal position to nearly every man who had campaigned actively against him. He appointed a printer who was also an opposition leader to a clerkship at city hall, a driver from the opposition camp to the city police barns at a lucrative salary, and the opposing candidate himself to a comfortable position in the city construction department. It was difficult to defeat a man with such political resources. Reform of the Nineteenth Ward had to wait for forces stronger than Miss Addams and her colleagues.

The rise and demise of the machine

Johnny Powers' operation in the Nineteenth Ward was one example of the urban party machines that dominated many American cities during the years of rapid urbanization and immigration. The party machine is both the best-known and the least-understood aspect of urban political life. Banfield and Wilson have defined it as a "party organization that depends crucially upon inducements that are both specific and material."[14] Specific inducements are those (like jobs in city government) that can be given to some and withheld from others; material inducements are those that are monetary or readily convertible into money. This definition, however, understates the importance of nonmaterial inducements in generating support for the machine. Banfield and Wilson themselves have noted that one very important resource of the ward captain was "friendship."

Fred I. Greenstein has offered the following more general definition of the machine from a structural and functional point of view:[15]

1. There is a disciplined party hierarchy led by a single executive or board of directors.

2. The party exercises effective control over nomination to public office, and, through this, it controls the public officials of the municipality.
3. The party leadership—which quite often is of lower-class social origins—usually does not hold public office and sometimes does not even hold formal party office. At any rate, official position is not the primary source of the leadership's strength.
4. Rather, a cadre of loyal party officials and workers, as well as a core of voters, is maintained by a mixture of material rewards and nonideological psychic rewards—such as personal and ethnic recognition, camaraderie, and the like.

The political machine is treated by reformers as an object of moral opprobrium, chiefly becuase of its presumably shady operations with the public tax dollar. Certainly many machine leaders have converted public funds to more or less private use, though there have been machines that were scrupulously honest and even puritanical. The difficulty with any assessment of the political machine that does not go beyond its shady dealings is that it ignores what Robert Merton has described as the "latent functions" of the machine.[16] Merton has distinguished between "manifest" and "latent" functions of an activity, the former being those that are intended and recognized and the latter those that are unintended and unrecognized. Even though the machine engaged in "honest graft"[17] at best and "dishonest graft" at worst, it nonetheless facilitated the government of urban America during a period of severe social tension. It functioned in an era when the official structures of local governments were inadequate to accommodate the strains of rapid urbanization and immigration. The machine filled a vacuum created by the fragmentation of legal power and responsibility in urban government. Edward M. Sait observed bluntly that "leadership is necessary; and since it does not develop readily within the constitutional framework, the boss provides it in a crude and irresponsible way from the outside."[18] At a time when the urban population was skyrocketing, when service needs occasioned by industrialization and immigration were expanding significantly, and when human relations were unusually tense, the machine provided a semblance of government in the city.

The machine also provided a welfare function for the dispossessed and did so with a personalism and intimacy that welfare bureaucracies have never equaled. Fires, unemployment, illness, and other human misfortunes were purely personal problems in the days before the welfare state. The political machines softened many of these misfortunes. They also provided an avenue of upward mobility for ethnic groups, helped them to become socialized in American culture, found jobs, and courted favors by providing a measure of status. Partly because of a strong strain of American "nativism," much of the private sector of society was closed to European ethnics. But the machine made mobility a reality. Politics was one of the most certain ways for Irishmen, Italians, and other ethnics to obtain acceptable positions. Although the party leaders themselves (in the early days of the machines) were almost all white and native Americans, they knew that ethnics had critical resources to offer to the parties. Bosses offered jobs, favors, and status in exchange for votes. The machines thus performed certain latent functions, which were performed by no other social institution before the days of legal aid, unemployment compensation, and social security.

The urban party machine survives today principally as an anachronism. There are several reasons why the machine has declined almost everywhere. Affluence has meant a general decrease in the relative values of the rewards available through the machines. In the affluent society, menial jobs like census taker and city sanitation worker will not buy the votes they once did. The rise of the welfare state also emasculated the machine. Unemployment compensation, social security, and other benefits are more certain and more generous than were the occasional turkeys, hods of coal, and small favors handed out by a friendly neighborhood precinct captain. The Depression was a double blow to the machine, straining its scarce resources as well as leading to a federally organized, financed, and supervised welfare program that the party organization could not match. At the same time the machines were losing their welfare role, local governments had to perform a new range of services. Municipal governments hired skilled technicians and professionals. Party hacks cannot handle complex decisions, intricate financial procedures, computerized police protection, and other technical matters. As public management becomes more complex, mismanagement becomes increasingly embarrassing.

The impact of the reformers, and the institutions they advocated, also dealt heavy blows to the machine. Nonpartisanship made it more difficult for voters to know who was behind the names on the ballot and for the machines to keep unwanted candidates off the ballot. Elections at large organized politics around whole constituencies, rather than neighborhoods whose precinct captains could know voters by name. They also raised the costs of machine campaigning.

Furthermore, the advent of manager governments and the professionalization of city bureaucracies through the civil-service system removed the office of mayor from the arena of public choice, lessened the importance of political premises in decision making, and substituted the trained skills and judgments of professional managers. Civil-service reforms, as they took hold at the local level, increasingly removed middle- and low-level jobs from patronage.

But some hang on

Today there are few machines really worthy of the name, but a few hang on.[19] Anyone who lives in Chicago, for example, will be unwilling to write an obituary for the political machine. There, Mayor Richard J. Daley has maintained his organization by using all the traditional devices, but also by adapting to many reform programs.[20] A good part of the business community, which forms the natural base for reform movements, has been willing to tolerate Daley's politics and patronage in exchange for the mayor's support of civic boosterism. The Chicago machine demonstrates that it is possible, although not easy, to maintain machine-greasing patronage and satisfy business interests at the same time. But even the Chicago machine has fallen on hard times. The events of the 1968 Democratic convention did little to bolster the organization's public image. The machine suffered electoral troubles in the 1972 Illinois and Chicago races. Some thought they foreshadowed a last hurrah for the mayor and his organization. Edward Hanrahan, Daley's protégé and State's Attorney for Cook County, was the major figure in Chicago's law-and-order politics ("Criminals fear his election" was his campaign slogan). One of Hanrahan's police squads raided the Black Panther headquarters in Chicago, killing several Panther leaders. Eventually, the FBI and a federal grand jury determined that Hanrahan's raiders had emptied nearly a hundred bullets into the room, while the Panthers had fired but a single shot (and that, possibly, in self-defence). At first Daley kept Hanrahan on the ticket for the 1972 Democratic primary, but after Hanrahan's indictment, Daley dumped him and hastily secured 20,000 signatures in the space of six hours to put a new name on the primary ballot. But Hanrahan ran in the Democratic primary anyway and won nomination for a second term. His presence on the November 1972 ballot contributed heavily to a defection by Blacks and liberals, with disastrous results for Daley's organization. Many state and county offices (including the governorship and the state's attorney's office with its vast investigative powers) fell into the hands of the machine's enemies.

Nonpartisanship and elections at large

The political machine was anathema to municipal reformers. Not only did it affront their ethical values, but it also violated their conceptions of policy making by professional management ("There is no Democratic or Republican way to pave a street"). The machine was an institution that capitalized on social cleavages within the electorate and was therefore also at variance with the reformers' belief in the interest of the community as a whole.

The institutional choices that reformers advocated to eliminate the pernicious effects of the machine were the *nonpartisan election* and the *constituency at large*. In a nonpartisan election candidates are not identified on the ballot by party affiliation.[21] A constituency at large includes the whole city, and candidates run in the entire city rather than as representatives of geographically bounded wards or districts. Today, among cities with populations greater than 50,000, 63 percent use elections at large, and 67 percent use nonpartisan ballots. Only a minority of cities of this size retain the unreformed structures of partisan elections and ward constituencies.

Nonpartisan, at-large systems are likelier to be found in some kinds of cities than in others. Council-manager cities are more likely to use nonpartisan and at-large elections, whereas mayor-council cities are more likely to retain the ward and partisan systems. About 85 percent of manager cities use the nonpartisan ballot, whereas only about 50 percent of mayor-council cities are nonpartisan. Region seems to be another differentiating factor. Cities in the Northeast are much more likely to use partisan and ward systems, those in the South and West lean toward nonpartisan, at-large ballots, and those in the Midwest are more evenly split.[22]

Table 3.3 presents data on the social and economic characteristics of cities using reformed and unreformed election and constituency types. The most obvious differences are:

1. Reformed cities tend to be smaller in size and to grow more rapidly than do their unreformed counterparts.

Table 3.3 *Social and Economic Characteristics of Election and Constituency Types in American Cities with More Than 50,000 Population in 1960*

Characteristic	Election type		Constituency type	
	Partisan	Nonpartisan	Ward	At large
Population, 1960	270,800	155,800	246,900	153,000
Percentage population increase, 1950–1960	17.1	58.3	23.1	59.1
Median income of families, 1959	$5,996	$6,074	$6,297	$5,942
Median education, in years	10.6	11.2	10.9	11.2
Percentage of white-collar workers	43.5	46.7	45.2	46.3
Percentage of non-white population	13.0	11.5	9.8	13.0
Percentage of children of foreign-born or mixed parentage	17.5	16.9	18.9	13.4

SOURCE: Adapted from data in Robert L. Lineberry and Edmund P. Fowler, "Reformism and Public Policies in American Cities," *American Political Science Review, 61* (September 1967), 701–716. All figures are mean values of the particular characteristic. A few cities use combinations of ward and at-large elections; in this table such cities are classified as using ward constituencies.

2. Although there is a slight tendency for the reformed cities to contain more educated populations and more white-collar people, income variables do not appear as an important correlate of election and constituency type.
3. Racial composition does not show a consistent effect.
4. There is a slight tendency for unreformed cities to have larger proportions of European ethnics.

Despite these tendencies, it is reasonable to conclude that the socioeconomic compositions of partisan versus nonpartisan and at-large versus ward cities are not markedly different. Although popular wisdom holds that nonpartisanship is a special property of small, upper-middle-class, WASP suburbs, it is difficult to differentiate between partisan and nonpartisan cities on the basis of socioeconomic composition alone.[23]

The introduction of nonpartisanship, especially when coupled with elections at large, has a number of consequences for urban politics.[24] To a significant degree, the nonpartisan ballot fulfills the expectations of its designers. It weakens the traditional party structure and isolates local politics from national political tides. There are only a few exceptions (e.g., Chicago) to the rule that strong local party organization does not coexist with the nonpartisan ballot. In Newark, for example, the political party plays an active role in partisan contests for the state legislature but is dormant in nonpartisan municipal elections.[25] Nonpartisanship also tends to split the systems of campaign finance and candidate recruitment, with one set of funds and candidates for local nonpartisan office and another for partisan political posts.[26] This split has reduced the grass-roots organizational capacities of the political party and has made it difficult for the parties to permit aspiring politicians to get their feet wet in local office, thus retarding the development of a national party system. On the other hand, it was not until the local party strongholds were finally broken, in part through the influence of nonpartisanship, that a nationally organized party system could have much meaning, a fact less frequently recognized by critics of nonpartisanship. The dominance of parochial machines was a major impediment to the national organization of the party. Until recent decades the national conventions were largely congresses of fiefdoms, without much genuine power, and even today machines play a major role at conventions. Somewhat ironically, therefore, nonpartisanship has had a mixed effect on the national party system. It has helped to create the conditions (the demise of the local machine) under which national party government could in fact develop, but it has made it difficult for a national party to organize itself at the grass roots.

At the voter level, the nonpartisan ballot at large has increased the information cost to the voter, increased the financial cost of elections, and altered the structure of participation in local elections. The political party in the American system is a great economizer for most voters, because party labels tell something (though certainly not everything) about the candidates and their policy goals. When those party labels are unavailable, voters' information declines and their frustration increases. Kenneth S. Sherrill studied the levels of political information about local candidates in two Ohio cities, one with a partisan ballot and one with a nonpartisan ballot. Even though the nonpartisan city (Oberlin) had a very well-educated electorate and the partisan city (Amherst) a much less well-educated electorate, Amherst voters knew as much about candidates and local affairs as did Oberlin voters.[27]

It is not only the party label that supplies information; contacts with party workers, party efforts to propagandize for causes and candidates, and the tendency of parties to organize issues more clearly than does a nonpartisan system also contribute. In the absence of party labels, voters must rely upon other cues, and familiarity with names and ethnic identification become critical. In Newark, voters relied primarily upon party identification in picking candidates in partisan races and primarily upon ethnic identification in nonpartisan races.[28] Because familiarity with names alone is a significant factor in reducing information costs, nonpartisanship favors incumbents in local races.

Electoral turnout is significantly lower in nonpartisan cities than in partisan cities. Reduction in the size of the electorate in the nonpartisan city is not across the board or random but is concentrated particularly in lower-income groups and among those voters who would normally vote Democratic.[29] This group of voters relies most heavily upon partisan affiliation as a cue to voting and has fewest alternative sources of political information (like press reports, personal knowledge of the candidates, civic-club ties, and so on). Nonpartisan elections therefore attract larger proportions of middle- and upper-class citizens and a relatively smaller proportion of working-class citizens than do partisan elections. Another consequence is that the combination of nonpartisanship with elections at large lessens the ability of minority groups to engage in bloc voting.

These factors suggest that nonpartisanship probably increases the representation of middle-class interests in urban politics. Lee described the "composite councilman" in a California nonpartisan city as Republican, of the middle class, a veteran, a member of a civic club, engaged in business or professional pursuits, and having little or no previous political experience.[30] The typical councilman tended to be Republican by a three to two margin in a state that was Democratic by a comparable margin. Unfortunately, Lee's picture does not compare the pattern of incumbency in cities with partisan elections. Even so, it is reasonable to suppose that the nonpartisan, at-large system gives an edge to better-off candidates, if for no other reason than the increased expense of running in a city-wide constituency.

The electoral process

Having one's name put on a ballot for President of the United States is a task so difficult that even the mighty shrink from it. Having one's name put on a ballot for city councilman or mayor, the most common elective offices in American cities, is often as easy as dropping into a city clerk's office and paying a small filing fee. The most common method of nomination, especially in nonpartisan cities, is the simple device of filing by individual candidates; next is the voter petition, in which a specified number of registered voters (usually a proportion of the turnout in the previous election) sign petitions in support of each would-be candidate. These two methods almost exhaust the nominating methods in nonpartisan cities. About half the partisan cities use party primaries, and a lesser number use party conventions to nominate local candidates. Cities that use primaries and conventions have much more closed nominating systems than do those using individual filing of petitions. Where individuals can file petitions, "dark horses" can enter a race, and, given the limited information available to the local electorate, sometimes a very dark horse wins.

Urban election campaigns can have four possible effects on the voter: conversion, activation, reinforcement, and minor change. Some voters will be converted, that is, will change their preferences from one candidate or party to another during the campaign; others will be reinforced in their support for their initial choices; still others will become activated to take more supportive roles in work for candidates or parties; and some will modify their views, but not to the point of conversion. Most voters experience reinforcement or minor changes, a few are activated, but only a handful are converted. These categories, however, are more meaningful and useful in partisan cities. Party identification provides the voter with a ready-made cue for choice even before the campaign begins. In nonpartisan elections, in which less is known about the candidates and their positions, the influence of the campaigns is much more variable. In a nonpartisan election, it is often possible for a relatively unknown candidate to pull off a victory through an effective campaign. A common pattern is for familiarity with his name or ethnic affiliation to determine the results.

Adrian has provided a useful typology of nonpartisan cities.[31] In the *nominally nonpartisan* city, nonpartisanship is little more than a facade, more formal than real. Political parties in these cities retain the dominant role in the nomination process and generate resources for candidates; they inform the voters of party candidates, and have little serious competition from other groups. Chicago is the most notable example of the nominally nonpartisan city. Elsewhere, the electoral process is one where *slates of candidates are put up by both parties and other groups.* In these cities, parties are one of several factions competing for public office. A third type of nonpartisan system involves *slating of candidates by groups other than parties.* San Antonio is a good example of this quasi-party system. There, a group called the Good Government League slates and finances its own candidates. Since its organization in 1955, the GGL has elected its candidate in 77 of 81 local election contests. In the final type of nonpartisan city, a *free-for-all* pattern prevails, and neither parties nor groups regularly endorse slates. No stable coalitions exist in these cities, and the electoral rule is "every man for himself." The single label "nonpartisan" thus conceals a great deal of real variation among American municipal electoral patterns.

Parties, elections, and representation

If the purpose of elections and parties is to identify and represent mass interests in urban decision making, they fall rather short of their goal. The party, historically the great institution of democratization, has been a poor performer at the local level. While the machine had its virtues (as well as its vices), it paid little attention to representation of public interests. Moreover, the machine did little to uplift the socioeconomic conditions of its constituents. To have done so would have been suicidal, for the machine depended upon its ability to parlay the plights of people into political power. In the postmachine era, the party has been weak or ineffectual, especially in most nonpartisan cities. In most urban areas the parties do not offer even their traditional minimum choice between Tweedledum and Tweedledee. If the national parties are pilloried as disorganized, ideologically fuzzy, and inattentive to issues, then the role of the local party is even worse as a representative mechanism.

Unfortunately, the party's failings are not fully compensated by other components of the urban electoral system. Even granting the assumption that the mass public is tolerably informed about local issues, elections do not insure the transmission of those opinions to decision makers. In the first place, as we have already seen, electoral participation is uniformly low in most systems. The sparseness of turnout implies that some persons fail to register their sentiments and thus can be easily discounted by policy makers. Second, because of the unevenness of participation from group to group, elections do not provide random samples of public opinion. Some interests get counted more heavily than others. Third, except in the special case of referenda, elections do not present choices of policy, but only of candidates. In the time-honored tradition of American politics, candidates may deliberately blur their views on policy issues in order to discourage a minumum number of potential supporters. Fourth, even if candidates stood foursquare behind particular positions, voters have only one vote each and may agree with candidate Jones on law-and-order questions, but with candidate Smith on taxes. When there is a multiplicity of issues—usually none too clearly articulated by the candidates—it is virtually impossible to estimate the collective sentiment of the electorate. And, finally, even assuming that candidates spelled out their positions clearly and that voters voted clearly, there is no guarantee that successful candidates will, in fact, pursue voters' wishes.

Given all these limitations on the election as a representational mechanism, we may agree with Dahl's observation that:

a good deal of traditional democratic theory leads us to expect more from national [or local] elections than they can possibly provide. We expect elections to reveal the "will" or preference of a majority on a set of issues. This is one thing elections rarely do, except in an almost trivial fashion.[32]

Even with well-intentioned and well-informed voters and candidates, the information to be gleaned from election results is likely to be sketchy at best and utterly inexplicable at worst.

Interest Groups in Urban Politics

Arthur Bentley was the first proponent of the *group theory of politics* in modern political science. So convinced was he that all political life could be explained by the interaction of groups that he claimed: ". . . when the groups are adequately stated, everything is stated. And when I say everything, I mean everything."[33]

According to Bentley, an individual is merely the sum of his group interests, and government constitutes merely the equilibrium of group interests at a given time. Numerous political scientists have expanded, qualified, or elaborated on Bentley's formulation, but the original outline of the analysis of groups and political life was his. Bentley himself despised "definition-mongers," sneering that "he who likes may snip verbal definitions in his old age, when his world has gone crackly and dry."

Part of the difficulty with definitions that may have troubled Bentley is that the words *interest* and *group* seem either redundant or, from another perspective, contradictory. If we conceive of a political group as an organized body of people designed to influence public policy, *interest* becomes a meaningless adjective, for it is hard to imagine such a group without shared interests. On the other hand, if we emphasize the adjective *interest*, then it is equally clear that not all interests are organized into groups or, at least, that some clearly are better organized than others. A consumer, a poor man, and a commuter each has an

interest in common with fellow consumers, poor people, and commuters, but no group—or at least not a very effective one—represents
this interest. The term *interest group,* therefore, subsumes two somewhat
distinct ideas. The degree to which a particular interest is in fact
organized as a group to influence public policy is an empirical question.

More specifically, we conceive of a political group as an organization
attempting to influence public policies through application of political
resources. From either an individual or group perspective, an interest
encompasses a set of preferences about the direction of public policy.
The essential difference between groups and interests is that interests
are psychological, whereas groups are sociological, phenomena.
Interests may be more or less organized into groups; groups may share
more than one interest.

Because, as we argued in Chapters 1 and 2, local politics is often a
politics of economics, it is not surprising to find economic interest
groups surfacing as a dominant source of activity. Table 3.4 confirms
these impressions by reporting a study of city councilmen in the San
Francisco Bay Area. Anyone who suspected that the chamber of commerce was an important local political group will find his belief supported by the evidence there. Moreover, it is clear that the categories of
economic groups and special interests are somewhat overlapping, with
some special interests like developers, unions, and merchant associations exhibiting strong economic interests. In the text which follows we
discuss some of the major interest groups in urban political life, including businessmen, ethnics, labor, reformers, municipal employees,
neighborhood groups, and environmentalists. We discuss briefly the
principal interests and activities of each group, while recognizing their

Table 3.4   *Most Influential Pressure Groups Named by City Councilmen*

Type of organization	Frequency of mention
Economic groups (e.g., chamber of commerce, taxpayer groups, neighborhood groups)	43%
Civic groups (e.g., PTA, League of Women Voters, church groups, press, service clubs)	31
Special interests (e.g., conservation associations, builders, developers, senior citizens, unions, merchant associations)	23
Semi-official and official bodies (e.g., planning commission, advisory committees, etc.)	2
Total	100%

SOURCE: Adapted from *Local Interest Politics: A One-Way Street,* by Betty H. Zisk, copyright © 1973, by
The Bobbs-Merrill Company, Inc. Used by permission of the publisher. The data represent answers by
San Francisco Bay Area city councilmen. Total rounded to 100%.

variability from community to community, and assess the ways in which such groups contribute to the representation of interests.

Businessmen

Generalizing about the role of businessmen in the 80,000 units of local government in the United States is hazardous, for the term *businessman* subsumes the owner of a local nightspot as well as a half-million-dollar-a-year Detroit automobile executive.

Businessmen constitute a large proportion of interest-group membership in local politics. Charles Adrian and Charles Press have observed that "so many business groups exert pressure upon government that they would probably overshadow and overpower all the others if it were not that they spend so much of their time opposing one another."[34] Economic interests unite most businessmen some of the time (as in the desire to reduce the tax burden on local business), some businessmen all of the time, but rarely all businessmen for very long. Downtown merchants are interested in policies on mass transportation, urban renewal, and economic development that would infuse new life into the central city. Businessmen in the outlying areas tend to oppose such costly undertakings. Small businessmen, especially those who are downwardly mobile in the status system, are often hostile to downtown interests like department-store owners. Realtors are more concerned with zoning and subdivision regulation than with revitalizing sagging downtown areas. Businessmen who provide services over a wide area within the community—major wholesalers and producers, for example—are more interested in community growth, regardless of the direction that it takes.

BUSINESS INTERESTS   The two interests most likely to be shared by most businessmen are the quest for lower taxes and the desire to secure economic growth for the community. The first interest is hardly monopolized by businessmen and may be overstated in any case. Charles Gilbert, in a study of government in the Philadelphia area, noted that "in interviews, industrialists commonly aver that local and county taxes are a small part of the cost of doing business." Moreover, he reminds us that local taxes, because they are deductible from federal taxes, cost industry only fifty-two cents on the dollar.[35] We do not mean to suggest that businessmen are enthusiastic about high taxes, but they may be no more antagonistic to higher taxes than are, say, home owners. Moreover, businessmen, especially those in larger firms, see a need to make local communities as attractive as possible, in public services, as a means of increasing livability both for them and for their prospective employees.

Businessmen are perhaps most unified and vocal in their support for public policies promoting economic growth. More economic growth not only means more sales; it is also a visible and measurable sign of progress, especially to those accustomed to measuring progress in economic terms. Although not all businessmen share the economic-growth orientation toward local government, it appears to be a dominant theme of policy, especially in small and medium-sized cities.[36] Several years ago, one of the authors interviewed the mayor of a tiny southern town. During the conversation, the mayor, who was also a businessman, used a ream of charts and graphs to support his claim that his town was really "the hub of the South."

POLITICAL RESOURCES Local businessmen are usually organized in chapters of the Chamber of Commerce. One of the key political resources of the chamber is its inclusiveness, but this factor can also work to its disadvantage. For one thing, in a large group with no power to compel its members to action or even to maintain membership, individual members are inclined to let other members do the work, for all policy gains can thus be shared by all members at no cost to most individual members.[37] Second, groups with large and somewhat diverse memberships will usually be unable to formulate group positions on issues likely to divide the groups.[38] Chambers of commerce harbor numbers of conflicting interests behind the façade of a few unifying interests. Among the conflicting interests typically found in a business association are downtown versus suburbs; wholesalers versus retailers; small versus large business; and absentee versus locally owned businesses. Such internal differences tend to blunt the effectiveness of this or any relatively large and diverse organization.

Still, businessmen are a significant element in most local political systems. Businessmen are mostly from the upper and middle classes and participate in politics beyond merely voting; most local leaders, formal and informal, are recruited from the business and professional community.[39] Business interests are virtually guaranteed a hearing by local policy makers, and businessmen tend to be well educated, to have the social and verbal skills necessary to communicate effectively with bureaucrats and politicians, and to perceive higher than average stakes in community decisions.

Labor unions

Given the visibility and alleged importance of labor unions in national politics, it is surprising to discover the variability in their political influence at the urban level. Detroit is a one-industry city dominated by automotive manufacturers and the United Auto Workers. The UAW has played a fairly active role in local politics through its Committee on Political Education (COPE). But it appears to be much less effective in local affairs than in influencing Michigan state politics.

Kenneth E. Gray and David Greenstone, in their penetrating study of labor influence in Detroit, St. Louis, and Houston, concluded that "despite its power, COPE has had relatively little success in [Detroit] politics."[40] This study indicated that voters and politicians alike tend to view COPE as a self-interested group that does not represent the city as a whole. Also, and perhaps more significantly, Detroit's nonpartisan electoral system weakens the hold of union leaders on their followers. Even when the rank and file do know the union's candidates, many are reluctant to support leader-endorsed liberals for fear of increased property taxation and the possibility that such candidates will enact housing-integration ordinances.

Labor's experience in Toledo, Ohio, demonstrates the difficulty that unions have in securing rank-and-file backing for their endorsements. Some members, particularly the older and less well-educated unionists followed fairly closely the choices of the labor leaders, but for most members, "union involvement in local politics was remote and unimportant."[41] Party identification, rather than leadership endorsement, was the most important element in the voting choices of the members. Since 1953, Toledo's United Labor Committee has endorsed forty-three candidates in local contests, only twenty-three of whom have been elected. This batting average is only slightly better than chance alone would predict.

In Houston, whose population is relatively young and heavily white-collar, labor unions constitute the backbone of the liberal faction in the Democratic Party. Union attention is, however, directed much more to state than to city politics. One Houston AFL–CIO official claimed that "the closer politics is to the local level, the more we stay out of it."[42] If union attempts to wield influence in Detroit, Toledo, and Houston are typical, it seems reasonable to conclude that unions are much less effective in city than in state or national politics.

The interests and stakes of trade unions, as well as their political resources, help to account for their minimal (or variable) influence on local policy. As organizations, unions have relatively low stakes in local public policy. The key decisions, which are of concern to *all* union members, are those related to wages and hours, safety requirements, right-to-work laws, and purchasing power. These decisions are made not in city halls but by states and the federal government. Said a leader of one union in Toledo: "City government is not as important for us. We've got to think about state and national issues. The state is in many ways the most important, I think, since it handles workmen's compensation, unemployment, and such things."[43]

During an earlier era when local police broke up strikes and jailed picketers, unions were more concerned about local politics. Today the overriding concerns of unions as a whole are focused on higher levels of the American federal system. Many significant local political issues tend to divide rank-and-file unionists in ways that would permit no clear leadership position to prevail. Race relations, integration of schools and neighborhoods, and taxation are especially divisive issues. As these issues involve no direct threats to the position of the union as an organization, local leaders commonly avoid taking sides.

To a much greater degree than the local chamber of commerce, unions harbor multiple conflicting interests among their members, which impel them to steer fairly clear of local politics, particularly when their stakes are at higher levels of government anyway. As in all interest groups, limitations on political resources—votes, money, and organization, in particular—require that they be spent where they will have the greatest impact; for trade unions, local government is not that point.

One particular feature of the governmental structure of reformed cities—the nonpartisan ballot—also contributes to the weakening of trade-union influence. Nonpartisanship permits candidates to be more flexible in their issue positions, and it is therefore more difficult to identify a candidate as either pro- or antilabor. Voters in a nonpartisan system do not have the valuable cues of party identification to help them sort out candidates. Psychologically, therefore, it is easier for a rank-and-file member to vote for a candidate of somewhat conservative ideological bent, especially on race and tax questions, even though he might not vote for the same candidate if the Republican label were affixed to the ballot. Nonpartisanship thus weakens the potential influence of labor in city politics.

Ethnic groups

THE ASSIMILATION THESIS   Mark Twain is said to have grumbled, upon reading his own obituary, that "the rumors of my death are greatly exaggerated." The same may be said about the widely espoused theory of the *assimilation* of European ethnic groups. According to the assimilationist theory, second- and third-generation European immigrants have become so thoroughly socialized in the culture of middle-class America that their political attitudes and behavior are scarcely distinguishable from those of direct descendants of arrivals on the *Mayflower*.

Dahl has suggested that ethnic politics passes through three stages.[44] In the first stage, group members are "almost exclusively proletarian," few indigenous group leaders exist, and social homogeneity within the group produces great similarity in voting habits. In the second stage, group members become socially differentiated, as some members attain white-collar positions and status. People in such roles have different views from those in the first phase of assimilation, but there is still a high degree of ethnic consciousness among these upwardly mobile individuals. In the third stage, considerable heterogeneity develops, as large segments are assimilated into the nonproletarian classes. To these people, ethnic identification becomes a source of embarrassment. Socioeconomic class, rather than ethnic identification, begins to determine individual behavior patterns, and ethnic solidarity becomes a subject for historians. By the late 1950s, Dahl had concluded that ethnic politics in New Haven was on the wane and that any politician who pitched his appeal solely to ethnic groups would probably lose.

Superficially at least, assimilation now appears to be extensive. Although 19 percent of the American population consists of either first- or second-generation immigrants, the once-prominent European ghetto within the central city has almost disappeared. No longer are European and Asian ethnic groups crowded into city tenements as they once were. As have other Americans, these ethnic populations have moved to the suburbs and home ownership is extensive among them. In Chicago, Detroit, Los Angeles, and Philadelphia, the proportion of home ownership is higher among first- and second-generation immigrants than among Americans of native-born parentage.[45] Today there are as many ethnics residing outside CCs as in them. Although New York City still has more Italians than Naples and more Greeks than Sparta, the salience of many ethnic communities has declined. There were an estimated 1300 foreign-language newspapers in the United States in 1914. Today there are fewer than 400. There is also less political cohesion in the ethnic vote than in the past.

THE LIMITS OF ASSIMILATION   On the other hand, there is much evidence against too-hasty acceptance of the assimilation thesis. Ethnic politics has a tenacity that defies academic arguments about assimilation, absorption, and homogenization. Raymond Wolfinger reinvestigated the patterns of ethnic politics in New Haven and found that Italian-Americans still gave vigorous support to the Connecticut Republican Party in the 1940s and the 1950s.[46] Polish-American voters in urban and rural areas of Illinois will still cross party lines to vote for Polish names.[47] In nonpartisan local elections, ethnic identification takes on added importance, for it is one of the few available cues for voters.[48]

With the growth of civil-rights and Black Power movements among urban Blacks, European ethnic groups have produced counterorganizations, particularly in opposition to neighborhood and school integration. Chicago Congressman Roman Pucinski, of Polish extraction, has claimed that "The rise of Negro militancy has brought a revival of ethnic orientation in all the other groups."[49] That many police departments in cities with heavily ethnic populations include large numbers of Italians, Irish, Polish, and other ethnics heightens the frictions between the police and Blacks.

Considering the evidence against overemphasis on the assimilation theory, Wolfinger has formulated an alternative model of ethnic politics, which he calls "the mobilization theory" of ethnic political life. He argues that "the strength of ethnic voting depends on both the intensity of ethnic identification and the level of ethnic relevance in the election." The most important expression of ethnic relevance is the presence of an ethnic name on the ticket. But, because "middle-class status is a virtual prerequisite for candidacy for major office" and because "an ethnic group's development of sufficient political skill and influence to secure such a nomination also requires the development of a middle class,"[50] ethnic voting solidarity will not appear until some members of the group become candidates for middle-class status. The peak of ethnic solidarity in elections thus will come not during the first generation—when the group is uniformly of the lower class and subject to manipulation and cross pressures from competing factions—but during the second and third generations. This theory seems better able to explain why, in New Haven at least, there was an increasing solidarity of ethnic groups behind their parties over time. It also embodies recognition of political-leadership skills as a crucial ingredient in ethnic politics.

At least in the early years of ethnic solidarity, the ethnic group pursues mostly status goals, as distinct from ideological or material goals. The most important element of the collective mentality of an ethnic group is its uncertainty about its own status in the social system. The placement of a group leader at the top of a political ticket provides vicarious status mobility to all members of the group. The hiring of policemen or civil servants from the group, the awarding of contracts, the election to party posts, and the "Columbus Day appeal" of ethnic celebrations are all measures of a group's political status. Such matters as taxation, urban renewal, zoning, and crime prevention are also relevant to members of ethnic groups, but they do not benefit the groups per se. In identifying with his national group—although we must recognize that he may also play a number of other politically relevant roles—the ethnic voter will be most concerned with status rewards for his group. The conflict over status will be more intense if the community contains two or more ethnic groups vying with one another for outputs. The vigor of competition among ethnic groups is one explanation for the higher-than-average participation of such groups in local politics. As we noted earlier, European ethnic voters tend to vote more in local politics than do more traditional Americans. Moreover, where there is considerable political activism among ethnic groups, traditional Americans may also participate more, simply in response to this vigor.

Politics has long provided an avenue of upward mobility for ethnic minorities, even when opportunities in other parts of the social system have been limited. In a system of universal suffrage ethnics have votes and a ready-made basis for group loyalty. The leaders of urban party machines, which dominated politics in many cities during the early years of urbanization, took full advantage of the new immigrants' potential. For decades ethnics constituted the hard core of support for the machines, which explains, at least partly, why the reformers, who have been mostly more established white Protestants, have been so outspoken in their criticism of the machines. Through the exchange of status and service for votes and support, the machine and the ethnic groups forged a solid and mutually productive alliance. Most machines, like most ethnic groups, were Democratic (a curious exception is the Italians in New Haven), and the Democratic parties of eastern cities still draw consistent support from ethnic voters.

James Q. Wilson and Edward C. Banfield have emphasized that most European ethnic groups hold a set of attitudes toward government and policy that separates them from the views held by traditional Americans. They describe these two attitudinal syndromes as *private-regarding* and *public-regarding*.[51] Private-regarding attitudes emphasize personal politics, oriented toward the family, group, or subculture—involving a political style not unlike that provided by the machines for many decades. This conception of politics includes bargaining, trading off, and the material satisfaction of group interests, with heavy emphasis on political accountability. The public-regarding style, a view associated with a more traditional American value system, encompasses principles of abstract morality, honesty, efficiency, and the value of professional management. The public-regarding perspective on local politics is one basis for the reform movement in local politics.

Reformers

Nearly every major city and most minor ones (assuming that any city admits to being "minor") has its reform group. Where reformers are not organized in groups, there is still widely shared interest in the goals of the reform movement. Oklahoma City has its Association for Responsible Government, New York City has the Citizen's Union, and San Antonio has the Good Government League, each of which seeks to institutionalize the virtues of good government. (Because of these perennial cries for "good government," critics of the early reformers sometimes called them the "goo-goos.") Virtually every city has a chapter of the League of Women Voters, although the league is not always as influential as its spokeswomen believe. Not all the reformers have identical views about their goals, but most seem to share the following predispositions about local government:

1. An aversion to "politics" as a means of arriving at public-policy decisions and specifically to political parties and organized interest groups;
2. A holistic conception of the community as a whole to which special interests should be clearly subordinated;
3. A strong preference for professional management of community affairs, implying preference for public policy making by technical experts like the city manager;
4. A strong faith in the efficacy of structural reform.

The goal of the early reformers was to rationalize and democratize city government by substituting community-oriented leadership for the pernicious politics of the machine. They rejected the personal kind of political accountability associated with the machine, patronage, ward leaders, and demands for ethnic recognition. Instead, they stressed a political accountability modeled upon that of the business corporation (or their image of it), which would have a small policy-making body, the council (board of directors), directly responsible to the electorate (stockholders), without the intervention of parties and groups, and administration by professional experts. A manager (corporation president) would serve at the discretion of the council. Although a number of structural reforms were advocated by the reformers, the most lasting in their effects have been manager government, nonpartisan elections, and at-large constituencies.

The reformers became prominent in the latter years of the nineteenth century. They have remained so ever since, although there are some differences between the early and latter-day reformers. Businessmen, traditional groups, local chambers of commerce, and upper-class people were in the forefront of the early battles for reform. Harold Stone, in his survey of early adoptions of the council-manager plan, found in Jackson, Michigan, that "most of the campaign work [for the plan] was done through the Chamber of Commerce, which enlisted the support of all the Protestant reform agencies in the city."[52] In Rochester, New York, the campaign for manager government was "supported by the leading industrialist of the city, George Eastman, by the Bureau of Municipal Research which he financed, and by most of the civic, reform, and business associations of the city."[53] (One leader of the Rochester Communist Party also supported the manager plan, believing that it was one stage through which politics would have to pass before the dictatorship of the proletariat could be achieved.) Almost as surely as the manager plan was supported by traditional and business interests in the city, it was opposed by trade unions and ethnic groups.

Many contemporary studies of city politics have revealed the major role played by reformers or by those who share reformist attitudes. Wilson and Banfield have portrayed the reformers as public-regarding voters, actors, and thinkers who seek the good of the community as a whole, rather than benefits to particular interests.[54] Robert Agger, Daniel Goldrich, and Bert E. Swanson have described the rise of *community conservationists*, a group that sees the "values of community life maximized when political leadership is exercised by men representing the public at large, rather than 'special interests.'"[55] Robert C. Wood has described a similar set of attitudes in the "no-party politics of suburbia." Suburbanites seem to be characterized by "an outright reaction against partisan activity, a refusal to recognize that there may be persistent cleavages in the electorate, and an ethical disapproval of permanent group collaboration as an appropriate means of settling disputes."[56]

The terms *reformism, community conservationism,* and *public-regardingness* all describe the attitudes that pervade American communities among upper- and middle-class citizens in particular. The structure of local politics has been heavily influenced by these attitudes, particularly the emphasis on professional management and the choice of managerial government, nonpartisan elections, and at-large constituencies as models of political accountability.

Municipal employees

The 4.5 million employees of urban government in the United States are important subjects of inquiry. They have higher stakes than do most citizens in the municipal political system; they form interest groups that press for group benefits, particularly wage and salary improvements; and they are themselves decision makers who shape the policies of municipalities, school districts, counties, and other local governments.[57] We are less concerned here with their roles as decision makers (a subject that we shall cover in Chapter 5) than with their roles as citizens and interest groups.

As the recipients of nearly $2 billion in wages and salaries (by far the largest proportion of city expenditures) city employees have obvious stakes in the wage and salary decisions of municipal government. Many skilled, unskilled, and professional city employees have joined unions. As in the private sector, unionization is less extensive among the white-collar employees of municipal governments (e.g., teachers) than among the blue-collar and the unskilled, but white-collar unionism is growing. Many of these unionized city employees are members of the American Federation of State, County and Municipal Employees, an affiliate of the AFL–CIO. (Most unionized teachers belong to the American Federation of Teachers, also an AFL–CIO affiliate.) Many city employees who are not members of national unions are members of local organizations that attempt to secure collective benefits, and many large and medium-sized cities have organizations of policemen, modeled after New York City's Patrolmen's Benevolent Association.

It is a commonplace of American law that government employees are not permitted to strike. In recent years, however, cities have suffered sudden "epidemics" among employees involved in wage negotiations. (Among policemen, this phenomenon is commonly known as the "blue flu.") New York City has experienced more difficulties with its employees than has perhaps any other city, having endured prolonged strikes of both teachers and sanitation workers. New York City's "finest" have also developed to a high art the strategy of variable law enforcement. From time to time, enforcement of parking and traffic regulations slows to a snail's pace under advice from the leaders of the PBA, whereas at other times they instruct patrolmen to "enforce the law 100%."[58]

Even in the absence of these uncommon tactics of negotiation, city employees are a very attentive public. They possess more information about city politics than do most other citizens, and they are more likely to vote than are most other citizens. These resources weld city employees into an interest group well worth courting in municipal elections. One of the first considerations in normal municipal budgeting is, if resources permit, to figure in wage and salary increases for municipal employees.

Most professional employees of city government are affiliated with professional associations, most of which maintain staffs in Washington, D.C., to press for legislation oriented toward the particular policy concerns of the organizations. Housing administrators are vigorous in their support of public-housing legislation, planners support federal assistance for urban-planning activities, and other professional organizations attempt to secure federal legislation to further their professional interests.

In addition to support for federal and state legislation, these associations provide guidelines and cues to their members. Through newsletters, periodicals, conferences, and conventions, organizations provide channels through which members are kept abreast of one another's thinking. Organizations thus disseminate professional standards that influence members' behavior, whatever the particular ordinances and rules provided by city administrators and councilmen. To a librarian, there are right and wrong ways to operate a library regardless of the position taken by the city council. A planner relies on his training and professional standards for planning criteria, whatever views the manager or mayor may hold.

Neighborhood groups

Neighborhoods take on particular importance in cities with ward elections, but under certain circumstances neighborhood groups may be important in any city. There is a well-known tendency for people to sort themselves—or to be sorted by others—into relatively homogeneous areas. Because of this tendency neighborhood interests overlap social and economic interests somewhat. Neighborhood-based political organizations are found most often in working-class and lower-middle-class areas, rather than in lower-class or upper-middle-class areas. The lowest-status areas in a city usually lack the stability and the leadership skills to organize viable groups. For other reasons, the neighborhood is not commonly a basis for social organization in more cosmopolitan upper-middle-class areas; organization there is based more often on occupational, professional, or city-wide considerations.

Some neighborhood groups persist for years, are effectively led, and present cogent statements of their interests to the council, mayor, or bureaucracy. But the more typical pattern is the ad hoc neighborhood association organized in response to some perceived external threat. One of the most frequent spurs to sporadic neighborhood organization is the threat of a change in zoning ordinances, especially one that would change a neighborhood's status from single-family residential to multi-family residential or to commercial. Such ad hoc groups differ widely in the quality of their leadership, their staying power, and the resources they bring to bear on decision makers. Because of these differences, it is difficult to predict the outcome of their confrontations with planning boards or city councils.

Zoning is not the only public policy that stimulates formation of neighborhood groups. Joint federal-urban programs like model cities, the war on poverty, and urban renewal focus on certain neighborhoods. Federal legislation requires that each program involve some degree of citizen participation. Opposition by neighborhood groups has been one of the most significant obstacles to local urban-renewal agencies. Studies by James C. Davies in New York City have shown that an effective neighborhood organization led by articulate, politically sophisticated people can hamstring major renewal projects.[59] But, because renewal agencies rarely tackle neighborhoods where there are reservoirs of middle-class leadership skills, the relevant neighborhood groups are often ineffective.

The antipoverty and model-cities programs are also obliged to encourage citizen participation in program formation. The early experience of the war on poverty demonstrated that neighborhood participation is highly variable: Some neighborhoods oppose the program, others are basically apathetic, and still others are supportive. Partly because the antipoverty program had given neighborhood groups some experience in influencing decision makers, such groups have been more effective in shaping the direction of the model-cities program.[60]

There has recently been a renaissance of the neighborhood organization. As we have just noted it arises partly from public policies that take particular neighborhoods as their target areas. Some cities have deliberately facilitated this neighborhood resurgence by attempting to decentralize public administration and policy making, particularly in education. Another contributing factor is the resurgence of ethnic consciousness among racial and national groups, each of which seeks to assert its identity and viability as a community.

Environmentalists

The newest entrant in the local interest-group struggle is the environmentalist organization. As ubiquitous as the problems they attack and the "progress" they oppose, environmentalists can be found in freeway controversies, opposing new airports, maintaining open spaces against encroachment, and fighting skyscrapers. Colorado environmentalists successfully protested the Winter Olympics; San Antonio environmentalists fought a freeway that would have run within 90 feet of the zoo's bear pits (see our case study on pp. 280–281); San Francisco environmentalists advocated limitation of skyscrapers; and environmentalists everywhere have battled against the automobile. These causes have not endeared environmentalists to civic leaders accustomed to measuring municipal progress by the number of new sewer connections. While business and reform ideologies assume growth is the key to urban survival, environmentalists see growth as further exploiting or despoiling scarce resources.

Most Americans are, at least in the abstract, environmentalists. In opinion polls, a majority of Americans have described themselves as "deeply concerned" and another third as "somewhat concerned" about air and water pollution.[61] Abstract interest, however, is not always translated into concrete action. Environmentalism is a public-interest issue like consumerism, and there is often a tendency to "let George do it" (or Ralph Nader or the Sierra Club) when the interest is an abstract and long-term problem. Local interest groups concerned with environmental despoliation are, therefore, often small, but vocal, minorities. We shall have more to say about environmental politics and policy in Chapter 11.

Interest groups and representation

Political scientists are hardly in agreement about the power of groups to influence public policy. But there is good reason, we think, to reject literal acceptance of Bentley's observation that, "when the groups are adequately explained, everything is explained." This argument is true only in the trivial and tautological sense that, if attitudes, values, parties, electoral mechanisms, bureaucratic premises, and the like are defined as *groups* or *group-determined*, then everything indeed can be explained by explaining groups. If *everything* is a *group*, then the concept *group* can explain everything.

If we restrict ourselves to a more narrow and commonsensical meaning of the term *interest group* to denote formal organization, however, we do not find that interest groups are all-powerful. One of the most penetrating studies of policy making at the national level examined the influence on tariff policy of such associations as the Chamber of Commerce, the National Association of Manufacturers, the League of Women Voters, and the AFL–CIO; it found them surprisingly ineffectual.[62] More pertinent to city politics, John P. Crecine studied budgetary policies in three cities and found that decision makers rarely received any pressure from specific groups. When groups did argue for particular financial commitments, decision makers tended to believe that most requests were reasonable but that "you can't do everything everybody wants."[63] In a study of San Francisco Bay Area city councils, groups were found to play an important role upon occasion, but their influence depended heavily on the attitudes of councilmen toward the legitimacy of the group's activity.[64] These findings do not invalidate the assumption that groups are important elements in community decision making, but they cast doubt on any theory of urban politics which assumes the primacy of interest groups in determining the use of community resources.

As a representational mechanism, therefore, the interest group is (like the party and electoral system) limited. One of the interest group's most significant limitations derives from the paucity of group membership in a city. Mythology to the contrary, the United States is hardly a nation of joiners. The vast majority of American citizens belong to no political organization. This does not mean that they will go unrepresented, but the nonparticipant remains at the mercy of someone else's good will. There is, moreover, a strong correlation between group membership and socioeconomic status. Some, in other words, are better organized than others. The Chamber of Commerce is more tightly organized than the local consumers' association; the schoolteachers are better organized than the poor; the transportation industries are typically more organized than commuters. Even if a group is well organized, many city councilmen reject pressure and prefer to follow their own consciences. Thus, a number of interests in the city are not well organized into groups, and, even when they are, an organization does not assure effectiveness in shaping policy.

Political Protest

Almost by definition, protest is a weapon of groups that are weak in conventional political resources. Protest—violent and nonviolent—has a long history in American cities. Not all protest, of course, is violent, nor is all violence protest. Unfortunately, neither the causes nor the consequences of protest are more than dimly understood. Speculation abounds about the effects of protest on policy, but there is little hard evidence at present. A few things about the nature of protest activity, however, are clear.

In the first place, it seems that protest is a more complex activity than is commonly believed. Michael Lipsky argues that our understanding of protest movements cannot be satisfactory unless we pay attention to a multiplicity of actors.[65] The participants in any protest activity are not limited to the activists themselves and to the elite whom they wish to influence, but depend upon crucial third parties. All protest activities will wither on the vine without a means of communicating sentiments. The mass media thus plays a crucial role in focusing attention on grievances. The activists typically intend to energize sympathetic third parties, who in turn can be expected to bring pressure on decision makers. Martin Luther King, Jr., we presume, had little hope of winning over diehard segregationist southern governors, mayors, and elites. His success depended upon his ability to lay bare and expose injustices to crucial third parties, particularly the national elite and the federal government. This is also true of protest movements at the local level, which depend upon their capacity to focus attention upon the evils they experience, and to develop within the community a network of third parties who will enter the conflict on their side.

Nonviolent protest is at least as old as Henry David Thoreau, yet as contemporary as rent strikes, welfare sit-ins, political demonstrations, and antiwar marches. The late Saul Alinsky developed protest strategies to the level of an art form, complete with rehearsed scenarios, the use of the dramatic (e.g., carrying live rats to councilmen's doorsteps in one campaign), and the insistence on a sustained thrust. But while it may be increasing in usage, the protest strategy has remained highly unpopular with most Americans. Despite the horrors of what Chicago lawyer (now Illinois governor) Daniel Walker called a "police riot," most Americans felt that Mayor Daley's police used *too little* or the *right amount* of force on demonstrators at the 1968 Democratic Convention. A majority of Americans contend flatly that they would *disapprove* of even a lawful protest march, *sanctioned by local authorities.* [66] If nonviolent protest is to be effective, it will surely be in spite of, rather than because of, the attitudes held by a majority of American citizens.

Violence in the city

Black activist H. Rap Brown once observed that "violence is as American as cherry pie," and scholarly research seems to support him. The prophet Ezekiel observed that "the land is full of bloody crimes and the city is full of violence," and his words still ring true. Violent protest in American political history has included slave revolts, antiblack violence, labor-management conflict, nativism and anti-Catholicism, and war and draft protest. One student of comparative civil violence, Ted Gurr, ranked the United States seventh among 113 nations in the level of its domestic violence. [67] It also has been argued that the overall level of political violence is not much greater today than at earlier periods in American history. [68] Today, a large proportion of all collective violence is racial in character (see our discussion in the next section), and an unspecifiable proportion of individual violence has racial undertones.

Black Politics:
From Conciliation to Confrontation

Wilson has written that "any book on Negroes, particularly on their politics, ought to be published in a loose-leaf binder so that it can be corrected and updated on a monthly basis."[69] Change—its presence, its absence, and expectation of it—is the distinguishing feature of racial politics in American cities. The urbanization of the American black community, or perhaps more precisely its "ghettoization," is the most profound change since the abolition of slavery. In 1910, nine out of ten American Blacks lived in the South, primarily in the poor countryside. By 1966, nearly seven out of ten Blacks lived in SMSAs, almost all in the CCs.

The civil-rights movement secured a number of favorable outputs from the national government—the historic school-desegregation decision, a succession of civil-rights acts, and open-housing and public-accommodations laws. But to some black leaders and their followers, these gains have proved to be chimerical, more symbolic than genuine. Civil-rights decisions heightened aspirations among Blacks, but the intended policy gains did not always produce gains for individual Blacks; tension and frustration over the widening gap between aspirations and attainments found an outlet in the summer riots of the 1960s. Racial explosions pockmarked the physical and social landscape of most sizable American cities.

Political participation of black urbanites

Because of the relatively low status of most black Americans, we expect to find them participating in politics much less than do Whites. Yet in many cities Blacks vote about as regularly as do Whites, at least when there are no other barriers to their participation. Although southern Blacks have a record of not voting as a result of a heritage of discrimination, Blacks in some northern cities participate at levels that equal or exceed those of Whites. Sixty-one percent of the Blacks in St. Louis reported voting in some local elections; almost exactly the same proportion of Whites reporting voting. Blacks were only a small proportion of the total population in New Haven, but their voting participation exceeded that of Whites.[70] Despite the evidence of parity in voting participation in these cities, black participation rates lag behind white rates in many, if not most, other cities.

To what degree does voting strength affect urban policies benefiting Blacks as a group? The right to vote has been touted as "the most powerful instrument ever devised by man for breaking down injustice and destroying the terrible walls that imprison men because they are different from other men."[71] Such claims make good politics but poor social science. Participation through voting is but one of many means of enunciating political preferences, and public policy is determined by more than occasional elections. The importance of the vote in a scheme of ordered liberty notwithstanding, any claims for the efficacy of the franchise in achieving group goals should be subjected to careful empirical examination.

William R. Keech assessed the strengths and limitations of black voting as a political resource in a study of Durham, North Carolina. Durham Blacks have voted for many years and have skilled leadership and vigorous political organization. Still, Keech noted, "the really striking gains of Durham's Negro minority have come through resources other than votes."[72] Some policy decisions are influenced by votes, but "the vote is a far more potent instrument for achieving legal justice than social justice. The gains [that are] most susceptible to Negro voting have consistently been those which most clearly involved fair and just administration of existing laws. Social justice, however, demands more than this."[73] People have different perceptions of *social justice*, but, if the concept includes such things as comparable incomes for comparable jobs, courteous and equal treatment by fellow citizens, and opportunities for economic advancement, the vote in urban elections does not win social justice. The vote is much more influential in reducing disparities in treatment in the public sector than it is in changing behavior in the private sector through governmental action. Other strategies like litigation, boycotts, and demonstrations seem to be more effective than the vote in securing basic social changes.

Black leadership

If this book had been written two decades ago, the subject of black leadership would have been coupled with the topic of political machines, for most "leaders" of the black community drew their power from their ties with Democratic or (less frequently) Republican machines. The most resilient example of this older style of machine leadership is the organization of the late Congressman William L. Dawson. His hold on the Chicago black vote can be compared only to Mayor Daley's hold on the Chicago white vote. Wilson described the Dawson machine this way:

The Dawson machine, like all machines, is an organization whose purpose is the election of men to office and which is sustained mainly through the distribution of tangible incentives to its members. To a greater extent than any other Negro organization which acts in the public or civic areas, it is "issue-free" . . . Negro leaders tend to be conservative, and to share (with the exception of the importance they attach to race) the values of white conservatives. Few feel that there is anything at stake important enough to warrant an attack on the status quo.[74]

The persistence of the Dawson machine depends upon the survival of the larger Democratic machine in Chicago. Vigorous competition among contending white factions for control of Chicago government would probably fragment the black machine as well, but because such competition has been slow in developing, the Dawson organization has survived both the moralism of the civil-rights movement and the militance of the Black Power advocates. Still, attacks upon the black organization have increased in vigor in recent years.

Philadelphia has exhibited a different type of organization, but it is similar to Chicago in the issueless character of black politics. Philadelphia has vigorous machines in both the Democratic and Republican Parties but has never had a black machine per se. John H. Strange concluded that black leadership in Philadelphia was weak and relatively unconcerned with racial goals: "There has never been any significant legislation of any kind proposed by a Negro or Negro organization in Philadelphia, nor has the political activity necessary to pass any legislation been conducted under the direction of a Negro organization."[75] In fact, the major organizations supporting both the Philadelphia fair-employment practices law and the Philadelphia fair-housing ordinance were dominated by Whites.

Not all American cities have black organizations like those of Philadelphia or Chicago, which are at times weak and uninterested in racial policies. The Durham black community has been effectively and skillfully organized into the Durham Committee on Negro Affairs and has developed to a high art the strategy of bloc voting for maximum impact on electoral outcomes.[76] Durham Blacks have voted with a mean cohesion of 91 percent in recent years. They switch votes from one election to the next, delivering overwhelming majorities for a candidate in one election and against him in the next. This degree of cohesion is significant, although high cohesion also occurred in the Gary, Indiana, and Cleveland, Ohio, elections of black mayors in 1967 and in the elections of Kenneth Gibson in Newark in 1970, Tom Bradley in Los Angeles and Maynard Jackson in Atlanta in 1973.[77]

Where Blacks have organized to pursue racial ends, they have tried either coalition with liberal or conservative elements or achievement of an independent balance of power.[78] The Durham experience is an example of balance-of-power strategy. The black leadership in Atlanta once cooperated with the moderately conservative white leadership structure, hoping to capitalize upon the power and public-regardingness of the latter. In Houston, on the other hand, black leadership has worked with liberals, who have less power than do conservatives in city politics but whose ideological goals are more compatible with black interests. Each strategy has its own costs and advantages, depending upon the history and the context of local politics.

Black Power leadership groups in American cities vigorously oppose coalition politics. Statements and definitions of Black Power are as numerous as are its proponents (multiplied, perhaps, by its critics). One of the most articulate and widely read statements is that of Stokely Carmichael and Charles V. Hamilton. Their fundamental premise is a distinction between "individual" and "institutional" racism. This distinction parallels the difference between micro and macro levels of analysis in city politics. They contend that:

When a black family moves into a home in a white neighborhood and is stoned, burned or routed out, they are victims of an overt act of individual racism which many people will condemn—at least in words. But it is institutional racism that keeps black people locked in dilapidated slum tenements, subject to the daily prey of exploitative slumlords, merchants, loan sharks, and discriminatory real estate agents.[79]

Individual racism is direct, specific, and visible; individuals can be singled out and held culpable. *Institutional racism* is covert, indirect, collective, and nonspecific; it is difficult to pin responsibility upon a single group or individual. Carmichael and Hamilton have argued that even achievement of the traditional black goal of integration can deal only with individual racism. They note that it is possible to *assimilate* individuals but that only groups can be *integrated*. Individual assimilation merely siphons off the fortunate few who might otherwise have provided a source of leadership for the black community. Instead of integration, the Black Power philosophy rests upon the "fundamental premise" that "before a group can enter the open society, it must first close ranks."[80] In these authors' view coalitions have failed in the past because Blacks have permitted white coalition partners to define the interests of both parties. Black Power rests upon the Machiavellian notion that "a prince ought never to make common cause with one more powerful than himself." Black Power proponents say, "enter coalitions only *after* you are able to stand on your own."[81]

A TYPOLOGY OF BLACK LEADERSHIP   There have been several attempts to construct typologies of black political leadership. Wilson, for example, has drawn a distinction between *status* and *welfare* orientations. Status orientations emphasize class advancement for the black community as a whole, and welfare orientations stress individual material advances that may not improve the status of the whole racial community.[82] Matthews and Prothro provide the most elaborate and useful typology, reproduced in slightly modified form in Table 3.5. They identify three "pure types" based on four dimensions: social background, goals, strategies, and sources of influence.

There are relatively few *traditional* leaders in big cities, although the Chicago machine approaches this type. *Moderate* leadership is most characteristic of groups like the NAACP and the Urban League—the civil-rights organizations—and seems most appealing to the white middle class. The *militant* style is anathema to most Whites, partly because its proponents deny a major role to Whites in the quest for

Table 3.5 *Typology of Black Leadership Styles*

Characteristic	Leadership style		
	Traditional	Moderate	Militant
Social position			
Educational and occupational level	High or low	High	High or low
Economic independence from Whites	Low	High	High
Goals	Ameliorative action within a segregated system, where few benefit	Improvement of welfare of all Blacks; gradual desegregation; legal and political equality	Status goals; symbolic gains for Blacks; emphasis on integrity of black community
Strategies	Ad hoc, covert, individual approach to influential Whites	Continuous, overt, organized effort; voting cohesion; legal attacks on segregation	Mass protest movements and direct action; developing community autonomy first; independence of coalition
Sources of influence			
With Whites	Ingratiation; usefulness to white leaders	Control over black votes; legality	Publicity; boycotts; threats of violence
With Blacks	Access or prestige	Political ability and performance	Agitational, charismatic or forensic abilities

SOURCE: Adapted from Donald R. Matthews and James W. Prothro, *Negroes and the New Southern Politics* (New York: Harcourt Brace Jovanovich, 1966), Table 7-4.

equality and partly because they refuse to reject violence as a strategy. There has been an increase in the proportion of militant leaders, but even this term does not capture the essence of some factions of black leadership, like the Black Panthers and other paramilitary groups. The latter, because of their militance (in the literal sense of the term), are as apolitical in terms of the conventional political system and its values as are the traditional leaders.

Race, violence, and politics

Race riots did not begin in the 1960s with Watts, Detroit, Cleveland, and Newark. Racial conflagrations in East St. Louis in 1917 and in Detroit in 1943 matched in deaths and destruction most of the severe riots of the 1960s. Stanley Lieberson and Arnold R. Silverman counted seventy-six major racial disorders between 1913 and 1963.[83] The earlier riots differed from those of more recent vintage, however, in being mostly initiated by

Whites and involving direct violence against individual Blacks or black groups. Most were responses to perceived transgressions of the legal or social taboos of racial segregation. The riots of 1963–1968 (which by one count numbered 283 among cities of over 25,000 population) were more commonly outbursts generated within the ghettos themselves and directed against aspects of white society (particularly the police and ghetto merchants), rather than against whites as individuals or groups.

Whites and Blacks, surveyed separately by the National Advisory Commission on Civil Disorders (the Kerner Commission), were sharply divided on the "causes" of the riots. According to Table 3.6, two-thirds of the Whites thought that some particular group of "undesirables"— radicals, looters, or Communists—had provoked the riots. This micro-level explanation attributes riots to the perniciousness of men. Blacks, on the other hand, almost universally offered macro-level explanations of the riots, as results of social-structural factors, especially discrimination and unemployment. It thus appears that the premise of *institutional racism* is prominent in black explanations for the riots. It follows from the varying perceptions of causes that Whites and Blacks also favor different policy responses to the riots. When asked what could be done to prevent further rioting, Whites most frequently responded that "more police control" is essential, whereas Blacks preferred changes in the social and economic structures.[84]

As the data in Table 3.6 suggest, a number of white Americans (and their public officials) pictured the "typical" rioter as part of the "criminal element" or as "radical." This view, sometimes dubbed the *riffraff theory* of riot participation, includes three premises about riots: (1) Only a tiny fraction (1–2 percent) of the ghetto community participated in the riots; (2) most rioters were riffraff—unattached youths, people with criminal records, the unemployed, disoriented migrants from the rural South who are unable to adjust to an urban environment; (3) the black community as a whole deplores the violence, seeing it as pointless and counterproductive.[85] This theory is comfortable for white middle-class Americans and their public officials, but it is not supported by studies of riot participants. Evidence suggests that between a third and a fifth of the ghetto community participates in major riots. And, instead of being drawn largely from the criminal elements in the ghetto, the typical rioter is not much different from his fellow ghetto residents. Robert M. Fogelson and Robert B. Hill's study for the Kerner Commission found that the "typical" rioter

1. Was slightly better educated than were other ghetto residents;
2. Was likely to have been born in the community in which the riot occurred;
3. Was usually employed, although at a job requiring little education;

Table 3.6 *Black and White Responses to the Question "What Do You Think Was the Main Cause of These Disturbances?"*

Most frequent types of spontaneous response	Blacks		Whites	
	Men	Women	Men	Women
Discrimination, unfair treatment	49%	48%	22%	27%
Unemployment	23	22	13	13
Inferior jobs	13	10	5	5
Bad housing	23	20	15	15
Poor education	10	9	7	7
Poverty	10	8	11	9
Police brutality	10	4	2	1
Black Power or other "radicals"	4	5	26	21
Looters and other undesirables	11	11	34	34
Communists	0	0	8	5

SOURCE: National Advisory Commission on Civil Disorders, *Supplemental Studies* (Washington, D.C.: Government Printing Office, 1968), p. 48, Table V-b. Each reply to the question was coded separately, and, as some people mentioned more than one cause, the percentages do not total 100. Only reasons mentioned by at least 10 percent of a group are presented here, except for the response "Communist," which is slightly under this limit.

4. Had an income about equal to that of other ghetto residents;
5. Was no more likely than other ghetto residents to possess a "record."

After an examination of rioters in Newark and Detroit, Nathan S. Kaplan and Jeffrey M. Paige concluded that

the rioters are not the poorest of the poor. They are not the hard-core unemployed. They are not the least educated. They are not unassimilated migrants or newcomers to the city. There is no evidence that they have serious personality disturbances or are deviant in their social behavior. They do not have a different set of values.[86]

The rioter was not an atypical member of the ghetto community.

The third tenet of the riffraff theory is that the riots are condemned by most Blacks. Yet, despite the fact that a number of ghetto residents suffered personal or material losses during the riots, a significant minority approved of them, and a majority saw them as protests that would ultimately have positive results. In the aftermath of the Los Angeles riots, "a large minority (about one-third) approved of the rioting, and most Negro residents of the riot area felt it had been a meaningful protest, and most were optimistic about its effects on their life situation."[87] Blacks, whether or not they supported the riots, thought that the riots had helped dramatize their plight.

This belief on the part of Blacks appears to be a very serious misreading of white attitudes. Whereas Los Angeles Blacks thought the riots dramatized their grievances, the overwhelming majority of Whites thought that Watts had increased the gap between the races.[88] Overall, white reaction to the riots was anything but sympathetic, as the evidence in Table 3.6 shows. In the aftermath of the riots, Whites swept in to office several law-and-order mayors such as former police captain Charles Sventig in Minneapolis and Philadelphia's police chief, Frank Rizzo (well known for his definition of a conservative: "you know what a conservative is? That's a liberal who got mugged the night before"). In 1969, George Gallup surveyed "middle Americans," that is, white Americans with incomes in the $5,000 to $15,000 range. In response to the question, "Do Negroes today have a better or worse chance than people like yourself to get well-paying jobs?" 44 percent answered that Blacks have a *better* chance, 31 percent said Blacks have the same chance, and only 21 percent saw Blacks' chances as worse.[89] Related questions about housing, education, and governmental assistance revealed that similar pluralities of Whites perceived Blacks' chances as better than their own.

Yet, despite the riots and the sobering assessment of black and white opportunities, there appears to be an increasing gradient of white support for integration. Andrew M. Greeley and Paul B. Sheatsley reported on repeated surveys of white American attitudes in 1942, 1956, 1963, and 1970.[90] In every period, the number of Whites supporting integrationist sentiments in education, public accommodations, transportation, and even interracial marriage, increased. This was true in the South as well as in the North. In 1942, only 2 percent of white Southerners supported school integration. By 1970, a majority expressed support. Attitudes, of course, do not always predict behavior, and people do not always support in practice what they verbalize to an interviewer. But attitudinal change may be significant in altering the context of policy making.

The issue of community control

Although a majority of black urbanites still profess integrationist goals, they are pessimistic—or perhaps realistic—about white attitudes toward integration. The new pessimism is bolstered by the Black Power emphasis on racial identity and integrity. A significant manifestation of these parallel trends is the new demand for community control of political and social institutions.[91]

Although the concept of community control has implications for law enforcement, urban renewal, housing, model cities, public welfare, and other policies, education has so far been the main target. New York City, Detroit, and other cities have experimented with decentralization of public-school systems. Within carefully drawn limits of city and state standards, neighborhood school boards have been granted certain powers to establish programs and to hire and fire teaching personnel. A distinction should be made, however, between purely administrative decentralization and community control. Decentralization may include no more than the geographical reshuffling of administrative personnel and tasks from a central office to field offices. Store-front city halls may possess real power or may be no more than outposts of the central bureaucracy. Decentralization of administrative organization may or may not imply that power has been redistributed to community groups. Bringing bureaucrats into physical proximity does not bring them under neighborhood control. Many urban police departments are de-centralized at the precinct level, but advocates of community control do not have this sort of geographical decentralization in mind. Community-control supporters advocate a measure of actual policy control of city government operations and decisions that affect themselves, their children, and services that they require. Suburbanites, they argue, have genuine power to shape the policy and direction of their schools, police forces, tax systems and other concerns; central-city neighborhoods should enjoy the same kind of citizen influence over public policy.

Alan Altshuler has identified several major sources of opposition to the community-control movement, and it is a formidable list indeed.[92] Many public officials oppose community control because it threatens to undercut their own control over city budgets and policies. The estab-lished municipal bureaucracies—teachers, policemen, welfare workers, and others—see neighborhood control of service personnel as threaten-ing to their jobs. Municipal employees' unions like the American Federation of Teachers have been active opponents of modest schemes for neighborhood control of schools in New York City. Contractors who do a major portion of their business with city governments fear disrup-tion of their established relations with city hall. Large numbers of Whites oppose any program that might contribute to disruption of the status quo in race relations.

Although there is hard-core opposition to black demands for greater neighborhood participation in policy formation, the issue of community control cuts across many conventional political groupings. Liberal Whites who favor integrationist goals find themselves in a bind because their long-range commitments to integration are challenged by black separatism. To liberals and black moderates alike, the major unknown is whether the program will promote integration or apartheid in the long run. Many black leaders, pessimistic about the prospects for integration, see community control as the most immediately practical alternative. The late Whitney Young, executive director of the National Urban League, argued that "community control is the most crucial issue right now. Institutions have failed because control isn't in the hands of the people who live in the communities."[93] Bayard Rustin, on the other hand, has argued that "black community control is as futile a program as black capitalism. . . . The truth of the matter is that community control as an idea is provincial and as a program is extremely conservative."[94] To white segregationists, the program of black power over neighborhood institutions poses equally difficult issues. Some favor the idea as a diversion from further housing and educational integration, but others fear a new militance arising from black control.

From the point of view of Blacks, community control contains a built-in dilemma: the tensions between resources and control. Blacks already control the political system of Newark, where they constitute a majority of the electorate and elect the mayor. But there they have been unable to secure resources needed for change, as Newark is teetering on the brink of public poverty. The dilemma between control and resources is illustrated by Figure 3.1. Ideally, advocates of community control prefer a situation depicted by cell *A*, that is, a high degree of control over generous resources. Unfortunately, the availability of human and economic resources in the ghetto is limited. Some integrationists argue that a program relying exclusively on neighborhood resources would doom minorities to a permanent poverty of public services. Fiscal resources sufficient to maintain only symbolic programs are no substitute for ghetto needs for heavy investment in education, extraordinary levels of law-enforcement activity, and a high level of additional public services. On the other hand, advocates of community control maintain that the present system is simply minimal control over minimal resources (Figure 3.1, cell D) and this is the worst possible arrangement. Almost any change, therefore, represents an improvement.

The issue of community control, of course, is predicated upon the assumption that no major dispersal of the ghetto population is likely in

Figure 3.1 Control Versus Resources and the Issue of Community Control

Control over Policy

	High	Low
High (Resources Available to Community)	A	B
Low	C	D

the coming years. No public policies designed directly to disperse ghetto populations throughout the city have yet appeared, though some policies may have modest indirect effects (e.g., open-housing legislation may permit already comparatively well-off ghetto residents to buy homes they would not otherwise have access to). Indeed, some policies have directly or indirectly contributed to the maintenance of the ghetto (e.g., the construction of public-housing units in ghetto areas). We present evidence in Chapter 12 (see pp. 301–304) to demonstrate that the segregation of housing by race may be rising rather than falling in major cities. In light of the absence of a ghetto-dispersal policy and the operation of the private-housing market, it appears that the ghetto will be with us for some years to come.[95] The subject of community control of ghetto institutions will, therefore, be a major question of policy.

Summary

We have reviewed in this chapter the *input process,* the mechanisms by which opinions and interests are channeled into the political system. Perhaps the most significant point to emerge from this discussion is how limited is the informational input from large numbers of groups and individuals. Political participation, whether through elections or in more active forms, is much lower in local political life than in state or national politics, for reasons we have tried to indicate. Not only is individual participation somewhat low, but the institutional and organizational devices for presenting interests are also not as well developed at the local level as they are at higher levels of government. Labor unions, for example, though quite active in national politics, play only minor roles in most cities. Because of the influence of nonpartisanship and other factors, political parties may be active in national and state elections but may be quite dormant in municipal contests (except in a few cities). Generally, the relatively low participation levels, coupled with the fragmentary channels of interest articulation, make the costs of political information—information about groups and individuals and their policy preferences—quite high. Because of the incompleteness and distortion of information processed through the input mechanisms, municipal decision makers can rarely obtain more than a fragmentary sense of community preference about public policy.

As we have seen, however, there are diverse interests and strong intensities in the urban system. The often-conflicting interests of businessmen, white ethnics, Blacks, municipal employees, neighborhood groups, and environmentalists do not lend themselves to ready reconciliation. These conflicts impose high informational and resource costs on decision makers and make it difficult to accommodate the many parts of the urban political scene to one another.

Notes

1. James A. Bill, "The Plasticity of Informal Politics: The Case of Iran," *The Middle East Journal, 27* (1973), 131–151.
2. The special character and context of black politics, even more than its newsworthiness, argue for singling it out and giving it separate treatment in our study of urban politics. The black American does participate, of course, through conventional channels, but he merits our particular attention because he is, far more than businessmen, labor unionists, and members of the more politically established ethnic groups, seeking an "identity." How this identity crisis will ultimately be resolved is a matter of profound importance for the future of the American city.
3. Robert R. Alford and Eugene C. Lee, "Voter Turnout in American Cities," *American Political Science Review, 62* (September 1968), 796–813.
4. Daniel Katz and Samuel J. Eldersfeld, "The Impact of Local Party Activity upon the Electorate," *Public Opinion Quarterly, 25* (Spring 1961), 1–24.
5. Lester Milbrath, *Political Participation* (Skokie, Ill.: Rand McNally, 1965), pp. 16–18.
6. Angus Campbell, et al., *The American Voter: An Abridgment* (New York: Wiley, 1964), p. 142.
7. Milbrath, p. 21.
8. Robert R. Alford and Harry Scoble, "Sources of Local Political Involvement," *American Political Science Review, 62* (December 1968), 1192–1206; Robert A. Dahl, *Who Governs?* (New Haven: Yale University Press, 1961), p. 283.
9. Alvin Boskoff and Harmon Zeigler, *Voting Patterns in a Local Election* (Philadelphia: Lippincott, 1964), pp. 130–131; John C. Bollens, et al., *Exploring the Metropolitan Community* (Berkeley: University of California Press, 1961), chap. 11; and Howard Hamilton, "The Municipal Voter: Voting and Nonvoting in City Elections," *American Political Science Review, 65* (December 1971), 1135–1140.
10. Alford and Scoble, p. 1203.
11. Bollens, et al., chap. 11.
12. Robert E. Lane, *Political Life* (New York: Free Press, 1959), p. 239.
13. Our discussion of the Nineteenth Ward is based on the account in Allen F. Davis, *Spearheads for Reform* (New York: Oxford University Press, 1967), chap. 8.
14. Edward C. Banfield and James Q. Wilson, *City Politics* (Cambridge, Mass.: Harvard University Press, 1963), p. 115.
15. Fred I. Greenstein, "The Changing Pattern of Urban Party Politics," *The Annals of the American Academy of Political and Social Science, 353* (May 1964), 3.
16. Robert K. Merton, *Social Theory and Social Structure* rev. ed. (New York: Free Press, 1957), chap. 1, especially pp. 60–82.
17. The old boss of Tammany Hall, George Washington Plunkett, distinguished between "honest" and "dishonest" graft. Honest graft occurred when "I seen my opportunities and I took 'em," whereas dishonest graft was "carrying things to excess." Plunkett's example of excess was a case in which "The Republican superintendent of the Philadelphia almshouse stole the zinc roof off the buildin' and sold it for junk." See William L. Riorden, *Plunkett of Tammany Hall* (New York: Dutton, 1963; originally published, 1904), especially pp. 29–32.
18. Edward M. Sait, "Machine, Political," *Encyclopedia of the Social Sciences*, vol. 9 (New York: Macmillan, 1933), p. 659.
19. Raymond Wolfinger argues persuasively that the machine continues to perform functions for urban populations, and that it will not wither until it is no longer useful. See his "Why Political Machines Have Not Withered Away and Other Revisionist Thoughts," *Journal of Politics, 34* (May 1972), 365–398.
20. Mike Royko, *Boss: Richard J. Daley of Chicago* (New York: Signet, 1971). For additional discussion of Mayor Daley, see Chapter 5, pp. 156–158.

21. Banfield and Wilson, p. 151.
22. Raymond Wolfinger and John O. Field, "Political Ethos and the Structure of City Government," *American Political Science Review, 60* (June 1966), 312.
23. This conclusion is suggested both in Wolfinger and Field, *ibid.,* and in Robert L. Lineberry and Edmund P. Fowler, "Reformism and Public Policies in American Cities," *American Political Science Review, 61* (September 1967), 701–716.
24. There are a number of excellent treatments of the effects of nonpartisanship. Among them are Banfield and Wilson, chap. 12; Eugene C. Lee, *The Politics of Nonpartisanship* (Berkeley: University of California Press, 1960); Oliver P. Williams and Charles Adrian, "The Insulation of Local Politics under the Nonpartisan Ballot," *American Political Science Review, 53* (1959), 1052–1063; Robert Salisbury and Gordon Black, "Class and Party in Nonpartisan Elections: The Case of Des Moines," *American Political Science Review, 57* (1963), 584–592; and Gerald Pomper, "Ethnic and Group Voting in Nonpartisan Elections," *Public Opinion Quarterly, 30* (Spring 1966), 79–97.
25. Pomper, *ibid.*
26. Charles Adrian, "Some General Characteristics of Nonpartisan Elections," *American Political Science Review, 46* (September 1952), 766–776.
27. Kenneth S. Sherrill, "The Electoral Decision in Partisan and Non-Partisan Settings." Paper delivered at the Annual Meeting of the Midwest Conference of Political Scientists, April 27–29, 1967.
28. Pomper, *op. cit.*
29. Banfield and Wilson, p. 159, and Salisbury and Black, *op. cit.*
30. Lee, pp. 50–56.
31. Charles Adrian, "A Typology of Nonpartisan Elections," *Western Political Quarterly, 12* (June 1959), 449–458.
32. Robert A. Dahl, *A Preface to Democratic Theory* (Chicago: University of Chicago Press, 1956), p. 131.
33. Arthur Bentley, *The Process of Government* (Cambridge, Mass.: Harvard University Press, 1967; originally published, 1908), p. 208.
34. Charles Adrian and Charles Press, *Governing Urban America*, 3rd ed. (New York: McGraw-Hill, 1968), p. 125.
35. Charles Gilbert, *Governing the Suburbs* (Bloomington: University of Indiana Press, 1967), p. 145.
36. Oliver P. Williams and Charles Adrian, *Four Cities* (Philadelphia: University of Pennsylvania Press, 1963).
37. This argument is a major theme of the penetrating analysis of groups in Mancur Olson, *The Logic of Collective Action* (New York: Schocken, 1968).
38. Raymond A. Bauer, Ithiel de Sola Pool, and Lewis A. Dexter, *American Business and Public Policy* (New York: Atherton, 1964), chap. 22.
39. In the four communities studied by Robert Agger, Daniel Goldrich, and Bert E. Swanson, the proportion of community leaders who came from the managerial-professional-proprietorial occupations ranged from a low of 79 percent to a high of 100 percent. See their *Rulers and the Ruled* (New York: Wiley, 1964), pp. 332–333.
40. Kenneth E. Gray and David Greenstone, "Organized Labor in City Politics," in Edward C. Banfield, ed., *Urban Government* (New York: Free Press, 1961), p. 372.
41. Schley R. Lyons, "Labor in City Politics: The Case of the Toledo United Auto Workers," *Social Science Quarterly, 49* (March 1969), 827.
42. Gray and Greenstone, p. 378.
43. Jean L. Stinchcombe, *Reform and Reaction* (Belmont, Calif.: Wadsworth, 1968), p. 156.
44. Dahl, *Who Governs?*, pp. 34–36.
45. Stanley Lieberson, *Ethnic Patterns in American Cities* (New York: Free Press, 1963), pp. 98–99.
46. Raymond Wolfinger, "The Development and Persistence of Ethnic Voting," *American*

Political Science Review, 59 (December 1965), 896–908; and Abraham H. Miller, "Ethnicity and Voting Behavior: A Review of Theories and an Attempt at Reformulation," *Western Political Quarterly,* 29 (September 1971), 483–500.

47. Robert A. Lorinskas, et al., "The Persistence of Ethnic Voting in Rural and Urban Areas," *Social Science Quarterly,* 49 (March 1969), 871–899.
48. Pomper, *op. cit.*
49. Quoted in *Newsweek,* October 6, 1969, p. .33. For an examination of the relations between traditional ethnics and Blacks, see William Ellis, *White Ethnics and Black Power* (Chicago: Aldine, 1969).
50. Wolfinger, "Ethnic Voting," p. 905.
51. James Q. Wilson and Edward C. Banfield, "Public-Regardingness as a Value Premise in Voting Behavior," *American Political Science Review,* 58 (December 1964), 876–887. See also their "Political Ethos Revisited," *American Political Science Review,* 65 (December 1971), 1048–1062.
52. Harold Stone, et al., *City Manager Government in the United States* (Chicago: Public Administration Service, 1940), p. 25.
53. *Ibid.,* p. 35.
54. Wilson and Banfield, *op. cit.*
55. Agger, Goldrich, and Swanson, p. 21.
56. Robert C. Wood, *Suburbia* (Boston: Houghton Mifflin, 1959), p. 155.
57. Banfield and Wilson, chap. 15.
58. See, for example, *The New York Times,* August 13, 1968, p. 1. For an analysis of municipal labor troubles in New York, see Raymond D. Horton, *Municipal Labor Relations in New York: Lessons of the Lindsay–Wagner Years* (New York: Praeger, 1973).
59. James C. Davies, III, *Neighborhood Groups and Urban Renewal* (New York: Columbia University Press, 1966).
60. Roland Warren, "Model Cities' First Round: Politics, Planning and Participation," *Journal of the American Institute of Planners,* 34 (July 1969), 245–253.
61. See the discussion of attitudes toward environmental issues in Ronald O. Loveridge, "The Environment: New Priorities and Old Politics," in Harlan Hahn, ed., *People and Politics in Urban Society* (Beverly Hills, Calif.: Sage, 1972), pp. 499–530.
62. Bauer, Pool, and Dexter, *op. cit.*
63. John P. Crecine, *Governmental Problem-Solving: A Computer Simulation of Municipal Budgeting* (Skokie, Ill.: Rand McNally, 1969).
64. Betty H. Zisk, *Local Interest Politics: A One-Way Street* (Indianapolis: Bobbs-Merrill, 1973).
65. Michael Lipsky, *Protest in City Politics* (Skokie, Ill.: Rand McNally, 1970), especially chap. 1.
66. Philip E. Converse, et al., "Continuity and Change in American Politics: Parties and Issues in the 1968 Election," *American Political Science Review,* 63 (December 1969), 1105.
67. Ted Gurr, "A Comparative Study of Civil Strife," in Hugh Davis and Ted Gurr, eds., *Violence in America,* vol. 2 (Washington, D.C.: Government Printing Office, 1969), p. 448.
68. Sheldon Levy, "A 150-Year Study of Political Violence in the United States," in Hugh Davis and Ted Gurr, eds., *Violence in America,* vol. 1, pp. 65–77.
69. James Q. Wilson, *Negro Politics* (New York: Free Press, 1960), p. v.
70. The data on St. Louis are found in Bollens, et al., p. 226, and those on New Haven in Dahl, *Who Governs?,* pp. 294–295.
71. Lyndon B. Johnson, while signing the Voting Rights Act of 1965, quoted in *Newsweek,* August 16, 1965, p. 15.
72. William R. Keech, *The Impact of Negro Voting* (Skokie, Ill.: Rand McNally, 1968), p. 105.
73. *Ibid.,* p. 107.
74. Wilson, pp. 53, 57.

75. John H. Strange, "The Negro and Philadelphia Politics," in Edward C. Banfield, ed., *Urban Government*, 2nd ed. (New York: Free Press, 1969), p. 411.

76. Keech, pp. 29–39.

77. In the election of Carl Stokes in Cleveland, all-black wards produced an average vote for Stokes of 95 percent; in the Gary election of Richard Hatcher, the figure was 93 percent. See Jeffrey Hadden, Louis H. Masotti, and Victor Thiessen, "The Making of the Negro Mayors 1967," *Trans-action*, 5 (January–February 1968), 21–30; and Thomas F. Pettigrew, "When a Black Candidate Runs for Mayor: Race and Voting Behavior," in Hahn, pp. 95–118.

78. Harry Holloway, "Negro Political Strategy: Coalition or Independent Power Politics," *Social Science Quarterly*, 49 (December 1968), 534–548.

79. Stokeley Carmichael and Charles V. Hamilton, *Black Power* (New York: Vintage, 1967), p. 4.

80. *Ibid.*, p. 44.

81. *Ibid.*, p. 81.

82. Wilson, pp. 218–221.

83. Stanley Lieberson and Arnold R. Silverman, "The Precipitants and Underlying Conditions of Race Riots," *American Sociological Review*, 30 (December 1965), 887–898.

84. See the discussion of white and black perceptions of the riots in Angus Campbell and Howard Schuman, "Racial Attitudes in Fifteen Cities," in National Advisory Commission on Civil Disorders, *Supplementary Studies* (Washington, D.C.: Government Printing Office, 1968), chap. 5.

85. Our discussion of the riffraff theory is based upon data in Robert M. Fogelson and Robert B. Hill, "Who Riots?" in National Advisory Commission on Civil Disorders, *Supplementary Studies* (Washington, D.C.: Government Printing Office, 1968), chap. 3.

86. Nathan S. Kaplan and Jeffrey M. Paige, "A Study of Ghetto Rioters," *Scientific American*, 219 (August 1968), 19.

87. David O. Sears and T. M. Tomlinson, "Riot Ideology in Los Angeles: A Study of Negro Attitudes," *Social Science Quarterly*, 49 (December 1968), 502; Campbell and Schuman, p. 49.

88. Sears and Tomlinson, p. 499.

89. The survey is reported in *Newsweek*, October 6, 1969, pp. 34ff.

90. Andrew M. Greeley and Paul B. Sheatsley, "Attitudes Toward Racial Integration," *Scientific American*, 225 (December 1971), 13–19.

91. On the community control issue, see Alan Altshuler, *Community Control* (New York: Pegasus, 1970); Joseph Zimmerman, *The Federated City* (New York: St. Martins, 1972); and Milton Kotler, *Neighborhood Government* (Indianapolis: Bobbs-Merrill, 1969).

92. Altshuler, chap. 3.

93. Quoted in Altshuler, p. 61.

94. Bayard Rustin, "The Failure of Black Separatism," *Harper's* (January 1970), 28.

95. Anthony Downs carefully outlines some projections in his "Alternative Futures for the American Ghetto," *Daedalus*, 97 (Fall 1968), 1331–1378.

part **two**

The conversion process of urban political systems

The demands and resources of the socioeconomic and political environment do not automatically produce public policy. The process by which these inputs are translated into policies is the subject of Chapters 4 and 5. In Chapter 4 we describe the urban conversion process from a macro perspective, which includes the governmental institutions of the metropolitan area, together with the impact of state and federal governments on urban decision making. These structures are not neutral features of the urban system. They impose their own constraints upon the choices open to cities.

The formal structures of local government are not the only features of the conversion process. In Chapter 5, we shift to a micro perspective, analyzing the behavior of decision makers themselves. To some observers, there seems to be a conspiracy of power in local (and perhaps state and national) politics, in which upper-class citizens work in concert to shape public policy in their own interest. Whatever the truth of such allegations, the role of public officials (mayors, councils, managers, and bureaucrats) cannot be discounted. These roles, the resources that individual decision makers possess, their decision-making strategies, and the ways in which they cope with limited information and resources are the major topics of Chapter 5.

chapter 4

The structure
of urban government

Because governmental institutions are never neutral, the design of political institutions is beset with political controversy. Issues of political philosophy compete with calculations about short-range tactical advantages. The details of debate focus on the creation of new municipalities or special districts, development of new departments in city government, transfer of programs from one department to another, changes in the structure and authority of a local council or executive office, changes in the relationship between local governments and state or federal governments, and changes in budgeting and other administrative procedures.

Beneath these details lie beliefs about the proper way of designing local government. Political demands use symbols like *popular access, citizen control, strong executive, professionalism in government,* and *home rule.* At times, there is a concern about the structure of government per se but often the prime concern is with the expected impact of structure on the allocation of benefits. The determination of *who gets what* may turn on the institutional arrangements of government and decision making.

Premises of Urban Government

In this chapter we discuss four premises that consistently appear in disputes about the nature of local governmental structures: (1) the effort to maximize political accountability by keeping policy makers responsive to the voters, (2) the effort to maximize professional management and the efficient use of public resources, (3) the notion that local governments are properly subordinate to state governments and must be responsible to state authorities, and (4) the effort to maximize local governments' independence from state authorities.[1] The first and second premises are clearly in conflict (between "political" and "professional" government), and the third and fourth premises are also in conflict (between "state control" and "home rule"). In this chapter we show how a predisposition toward one or another premise influences the development of local institutions, and we illustrate some specific conflicts in local politics that grow out of these contradictory premises.

Political accountability

A desire to maximize political accountability is evident in many features of national, state, and local governments in the United States. It is the "democratic," or "Jacksonian," strain that runs throughout the political system, although political accountability may not be the dominant theme in governmental structures. At the national and state levels, it competes with the desire to maintain separation of powers and checks and balances (designed to limit the power of popularly inspired movements), as well as with the *professional management* theme. At the local level, political accountability competes, not only with the professional-management theme, but also with the belief that local governments are properly the subordinates of the state government and should be governed by the legislative and executive branches of the state.

Several devices are built into governments in order to keep policy makers responsive to popular sentiment: Elected legislators and executives establish the legal authority and budgets of administrative departments; elected officials select administrative subordinates who have supported their campaigns and who presumably will administer programs in ways that support the policies of elected officials. Elected officials are reluctant to develop rigid career lines within governmental departments. Instead of promoting long-time bureaucrats to leading positions, mayors often select businessmen, college professors, and other outsiders who may bring a fresh approach to local government. Of course, the theme of political accountability is not equally emphasized in all local governments. It must compete with other goals of governmental organization.

Some manifestations of political accountability are distinctively urban in nature, including selection of aldermen by wards; efforts by suburban communities to maintain their own governments apart from that of the central city; and demands from some neighborhoods within the central city for community control of schools, welfare programs, and the police.

Selection of aldermen by wards is common in about one-third of the cities with more than 50,000 population; it is designed to give each neighborhood a separate voice in city hall and thus to facilitate its demands for improvements in streets, playgrounds, schools, garbage collection, police protection, and other services. When a city is governed by a machine, the ward representatives provide a medium for transmitting local demands to the boss and for the machine's mobilization of voters on election day.

The independence of suburban communities is a constant element in the politics of metropolitan areas. We mentioned it in Chapter 2 in connection with the separation of economic resources and service demands. Here we shall view it as a feature that permits urban residents to maintain control of their most immediate government. Suburbanites voice several reasons for keeping their governments apart from that of the CC: to avoid the high taxes necessary to support the welfare, police, health, and educational services of low-income neighborhoods; to keep government small and in the hands of familiar officials; and to facilitate residential exclusiveness—either by keeping out public housing for low-income residents or by zoning restrictions that force up the costs of private-home building.[2]

The desire of ghetto residents in the central city to have neighborhood control of municipal services springs from the same roots that cause suburbanites to opt for separation. Of course, the details differ: Whereas suburbanites demand separation in order to free themselves from the costs of public health and welfare and to maintain high-quality education, ghetto residents demand neighborhood control of municipal services in order to ensure that education, health, welfare, and police services are commensurate with their needs. Both suburbanites and ghetto residents, however, identify specific urban areas with relatively homogeneous needs for public services and seek control over those services.

Professional management

A second influence on the design of local government structures is a management theory that likens government agencies to private firms. Its most prominent features are an insistence on *professional* (as opposed to *political*) criteria for selecting personnel, a hierarchical organization based on efficiency in provision of public services, and attempts to take local government out of politics and to put it on a businesslike basis.

Several structural aspects of local government reflect emphasis on professional management: the council-manager form of government; nonpartisan elections; selection of councilmen from the city at large, rather than from separate wards; selection of administrative employees according to merit; and efforts to consolidate the territory of several adjoining communities into one jurisdiction. The appointment of a professional city manager and the use of merit criteria in selecting employees are the most prominent of the businesslike features of local governments. They eliminate partisanship from local administration and restrict political accountability to the elected legislature. Where this body is selected by nonpartisan ballot and from the entire community at large rather than by wards, local policy making is likely to be even farther removed from partisan politics. The service demands or partisanship associated with particular neighborhoods are not guaranteed hearings in the local legislature, and the interests of the entire community are supposed to prevail.

People who advocate the consolidation of several communities into single jurisdictions hope to broaden the tax and service bases for governmental programs and rationalize their administration. Encompassing a larger territory broadens the financial support available for a service and thus makes it more economical. Where it is not feasible to extend the territory of a municipal government and to offer its full range of services to a larger clientele, individual services may be separated from a municipality and offered to larger areas. Special districts govern education, libraries, parks, police, hospitals, airports, highways, and sanitation in extensive areas within metropolitan areas.

The symbols that are used to defend the management role of local governmental structures reflect the interests and socioeconomic backgrounds of their advocates. *Businesslike, professional,* and *management* are terms that describe the occupational groups that most often favor council-manager structures and the merit selection of city employees. *Nonpartisan* takes on defensive connotations when used by middle- and upper-income supporters of these structures. The truth is that the conservative and Republican tendencies of professional-management supporters would not often be satisfied if city elections were conducted on a partisan and overtly political basis. This group is inclined toward low-spending policies, toward economy. We discussed these and other motivations of reformers in Chapter 3 (see pp. 75–77).

There are latent tensions between the political-accountability and professional-management modes of local government. The first reflects reverence for popular control of local public services, whereas the second reflects faith in objective measures of proficiency and efficiency. The two can exist in some form of accommodation. Local politicians are more often concerned with getting along than with pushing a form of governmental organization that has only abstract appeal. Yet the tensions burst into prominence when the advocates of one or the other mode feel their essential demands are threatened. The teachers of New York City struck for most of the fall of 1968 on behalf of professional management; they felt threatened by the actions of neighborhood school boards. On the other side, local boards exerted intense pressure for control over teachers; they viewed the academic approach of many teachers as irrelevant to ghetto children.

REFORMISM IN LOCAL GOVERNMENT   The concerns for political account- ability and professional management have motivated reform move- ments that have swept across the urban scene. Depending on the time and the then-perceived evils of the status quo, the desires of reformers have focused on one or another mechanism for accountability or pro- fessionalism. At some times and in some places, for example, it seems desirable to establish ward constituencies for council members in order to give neighborhoods a direct representative in their government; at other times it is said that ward representatives are the captives of special interests or machine bosses, and that council members should be elected on an at-large basis. In this book we recognize the shifting and relative nature of *reformed* and *unreformed* local governments, but we use the terms to denote the following traits of governments that maximize values of professional management:

	Reformed	Unreformed
Elections	Nonpartisan	Partisan
Constituency of council	At large	Ward
Executive	Manager	Mayor

Local control versus state control

The third and fourth premises of local governmental structures are clearly in conflict. Most of the legal powers are on the side of the state governments, but there are substantial—and perhaps increasing— political resources on the side of the cities. The subordination of local to state governments is shown in the lack of specific provision for local governments in the U.S. Constitution; by the acceptance in many state courts of *Dillon's rule,* which limits local governmental powers to those explicitly provided by state constitutions and statutes; and by the failure of local governments to raise sufficient revenues to meet their citizens' service demands, even when their jurisdictions include abundant private wealth.

THE LEGAL BASIS OF LOCAL GOVERNMENT   The structure of government established by the Constitution recognizes the nation, the states, and the people; the Constitution provides certain guarantees to each. There are no provisions for local governments. Municipalities were considered to fall under the umbrellas of their states and to be subject to whatever powers and restrictions the state constitutions and laws provided. The charter of a municipality is the state statute that affects it most directly, but other state actions also apply. They include general laws pertaining to all local governments and numerous local bills pertaining to specific municipalities. The standard interpretation of local government powers is Dillon's rule:

It is a general and undisputed proposition of law that a municipal corporation possesses and can exercise the following powers, and no others: First, those granted (by the state) in express words; second, those necessarily or fairly implied in or incident to the powers expressly granted; third, those essential to the accomplishment of the declared objects and purposes of the corporation—not simply convenient, but indispensable. Any fair, reasonable, substantial doubt concerning the existence of power is resolved by the courts against the corporation, and the power is denied.[3]

This severe standard resolves even reasonable doubts against the local government.

Where the state constitution is restrictive in its general grant of power to municipalities, the state legislature is a busy enactor of local laws; it may approve specific sites for local schools and other public facilities, condemn private property, and define local employees' salaries and working conditions. Under this kind of arrangement, the legislators who represent an urban area become an important—if informal—adjunct to the local government; they can modify those items that municipal officials ask them to introduce in the legislature and can select proposals to steer personally through the legislative process.

Even the most permissive state constitution restricts the nature and extent of local government taxation or indebtedness. All typically limit municipalities to property taxes and perhaps to small levies on retail sales and personal incomes. In an era when the most dramatic social demands are made in urban communities, the governments most closely affected by these demands do not have the authority to raise sufficient revenues from local resources. Local officials lack access to the wealth from high personal incomes and lucrative commercial transactions if they cannot tax income or sales. In New Mexico, before the state adopted home-rule provisions for city governments, it took state laws to:

1. Permit cities to destroy weapons and narcotics confiscated by police;
2. Authorize cities with populations over 100,000 to acquire and operate their own bus systems;
3. Allow municipalities to discontinue water service to customers who had not paid their bills;
4. Permit cities to zone for flood control.

HOME RULE   About half the states have written provisions into their constitutions that are designed to increase the discretion of local officials. The term *home rule* suggests a large grant of authority to local governments, but this image is more generous than the actual grant of authority. The home-rule movement began in Iowa in 1851, and such provisions were first adopted into a constitution in Missouri in 1875. By 1960 it had become part of the constitutions of twenty-three states, and cities in twenty-one of these states had taken advantage of its provisions. When a city operates under home-rule provisions, it can change its own powers and operations without first going to the state legislature for consent. The mechanism for changing local powers is typically a citizens' referendum. Some home-rule cities can change the form of their local governments, including the nature of local elections; can annex fringe areas; and can regulate public health, safety, and morality.

The practical significance of home rule is not as great as many of the reformers originally anticipated. State reins on local authorities remain short and can be tightened at the convenience of the state legislature. Some local authorities view their narrowly defined home-rule provisions as disadvantageous in that they preclude some imaginative efforts that would be permitted by more broadly defined provisions. Yet home-rule provisions may raise a psychological deterrent to state legislators. The broad connotations of the term may benefit cities, especially during an era when urban problems and reapportionment at the state level may heighten legislative support for local authorities. At the least, home-rule provisions relieve local officials of the nuisance of having to go to the state legislature for many detailed enactments.

To some observers, state control over local authorities seems to reflect deep-seated features of American politics: distrust of all cities and urban governments. Our cities are widely viewed as dangerous, unhealthy, and even "sinful," governed by bosses or party machines, and populated by alien groups. The flight of middle-class Whites (and a few Blacks) to the suburbs and the reluctance of state legislatures to reapportion themselves in accordance with population changes reflect this antiurban sentiment, as David Danzig and John Field have noted:

Great American cities, unlike such European counterparts as London, Paris, Rome, and Moscow, have not played a dominant part in the history of the nation. American history has not been made by the cities, nor have the cities supplied any of our heroes. European kings and rulers have always been largely urban; in contrast, no American President has been identified with the city. Franklin Delano Roosevelt, whose political power was heavily based on the cities, preferred the image of the Dutchess County gentleman farmer, while John F. Kennedy, instead of being taken for Boston Irish, chose to show his Harvard-Hyannisport profile to the public. Only in the veins of the East Side's defeated Al Smith did the blood of the city course unashamedly. . . . At a recent Washington conference, which was given the neighborly title of "Town and Country" to avoid the unpleasant term city, the Secretary of Agriculture seemed not to offend anyone when he spoke of the "garbage can life in the inner city"; nor, on another occasion, did New York State Senator William E. Adams provoke any public ire when he attributed the growth of welfare cases in the suburbs to the spread of "the welfare rot of the central cities." Obviously, the historic "shame of the cities" is still with us, although the "wicked city" has now become the "asphalt jungle" and what was once the slum is now "the rotting cancer" of the inner city.[4]

The cities are not without some clout in their competition with state governments. Some of this power is intangible and reflects only the revered position of local control and home rule in American traditions. The cities also benefit from whatever attachments there are to political accountability as a mode of governmental organization. Insofar as local residents are thought to be most aware of their needs, they are considered to be the most suitable governors of local activities. Much of the time, however, such strengths are not sufficient to free the cities from the hard bonds of law and precedent that subordinate them to the states.

Recently cities have gained some ground in their competition with the states. Their victories—which promise even greater gains in the future—include a series of federal court decisions, since *Baker* v. *Carr* in 1962, that have vastly improved the representation of urban areas in state legislatures and an increasing willingness in Congress to establish grant-in-aid programs that are national-local in character and involve only minimal participation for state governments. Although the impact of legislative reapportionment on state governments' treatment of the cities is yet to be demonstrated,[5] it has at least increased urban representation in the legislatures. Optimists predict increased state sensitivity to urban needs and more permissive legislation pertaining to city revenues. The federal government started to provide direct aid to the cities through housing legislation in the 1930s, and more recently there have been substantial increases in federal aid to cities for primary and secondary education, preschool classes, job training, highways, mass transit, and community action, as well as the assurance that cities will receive a share of federal revenue sharing (see pp. 119–123).

Structures and Consequences

The structure of city government

The structures of most urban governments reflect the influence of political accountability or professional management or—more typically —a mixture of the two. Here we shall outline the principal institutions of local governments. In Chapter 5 we shall return to this topic and describe the personal traits and decision-making procedures of office holders.

MAYOR-COUNCIL FORMS   The classic model of local government combines an elected mayor with an elected council. Figure 4.1 portrays the relations of a typical mayor and council with the voters and with the

Figure 4.1 Simplified Government Structure in a Strong Mayor-Council City

departments of the city government. Depending upon the predominant influences at work in the initial design or later modification, these structures may reflect emphasis on political accountability or professional management. Offices may be filled through partisan or nonpartisan ballots; the personnel of administrative departments may be selected by the chief executive according to political criteria or according to professional personnel standards and protected by a merit system; the legislators may be elected at large or from individual wards.

Mayor-council cities may also differ in the formal powers given to the mayor and council. In *weak-mayor governments*, the selection of department heads and the responsibility for administrative policies are usually given to boards or commissions, whose members are chosen by direct election or by the mayor and the council. Mayors can also be weakened by being denied a veto over the actions of the council or by being required to share responsibility for preparing the budget with the entire council or a council committee. An individual executive can also be made stronger or weaker by virtue of the staff he is allowed to hire. Where he is permitted an extensive, well-paid, and professional cadre of assistants, he can use the high-quality information they provide to assert himself in dealings with the council or administrative departments.

A local government reflecting the primary influence of political accountability would tie the mayor and council to the voters and minimize the authority of any local official to make policy on his own initiative. It would have partisan elections for the mayor and council, councilmen elected from wards, selection of administrators according to political criteria, control of departments by the elected chief executive, but budgeting and other policy-making functions shared by the mayor and the council.

THE MANAGER FORM   The extreme expression of the professional-management doctrine is the council-manager form of government. This form is depicted in Figure 4.2. It typically combines a small council, elected at large by nonpartisan ballot, along with a professional administrator who is selected by (and responsible to) the council. There is often also a mayor, who performs ceremonial functions as head of the local government. He may preside at meetings of the council, represent the city on public occasions, and sign legal documents for the city. He may be elected by the voters or selected by the council from among their own members (see Table 5.2 for details). The typical manager has the power to appoint (and remove) the heads of administrative departments; to prepare the budget for the council's consideration and to allocate funds after the budget's approval; and to make investigations, reports, and policy recommendations to the council on his own initiative or at its request. The professional-management ideal is even more nearly realized when administrative personnel are selected on the basis of professional competence and protected from political dismissal and when the manager has the budget and authority to hire competent staff.

As the council-manager plan was originally designed, the manager was expected to administer but to remain assiduously aloof from politics or policy making. In recent years, however, it has become evident that the manager is inevitably involved in controversial issues. Even the most careful manager encounters politics when he conducts policy-oriented research for the council, formulates a budget for the council's deliberation, interprets the council's preferences in allocating funds to

Figure 4.2   Simplified Government Structure in a Council-Manager City

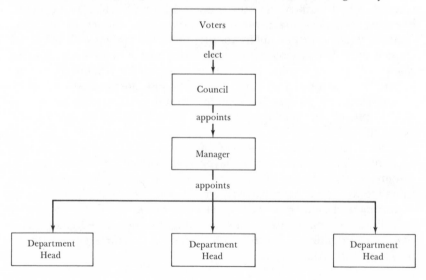

the departments, or seeks to change a department's procedures in rendering service. The manager's role in policy making is heightened when the council depends upon his professional judgment. Council members are typically part-time officials not professionally trained to make policy decisions nor to supervise their implementation. Although most—if not all—managers do involve themselves in politically charged issues, they differ markedly in style. Some shape the basic policies of their governments and enlist the aid of interest groups, private citizens, and councilmen in their efforts. Others work more narrowly through official channels. Managers have no tenure in their positions; they can be dismissed by majorities of their councils or forced to resign by intensely hostile minorities. Some managers define success by their ability to remain in office, whereas others define it by the innovations they have guided through local politics.[6]

THE COMMISSION FORM   The third form of local government, the city commission, departs radically from the distinctive American pattern of separate legislative and executive branches. This structure is portrayed in Figure 4.3. It consists of a small group of elected commissioners, each heading an administrative department, as well as sitting as a member of the local legislature. There is no strong executive, although one member of the commission is designated the nominal head of government. In some cities, the chairman's position rotates periodically among the commissioners. At one time this form of government was the darling of good-government reformers. It was first developed in Galveston in 1900 and was in use in 108 cities by 1910. It is said that commission cities suffer from a lack of administrative integration. Separately elected department heads and the absence of a real central

Figure 4.3 Simplified Government Structure in a Commission City authority provide no focus of coordination. Vote trading and "you stay out of my department, and I'll stay out of yours" characterize the style of government. The plan has lost its appeal to reformers, most of whom have switched their allegiance to the council-manager form. The commission is now used by only thirty-seven cities with populations over 50,000 plus a smattering of smaller cities, mostly in the South.

The absence of hierarchy in American cities

Although the professional-management approach to local government has shown its success in the widespread acceptance of the council-manager form of government, it has not been notably successful in implanting principles of hierarchical management. The lack of hierarchy is evident in two ways: First, no chief executive of a major city has sufficient control over personnel and funds to exercise direction of his own administration comparable to that of the national President or most state governors, and, second, the multiplicity of jurisdictions in any metropolitan area limits whatever powers the city executive does possess to the artificial borders of his municipality. President Lyndon B. Johnson is said to have commented in one of his most harried moments that "things could be worse. I could be a mayor."[7] A mayor of Milwaukee once observed that "the central city mayor survives only when he has the psychological capacity to handle at one time three man-eating gorillas of crises and two of the paper tigers that, it seems at times, are thrown upon his back just to test him."[8]

Much of the difficulty in appraising our mayors is that we are influenced by the *myth of hierarchy*, which does not describe American city government. Although the President and most governors have at least nominal hierarchical controls working for them, American cities are surrounded and beset by formal pluralism.[9] In the first place, city governments are only one of multiple types of governments in urban areas. Milwaukee County has forty-six taxing units of local government: the City of Milwaukee; eighteen suburban municipalities, "each proudly waving its own flag of suburban independence emblazoned, 'Don't invade me'"; twenty-two suburban school boards; two sewage commissions; two city school boards; as well as the county government.[10] Even if a mayor reigned supreme in his own bailiwick, he would thus be at best a feudal lord in a castle, beset by numerous other claimants to the throne.

Within what we call city government, there is also fractionalization of power, with the mayor being both limited in his powers and compelled to share responsibilities with other decision-making agencies, particularly the council and perhaps also a manager. Also there may be other decision-making officers elected by the public and thus not beholden to the mayor. (For further discussion of the mayor's political-leadership role, see Chapter 5, pp. 156–161.)

Incidence and significance of governmental structures

Politicians, journalists, and political scientists have argued the merits of one or another form of local government for many years. There are various allegations about the democratic features of governments dominated by political accountability, and about the businesslike efficiency to be expected from governments dominated by professional management. As we have noted, however, these elements are generally mixed in the structures of individual municipalities. The best we can do in assessing them is to compare local governments showing traits that have been reformed in the name of professional management with those that have not. Unreformed cities have mayor-council governments, ward selection of councilmen, and partisan ballots for mayor and council. Reformed cities have either manager-council or commission governments, selection of councilmen at large, and possibly nonpartisan ballots. The incidence of each element in cities with populations over 50,000 is shown in Table 4.1.

There has been some research into the kinds of cities that have adopted each form of government. Table 4.2 shows the distributions of various features by size of city over 5000 population. Unreformed mayor-council forms dominate in both the smallest and largest cities, whereas the council-manager and commission forms together dominate the middle-sized ones. Council-manager forms are by far the most common among reformed institutions. As we have noted, commission forms are a small minority and are concentrated in middle-sized cities.

There are two separate explanations for the predominance of mayor-council governments in small and large cities. In the former there is seldom enough revenue—or enough work—to justify employment of a professional manager. Both the mayor and the council in towns under 10,000 are typically part-time officials, receiving little or no salary. In the largest cities there may be too much social and economic heterogeneity to escape severe political tensions. Political accountability seems most

Table 4.1 *The Incidence of Government Forms in 200 Cities of over 50,000 Population*

Institutional form	Reformed		Unreformed	
Form of government	Manager	45%	Mayor-council	43%
	Commission	12		
Type of election	Nonpartisan	67	Partisan	33
Type of constituency	At large	63	Ward or mixed[a]	37

[a]Includes a small proportion of cities that use a combination of ward and at-large elections.
SOURCE: Robert L. Lineberry and Edmund P. Fowler, "Reformism and Public Policies in American Cities," *American Political Science Review, 61* (September 1967), 705–706.

Table 4.2 *Distribution of Government Forms in Cities of over 5,000 Population*

	Mayor-council (%)	Manager (%)	Commission (%)	N^a
1,000,000+	100.0	—	—	5
500,000–1,000,000	73.7	26.7	—	15
250,000–500,000	40.0	43.3	16.7	30
100,000–250,000	37.5	48.8	13.8	80
50,000–100,000	35.3	50.5	14.2	190
25,000–50,000	34.0	52.8	13.1	388
10,000–25,000	49.7	40.3	10.0	1005
5,000–10,000	66.7	28.1	5.2	1257

^aN = Number of cases.
SOURCE: John H. Kessel, "Governmental Structure and Political Environment: A Statistical Note About American Cities," *American Political Science Review*, 56 (September 1962), 615.

suited to such a community: Major offices go to the coalition of interests that can muster a plurality at the polls. Strong factions are unlikely to accept a professional manager who would take the key offices out of their reach.

There is also a regional bias in the selection of local government structures. Mayor-council cities dominate in the Northeast; council-manager cities are found most often in the South and West; the Middle West shows a mixture of the two forms.[11] These differences may reflect the ages and social compositions of cities in each region. Northeastern cities are most likely to be old and to have large European ethnic communities. The mayor-council structure has the legitimacy of tradition, and competition among distinct European ethnic communities (now joined by politically sophisticated black enclaves) ensures that politics remains in local government. In contrast, a number of cities in the South and West have reached substantial size only during this century. They have faced an obvious need to reexamine their governmental structures because of population increases during the period when reformers were working hardest for council-manager (or commission) forms. In the South, moreover, the ethnic situation favors professional management. Because of sizable black communities in the cities, entrenched Whites have regarded the professional manager as a device to isolate local government from the potential black vote.

A number of scholars have examined the formal structures of governments as they affect the nature of local politics and public policies.[12] To the extent that high (or low) scores on the measures of politics or policy coexist in those municipalities that have certain kinds of governmental structures, we can infer that structure has something to do with the scores. Yet it is also possible that such findings reflect nothing more than the influence of a peculiar social or economic environment. The coexistence of structural features with particular politics or policy may be a happenstance that does not indicate the influence of governmental structure. Local political life may affect the choice of governmental structures, or features of the social or economic environment may be powerful enough to affect a certain kind of politics or policy, as well as to affect the development of governmental structure. This possibility is recognized in some of the research, in which refined analytic techniques are used to identify the strengths of relationships between structure and policy that are independent of influences from social or economic environment. Some findings are ambiguous, however, and generate controversies about the validity of the measurements or about the sensitivity of the analytic techniques used.

There is some evidence that cities with reformed governmental structures have lower rates of voter turnout[13] and that their officials are less responsive to the demands of social and economic groups.[14] These findings square with the expectations of the reformers themselves. The features of council-manager government, nonpartisan elections, and selection of councilmen at large were expected to put local government on a professional-management basis and to keep it out of politics. They mask the cleavages that exist within the local electorate and make it difficult for voting blocs to gain control of particular officials in the municipal government. Local politics must develop its own language, with disputes expressed in terms other than the labels of the major national parties. Such debate is difficult to follow for those whose marginal interest in politics leads only to identification as Democrats or Republicans. Reduced voting turnout is a natural result, as is municipal government that operates at some distance from popular demands.

Partisan electoral systems, when combined with ward representation, increase the access of two kinds of minority groups: those which are residentially segregated, and which may as a consequence of the electoral system demand and obtain preferential consideration from their councilmen; and groups which constitute identifiable voting blocs to which parties and politicians may be beholden in the next election. The introduction of at-large, nonpartisan elections has at least five consequences for these groups. First, they remove an important cue-giving agency—the party—from the electoral scene, leaving the voter to make decisions less on the policy commitments (however vague) of the party, and more on irrelevancies such as ethnic identification and name familiarity. Second, by removing the party from the ballot, the reforms eliminate the principal agency of interest aggregation from the political system. Hence, interests are articulated less clearly and are aggregated either by some agency or not at all. Moreover, nonpartisanship has the effect of reducing the turnout in local elections by working class groups, leaving office-holders freer from retaliation by these groups at the polls. Fourth, nonpartisanship may also serve to decrease the salience of "private-regarding" demands by increasing the relative political power of "public-regarding" agencies like the local press. And when nonpartisanship is combined with election at-large, the impact of residentially segregated groups or groups which obtain their strength from voting as blocs in municipal elections is further reduced. For these reasons, it is clear that political reforms may have a significant impact in minimizing the role which social conflicts play in decision-making. By muting the demands of private-regarding groups, the electoral institutions of reformed governments make public policy less responsive to the demands arising out of social conflicts in the population. [15]

There are some findings about the substances of policies enacted in cities with reformed and unreformed structures. One study finds lower *expenditure effort* (expenditures as a percentage of aggregate personal income) in communities governed by city managers than in those governed by elected mayors. [16] This finding suggests that the city-manager form of government occurs in business-minded, conservative communities and that it works against high taxes and expenditures, although a study of school-board expenditures reveals the highest spending in communities governed by city managers. [17]

Vertical Intergovernmental Relations

Cities and the federal system

The city's relations with national and state governments are a dimension of governmental structure that has profound implications for the resources and policy options available to local officials. Under the American system of checks and balances, no governmental unit can make decisions in isolation from other units. National and state governments are protected from each other by the bulwarks of the federal system and can exert only strong pressures and constraints on each other's policies. Local governments enjoy no specific federal protections, however, and are more open to state demands and controls through constitutions, statutes, and administrative acts. Yet the officials of local governments enjoy the extraconstitutional protections of local customs and political institutions. These latter combine with the formal components of federalism to protect the officials of each government against those of other governments, even while each is partially dependent upon the decisions of others. The result is something of a muddle: A "marble cake" is a common and accurate analogy for relations among national, state, and local governments. [18] No understanding of policy making in local governments can be complete without some comprehension of the links, barriers, assistance, and influence between local authorities and their national and state "superiors."

Every major nation in the world has both central and local units of government. A federal arrangement is peculiar, however, in that it provides certain assurances to both levels of government involved. It is common to speak of the American national and state governments as "superior" and "subordinate" to each other, but this terminology is inaccurate. On some dimensions the national government has prerogatives reserved to it alone. The states are not the creatures of the national government, however. Some states predate the current national government, and those that postdate Independence enjoy the same guarantees as do the original states.

The federal nature of American politics is supported by a combination of constitutional provisions, laws, extralegal political institutions, and customs. Constitutional guarantees provide for equal representation in the U.S. Senate (which is protected from the normal procedures for amending the Constitution), selection of members of the U.S. House of Representatives by state, a role for the states in the Electoral College and the process of constitutional amendment, and provision in the Tenth Amendment that certain powers are "reserved to the states." Some of these prerogatives provide direct grants of authority to state governments, whereas others protect the states by ensuring their citizens a role in important decisions by the national government. The use of states as the electoral units for the House, Senate, and President permits the leading politicians in each state to exact promises from candidates in exchange for their own campaign support. Candidates are frequently oriented toward the demands of state populations by the need to win elections within state jurisdictions. Insofar as the officials of leading cities have some influence over their states' political parties (Chicago's Mayor Daley is the best example), this consultative role of the states in national politics also serves the interests of the cities.

Whereas the constitutional provisions merely set the stage for the protection of state and local interests within the federal structure, a series of laws, customs, and political institutions provide the detailed bulwarks for these interests. The laws establishing grant-in-aid programs recognize the demands made by state and local officials who testified before Congress, and federal laws may require subsequent hearings about the standards set by the federal agencies.

Prominent but extralegal bulwarks of state and local governments include the political parties and "civic societies" that use the institutions of state and local government to pursue or protect their own goals. The American party system has its roots within the states, congressional districts, counties, and municipalities and serves to protect state and local interests in national councils.[19] Members of the House and Senate, as well as candidates for the presidency, owe their political obligations to the leaders of state or local party organizations, rather than to national party leaders. The national parties are composed of fifty state parties, which are themselves composites of separate organizations based on counties, municipalities, or legislative districts. Nominations and financial support for candidates come from state or local party organizations, which may be no more than personal organizations focused on the careers of single politicians. The national party offers few tangible incentives for state or local cooperation and exerts no formal sanctions against state or local recalcitrants. Some congressmen, governors, and mayors campaign openly in opposition to the presidential nominee of their party, and some congressmen compile voting records sharply at odds with the program of their party's President.

State populations have shown their loyalty to regional parties in the face of outside pressure.[20] This loyalty is most pronounced in the South but is not limited to that section. Officials of state and local governments in the South have responded in concert with private organizations against federal statutes and administrative guidelines that require racial integration. In every state numerous groups seek federal contracts for industries or federal expenditures on military installations or public works. These efforts involve chambers of commerce, elected officials of state and local governments, congressmen, and individual businessmen.[21]

A feature that heightens the importance of federalism in local politics is the mixture of governmental responsibilities in each field of public service. There is no important domestic activity that is manned or financed solely by federal, state, or local government. The activities that consume most domestic expenditures—education, highways, welfare, health, natural resources, public safety—are funded by combinations of federal grants or loans, state and local taxes, and service charges.

The combination of a viable federal structure, political values that respect home rule and local self-government, and shared responsibilities for major domestic services means that policy makers at any level of government must be alert to inputs from other levels of government. Federal grants and program requirements provoke state and local officials to action, whereas the demands or unwelcome decisions of state and local officials often provoke federal authorities. It is not simply elected officials who engage in intergovernmental relations. The list of important actors includes administrators at each level of government, plus members of the staff agencies of each chief executive and legislature. For local administrators intergovernmental relations may take the form of requests, demands, or appeals to state or federal agencies, legislatures, or executives. These communications may go directly to federal or state administrators or be routed through the political contacts of local authorities in the national or state legislatures.

Urban policy makers take an active—and often aggressive—role in intergovernmental relations. Joseph A. Doorley, the mayor of Providence, Rhode Island, once documented his style of federal system politics for a training session sponsored by the U.S. Civil Service Commission as follows:

. . . On the national scene . . . I represent my state as a member of the Democratic National Committee . . . I do not hesitate to ask for special treatment for
my city. . . .

The political relationship which Providence has with national political figures
has on more than one occasion provided me with the key to government officials
who administer non-political programs. Having met them at congressional campaign dinners, national party affairs, or even on social occasions, has given me
the opportunity to point out the political importance of moving some project
along on a priority basis.

I do not mean to convey the impression that my urban renewal programs or
my antipoverty programs receive approval solely because of this association,
but rather frankly admit it can expedite a proposal or project.

I am unalterably committed to exerting every possible bit of political muscle I
have to secure federal aid for my city. . . . During the lifetime of our beloved
John Fogarty, late a congressman from Rhode Island's Second District, I
managed to finance one of the most comprehensive antipoverty efforts in the
country . . . Congressman Fogarty was a brother Irishman who belonged to
many of the same societies, clubs and groups with which I am associated. . . .
Fogarty's never-ending concern to keep Providence in the forefront required
him to rattle more than one federal administrator who might be sitting on some
Providence proposal.[22]

FEDERAL AIDS TO THE CITIES   Grant-in-aid programs are the single most
prominent feature of federal relations with state and local governments.
In 1973 they amounted to $45 billion. Table 4.3 shows how $31.4 billion
in federal grants and other aids to urban areas were to be distributed
through numerous programs during 1974.

Federal grants have several distinct features, each of which has certain
implications for the recipient. Each program has a specific purpose;
there is no general support for local activities except for revenue-
sharing. Recipient agencies must provide some of their own resources to
support the program and must administer it according to prescribed
standards. The tying of federal grants to purposes and the requirements
that go with them are frequent sources of conflict between federal and
local administrators. It is alleged that the federal carrot leads recipients
to undertake activities that are not in their own best interests and that
requirements are frequently inconsistent with the local social or economic problems. Federal money is not "free." Recipients must pay some
economic and political costs in order to receive its benefits.

The year 1972 saw a major new departure in the nature of federal aid.
Revenue sharing began with grants of $2.6 billion to the states, with
two-thirds earmarked for local governments. At this writing, total
allocations to state and local governments under revenue sharing are
scheduled to reach $30.2 billion over the 1972–1977 period. The allot-
ments to individual localities reflect various factors. Revenue increases
with the size of a community's population, the effort it shows in taxing
locally available resources, and its poverty as reflected by per capita
income.

Table 4.3   *Federal-aid Outlays in SMSAs (in Millions of Dollars)*

Function and program	1961 actual	1964 actual	1969 actual	1974 estimate
National defense	10	28	30	62
Agriculture and rural development:				
Donation of surplus commodities	128	231	313	443
Other	27	40	104	132
Natural resources and environment:				
Environmental protection	24	8	79	1,252
Other	30	10	101	227
Commerce and transportation:				
Economic development	—	158	104	181
Highways	1,398	1,948	2,225	2,594
Airports	36	36	83	187
Urban mass transportation	—	—	122	438
Other	1	5	5	101
Community development and housing:				
Funds appropriated to the President	—	—	432	244
Urban renewal	106	559	786	788
Public housing	105	136	257	947
Water and sewer facilities	—	36	52	80
Model cities	—	—	8	567
Other	2	17	75	207
Education and manpower:				
Education revenue sharing—	—	—	—	1,185
Elementary and secondary	222	264	1,262	449
Higher education	5	14	210	54
Vocational education	28	29	179	256
Employment security	303	344	449	315
Manpower revenue sharing	—	—	—	663
Manpower activities	—	64	530	624
Other	3	7	333	1,209

(continued)

Revenue sharing differs most dramatically from traditional federal aids in its lack of "strings." The money goes to communities as a matter of right, without detailed applications. Recipients can spend the money at their discretion, subject only to the following restrictions:

1. Local governments must spend their allotments within certain "priority" areas: public safety, environmental protection (including sanitation), public transportation, health, recreation, libraries, social services for the poor and aged, financial administration, and "ordinary and necessary" capital expenditures.
2. Discrimination on the basis of race, color, national origin, or sex is not permitted in any program financed with revenue-sharing funds.
3. Funds may not be used to match federal funds provided under other grant programs.

Table 4.3 *(Continued)*

Function and program	1961 actual	1964 actual	1969 actual	1974 estimate
Health:				
Health services and planning	48	66	109	159
Health services delivery	47	82	219	486
Mental health	4	8	77	313
Preventive health services	—	—	—	27
Medical assistance	—	140	1,731	3,209
Health manpower	—	—	107	246
Other	—	4	54	30
Income security:				
Vocational rehabilitation	37	61	247	611
Public assistance	1,170	1,450	3,022	5,380
Child nutrition, special milk, and food stamps	131	168	482	1,940
Other	3	16	148	546
General government:				
Law enforcement (including law-enforcement revenue sharing)	—	—	17	615
National Capital region	25	38	85	307
Other	—	9	27	115
Other functions	—	2	—	15
General Revenue Sharing	—	—	—	4,225[a]
Total aids to urban areas	3,893	5,588	14,045	31,429

[a]Tentative estimated impact.
SOURCE: *Special Analysis, Budget of the United States Government, Fiscal Year 1974* (Washington: Government Printing Office, 1973), p. 219. Note that "1974 estimates" represent the requests being made by the President in this submission to Congress.

4. Construction workers paid with revenue-sharing funds must be paid at least the wage prevailing on similar construction activity in the locality.
5. Recipient governments must publish plans and publicly account for the use of revenue-sharing funds.[23]

While the lack of detailed controls on revenue sharing appeals to local officials, this feature imposes costs on other actors in the local arena. Supporters of individual programs have no guarantee that the money will be spent on their favored projects. With the traditional grants-in-aid, program supporters could concentrate their efforts at the national level, and count on state and local officials carrying out the requirements in the federal statutes. For fiscal year 1974, President Nixon's budget proposed to increase revenue sharing while reducing allocations for certain grants-in-aid. This would mean that supporters of aided programs must battle in hundreds of local arenas to acquire some of the revenue-sharing funds for the programs that had been guaranteed support under grants-in-aid.

Federal grants-in-aid and revenue sharing are only two of several devices for providing financial and technical assistance to state and local agencies. Federal loans, loan guarantees, tax credits, deductibility of state and local taxes from federally taxable income, and direct federal benefits to urban residents are additional kinds of aid. Some programs mix grants-in-aid with other features to provide different options to recipients. In the public-housing program, for example, federal guarantees of private loans have supported the bulk of most projects, whereas outright grants covered additional costs. Some programs make available direct loans from the U.S. Treasury if federal guarantees will not allow recipient agencies to contract commercial loans at desirable interest rates.

Many taxpayers do not recognize the subtle federal aids that are written into the income-tax code. In computing income subject to federal taxation, a citizen can deduct any amounts paid as state or local income or sales, excise, or property taxes. Furthermore, any income received from interest on state or local government bonds is not subject to federal taxation. These provisions lessen the impact of state and local taxes and permit state and local agencies to pay lower than commercial interest rates for the money they borrow.

Several other federal programs provide indirect, or subtle, forms of aid to state or local agencies. The direct provision of federal benefits to institutions or private citizens relieves states and municipalities of demands for services that otherwise would come to them. In this category are federal grants, loans, or loan guarantees to institutions of higher education for the construction of instructional facilities and dormitories; loans and scholarships to the students of these institutions; and federal insurance payments for the aged and disabled.

FEDERAL URBAN POLICY   One charge made against the urban programs of the federal government is that they are not coordinated among themselves. Frederic N. Cleaveland and his colleagues have reported that, "in comparison to established policy fields like agriculture policy, foreign trade policy, or labor policy," the federal structure for making urban policy is "vague and hopelessly diffuse."[24] Wilson sees various federal urban programs as working consistently at cross purposes:

> . . . the new Department of Housing and Urban Development stands squarely in this tradition. Under its previous name (the Housing and Home Finance Agency), it subsidized the flight to the suburbs with FHA mortgage insurance, while trying to lure back suburbanites to the central city with subsidies provided by the Urban Renewal Administration. The Public Housing Administration built low-rent units for the poor while urban renewal was tearing them down.[25]

Examples of apparent contradictions in federal urban policy could be multiplied almost indefinitely. While trying to reduce air pollution, the federal government nonetheless encourages more automobile traffic by constructing new superhighways; while claiming to improve the housing of the poor through public housing, it benefits the middle classes through tax write-offs on home-loan interest; while funding public-welfare programs, it also subsidizes Community Action Agencies that attack welfare bureaucracies.

Problems of coordination seem endemic in a federal system having three levels of government and 81,000 jurisdictions, each trying for its piece of the action. Some efforts by the national government to foster coordination have produced further confusion. The regional offices of federal agencies are designed to smooth intergovernmental relations. Yet the regional offices have become the target of further competition among states and localities. Cities view the offices as economic prizes that offer steady payrolls, plus attractions for visiting officials who patronize hotels and restaurants. Until recently, Congress and the administration have spread these benefits to a large number of cities. Local governments in Kentucky, for example, have been served by the regional office of HUD in Atlanta, Georgia; HEW in Charlottesville, Virginia; the Bureau of Employment Security in Cleveland, Ohio; the Bureau of Work Programs and OEO in Washington, D.C.; and the Economic Development Administration in Huntington, West Virginia. Problems arise when a city official must visit separate regional centers to negotiate a related set of projects that involve separate federal agencies. Moreover, a federal official cannot call an interdepartmental regional meeting to consider a common approach to a city's project without bringing people from several localities, and then seeing them scatter across a third of the country once the meeting is over.[26]

Although these and other contradictions occur in federal urban policy, some of them are the inevitable by-products of politics itself, or of politics in a relatively democratic system. There are, after all, multiple constituencies in each field of policy, and efforts to provide at least some "goodies" for all seem bound to produce inconsistencies in terms of some abstract ideal. Moreover, it is not clear that urban policy is any more fragmented and inconsistent than are other federal policies. Policy making in foreign trade shows elements of logrolling and "every man for himself" instead of well-ordered consistency. Farm policy shows inconsistent mixtures designed to benefit both commercial enterprises and less profitable family farms. Federal urban policy may be fragmented and inconsistent. But so, as we saw in Chapter 3, are the interests of various groups within the urban area.

STATE AIDS TO THE CITIES   The array of state aids to municipalities includes many patterned after federal aids to state and local governments. But state aids emphasize shared taxes and *bloc grants* (for broadly defined types of programs), rather than grants-in-aid for specified projects. A fixed portion of taxes revert to the local government in whose jurisdiction they were collected. As bloc grants and shared taxes are used by most states, they provide more freedom to local governments than do federal grants-in-aid. They are awarded not for specified projects or in response to detailed applications but go automatically to local governments according to certain criteria and may be used for any programs within generally defined areas (e.g., education, roads and streets) or even for any local government activities. State aids are generally free, and no matching by locally raised revenues is required. For the most part, local governments receive state aid as a matter of right; there are few application procedures and few limitations on expenditures. The financial relations between state and local governments are not, however, free from disputes over local and state control.

State governments use various criteria to allocate financial aids to each local government. Some redistribute economic resources from have to have-not communities; some merely return to communities certain proportions of state taxes collected there; some reward communities that make some effort to use their own resources in support of certain programs; some award funds equally according to arbitrary criteria (like population); and some rely on special considerations of emergency or agreements between state and local agencies. Table 4.4 shows the distribution of funds to city governments according to the criteria used in California, Massachusetts, and Pennsylvania during 1962. California and Pennsylvania did not offer great rewards for local effort. California distributed almost 70 percent of its funds on the basis of local sales of taxed items or licenses or in equal amounts to all jurisdictions. Pennsylvania distributed almost 22 percent according to population and another 49 percent according to local sales of taxed items or licenses and local road mileage. California distributed only 22 percent according to criteria that reward local effort (ratio to local expenditures for the aided function) and Pennsylvania only 19 percent. In contrast, Massachusetts awarded almost 59 percent of its aid according to local-effort formulas. It also awarded almost 13 percent of its aids in a way that redistributes economic resources from have to have-not areas.

The concept of *state aid* is necessarily loose because of the wide variety of programs and techniques in fifty state governments. In many states, the aid granted to local governments represents only a small portion of the services that state governments provide to local residents. State governments vary in the kinds of services they provide themselves and the kinds they leave to local authorities. In education, for example, some state governments pay the entire cost of supporting public junior colleges, whereas others provide only some of the costs to county or municipal governments. In public welfare, some state governments pay for all aid payments not covered by federal grants, whereas other states share these costs with local governments. The most complete record of

Table 4.4 *State Payments to Municipalities by Percentages Distributed According to Various Standards, 1962*

Standard	California	Massachusetts	Pennsylvania
Population of local jurisdiction	69.9%	0.4%	21.5%
Sales or licenses in local jurisdiction (for example, sales of alcoholic beverages, tobacco, or other taxed items and the number of auto or drivers' licenses issued locally)	6.7	—	17.1
Road mileage	—	—	32.3
Amount of state-owned land in local jurisdiction	—	0.4	—
Equal aid to all jurisdictions	1.4	—	—
Contractual arrangements with specific cities for services provided to state institutions	0.2	—	—
Specified rate of aid per unit of service provided (e.g., per patient day in city hospital)	0.1	1.8	—
Assessed value of certain types of property (e.g., industrial property)	—	22.6	—
Local fiscal ability	—	12.6	—
Ratio to local expenditures for aided function	21.8	58.8	18.9
Need as determined by state agency	0.3	3.1	—
Criteria undefinable by available data	—	0.2	11.0
Total[a]	100.4%	99.9%	100.8%

[a]The columns do not add up to exactly 100 percent because the separate percentages within the table have been rounded.

SOURCE: Ira Sharkansky, *Public Administration: Policy-Making in Government Agencies*, 2nd Edition, Chicago: Markham Publishing Company, 1970, 1972, p. 288. Reprinted by permission of Rand McNally Publishing Company, Chicago.

state involvement in the support of public services shows the percentage of total state and local government revenues that are raised or spent at the state level. Table 4.5 shows the record of revenue raised for each state during 1969–1970.

There is considerable variation in the role that state governments play in raising revenues for themselves and local governments. The nationwide average is 55.5 percent of total state and local revenues raised by the state government. But the range extends from 79.3 percent in Delaware to 38.5 percent in New Hampshire.

There is a tendency for low-income states to rely heavily on state revenues. In Louisiana, North Carolina, South Carolina, and Vermont,

Table 4.5 *State-Government Portions of State-Local Total Tax Revenues, Fiscal 1969–1970*

United States	55.5%		
Alabama	73.7	Montana	46.6
Alaska	68.1	Nebraska	44.4
Arizona	62.9	Nevada	58.0
Arkansas	72.6	New Hampshire	38.5
California	49.2	New Jersey	41.5
Colorado	50.8	New Mexico	74.9
Connecticut	50.4	New York	51.4
Delaware	79.3	North Carolina	75.3
Florida	60.3	North Dakota	52.4
Georgia	65.7	Ohio	46.5
Hawaii	77.2	Oklahoma	64.1
Idaho	62.9	Oregon	51.5
Illinois	53.0	Pennsylvania	58.6
Indiana	54.0	Rhode Island	58.0
Iowa	50.9	South Carolina	76.5
Kansas	48.5	South Dakota	42.4
Kentucky	73.0	Tennessee	62.6
Louisiana	69.5	Texas	55.7
Maine	54.9	Utah	63.3
Maryland	57.2	Vermont	64.5
Massachusetts	49.2	Virginia	60.4
Michigan	58.0	Washington	68.0
Minnesota	60.7	West Virginia	73.3
Mississippi	74.0	Wisconsin	59.3
Missouri	51.1	Wyoming	58.6

SOURCE: U.S. Bureau of the Census, *State Government Finances in 1971* (Washington, D.C.: Government Printing Office, 1972).

there are numerous local governments (especially rural counties) that are hard-pressed to support minimum levels of public services with the economic resources available within their borders. Perhaps because many local authorities in these states must rely upon state aid, all local governments are inclined to view the state governments as the prime sources of funds. It is therefore probably easier to pass a state-aid bill when there is something in it for the constituents of most legislators. At the other end of the income scale, local governments in the well-to-do states of New York, New Jersey, Massachusetts, and California carry a larger than average share of state and local financing.

Apparently out of step with the general pattern is Delaware. This state has one of the highest levels of personal income per capita in the nation but is also the heaviest user of state revenues. It thus reflects the pattern of its southern neighbors. Southern states have been centralized historically, owing partly to colonial experience of dispersed population and a plantation economy that did not nurture the development of strong, autonomous towns. Nebraska is another state that deviates from the normal association between low income and high reliance on state revenues. It ranks below the national average on several measures of economic resources but close to the top in the proportion of revenues raised locally. There a strong local orientation, together with fiscal conservatism, seems to have retarded the development of sources of state revenue. Nebraska was one of the last state governments to abandon its reliance on locally raised property taxes.

State aids to cities are on the increase, especially to the largest cities. Table 4.6 shows the growing benefits to bigger cities, both in per capita terms and in the percentage of local revenues that are coming from state governments. The decade of the 1960s saw the largest cities increasing their per capita state aid by more than five times. Now it is cities below 50,000 population that are distinctly second-class citizens in the state-aid competition.

Also during the 1960s and early 1970s, an increasing number of states changed their constitutions to permit local governments greater freedom in raising their own revenues. Cities still rely most heavily on the property tax. As of 1970, however, the local governments in twenty-two states collected a sales tax, and local governments in ten states collected an income tax. In most cases, the state revenue department actually collects the revenues for the locality, according to options chosen by the local units. Further state efforts have improved the administration of local property taxes. Forty states make periodic comparisons between market values (as determined by actual sales) and local property assessments. These sales-assessment studies can help local governments and their citizens in several ways: They can indicate areas of inequality in tax

Table 4.6 *State Aids to City Governments, 1960 and 1970–1971*

	1960		1970—1971	
City size	Per-capita state aid	State aid as percentage of city revenue	Per-capita state aid	State aid as percentage of city revenue
1,000,000 plus	$35.95	17.8	$197.67	36.3
500,000–999,999	23.48	16.4	65.55	19.2
300,000–499,999	14.11	13.2	43.94	17.8
200,000–299,999	12.28	11.4	45.81	18.6
100,000–199,999	14.77	14.2	41.08	18.3
50,000–99,999	13.91	15.0	31.44	17.3
25,000–49,999	11.27	14.3	} 21.20	17.8
less than 25,000	8.62	17.0		

SOURCES: U.S. Bureau of the Census, *Compendium of City Government Finances in 1960* (and 1970). (Washington, D.C.: Government Printing Office, 1961 and 1971.)

assessments between communities; they can equalize the distribution of those state aids that go to communities on the basis of local property values; and they can reduce tax competition between adjacent communities in metropolitan areas.[27]

Horizontal Intergovernmental Relations

The metropolitan problem

Metropolitan areas are the most frequent settings for horizontal relations among local officials, reflecting the high population density and the demands for policy that are thus generated, as well as the proximity of many separate governments with policy problems that depend partly on one another's actions. In Chapter 2 we discussed the social and economic differences between central cities and their suburbs and mentioned some features that hinder the smooth coordination of local activities in metropolitan areas. Here we return to the subject of metropolitan areas, this time to focus on problems and opportunities in governmental integration.[28]

The number and density of governmental units in metropolitan areas (see Table 4.7) are the primary conditions that beg for coordination. The Chicago SMSA has the dubious distinction of containing the most units. Its 1113 jurisdictions were divided among school districts, counties, municipalities, townships, and special districts as shown in Table 4.7.

The "metropolitan problem" has been studied and decried by a generation of urban scholars. The fundamental problem they identify is the *noncongruence of policy-making units and problem units.* Municipal borders follow railroad tracks, creeks and rivers, streets and alleys, and other artificial lines of demarcation; but problems of crime, pollution, poverty, transportation, and so forth, do not respect these boundaries. Lineberry[29] has identified four basic aspects of governmental fragmentation in the metropolitan area: externalities, fiscal and service inequities, absence of political responsibility, and lack of coordination.

EXTERNALITIES   Because the metropolis is an interdependent system, policies undertaken by independent municipal corporations or special districts may produce changes, sometimes unintended, in other parts of the total region. Economists call such consequences *externalities*, or, more descriptively, *spillover effects*. Land-use and zoning policies are examples. Sophisticated manipulation of zoning requirements is regularly used to produce the most desirable mix of residents and commerce, while shifting burdens to other areas in the metropolis, particularly to the central city. The "zoning game" may thus be used to maximize the benefits to one's own community while shifting the costs to other "players," particularly the less fortunate ones (see our discussion of the

Table 4.7 *Number and Types of Local Governments*
in United States and in the Chicago SMSA

	United States		
Type	1962	1967	Percentage change, 1962-1967
All local governments	91,186	81,248	−10.9
School districts	34,678	21,482	−37.2
Other	56,508	59,466	5.2
Counties	3,043	3,049	0.2
Municipalities	18,000	18,048	0.3
Townships	17,142	17,105	−0.2
Special districts	18,323	21,264	16.1

Chicago SMSA	
	1967
All local governments	1,113
School districts	327
Other	
Counties	6
Municipalities	250
Townships	113
Special districts	417

SOURCE: U.S. Bureau of the Census, *Census of Governments 1967:* vol. 1, *Governmental Organization* (Washington, D.C.: Government Printing Office, 1968), Tables 1 and 19, pp. 23, 126 ff.

zoning game in Chapter 12, pp. 295–299).[30] Although zoning decisions especially illustrate the spillover effects of municipal policies, decisions in numerous other functional areas, including crime prevention, transportation policy, pollution control, schooling, and industrial attraction, may also entail externalities for other communities.

FISCAL AND SERVICE INEQUITIES We noted in Chapter 2 the problems resulting from the segregation of economic needs and resources in the metropolitan area. To reiterate by example, in Detroit, twenty-five suburban school districts spent up to $500 more per child per year to educate their children than did the city of Detroit. In the CC of Detroit, on the other hand, nearly a third of the public-school buildings were built during the administration of President Ulysses S. Grant.[31] One New Jersey community had an assessed valuation of $5.5 million per pupil, and a neighboring community had a valuation of $33,000 per pupil.[32]

ABSENCE OF POLITICAL RESPONSIBILITY When there is a plethora of governmental units, citizen control of decision makers is diffused. A citizen of Fridley, Minnesota, a Minneapolis suburb, is expected to exercise informed control over eleven local governments, in addition to the state and national governments. In the absence of an overarching metropolitan government there is no policy-making body to hold accountable for broad metropolitan problems or for failures arising from governmental action or inaction. Such fragmentation of the citizens' attention can hardly contribute to responsible democratic government.

LACK OF COORDINATION The construction of public policy requires at least minimum coordination both among functions and among decision-making units. The absence of both types of coordination in the metropolis suggests that it will be unable to realize all the benefits of coherent policy and the consequent economies of scale that larger units should be able to secure. If communities fail to coordinate air-pollution control, for example, a municipality downwind may have the most advanced regulation yet still suffer the effluence of its upwind neighbor.

The politics of metropolitan reorganization
There are ten major alternative forms of metropolitan reorganization, ranged here from the least to the most extensive:[33]

1. Municipal extraterritorial regulation of real-estate developments in the rural fringe outside municipal borders;
2. Intergovernmental agreements;
3. Voluntary metropolitan councils;
4. The urban county;
5. Transfer of functions to state governments;
6. Metropolitan special districts;
7. Annexation and intercity consolidation;
8. City-county separation, that is, separation of the urbanized and rural areas;
9. Consolidation of the city with the urbanized county surrounding it;
10. Federation of several municipalities.

Measured in terms of the oceans of ink used by reform advocates, the reorganization movement has been only modestly successful. Without attempting to construct a theory of metropolitan reform ourselves, we may still cite some propositions showing that metropolitan government is a volatile and divisive issue and fundamentally political. The following explanations of the overall failure of reorganization schemes are offered.

First, *public officials and the "power structure" of the metropolitan area rarely initiate reform.* Although city officials do sometimes initiate reorganization proposals, more typically a group like the League of

Women Voters, a civic-betterment association, a newspaper, or a band of intellectuals initiates the movement. Yet, without the support of elected officials and community power structures, a reform campaign begins with at least one strike against it. If public officials are relatively unconcerned about reorganization, voters will be even less enthusiastic.

Second, *voters are often apathetic about metropolitan organization and place higher values upon other goals (like community autonomy) than upon reform (for efficiency and the like).* Studies of several metropolitan areas[34] suggest that citizens (except for residents of racial ghettos)[35] are quite satisfied with levels of municipal services. Voters seem to be more impressed by arguments concerning loss of community autonomy and by fear of higher taxes than by abstract arguments in favor of metropolitan consolidation. Moreover, voter information about metropolitan reform tends to be minimal and inaccurate. Evidence from survey data suggest that in one Miami campaign less than a third of the electorate had heard of the reform proposal and "had a sliver of a correct idea about it."[36]

Third, *suburban officials form a hard core of opposition to change.* In the St. Louis consolidation effort, the major source of organized opposition was the Citizen's Committee for Self-Government, dominated by municipal officials and Republican Party leaders from the county. Also, political party leaders, though they have sometimes (as in Cleveland) supported change, tend to be either apathetic or antagonistic to it. It is well known that the central cities of larger metropolitan areas outside the South are dominated by the Democratic Party and that suburban areas are generally Republican. The merging of central cities and fringe areas into a single metropolitan entity would almost certainly decrease predictability for local party leaders. In some areas it would also benefit the Republican Party. As Banfield has concluded:

Even if the proportion of Republicans declines sharply in the suburbs, metropolitan government north of the Mason-Dixon line would almost everywhere be Republican government. In effect, advocates of consolidation are asking the Democrats to give up their control of the central cities, or at least to place it in jeopardy.[37]

Labor unions also tend to oppose metropolitan reorganization. Much of their political clout comes from union members living in the central city. Union spokesmen would find themselves representing a smaller percentage of the new electorate, and having to deal with Republican power bases in the suburbs. The inevitable changes in personnel and alignments on the council would reduce union access to decision makers, and would require changes in their political tactics.

Finally, *black leaders and voters are almost always opposed to reorganization.* Given the national policy commitment to betterment for black Americans and the increasing concentration of Blacks in the central cities of the metropolitan complex, the opposition of black leaders and voters merits special attention. No study of a proposal for metropolitan reorganization, successful or not, has found a majority of black voters on the side of restructuring. The most impressive evidence of this opposition comes from a study of voting on reorganization proposals in Cleveland-Cuyahoga County. For a succession of ten reorganization proposals over a twenty-five-year period, black support declined with each election.[38] This increasing opposition was contemporary with a proportional increase in black voting strength in the city itself, culminating in the 1967 election of Carl Stokes as mayor. Black resistance to such reform is based on two beliefs about the consequences of metropolitan merger. First, Blacks anticipate dilution of their voting strength in any larger-area government. They also fear redirection of urban public policy away from the issues of poverty, ghetto rehabilitation, and civil rights.

There are two factors in the socioeconomic structures of metropolitan areas that are especially relevant to metropolitan reform. First, *the larger the metropolitan area, the smaller is the probability of a successful reform campaign,* and, second, *the sharper the socioeconomic differences between suburban and central city areas, the smaller is the probability of reform.* In the largest metropolitan areas, where there are distinct social-class differences between central cities and fringe areas, metropolitan integration would be most difficult. These observations are substantiated by studies of school-district mergers and municipal annexation. Where the central-city and suburban population resemble each other, annexation seems more feasible than where the two populations represent distinct social and economic compositions.[39] Annexation seems most difficult where the central-city population is distinctly less well educated and employed in less attractive occupations than are the suburbanites. Under these conditions suburbanites seem to resist entering the same government unit with central-city residents. Opponents of annexation argue that suburban voters will be forced to pay the high costs of welfare, police, and fire protection required for residents of the central city, especially of its slums. As these problems are the ones that many suburbanites left the city to escape, they are hardly likely to welcome reaffiliation with the central city. In the minds of many suburbanites, the city means undesirable people and the high taxes necessary to provide services for them. Annexations are also impossible in older cities already surrounded by incorporated suburbs. Where all the fringe area is incorporated, the central city may be literally hemmed in and blocked from taking new land outside its borders. Very few of the major central cities can take advantage of annexation provisions.

Metropolitan government in practice

Even though metropolitan government reorganization has been urged upon urban areas by a generation of political scientists, the record of accomplishment has not been impressive. Almost fifty referenda have been held on metropolitan reorganization proposals in the post-World War II years,[40] but only a minority of them have passed. City-county consolidations have succeeded in several areas of Virginia, in Baton Rouge, in Nashville, and in Jacksonville; a federation of several governments was adopted in the Miami area. Most recently a modified city-county consolidation was imposed on Indianapolis-Marion County by the state legislature, one of the rare cases in which a referendum was not required.

Each of these metropolitan governments has taken significant steps toward eliminating fiscal and service disparities, lack of coordination, absence of political responsibility, and the problem of externalities. Yet, as we have seen, adoption of these metropolitan reforms requires overcoming so many legal and political hurdles that it is rare. Williams, a leading student of urban government, has observed that "through the second quarter of this century many political scientists were writing on why metropolitan areas needed to be politically integrated through local government consolidation. Thus far, in the third quarter, a major theme has been documentation of how thoroughly this advice has been rejected by the American people."[41]

Federal policy and the metropolitan problem

In recent years several federal policies have been directed toward the problems of fragmented government in the metropolis. The substance of federal metropolitan policy has been to encourage metropolitanwide planning and councils of government. Federal encouragement of area planning may be traced to the "701" assistance program of the Housing Act of 1954, but the most extensive requirements are contained in the Demonstration Cities and Metropolitan Development Act of 1966.

The act requires that all applications for federal grants or loans in nine categories of assistance be submitted for review to an area planning agency, which must be "to the greatest practicable extent, composed of or responsible to elected officials" of the governmental units of the area. If no such area agency exists, applications must be reviewed by a state planning agency. A total of 100 specific federal assistance programs come under the purview of the Demonstration Cities and Intergovernmental Cooperation Acts.

A common result of federal involvement in metropolitan affairs is the *council of government.* Examples include the Association of Bay Area Governments (ABAG) in the San Francisco–Oakland area and the Association of Central Oklahoma Governments (ACOG). The councils of government (COGs) usually include elected officials from counties, school districts, municipalities, and special districts. Their most important function is to approve or disallow applications for federal grants-in-aid based upon the consistency of the submitted proposals with metropolitan-area objectives. Before any single governmental unit in the area can receive federal assistance, its application must be reviewed by the COG. Typically, the COG has prepared, or is in the process of preparing, an overall plan for metropolitan development.

Most of the powers of the metropolitan COGs are, therefore, negative, rather than positive. They can reject local grant applications that are inconsistent with sets of (sometimes vague) metropolitan criteria, but they cannot compel any local government to do anything against its wishes. Practically, their limited powers extend only to matters involving federal money and not to local decisions on zoning, taxation, spending, and other policies that do not commit the U.S. Treasury. Although they have the organizational potential for effective metropolitan coordination, they are at present little more than metropolitan planning agencies, with no real basis of authority beyond their power to disapprove grant applications. They still lack the effective power actually to coordinate the activities of the numerous local governments in the metropolis. As Banfield has described the difficulty of metropolitan planning agencies, "the catch is that the making of a plan is precluded by the very problem—lack of coordination—that the plan is supposed to solve."[42] Plans are often, in Norton Long's words, little more than "civic New Year's resolutions." Even if metropolitan COGs and planning agencies were truly effective coordinators of local policies, they would still be a long way from solving the deeper problems of the absence of political responsibility and the presence of fiscal and service disparities within the metropolis.

Summary

In this chapter we have outlined the structural context of urban policy making. We have not simply described governmental institutions but have also shown how different kinds of structures grow out of basic notions about governmental organization and how they interact with local politics and public policy. The premises of local organization include the desire to maintain the political accountability of local officials, the desire for professional management, and the desire to maintain either local or state control of city affairs.

The three prominent models of local governmental organization are the mayor-council, council-manager, and city-commission types. These basic models can be combined with any number of secondary features, each of which may be the subject of political controversy because of its implications for local policy making: the use of partisan or nonpartisan ballots; selection of legislators at large or by wards; executive veto of legislative actions; assignment of personnel and budgetary controls to the legislature, executive, or semiautonomous boards; and the use of partisan or professional criteria in selecting the heads and employees of administrative departments.

Many issues of local governmental structure involve the cities' relations with national and state governments: vertical intergovernmental relations. Others involve relations among officials of different local jurisdictions: horizontal intergovernmental relations. Both have enormous relevance for local policy making. Local officials seldom make important decisions without considering the resources or requirements available from national and state authorities. And, particularly in metropolitan areas, few officials can work for long without having influence on—or feeling the influence of—officials from other local jurisdictions.

Notes

1. This discussion about the roots of local government structures borrows from the work of Herbert Kaufman, especially "Administrative Decentralization and Political Power." Paper delivered at the Annual Meeting of the American Political Science Association, Washington, D.C., 1968. See also Ira Sharkansky, *Public Administration: Policy-Making in Government Agencies* (Chicago: Markham, 1972), chap. 4.
2. Scott Greer, *Governing the Metropolis* (New York: Wiley, 1962), chaps. 3 and 5.
3. Quoted in Duane Lockard, *The Politics of State and Local Government* (New York, Macmillan, 1963), p. 132.
4. David Danzig and John Field, "The Betrayal of the American City," *Commentary*, (June 1968), 52–59.
5. See Ira Sharkansky, "Reapportionment and Roll Call Voting: The Case of the Georgia Legislature," *Social Science Quarterly, 51* (June 1970), 129–137, and the literature cited therein.
6. See Karl Bosworth, "The Manager Is a Politician," *Public Administration Review, 18* (Summer 1958), 216–222; and Ronald O. Loveridge, *City Managers in Legislative Politics* (Indianapolis: Bobbs-Merrill, 1971).
7. *Newsweek*, March 13, 1967, p. 38.
8. Henry Maier, *Challenge to the Cities: An Approach to a Theory of Urban Leadership* (New York: Random House, 1966), p. 190.
9. For some appropriate qualifications on the hierarchical controls available to the President and governors, see Ira Sharkansky, *Public Administration*, chap. 4. The point is that mayors have even fewer such controls, not that they are the only American chief executives who lack them.
10. Maier, p. 23.
11. Raymond E. Wolfinger and John O. Field, "Political Ethos and the Structure of City Government," *American Political Science Review, 60* (June 1966), 206–226.
12. *Ibid.*; see also Robert L. Lineberry and Edmund P. Fowler, "Reformism and Public Policies in American Cities," *American Political Science Review, 61* (September 1967), 701–716, and the literature cited there.
13. Robert Salisbury and Gordon Black, "Class and Party in Partisan and Nonpartisan Elections: The Case of Des Moines," *American Political Science Review, 57* (September 1963), 584–592; and Robert R. Alford and Eugene C. Lee, "Voting Turnout in American Cities," *American Political Science Review, 62* (September 1968), 796–813.

14. Lineberry and Fowler, *op. cit.*

15. *Ibid.*, pp. 715–716.

16. *Ibid.*

17. Thomas R. Dye, "Governmental Structure, Urban Environment, and Educational Policy," *Midwest Journal of Political Science*, 11 (August 1967), 353–380.

18. Morton Grodzins, "The Federal System," in The President's Commission on National Goals, *Goals for Americans* (Englewood Cliffs, N.J.: Prentice-Hall, 1960).

19. See Morton Grodzins, "American Political Parties and the American System," *Western Political Quarterly*, 13 (December 1960), 974–998.

20. See Daniel J. Elazar, *American Federalism: A View from the States* (New York: Crowell, 1966), chap. 1.

21. Wallace S. Sayre and Herbert Kaufman, *Governing New York City* (New York: Norton, 1965), pp. 559–562.

22. Quoted from Douglas M. Fox, ed., *The New Urban Politics: Cities and the Federal Government* (Pacific Palisades, Calif.: Goodyear, 1972), pp. 90–92.

23. *The Budget of the United States Government, Fiscal Year 1974* (Washington, D.C.: Government Printing Office, 1973), p. 163.

24. Frederic N. Cleaveland et al., *Congress and Urban Problems* (Washington, D.C.: Brookings Institution, 1969), p. 375.

25. James Q. Wilson, "The War on Cities," in Robert Goldwin, ed., *A Nation of Cities* (Skokie, Ill.: Rand McNally, 1966), p. 19.

26. See James L. Sundquist, *Making Federalism Work* (Washington, D.C.: Brookings Institution, 1969); and Ira Sharkansky, *The Maligned States: Policy Accomplishments, Problems, and Opportunities* (New York: McGraw-Hill, 1972), pp. 46–50.

27. See Sharkansky, *The Maligned States*, pp. 146–147.

28. This discussion is based on Robert L. Lineberry, "Reforming Metropolitan Governance: Requiem or Reality?" *Georgetown Law Journal*, 58 (March–May 1970), 675–718.

29. *Ibid.*, pp. 676–681.

30. See Seymour Sacks and Alan Campbell, "The Fiscal Zoning Game," *Municipal Finance*, 35 (1964), 140–149; and David Ranney, "Regional Development and the Courts," *Syracuse Law Review*, 16 (Spring 1965), 600–612.

31. National Commission on Civil Disorders, *Report* (Washington, D.C.: Government Printing Office, 1968), p. 241.

32. Robert C. Wood, *1400 Governments* (Garden City, N.Y.: Doubleday, 1961), p. 55.

33. Advisory Commission on Intergovernmental Relations, *Alternative Approaches to Governmental Reorganization in Metropolitan Areas* (Washington, D.C.: Government Printing Office, 1962).

34. See, for example, John C. Bollens et al., *Exploring the Metropolitan Community* (Berkeley: University of California Press, 1963), pp. 188–190; and Metropolitan Community Studies, *Metropolitan Challenge* (Dayton, Ohio, 1959), p. 241.

35. National Commission on Civil Disorders, pp. 79–83.

36. Edward Sofen, *The Miami Metropolitan Experiment* (Bloomington: University of Indiana Press, 1963), p. 76.

37. Edward C. Banfield, "The Politics of Metropolitan Area Organization," *Midwest Journal of Political Science*, 1 (May 1957), 77–91.

38. Richard A. Watson and John H. Romani, "Metropolitan Government for Metropolitan Cleveland," *Midwest Journal of Political Science*, 5 (November 1961), 365–390.

39. Thomas R. Dye, "Urban Political Integration: Conditions Associated with Annexation in American Cities," *Midwest Journal of Political Science*, 8 (November 1964), 430–446; and Basil Zimmer and Amos Hawley, *Metropolitan Area Schools* (Beverly Hills, Calif.: Sage, 1968), p. 307.

40. Lineberry, *op. cit.* For discussions of the major reforms, see Sofen, *op. cit.;* Brett Hawkins, *Nashville Metro* (Nashville, Tenn.: Vanderbilt University Press, 1966); and William C. Havard, Jr., and Floyd Corty, *Rural-Urban Consolidation: The Merger of Governments in the Baton Rouge Area* (Baton Rouge: Louisiana State University Press, 1964).
41. Oliver Williams, "Life Style Values and Political Decentralization in Metropolitan Areas," *Southwestern Social Science Quarterly, 48* (December 1967), 299.
42. Edward C. Banfield, "The Uses and Limitations of Metropolitan Planning in Massachusetts," in H. Wentworth Eldridge, ed., *Taming Megalopolis* (Garden City, N.Y.: Doubleday, 1967), p. 716.

chapter 5

Decision making in urban government

Decision making is a two-sided process, involving both input from the political system and outputs of public policies. Decisions are choices among alternative courses of action that shape the outputs of the urban system. Policy makers are not free to make whatever decisions suit their fancies, for they are confronted with numerous demands and have only limited resources of time, information, money, and authority with which to meet them. Administrators, legislators, executives, and members of informal power structures must therefore develop various strategies for coping with this complexity. These strategies are the subject of this chapter.

Inevitably, procedures for coping with inputs will represent compromises with a strictly rational model of decision making, for the strictures of rationality are ordinarily too severe for operating political systems. Before we begin to address the important issues involved in the decision-making process, however, we shall need to clear some difficult preliminary ground. It will be useful if we understand something about the nature of political power, particularly its role in the urban political system. Then we can examine the application of power to decisions. Because a variety of people in a community besides the formal office holders may hold power, we shall also have to discuss the structure of community power. What may seem at first to be a relatively simple matter—the identification of power holders in an urban area—is really quite complex.

The Structure of Community Power

Formal decision makers (those who hold significant public offices) may or may not be the "real" decision makers in a political system. Sociologist C. Wright Mills won considerable notoriety with his argument that "the power to make decisions of national and international consequence is now so clearly seated in political, military, and economic institutions that other areas of society seem off to the side and, on occasion, readily subordinated to these."[1] Mills argued that elected office holders are essentially subject to historic decisions made by the big three institutions of government bureaucracies, military commanders, and economic elites. Whether Mills was right or wrong need not concern us here, but his implication that power may not always reside with the occupants of formal positions is clearly relevant to the study of urban politics. The degree to which formal office holders actually exercise power is a most significant empirical matter.

The concept of power

Power is a commonplace analytical focus for political scientists, political activists, and ordinary citizens. It is as ancient as Aristotle and as current as Black Power and student power. It is as ambiguous as it is ubiquitous, as elusive as it is useful. There is much controversy over the definition of power, but most contemporary efforts are based on that of the German sociologist Max Weber: "'Power' is the probability that one actor within a social relationship will be in a position to carry out his own will despite resistance, regardless of the basis on which this probability rests."[2] One of the most penetrating students of power in American communities, Dahl, has relied upon Weber's formulation: "My intuitive idea of power, then, is something like this: A has power over B to the extent that he can get B to do *something that B would not otherwise do.*"[3]

Power can be a micro (individual) property or a macro (community) property. It is both a capacity of the individual to alter his environment and a capacity of the community itself to manipulate the economic, social, and cultural spheres in which the individual operates.

Anticipated reactions and nondecisions

There are a number of problems in the analysis of political power. Power cannot be directly observed but can only be inferred from behavior or from reports. The problem of *anticipated reactions* means, however, that B will take account of A's possible reactions, even if A makes no visible effort to apply power, force, or influence. B may respond even when A does not communicate his preferences verbally. In their appointment of Supreme Court justices, for example, Presidents anticipate the reactions of the Senate. In preparing municipal budgets, the city council and the manager anticipate the reactions of taxpayers, interest groups, and service personnel.

The problem of *nondecision* reflects the social context of power and directs attention away from *A*'s overt attempt to influence *B*'s behavior. Nondecision occurs when decision makers choose not to embark upon a program that might offend an important group of the community's residents. These and other problems do not render power a worthless concept, but they suggest that essentially superficial observations like "Smith (or Mayor Daley or Senator So-and-So) has a lot of power" may be so oversimplified as to be misleading.

It is helpful to conceive of power as a relation persisting through time and depending upon the situation. Because power relations do persist through time, *A* and *B* usually coexist in a reciprocal relation. A manager depends upon his council to fund the programs he proposes to undertake, but the council depends upon the manager for policy recommendations. Because the power relationship persists, the wise strategist will not exhaust all his resources in a single attempt at influence. Although, for analytic purposes, we may be interested in a single decision and a successful application of power by *A*, it is probable that the specific outcome has been affected by a series of previous interactions between *A* and *B* and has implications for future attempts by each to obtain favorable decisions from the other.

Just as it is difficult to wrench decisions out of the time dimension, so too is it difficult to ignore the situational elements in a power relationship. A few salient situational factors that may influence the success of an attempt by *A* to influence *B* include:

1. *B*'s legal, contractual, or political authority to make an agreement with *A*;
2. The probability that *C*, *D*, and *E* might be activated in a manner unacceptable to *A*, *B*, or both;
3. The accuracy with which *B* perceives the outcome that *A* seeks;
4. The availability of resources to *A* and *B*;
5. The power of other actors over both *A* and *B*.

These considerations suggest that the analysis of any single attempt at exercising power is complex and that examination of the myriad influence patterns in an urban system is a staggering enterprise. That is why the proposition "*A* has a lot of power" is much less useful than is the proposition "*A* has power over *B* with respect to *Y*, under conditions *p*, *q*, and *r*."[4]

Community power structure

A community power structure may be defined as the power relations among political actors in the community persisting through time. Note that this definition pertains to the community as a whole and not only to the public or political sector. The most important single finding of the research on community power is that power does not reside in the governmental sector alone. To restrict our definition to governmental office holders would be to make an assumption about the power structure that might or might not be accurate.

The initial problem faced by students of community power has been to "operationalize" the concept of power in order to render it amenable to measurement and investigation. Though most researchers have developed their own measures, the major approaches to identification of power holders fall into three types: positional, reputational, and decisional.[5]

THE POSITIONAL APPROACH   The oldest and simplest method of studying community leadership is through the positional approach. Although it has been replaced by more sophisticated techniques in the social sciences, it is still used widely by laymen and journalists. It assumes that leaders perform specified governmental and organizational roles. When, for example, Samuel Stouffer wanted to know whether community leaders or the public were more tolerant of minority rights, he drew up a list of formal roles, including the mayor, the chairman of the local Parent-Teacher Association, party leaders, the school- and library-board presidents, the newspaper publishers, and others. Each occupant of the designated position was interviewed, on the assumption that he was, in fact, a community leader.[6] Other studies have assumed that occupants of such positions as mayor, councilman, newspaper editor, banker, chamber-of-commerce president, League of Women Voters officer, school-board member, superintendent, and labor-union leader are community leaders.

The positional approach has several advantages: It is simple and economical to apply and it does not presume any particular knowledge about the social and economic structure of the community being investigated. Moreover, it rests upon the probability that holders of governmental and organizational positions will actually exercise influence, which, though not totally justified, is not altogether unrealistic.

The major difficulty with the approach is that it may be both too inclusive and too exclusive. Without independent verification, one never knows whether he has included leaders who are merely titular or excluded some who may exercise considerable power. A particular set of positions may encompass the real leaders in one community but not in another. The positional approach also assumes that all office holders are approximately equally powerful on every issue. A likelier possibility is that governmental office holders may be most influential on some issues (e.g., on how much money to spend on road construction) and that nongovernmental leaders may dominate on other issues (e.g., minority employment opportunities). The positional approach is thus a rough-

and-ready technique, useful for some purposes but doubtful as a means of identifying the real power holders in a community.

THE REPUTATIONAL APPROACH   The reputational method of identifying community leaders has several labels: the *sociometric approach* (after its technique), the *sociological approach* (after its major academic proponents), and the *elitist*, or *power elite*, approach (after its major findings).

The earliest and still the most significant reputational study of community power structure is Floyd Hunter's study of Atlanta.[7] Hunter's method, which inspired countless reputationalists, involved using a panel of informants to identify the most influential men in the community that he studied. The informants might be either a random sample of the population or a specific panel believed to be particularly informed about local decision making (as newspaper editors or chamber-of-commerce officials would be). By culling newspaper accounts of community decision making and organizational rosters and minutes, Hunter arrived at a list of 175 possible leaders and then submitted this list to a panel of informants. These informants were told to pare down the list, and forty people were finally identified as the community "influentials" of Atlanta. Once the list of forty had been compiled, Hunter interviewed as many of its members as possible in an effort to identify the "top leaders." The principal question he asked each person on his list was "If a project were before the community that required *decision* by a group of leaders—leaders that nearly everyone would accept—which

Table 5.1   *Occupational Characteristics of Top Leaders in Atlanta, Georgia*

Occupation	Number of leaders	Positions held
Banking, finance, insurance	7	President, executive vice-president, etc.
Commercial	11	Board chairman, president, editor, etc.
Government	4	Mayor, superintendents of city and county schools, county treasurer
Labor	2	Local union presidents
Leisure	5	Social leaders
Manufacturing, industry	5	Board chairmen, presidents
Professional	6	Attorneys, dentist
Total	40	

SOURCE: Adapted from Floyd Hunter, *Community Power Structure* (Chapel Hill: University of North Carolina Press, 1953), Table 4.

ten on this list of forty would you choose?" Twelve men were identified consistently enough by the forty "reputational leaders" to convince Hunter that they constituted the top leaders in the community power structure.

The key leaders in the power structure of Atlanta were men from the private, rather than the public, sector. Table 5.1 shows the occupational composition of this leadership group. Only four of the forty on the original list had roles in the public sector. Most held positions in commerce, banking, manufacturing, and the professions. Not only were the political officeholders a small proportion of the total leadership, but also, Hunter argued, they were mainly second-level leaders, whose major responsibility was execution of decisions made by economic "dominants." The political and governmental realm was thus secondary to the economic one. In Atlanta, according to Hunter:

the dominant factor in political life is the personnel of economic interests. It is true that there is no formal tie between the economic interests and the government, but the structure of policy-determining committees and their tie-in with the other powerful institutions and organizations of the community make government subservient to the interests of these combined groups. The government departments and their personnel are acutely aware of the power of key individuals and combinations of citizens' groups in the policy-making realm, and they are loath to act before consulting and "clearing" with these interests.[8]

The picture of community power painted by Hunter and other reputationalists is one in which realities of power are at variance with the democratic theory of political accountability. Instead of decision making by elected office holders, power is wielded by economic dominants who are relatively invisible to the public and are not subject to electoral control. Rather than a wide distribution of political power among the citizens, power is held by a relatively small upper class.

The reliability of such conclusions depends upon the validity of the reputational method. Its defenders argue that it is relatively efficient and economical to use, whereas its principal rival, the decision method, may involve years of observation.[9] Moreover, the reputational approach depends upon reports by presumably informed observers of the local decision-making process. Nonetheless, critics of the reputational approach have leveled serious charges against it.

Perhaps the most serious charge is that the approach predetermines its findings by incorporating the a priori assumption of a single power elite. To ask "Who are the top leaders here?" is to assume that some particular group holds top leadership positions. Critics believe that it is no coincidence that the method usually identifies a single cohesive set of leaders. They claim that the existence of a single elite is an empirical question that must itself be tested, rather than being incorporated into the methodology of a study.

Second, ignoring the possibility that power may vary from one policy domain to another, the reputational approach falsely assumes that the power structure identified controls all major issues. Actually, leadership may be specialized, and one group may be influential in one policy area and other groups in other areas.

Third, the reputational approach measures not power per se but rather the reputation for power. Some case studies of decision making have shown that economic dominants are widely perceived as powerful but are not active participants in the decision-making process.[10]

Fourth, there is an inevitable arbitrariness in any particular cutoff point in defining the limits of the power structure. Why, for example, should Hunter have selected just forty leaders? Why not draw the line at 400 or 4000 members of the community power structure?

Fifth, the method is primarily subjective, rather than behavioral and empirical. It rests upon the assumption that what informants observe and report accurately reflects what really occurs.

THE DECISIONAL APPROACH   The decisional approach has been stimulated by the work of Dahl and his associates at Yale University.[11] It is also called the *event analysis*, or *decision-making* approach (after its method), the *political science* approach (after its academic proponents), and the *pluralist alternative* (after its usual findings).

The decisional approach begins with the selection of certain key issues in the community and then identifies the people who seem significant in affecting their outcomes. Current decisions may be selected by the researcher from meetings, newspaper accounts, and interviews of participants. Past decisions may be reconstructed through similar procedures and from the minutes of past meetings.

Dahl identified three basic issues in New Haven during the period of his study: school decisions, an urban-renewal decision, and political nominations. His principal conclusions about power in New Haven are, first, that a leader in one issue area was not likely to be influential in another and that, if he was, he was probably a public official and most likely the mayor; and, second, that leaders in different issue areas did not seem to be drawn from a single homogeneous stratum of the community.[12] No identifiable, cohesive elite dominated by economic and social notables appeared in Dahl's study of New Haven. The power structure included multiple centers. Different sets of decision makers operated in each arena, and the arenas were bridged only by the mayor. In New Haven, Dahl concluded, economic and social notables had "relatively little direct influence on government decisions."[13] As public officials tended to be the major power brokers, it followed that there was a high degree of mass control over decision makers. Such political accountability is unlikely when decision making is controlled by an elite in the private sector.

Dahl's study of New Haven presented a more benign picture of power in an American community than did Hunter's study of Atlanta. But the reputationalists have responded with both methodological and substantive criticisms of the decisional approach and its findings. They have claimed that, despite Dahl's criticism of Hunter, the decisional approach still relies upon reputational methods: People are asked for reports of their own and others' behavior with regard to particular decisions, the reports of journalists are used, and the reconstruction of past decisions may reflect severe distortions of memory and perception.

Second, the approach rests upon an arbitrary choice of issues. That Dahl identified three major issue areas in New Haven, whereas other decisionalists have identified dozens, suggests that standards for a key issue are not well defined. Just as one limitation of the reputational approach involves the initial selection of informants, a critical weakness of the decisional approach involves somewhat arbitrary selection of issues.

Third, by emphasizing the key, or controversial, decisions, the approach ignores the cumulative significance of routine decisions. If the best teachers are continually assigned to schools serving upper-income neighborhoods, lower-income children will study under the worst teachers—a routine decision with potentially significant consequences.

Fourth, the approach ignores leadership ideologies. If there is no ideological divergence among the power structure, it makes little practical difference whether all the leaders participate in every decision or whether there is a division of labor among the elite. Accountability to the public depends upon a choice of leaders, and there is no meaningful choice when all leaders share similar ideological perspectives.[14]

Fifth, the decisional approach implies, but does not demonstrate, that elections control the nature of public policy by governing the selection of public officials. In an earlier statement, Dahl himself argued that elections are severely limited as devices for the registering of public opinion.[15] Our discussion of local elections (pp. 65–67) also suggests that they are quite imperfect instruments for insuring political accountability.

General problems in the analysis of power structures

Some additional problems plague both reputational and decisional studies of community power: the *self-fulfilling prophecy*, the *limitations of the case study*, an *absence of longitudinal analysis*, the problem of the *two faces of power*, and inattention to *constraints upon power structures*.

Some recent evidence suggests that both the reputational and decisional approaches imply self-fulfilling prophecies. John Walton reviewed analysis of the power structures of fifty-one communities and found that political scientists used the decisional approach just as consistently as their sociological cousins used the reputational approach. The difficulty, however, is that the type of power structure identified, whether pluralist or elitist, was highly correlated with the choice of method. He concluded that "the disciplinary background of the investigator tends to determine the method of investigation he will adopt, which, in turn, tends to determine the image of the power structure that results from the investigation."[16]

The problem of the self-fulfilling prophecy is compounded by the limitations of the case study. It is not clear whether Atlanta, New Haven, or any single city is typical of most American cities. One recent study with a sample of sixty-three American cities concluded that New Haven was an extreme case of decentralized decision making.[17] There are two ways to cope with the limitations of case studies. The first is to analyze them as sources of data in their own right. Claire Gilbert examined 166 case studies of community power and concluded that "there is very strong evidence that political processes are tending to be more pluralistic" over time.[18] The other solution is to study several communities utilizing a single research design. Agger, Goldrich, and Swanson studied four communities, two in North Carolina and two in Oregon.[19] The Permanent Community Sample of the National Opinion Research Center has been used to study power structure and decision making in a large number of cities.[20]

Studies done at a single point in time also suffer from limitations analogous to those of a snapshot. If a power structure is cohesive and truly coercive and entrenched, it should be relatively stable. But without longitudinal analysis we do not know whether the power structure changes from year to year or persists over longer periods of time. The limited evidence from Agger, Goldrich, and Swanson's analysis of four communities over a fifteen-year period suggests that communities may have different power patterns in the space of a single decade.[21] And, until more longitudinal analyses are available, it will be impossible to identify the factors that change the distribution of power.

The problem of the two faces of power was first identified by Peter Bachrach and Morton Baratz. They argued that "there are two faces of power, neither of which the sociologists [reputationalists] see and only one of which the political scientists [decisionalists] see."[22] They agree with the decisionalists that the reputational approach suffers the fatal defect of confusing potential, with actual, power. But, they insist, there are serious objections to the decisionalists' own methodology, because the latter approach "takes no account of the fact that power may be, and often is, exercised by confining the scope of decision-making to relatively 'safe' issues."[23] Those who establish the public agenda may exercise the most important power through their capacity to prevent issues from entering the political system. What the decisionalists call key issues may actually be minor matters that do not threaten the basic distribution of values in the community. The existence of the private-property system, the legitimacy of wealth, and the validity of the social-incentive system are matters so fundamental that they are missed by the student of the controversial issues facing the city council. Had the decisional approach been used to study community power in a southern town in the 1940s, for example, it might have been discovered that the key decisions involved fluoridation, the location of a new high school, and the dismissal of the city manager. The latent, yet potentially explosive, issue of the distribution of values between the races would have been ignored because it was so tightly entwined in the status quo that it was not an issue at all and did not become one until some years later. In sum, the decisional approach ignores the "values and biases that are built into the political system . . . and the dominant values and the political myths, rituals, and institutions which tend to favor the vested interests of one or more groups, relative to others."[24] An examination of the other face of power requires a determination of the economic, social, and ideological underpinnings of the status quo.

That power is to be located in institutions, as well as in individuals, suggests constraints upon even the most powerful structures. In his analysis of the presidential decision-making process, Theodore Sorensen has emphasized that American Presidents—powerful as they are—are constrained by permissibility, the implications of previous commitments, and the availability of time, resources, and information.[25] If powerful American Presidents are constrained by factors in their environment, then we might expect to find that even monolithic community power structures are limited in their capacities. Urban power structures are no doubt constrained by the same sets of factors that limit all decision makers, ranging from imperfect information to inadequate resources and including constraints imposed by state and national systems.

Antecedents and consequences of variations in power structure

ANTECEDENTS   Are certain kinds of communities more likely than others to have monolithic power structures? Does the structure of community power make any difference in the kinds of public policies pursued by local government? These questions have received considerably less attention than have questions of the shape or structure of power and the mere identification of power holders. Nor is either of them easily answered. In some obvious respects, however, there are remarkable similarities between Atlanta and New Haven. Both have recently been governed by mayors nationally regarded as progressive (Ivan Allen and Richard Lee respectively). Both are central cities where parks are built, police patrol neighborhoods, fires are fought, and hospitals and public utilities are maintained. Although neither city is usually singled out as an extreme case of discrimination, racial disorders have occurred in both. What are the antecedents and consequences of variations in community power structures, and can they be identified?

This question can be answered more directly if we classify power structures on a continuum ranging from monolithic to pluralistic, as indicated in Figure 5.1. Although several classification schemes have been suggested,[26] the one adapted from Charles M. Bonjean's and David M. Olson's analysis of power structures captures the major disagreements among the researchers; it uses the dimensions of *legitimacy, visibility, scope of influence,* and *cohesion.*[27] The two models of pluralistic and monolithic power structures represent extreme points on a continuum. It is doubtful that any existing power structure is completely monolithic or pluralistic. Given the classification scheme, the question then becomes, what variables are associated with power structures that tend toward one or the other extreme? Several antecedents of power structures may be suggested in the form of propositions.[28] These propositions are only tentative generalizations rather than absolute laws of social structure. Each community possesses certain features that make it unique and imperfectly comparable to other communities. What is really important may be not the presence of particular factors but their combination and interaction in a particular setting. Moreover, these generalizations are derived from a wide assortment of studies that differ among themselves on the most appropriate methodology for studying community power. The propositions, therefore, are better viewed as tools for analysis than as iron laws of power distribution in the city.

1. The larger the number of inhabitants in a community, the more pluralistic is the power structure.

Figure 5.1 Four Dimensions of Power Structure

"Pluralist" Structure	DIMENSION	"Monolithic" Structure
Leaders hold public or associational office	LEGITIMACY	Leaders do not hold public or associational office
Leaders are recognized by general public	VISIBILITY	Leaders are unknown to general public
Leaders do not form a cohesive, interacting group	COHESIVENESS	Leaders form a cohesive, interacting group
Leaders are specialized and exercise power in one or a few policy areas	SCOPE OF INFLUENCE	Leaders are general and exercise power in most or all policy areas

SOURCE: Adapted from Charles M. Bonjean and David M. Olson, "Community Leadership: Directions of Research," *Administrative Science Quarterly, 8* (December 1964), 291–300.

The evidence from case studies is mixed. However, Terry N. Clark's analysis of decision-making structures in fifty-one cities has revealed a moderate relationship ($r = .384$) between community size and a measure of pluralistic decision-making structures.[29] The smaller the community, the greater is the probability of dominance by a monolithic structure. One study of a tiny upstate New York village has identified a small clique of influentials who controlled the village government.[30] On the other hand, the relationship between size and type of power structure is not perfect. Reputational studies of Atlanta and Dallas have concluded that monolithic power structures dominate those communities.[31] Size per se may be less important than certain structural characteristics associated with size. Large cities are ordinarily more socially and economically heterogeneous. It may be this heterogeneity, rather than size alone, that is associated with pluralistic power structures. We can frame this argument in terms of a proposition.

2. The more diversified the economic system within a community, the more pluralistic is the power structure.

The evidence for proposition 2 ranges from a slight tendency to strong support.[32] The logic of the proposition suggests that multiple economic centers in the private sector produce alternative resource bases for competition in community decision making. One particular feature of the economic structure that seems relevant to the structure of power is the degree of industrialization.

3. The more industrialized the community, the more pluralistic is the power structure.

Almost by definition, industrialization will broaden the economic base of a community beyond commercial and service-oriented enterprises and will introduce another potential center of power in the economic system. Moreover, industrialization is usually (at least outside the South) associated with labor unions, which offer an additional source of power in community decision making.[33] The implication can also be framed as a proposition.

4. The stronger labor unions are in a community, the more pluralistic is the power structure.

One other proposition relates community power distribution to the economic system.

5. The larger the proportion of absentee-owned enterprises in a community, the more pluralistic is the power structure.

Perhaps the most monolithic power structure ever identified was that in "Middletown," where a single local family owned the major source of livelihood for the town's entire population and dominated nearly all facets of community life.[34] In cities dominated by absentee ownership, the executives of such nonlocal firms tend to have lower stakes in community activities and to play less active roles.

Social heterogeneity parallels economic differentiation in its association with more pluralistic forms of power.

6. The more socially heterogeneous the community, the more pluralistic is the power structure.

However, a community where elites do not value political equality and mass participation is unlikely to fit proposition 6. A community dominated by racists is not a likely candidate for social pluralism. So:

7. Pluralism is promoted by community and, particularly, elite attitudes emphasizing widespread participation and political equality.

A well-developed network of secondary associations—civic groups, social clubs, ethnic and religious organizations, political action groups, and so on—provides multiple channels for expression of opinion, as well as an organizational basis for alternative leadership structures.[35] Another proposition therefore follows:

8. The larger the number of secondary associations in the community, the greater is the probability of pluralism.

There has been too little research on the relation between governmental structure and power structure to permit confidence in any generalization. Nonetheless, several writers suggest that governmental reformism, particularly nonpartisanship, is associated with monolithic power structures.

9a. Nonpartisanship is more commonly associated with monolithic structures of power.
9b. Competitive party politics is more commonly associated with pluralistic structures of power.

John Walton found a strong relationship between competition among local parties and pluralism in community power.[36] Clark's study of fifty-one communities went even further in relating reformism to monolithic structures.[37]

10. The higher the level of reformism of political institutions (form of government, type of elections, and type of constituencies), the more monolithic is the decision-making structure.

The degree of governmental reform was the strongest predictor of power structure in Clark's fifty-one cities. Certain features of the reformist syndrome seem to produce less pluralism in community decision making. Among them may be the elimination of competition among parties through the nonpartisan ballot, the depoliticization of the mayor's office, and the reduction in working-class voting turnout associated with reformed institutions.

A significant consequence of community power structure is its impact upon citizen participation, as several studies have indicated.

11. Competition among different elements of the power structure is a necessary condition for widespread citizen participation.

Agger, Goldrich, and Swanson concluded that "a competitive political leadership is necessary . . . for the existence of a power structure of the mass type."[38] If the cohesion dimension of leadership changes from competitive to consensual, the distribution of political power in the community will thus change from relatively broad to relatively narrow. This finding is consistent with much writing by democratic theorists who stress competition among elites as the sine qua non of democratic government.[39]

CONSEQUENCES FOR POLICY   Whatever the nature or source of a community's power structure, its relation to the level or distribution of urban public policies is not well established. In discussing the consequences of power structure, Bonjean and Olson deplored the fact that "even fewer studies have been concerned with consequences of leadership structure characteristics than with antecedents."[40] This neglect is particularly unfortunate if, as we believe, the central task of urban political analysis is the understanding of policy outcomes.[41]

Perhaps power structures do not make much difference in the outputs of community political systems. Many decisions by local governments are automatic responses to the requirements of state and federal statutes and prior financial commitments. Regardless of the concentration or dispersion of power, local governments are constrained by Dillon's rule, by tax rates and municipal indebtedness, and by the laws and administrative rulings of states and the federal government. Yet several hypotheses suggest variations in the effects of power structure on policies. Cities with monolithic power structures may furnish fewer public services to poor neighborhoods (unless, of course, the power structure is public-regarding), may emphasize economic-development over social-welfare policies, and may tax and spend at lower than average levels. But, until we have more data, we cannot demonstrate that policy choices in monolithic cities are notably different from those in pluralistic cities.

A triangular view of community power

Most research on community power structure, implicitly or explicitly, subscribes to a bipolar notion of the possibilities. Power structures are said to range from tight, monolithic, and elite-dominated at the one extreme to slack, pluralistic, mass-dominated (or at least competitive) at the other. According to Hunter, the monolithic structure is centered in

Figure 5.2   A Triangular Model of Community Power

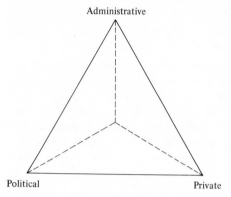

the private sector, while the pluralistic, according to Dahl, is rooted in the political sector. In our view, these possibilities are oversimplified and misleading. They recognize only two major centers of power (the private and the political), and ignore a third: the administrative. Instead of being located along a continuum from monolithic and private to pluralistic and political, the power structures of any given city might best be charted within a triangular model as in Figure 5.2.

Some cities (perhaps Atlanta) might fall near the private pole, while others (perhaps Chicago and New Haven) would be dominated by their political elites. Still others (perhaps New York) would appear nearest the administrative pole. As critics of power-structure studies have long recognized, of course, dominance in one policy area does not equal dominance in others. Chances are that law enforcement in many cities would show the dominance of public bureaucracies, and that other areas (e.g., urban renewal and economic development) would show greater roles for private and political elites. In any case, a perspective on power that assumes bureaucrats are dormant or dominated by private and political elites misses the important legacy of reform movements that emphasized the goals of professional management. As we shall see later in this chapter, bureaucracies are a significant force in urban policy making. Yet a casual reader of the power-structure literature would scarcely know of their existence.

We now move from a discussion of informal decision makers—community power structures—to discussion of formal decision makers, councils, mayors, managers, and bureaucrats. Even if a city contains a sub rosa power elite, the formal decision makers must at least execute decisions made elsewhere. In all cities the formal decision makers manage the routine decisions. And, in the final analysis, these routine choices—involving as they do spending and taxing, zoning, distribution of services, and the like—may have as much impact as do the allegedly big decisions made in a behind-the-scenes power structure. In Chapter 4 we discussed the governmental structures of urban areas. We shall now deal with the roles, resources, and behavior of occupants of formal decision-making positions.

Formal Decision Makers: The Council

The councilman

It is difficult to describe a *typical* councilman. Councilmen come from varying income, educational, occupational, and ethnic backgrounds; have different views about municipal government; and, depending upon the particular states and municipalities in which they hold office, exercise different powers and responsibilities. Yet we can gain perspective on the city councilman by positing some characteristics of a typical councilman and then suggesting factors responsible for deviations from those characteristics. Typically, a councilman is male, middle-aged, a businessman or professional, relatively well educated and well-to-do, white, active in civic associations, and Republican. A study of councilmen in St. Louis County revealed that 70 percent of the councilmen were at least high-school graduates and that 53 percent had completed college. About half were from managerial, professional, or proprietary occupations, and another 22 percent were from white-collar occupations.[42]

The use of ward or at-large elections also affects the composition of the council. Ward systems tend to increase the representation of lower socioeconomic groups and minorities. Sloan found that cities using ward systems elected larger proportions of councilmen from minority groups than did cities using at-large elections.[43] The at-large system increases the costs of elections and forces all contenders to run before a constituency of the whole. Minority-group candidates in many cities thus face a white Protestant majority. Even when minority-group candidates are successful, under the at-large system they are usually the more moderate ones.

Factors other than these class and election procedures influence the types of people chosen for the council. Some of these factors are specific to a particular city or even to a particular campaign. But among the more general ones are (1) the degree to which labor unions and ethnic and racial groups are organized and involved in local politics, (2) whether the city pays councilmen enough to sustain working-class representation on the council, (3) whether the party system facilitates representation of various social groups, and (4) whether a covert power structure recruits or prevents recruitment of certain kinds of candidates.

Roles and resources

RESPONSIBILITIES *The New York Times Magazine* once entitled a story about a New York councilman "Man in a Wind Tunnel."[44] Its focus was the multiple pressures constantly buffeting an office holder in the nation's largest city. In smaller and less heterogeneous communities these pressures are less intense. A better analogy is perhaps life in a partial vacuum. Whatever the appropriate metaphor, the council and its members are legally responsible for making all ordinances pursuant to state law and the municipal charter. Yet this statement leaves much unsaid, just as a description of the U.S. Congress solely in terms of its constitutional responsibilities would be incomplete or even misleading.

In the broadest sense, the city council makes policy for the city; that is, it chooses among alternative courses for taxing people, spending money, and the like. In a narrower sense, the formal powers of the council vary a good deal from one form of government to another. The council operating in the council-manager city is supposed to make policy but to leave questions dealing with administration to the city manager and his administrative agencies.

The council-manager plan enshrines the alleged dichotomy between policy and administration. In the strong mayor-council form of government, the initiative for policy is still more likely to come from the mayor than from the council, although the latter is not confined so narrowly as in the council-manager city. The scope of the council's power is probably greatest in the weak-mayor system. Here the mayor shares his power with other elected officials, and the council itself sometimes appoints officials, prepares the budget, or performs tasks that are considered administrative in other forms of government. A commission government fuses legislative and administrative authority in the council; each councilman is also the administrator of some particular branch or department of the city government. Commissioners are prone to mind their own bailiwicks and to let others do the same, which promotes mutual noninterference at the council level.

As do all legislative bodies, the municipal council performs an important representative function. Yet different councilmen will have different views about the proper role of the representative, and the formal structures of municipal government foster particular styles of representation. In the ward system, representation is likely to mean a narrow bricks-and-mortar orientation: Ward councilmen tend to look after their constituencies' desires for paved streets, parks, school facilities, and other tangible outputs of municipal government. In one Michigan city using the ward system, one councilman shouted to another at a meeting, "You bastard, you had three more blocks of black-topping in your ward last year than I had, you'll not get another vote from me until I get three extra blocks."[45] One New York City councilman, explaining his approach to the city budget, said:

> . . . the first thing I look for is the budget items involving my district. Are we getting what we're entitled to? Are we being shortchanged on a library or not getting a school we were promised? . . . It's only after I've done all I can for my own area that I look into the rest of the budget.[46]

In the constituency at large, a councilman's political future depends less upon material gains for a small area. A councilman at large can afford to align himself with broad social, economic, or political interests, rather than binding himself to geographical interests.

ROLES   The ways in which a municipal councilman attempts to represent his constituency depend upon his representational role. Political theorists debate the extent to which a representative should be either a trustee or a delegate. The trustee role emphasizes the representative's obligation to vote according to his conscience and best judgment, regardless of whether his vote happens to follow his constituents' preferences. The delegate role obligates the representative to vote according to his perception of his constituents' sentiments, regardless of his own views.

Studies of city councilmen suggest overwhelming support for the trustee orientation toward representation.[47] Almost three-quarters of St. Louis area councilmen said that they made decisions on the basis of their own judgment or principles. Councilmen seem to prefer their own to their constituents' thinking on matters of public policy, and Downes has hypothesized that this attitude may reflect councilmen's own belief that "they act as councilmen in their spare time and receive little or no monetary compensation." Therefore they can "ignore the blandishments of neighborhood, ward, or other specialized interests."[48] It may also reflect the very imperfect information on public preferences that councilmen receive. When input institutions like elections, parties, and interest groups provide vague or conflicting intimations of public opinion, the councilman may find it easier to use his own judgment as a guide to policy.

Partly because most councilmen have trustee orientations, they are relatively free to ignore the sentiments of their constituents. But Kenneth Prewitt finds that councilmen also share an ethic of *volunteerism*, which further immunizes them from the necessity of responding to constituent attitudes.[49] It is easy for a councilman whose political ambitions are negligible to vote his own policy preferences and to ignore his constituents' wishes. Prewitt's councilmen hold elected offices, but are not always veterans of tough contests. About one-fourth of the councilmen in his sample had been initially appointed to their office upon a predecessor's resignation, and if they ran for reelection it was with the advantages of an incumbent. Further, only a minority expressed a wish for a political career extending to higher offices.[50]

When asked if it was easy or difficult to go against majority preferences in policy making, one councilman said: "Easy, I am an independent type of individual. I don't feel the weight of voter responsibility. I am not all fired up for a political career." Such councilmen do not fear the ballot, which makes electoral accountability and reprisals difficult. Although volunteerism may be more widespread in suburban, middle-class areas than in big-city politics, its prevalence does not make it easier for the electorate to control local government.

RESOURCES   The city councilman's major political resource is his legal authority to make policy. Whatever influence other elements of the city's political system may have, it is still the legal responsibility of the council to pass ordinances (consistent, of course, with the city's own charter and the laws of the state), to enact the city budget, to hire and fire the manager in a council-manager city, and so forth. Councilmen may also possess as individuals great political skill, some prestige, and experience in the procedures of decision making. But most councilmen are limited in their resources of time and information, particularly technical information. Serving as a city councilman is a full-time job only in the largest cities. Elsewhere the councilman must divide his time between his private occupation and his public service. Staff assistance is minimal or nonexistent on almost all city councils. Individual council members find it tempting, and necessary, to rely on the recommendations of their professional city manager or department administrators, or the full-time mayor who can rely, in turn, on the advice of staff assistants. Moreover, councilmen face increasingly complex and technical policy issues with only their own wits and political wisdom to guide them. Many of these issues are too broad in scope for the council —or any other city officials—to tackle by themselves. Issues such as air and water pollution and mass transportation involve areawide coordination and a scale of financial resources that make state and federal governments the prime actors, and may reduce city councils to the role of observers.

Formal Decision Makers: The Mayor

The two most controversial urban chief executives in recent years, John Lindsay of New York and Richard Daley of Chicago, illustrate the great differences among mayors.[51] Mayor Daley is surely one of the most controversial figures in American politics, partly because of his role in the confrontation between police and demonstrators at the 1968 Democratic National Convention in Chicago. He is a product of ethnically heterogeneous Chicago, hailing from an Irish community called Bridgeport. The son of lower-class immigrant parents, Daley, following many ethnic sons of an earlier day, found an avenue of upward mobility in politics. He emerged as a major figure in the nation's largest extant urban political machine in the early 1950s, when he was clerk of Cook County. In that position he served as a combination "secretary of state" and "chief of staff" for the county machine. Daley's position as mayor of Chicago, combined with his mastery of the party organization, makes him as powerful a figure as exists in any American city. Unlike some other machine leaders, he has built upon his inheritance of power. Some potential opponents have been absorbed into the party apparatus in positions of political responsibility. Daley and his organization survive precisely because he has used key opportunities for reform. Chicago's merit system for employees coexists with an extensive patronage system; professional-management techniques are well developed; growth and development policies have won the support of businessmen.[52]

Daley's machine is concerned partly with its own maintenance. Social problems and policies are subordinated to the organizational needs of the party. Aggressive pursuit of social change would, in all probability, threaten the stability of the machine by introducing unpredictable changes in its environment. These factors give Daley and his organization an orientation to the status quo that is reinforced by Daley's own personal values, which center on the home and the faith. According to David Halberstam, Daley

is deeply religious, but his religion is Pre-Ecumenical, pre-John XXIII, where there is individual sin, but little social sin. He can tolerate small and petty graft, but he cannot excuse adultery, and cannot understand or tolerate a man who fathers a family and then deserts it. He seems unable to understand the forces which create these failings.[53]

The Mayor of Chicago has great appeal to established second- and third-generation Americans. He is a man of politics but not a man of action or rhetoric. Indeed, he is a master of malaprop. "We must rise," he once said, "to higher and higher platitudes." Mayor Daley's prominence as a symbol of veneration and enmity for opposing groups has given rise to folklore built partly on statements by or about him. In the words of one admirer among the city councilmen of Chicago: "Thank God for Mayor Daley." One of Chicago's delegation in the U.S. House of Representatives has said: "I don't even go to the bathroom without checking first [with Daley]." The mayor's view of himself seems to combine strength with thinly veiled humility in the style of a *pater familias*:

"You'll need another haircut" (commenting on an alderman's hairstyle in response to the alderman's attempt to raise a point of order at a council meeting).

"Put the alderman of the 40th ward in his seat if he refuses to obey the rules."

"*Boss* should apply to someone who unreasonably imposes his way. I thought I was the leader of the city. You don't call the leader of a church or synagogue a boss."[54]

There is some irony in finding John Lindsay a more vocal crusader for social reform than is his Chicago counterpart. Daley is a man of the working class, presumably cognizant of its problems, but Lindsay comes from an affluent background. He is a white Anglo-Saxon Protestant who governs a city with even more ethnic diversity than Chicago. The Mayor of New York, unlike the Mayor of Chicago, lacks the backing of a potent political machine. In campaigning for his first term, Lindsay relied on the Republican Party (a minority in Democratic New York City) in coalition with the Liberal Party. The Republican Party denied him renomination for a second term in 1969, and he then relied on the Liberal Party and his hastily forged Urban Party. The city council and board of estimate are solidly Democratic; the municipal bureaucracy has been shaped by a string of Democratic administrations and is composed of relatively autonomous agencies, each of which resists coordination in any form.[55] These factors support the widely held view that New York is ungovernable. In fact, even when Mayor Lindsay became an enrolled Democrat, few of his political problems went away. In such a context, any effort at change is difficult. Lindsay possesses no organization permeating the interstices of the political system, as does the Chicago machine, and his policy-oriented style is thus blocked by the inertia and sheer weight of a massive public bureaucracy.

Roles and resources

THE MAYOR'S POLITICAL RESOURCES   Daley and Lindsay illustrate that the personality and political bases of the mayor are important in determining the kinds of influence that he can exercise. But the roles and resources of the mayor are affected by other factors as well. Some of the city-to-city variation in the mayor's office reflects the form of government. The mayor of a council-manager city is normally no more than a titular leader, first among equals on the city council, responsible more for ribbon clipping than policy innovation. The differences between the mayors in a strong-mayor city and in a weak-mayor city are, of course, matters of degree. The weak mayor can rarely be called a chief executive. He shares administrative power with separately elected officials, with independent boards and commissions, and with the council itself. Often he has no central role in budget making but shares power equally with other officials. In Milwaukee, for example,

. . . the mayor does not prepare an executive budget as is done in cities of the "strong mayor" type. Instead, a number of cooks are involved in the making of the budget pie. The Budget Department goes over requests with individual department heads, usually paring their requests sharply. The formal budget is prepared at hearings conducted by the Budget Examining Committee of the Board of Estimates, on which the mayor serves as chairman, together with the council's Finance Committee, the Comptroller, and the Budget Supervisor as secretary.[56]

In a strong-mayor city, the mayor plays a more crucial role in both policy initiation and administration. He typically dominates the budget-formulation process and key administrative appointments. To be sure, these formal differences do not always predict accurately the power relations at city hall. Sometimes, as in Chicago and New Haven, politically strong mayors operate within weak-mayor systems. Still, however, the formal powers of the mayor make it easier or more difficult for him to influence policy making.

Table 5.2 provides data on three specific features of the formal governmental structure that may affect the mayor's potential power. It is reasonable to assume that a mayor is most effective when he is directly elected and can claim a popular mandate, when he possesses some veto power, and when he has a longer term of office.

Mayors in mayor-council systems are more likely to benefit from these features than are mayors in either commission or manager cities. Formal structural factors do not exhaust the mayor's resources. Items like political information, experience, strong political organization, ability to bargain, and intelligence cannot be readily measured. But they are no less—and are perhaps more—important than are the structural features of office.

LEADERSHIP ROLES   Some mayors convert limited political resources into significant bases for political leadership; others, perhaps endowed with more generous resources, rarely use them to lead their cities in new directions. We have described the roles of councilmen primarily in terms of their views of representation. As conventional wisdom pictures the mayor as the political leader of the city, his choice of roles reflects his views on policy leadership. Duane Lockard characterized big-city mayors as reformers, program politicians, evaders, and stooges.[57]

Table 5.2   *Selection, Veto Powers, and Tenure of Mayors in American Cities of Populations of 5000 or More in 1960, by Form of Government*

Form of government	Method of selection[a]		Veto power[b]		Term of office	
	Directly elected	Selected by council	No veto	Veto	1-2 years	3 or more years
Mayor-council	95.6%	3.9%	32.6%	67.4%	56.3%	43.7%
Commission	76.1	23.0	91.4	8.6	22.8	77.2
Council-manager	51.1	47.8	71.4	28.6	73.3	26.7

[a]Percentages do not total 100, for about 1 percent of cities designate the candidates receiving the highest number of votes in city-council elections as "mayors."
[b]Excluding cities in which mayors are not directly elected.
SOURCE: Orin F. Nolting and David S. Arnold, eds., *The Municipal Year Book 1967* (Chicago: International City Managers' Association, 1967), pp. 104–105.

The reformer rides into office in a campaign against corruption, bossism, or the machine. His style is often flamboyant, but he is usually a capable organizer who can weld together an effective following. There is considerable variety among reform mayors, from the dashing and charismatic Fiorello La Guardia (Mayor of New York City from 1934 to 1945), to the blue-blooded Joseph S. Clark and Richardson Dilworth (Mayors of Philadelphia during the 1950s). The policy orientations of reform mayors vary as much as do their social backgrounds. Some mayors are conservative and limit themselves to honest, efficient, and businesslike administration of city services. Others are social reformers who try to upgrade services for the poor.

The *program politician* is an activist-entrepreneur, whose political style includes generous doses of public relations and promotional techniques to secure policy changes. Often the program politician dedicates his administration to a miniature urban version of a Great Society or a New Frontier. One example is Carl Stokes' "Cleveland Now!" Some of the more prominent program politicians have included New York's John Lindsay, Newark's Kenneth Gibson, Cleveland's Carl Stokes, Milwaukee's Henry Maier, Los Angeles' Tom Bradley, New Haven's Richard Lee, and Detroit's Jerry Cavanaugh. Sometimes political fortunes are hard on such innovative mayors. Aggressive advocacy of change alienates certain elements in the municipal electorate.

The political style of the *evader* is avoidance of conflict. Sometimes reformers become evaders once they are secure in their posts. A frustrated program politician may find it easier to play an evader's role. To some degree, the fragmented structure of government in American cities (especially in the weak-mayor system) tends to encourage evasion.

The *stooge*, who is merely a front man for a political machine or power structure, seems rarer today than in the past. The demise of the machines in most cities, together with the increased pressure on and visibility of the mayor's office, has made it more difficult for an informal organization to place a stooge in public office. Yet continuing allegations that some mayors are "owned" by organized crime and the recent indictments and convictions of some mayors suggest that the role of stooge is still with us.

POLITICAL LEADERSHIP In examining the current leadership potential of big-city mayors, Alexander L. George has written:

The nature of the urban political environment makes intense demands on the mayor for special leadership skills of a high order if the need for social change is to be met; at the same time, however, the realities of urban political life make it difficult for him to perform these role requirements effectively and consistently. The root of this paradox lies in the considerable fragmentation of authority and dispersal of power characteristic of the formal governmental structure of American urban areas. In the larger cities, governmental authority is divided and dispersed among federal, state, county, and city jurisdictions; among mayor, council, and various independent officials, boards, and commissions designated by the electorate to deal with specific services and functions.

In few cities today . . . does the mayor have *formal* authority and resources commensurate with the responsibilities and tasks which face him.[58]

Above all else, the weakness of the big-city mayor is a function of the limited political resources at his disposal. In the heyday of the political machine, the mayor—assuming that he dominated the machine—could offer material incentives in the form of patronage positions to countless claimants upon the public pocketbook. Even today Mayor Daley of Chicago, the boss of the only major city machine still in operation, has an estimated 35,400 patronage positions (ranging from menial census takers to prestigious judgeships) at his disposal. Daley, however, is the exception. Most mayors have lost to well-developed civil services most of their control over their bureaucracies. Having also lost the support of vigorous political parties, today's mayors must spend much of their time (also a valuable political resource) engaged in generating and maintaining political support for the next elections.

Most contemporary mayors lack the formal powers conferred on both the President of the United States and most state governors. Fully half of all mayors lack veto power of any sort; half are elected to only two-year terms; and nearly half of all cities elect other executive officials (including treasurers, clerks, police chiefs, assessors, and attorneys) who may compete with the mayors for political leadership.

The mayor's powers are circumscribed most sharply in the council-manager system, in which he ordinarily functions as a symbolic leader (having thus about the same amount of political muscle as does the Queen of England). Richard Neustadt has observed that American presidential power is nothing more than the "power to persuade." The central difference, however, is that the President ordinarily has the political resources to add that extra touch to his persuasiveness; the mayor merely persuades.

Formal Decision Makers: The City Manager

The manager plan

The city manager is a professional city administrator who is also chief executive in the council-manager city. The professional organization of city managers is the International City Management Association (formerly the International City Managers' Association). For many years, the ICMA has provided a model city charter, which outlines the ideal relations between the manager and the council and is the basis of numerous actual city charters and many state-enabling statutes.

The city manager is hired by the council and serves at its discretion. He is subject to removal at any time by a majority vote of the council. In the early days of the council-manager plan, most managers were civil engineers by training. Today most city managers have been trained in graduate programs of public administration. They are familiar with financial administration, personnel management, municipal law, and planning. Like many professionals in American society, city managers tend to be highly mobile. Only a minority are hometown boys. The career of a typical manager might include work as a staff assistant to an established manager, then a post as assistant city manager, then appointment as manager in a small town, and, finally, similar posts in larger or more prestigious communities.

The official responsibilities of a manager are specified in the city charter. They include (1) overseeing the execution of policy made by the council, (2) preparing and submitting the budget to the council, (3) appointing and removing the principal department heads (the police and fire chiefs, the personnel and budget officers, and so on), and (4) making recommendations on policy to the council. It is the last point that receives the most varied interpretations. The underlying philosophy of the manager plan specifies the responsibility of the council to make policy and of the manager to administer it. The manager is expected to shun interference in the policy choices of the council. The most egregious violation of the managers' code of ethics is participation in partisan politics. But, if the manager is expected to make recommendations to the policy-making council, where is the line drawn between the roles of manager and council?

In practice, of course, there is no clear line between policy and administration. The manager's persuasiveness in his policy recommendations can make him the most powerful figure in a city's policy-making process. Matters ordinarily regarded as administrative are laden with policy implications. The cumulative effect of bureaucratic, or administrative, decisions—many of which are made by the manager's subordinates in the operating units of the city government—may be as significant as any general policy selected by the mayor or council. For example, police treatment of minority groups may have more effect on minority group attitudes toward law enforcement than does any policy of equal treatment enunciated by the city council.

Roles and resources

In order to define more precisely the roles and behavior of the city manager, Deil S. Wright conducted a survey of forty-five managers in cities with populations larger than 100,000. "The behavior of city managers," he wrote, can be "fully and exhaustively characterized by three role categories: managerial, policy, and political."[59] The first managerial role involves his relation with the municipal bureaucracy, including supervision and control of policy administration and personnel. The policy facet of the manager's role includes his relation with the city council, particularly as he is the source of policy recommendations. His political role includes efforts as a community leader and as a representative of community needs and interests before the local council, the community at large, and other units of government. Wright's survey of managers uncovered variations in the ways that they view and perform these three roles.

In his performance of the managerial role, "the capacity of the manager to control the bureaucracy is linked to his abilities to secure information, allocate resources, and impose sanctions (or grant rewards)."[60] The major formal resources available to him in his administrative capacity are his professional staff, his control over the budget, and his power to appoint and remove department heads. Each of these resources may be used to impose constraints and to offer incentives to the municipal bureaucracy. In most council-manager cities, the manager has nearly complete autonomy in his performance of the administrative role. This autonomy is, more than any other factor, at the core of the council-manager system. Many managers guard their administrative autonomy jealously.

The underlying philosophy of the council-manager plan is more ambiguous about the role of manager in policy initiation and recommendations. Still the manager does play a significant role in initiating policy. Wright has concluded that the manager is the dominant policy initiator in most council-manager cities. More than two-thirds of the managers that he surveyed said they set the agendas of the city councils. This task helped them to control the kinds of questions that were raised and the policy options that were considered. The same proportion of managers reported that most items considered by the council were on the agendas at the behest of managers. The city manager is probably the major source of information for any city council. He bears most of the responsibility for creating the "menu" of policy alternatives to be considered. The council will not accept everything on the menu, but the menu does set forth the policies likely to be considered seriously.

Wright has divided the manager's political-leadership role into two components: vertical (extracommunity representation) and horizontal (intracommunity leadership). In dealing with other units of government (particularly the states and the national government), the manager interacts with state or federal bureaucrats. The mayor usually serves as spokesman to elected state or national officials. On the horizontal dimension the manager plays a major role in representing and explaining community policies to the public at large. He ordinarily has no special expertise or information on the political interests of the community, however. His information is technical, not partisan.

Wright found that the manager is most at home in his administrative role, and he devotes more of his time to administrative tasks. Managers report that they obtain more personal and job satisfaction from their administrative than from their other roles.[61] This attitude reflects their basic professional orientation toward efficient management and delivery of public services and towards detailed financial accounting and personnel administration. Their skills are administrative, and their major resource is technical expertise. Their commitments are greatest in matters of capital improvements (bricks and mortar) and established programs. They shoulder responsibility for the formulation of social policy and the burdens of community leadership with less enthusiasm and, perhaps, with less competence. Karl Bosworth wrote some years ago that "the manager is a politician."[62] This view is a useful corrective to myths about apolitical managers. In Wright's study, however, managers appear primarily as administrators; they are more interested in administrative than in political responsibilities.

Ronald O. Loveridge adds to our understanding of city managers with his information from the San Francisco Bay Area. He finds that managers espousing a political role for themselves are more likely than self-perceived administrators to have majored in the social sciences in college, and to have pursued graduate training in public administration. They are also more likely to be newcomers to local government. Managers oriented to administrative roles, in contrast, are more likely to have begun work without a college degree, and to have moved up in municipal administration through such jobs as public works director, building inspector, city engineer, or personnel director.

Loveridge finds that managers and council members differ sharply in their views of proper managerial behavior. While most of the managers (even those feeling most comfortable as administrators) claim some prerogatives as policy leaders, council members express the older view of management as being strictly administrative and subordinate to the council. The result of these disharmonious views is compromise; neither party acts within the strict boundaries of his role conception. Managers sense the limits of activity that council members will permit; they feel out the situation; work behind the scenes; advise council members in private; educate the council in regard to issues and alternative policies; and generally seek to maintain the council's support. Specific strategies of the manager include the introduction of his policies in the budget that he recommends to the council; writing formal reports to introduce new issues onto the council's agenda; and selecting an outside consulting firm to make recommendations. With each of these actions, an astute manager may appear to be removed from the debate about major policy changes, even while he induces the council to consider a problem, defines the terms of its consideration, and structures the presentation of alternatives to highlight his own preferred course of action.[63]

Formal Decision Makers: Bureaucrats

Roles and resources

Virtually every policy decision of urban government depends for execution upon the capacities and willingness of the bureaucracy. Few important decisions are self-executing. But bureaucrats do more than simply implement policy. They are a highly attentive and interested public with unusually high stakes in policy outcomes; they form an interest group that favors certain policy directions.[64] We have previously met the municipal bureaucracy in our discussion of its roles as urban interest group and decision maker. It is often dominated by two motivations: first, the desire to maintain its autonomy, security, and freedom from political interference and, second, an interest in program expansion. These motivations give bureaucrats both conservative and expansionist interests in the policy process. Sayre and Kaufman found that in New York City "bureaucratic groups, especially as they mature in their organization and in their self-awareness as cohesive groups, share with all other groups the aspiration to be self-sufficient and autonomous. In fact, bureaucracies appear to present one of the strongest expressions of this general tendency."[65]

Expertise—knowledge of how to lay out a highway network, how to fight fires, how to organize an educational system—is the major resource of the technical specialist. Bureaucrats resist encroachments on expertise as a premise of decision making. They also follow strategies that help to maintain autonomy. By insisting on stringent rules for entrance, promotion, and seniority in the bureaucracy, they reduce the opportunities of elected officials to appoint political and nonprofessional department heads. The appointment of someone other than a career public servant is regarded as political manipulation. Another strategy is the demand for participation in policy formulation. Police administrators seek to impress their own judgments about law enforcement upon the council; school administrators do the same with educational policy, and so forth. As a source of technical information, bureaucracies almost always play some role in policy formulation. It is seldom that policy makers consciously pursue policies that are opposed by the concerned administrative heads. It seems to be more often that the formal policy makers seek—and accede to—the advice of administrators on matters of program formulation.

At the same time that bureaucrats resist disruption of their established ways of doing things and seek to "minimize innovation and change,"[66] they often seek to expand their budgets and activities. There is no better spokesman for the interests of policemen than the local Policemen's Benevolent Association or its equivalent. Bureaucrats are their own best lobbyists, although they also commonly align themselves with organized clients and other interest groups. Educational administrators and teachers seek the support of parent-teacher associations, and planners often seek the support of the local chamber of commerce. A major source of pressure for expansion comes from the agency itself and its administrative heads.

As administrators

By far the most important bureaucratic resource in directing actual policy is its control over the day-to-day execution of programs. Some people think of bureaucrats as neutral automatons who merely carry out policies laid down at higher levels, exercising no choice or discretion. In reality, according to Sayre and Kaufman,

> it is in execution that the bureaucrats have their most nearly complete monopoly and their greatest autonomy in affecting policy. They give shape and meaning to the official decisions, and they do so under conditions favorable to them. Here the initiative and discretion lie in their hands; others must influence them.[67]

Many bureaucrats—from department heads to the lowest clerks—possess considerable discretion. In fact, studies of traffic-law enforcement and ticketing policies by John A. Gardiner and of local welfare administration by Martha Derthick suggest that top administrators enjoy striking degrees of discretion.[68] Gardiner noted extreme variations in the number of traffic tickets dispensed in cities with nearly identical populations. Boston and Dallas both have populations of about 700,000, but in one year Dallas policemen wrote twenty-four times as many tickets as did those in Boston! No doubt some of this variation may be attributed to variations in state laws and local traffic ordinances or to different habits of Boston and Dallas drivers, but it is unlikely that such factors account for such a large differential. In fact, between two adjacent Massachusetts cities with similar populations (Cambridge and Somerville) there was a 700 percent differential in ticketing rates. The most important factor accounting for wide differences in law-enforcement policies has proved to be the attitude of the police chief toward traffic ticketing. "In general, the rate of enforcement of traffic laws reflects the organizational norms of a police department—the extent to which superior officers expect and encourage particular policies regarding ticket-writing."[69] Gardiner has reported the change in one New England city from a police chief who viewed detective work as the only really important police function to another who was a zealous advocate of traffic enforcement. During the last year of the first chief's tenure the whole force wrote 480 tickets. After the new chief took over, the figure shot up to 4569, which shows the influence of administrative discretion on the performance of lower-level bureaucrats.

Opportunities for discretion are not monopolized by senior bureaucrats and agency heads. Street-level bureaucrats like teachers, policemen, and social workers often exercise discretion in crucial matters for their clients or citizen contacts.[70] Social workers can facilitate or discourage an application for public assistance; school teachers can be supportive or severe in dealing with students having little motivation. James Q. Wilson has analyzed the discretion of beat patrolmen.[71] He discovered that officers have relatively little discretion when they confront clear transgressions of unambiguous laws: armed robberies, murders, dope peddling, and so on. But, in maintaining order and dealing with transgressions against vague standards of public peace and serenity, their discretion increases. In the case of a clear violation, an officer approaches the situation by enforcing the law; in other matters, he is free to handle the situation.

In the final analysis, however, the bureaucrat is not totally free to do whatever he wants. Lower-level bureaucrats—as the traffic-ticketing study indicates—are clearly constrained by the expectations of their superiors, and even their superiors have only finite amounts of discretion. Bureaucrats are not neutral automatons, but neither are they wholly independent in their actions. Certain kinds of policies or circumstances permit greater discretion than do others. When administration can easily be routinized, there is less room for discretion. The maximum welfare payment, the speed that breaks the legal limit, and attendance in school are subject to exact specification. On the other hand, bureaucratic decisions involving determination of what constitutes undesirable behavior as grounds for eviction from a housing project or how to handle a scuffle outside a bar do not lend themselves to uniform responses. In much of the administrative process there are continuing attempts at routinization in order to minimize the discretion of subordinates.

The "new machines"

We have repeatedly mentioned the demise of urban party machines. We have also noted the formal fragmentation of the municipal governments that survive the machines. This fragmentation is characterized by relative decentralization, weakening of the formal and political powers of the mayor's office, and proliferation of independent boards and commissions. The disappearance of the machines left in its wake considerable disorganization of the policy-making process. City government is characterized not by absence of political resources but by their dispersion in countless hands; centralized leadership from political officials is difficult to obtain. One effect of this dispersion is that the greatest single combination of organized resources now resides in public bureaucracies. They are, according to Theodore Lowi, the new machines in urban politics: "The legacy of Reform is the bureaucratic city-state," in which cities "become well-run but ungoverned."[72] The new machines are different from the old machines in their low tolerance for inefficiency and corruption. They also have a resource base of formal authority rather than votes. But, according to Lowi,

> The New Machines are machines because they are relatively irresponsible structures of power. That is, each agency shapes important public policies, yet the leadership of each is relatively self-perpetuating and not readily subject to the controls of any higher authority.
>
> The New Machines are machines in that the power of each, while resting ultimately upon services rendered to the community, depends upon its cohesiveness as a small minority in the midst of the vast dispersion of the multitude.[73]

New York is a prototype. Sayre and Kaufman describe the public bureaucracies of New York City as relatively autonomous islands of power, in which resistance to innovation is the first operating premise.[74] Many of the old machines were run by the mayors. Now, however, any mayor with an innovative turn of mind must confront the new machine, in which he is permanently denied membership.

Making Public Policy:
An Overview of the Decision Process

The sheer number and variety of inputs that come to decision makers complicate their task. Citizen demands, budgetary constraints, pressures from state legislatures and the federal government, the threat of violence, pressures from growth or decay, and a myriad of other factors impinge on the decision maker. No simple procedure for making decisions can accommodate all of these inputs. Decision making demands a capacity to cope with complexity.[75]

Why urban decision making is rarely "rational"

Rationalism receives wide respect in our social system. The demands of a completely rational decision are severe, however. It is costly to be perfectly rational, and few decision makers have sufficient resources to inform themselves about all possible opportunities and all possible consequences of each opportunity. There are five major reasons why decisions in public (or private) bodies rarely measure up to the exacting standards of pure rationality:

1. The sheer pressures of time;
2. The costs of obtaining adequate information about the various acceptable goals and policies;
3. The mixture of sometimes incompatible or incommensurable goals that are pursued simultaneously within an urban system;
4. Structural features of the political system that frustrate coherent and coordinated policies;
5. The constraints of political feasibility.

These five items are not entirely separable in practice, but each does impose its own limitations upon pure rationality, and each is worth separate consideration for analytical purposes.

TIME PRESSURES   Most features of the urban environment that we consider to be problems—high population density, inadequate transportation, pollution, decay—did not appear overnight and will not be eliminated overnight. But policy makers are pressed for action, for policies, and for solutions. Planners and other bureaucrats may be able to look to the future and to deal with models covering spans of several decades; politicians, however, must look to the next election. Academicians have time for reflection, but decision makers are expected to act with dispatch. The press of time is an obvious enough problem, and it is probably the first and paramount reason why public policies cannot be formulated according to the rational model. There simply is not enough time to accumulate the information, survey all the possible alternatives, and select from among them.

COSTS OF INFORMATION   A second factor that makes rational decision making impossible is the high cost of obtaining information. There are basically two types of information: political (on the needs and preferences of the community and interests within it) and technical (on the most efficient ways of reaching goals). Anthony Downs has listed three conditions that generally prevent bureaucracies and other decision-making bodies from acquiring the types of information required by the rational model:

1. Information is costly because it takes time, effort, and sometimes money to obtain data and comprehend their meaning.
2. Decision-makers have only limited amounts of time to spend making decisions, can consider only a certain number of issues simultaneously, and can absorb only certain amounts of data on any one problem.
3. Although some uncertainty can be eliminated by acquiring information, an important degree of unpredictability is usually involved in making decisions.[76]

Not only is information costly to gather and process, but also different types of information may imply contradictory policy decisions. A common problem is that political information implies different decisions from those implied by technical information. Technical information on access, noise, and similar criteria may suggest the location of a new airport in a particular district, but political information may suggest that it would be wiser to choose another site.

As capacities for obtaining information are limited by the availability of resources, the important questions are, When does a decision maker stop gathering information? And when does he stop assessing what he has gathered? The answer to both these questions may be never. But, at some point in the formulation of a new policy, the information-search process will have to be replaced by the decision and action process. Often, decision makers will cut off their search when they discover a mode of operation that involves the least profound change in their established programs. They do not search all possible alternatives until they find the one best mode of operation. Instead they search until they find something that will work, that will provide some relief from the perceived difficulties without threatening undesirable unrest within the bureaucracy and among other decision makers and interest groups. In the words of one student of decision making, the search proceeds until the participants can "satisfice."[77] It is simply too expensive (and the demands for action are too great) to search until the one optimum combination of goals and policies has been identified.

INCOMPATIBLE AND INCOMMENSURABLE GOALS   Urban (and other) governments pursue numbers of policies simultaneously, some of which are almost certain to be incompatible with others. This fact is certainly not surprising and is perhaps fortunate when we realize that governments serve multiple interests and respond to numerous demands for service and conflict resolution. At least in the abstract, there is some inconsistency in community policies that encourage the dispersion of population to the urban periphery, while other policies are aimed at salvaging a decaying downtown area. Sometimes, however, such inconsistent goals must be served by a single policy or agency. An example is urban renewal. Among the goals that some people think it should accomplish are such disparate efforts as improving the city's tax base, attracting new industry, reversing suburban migration by providing middle-income housing, and improving the housing plight of low-income families. It is clear that a single urban-renewal program cannot serve each of these goals equally; even if it could, it would fall short of any strict standard of rational policy making.

Not only are goals of a community or a particular agency sometimes in conflict, but they are even more consistently incommensurable. By *incommensurable*, we mean they are difficult or impossible to compare. There is both insufficient consensus on the goals themselves and a highly inefficient system for their measurement. Each of these factors impedes comparability. Decision makers have little notion of whether another dollar invested in urban renewal would reap more payoffs than would another dollar invested in education. Even if the goal is supported by a relative consensus, as is the reduction of poverty, there is still incommensurability among policies. There is no very clear evidence that any one strategy for reducing poverty will be more effective than would any other strategy. Because most goals and policies do not lend themselves to ready measurement, it will be nearly impossible to meet standards of rationality that require comparison between alternative goals and policies.

STRUCTURAL BARRIERS TO RATIONALITY   If rational decisions require the capacity to organize public processes of selection toward certain goals rather than others, the structure of urban government is not geared to maximize rationality. Instead, there are countless local governments in a metropolitan area, as well as the state and federal governments, each of which may be pursuing different policies to achieve the same or different goals. Within the city government itself, fragmentation of legal authority means that various decision makers can each pursue different strategies and policies, without too much concern for checkmate by superior authority.

POLITICAL FEASIBILITY   In the last analysis, the determination of what to do about a particular problem is made not by what is rational but by what will "sell" to the electorate and to political influentials. Public attitudes toward taxation are likely to be a major constraint upon any purely rational approach to problem solving. Feasibility depends to a considerable degree upon familiarity. According to Ralph Huitt, "what is most feasible is what is purely incremental, or can be made to appear so. . . . Paradoxically, it is politically attractive to tout a proposal as 'new' so long as it is generally recognized that it is not new at all, but a variation on a familiar theme."[78] Elected officials are rarely willing to sacrifice their chances for reelection upon the altar of rationality, especially when justifications abound in democratic theory for adhering to the voice of the people. Perhaps the most rational way to grapple with the problem of poverty in the American system is through a form of guaranteed high-level income for all. Politically, however, such a proposal is likely to generate enough hostility to be considered unfeasible by most politicians, even if they might support the notion on other grounds.

   Although politicians are said to seek power, the complexity of their environments may make it difficult to reach a decision. Deciding what is *feasible* may be as difficult as deciding what is *right*. It is often advantageous for decision makers to avoid conflict and delay decision. William L. C. Wheaton suggests that conflict avoidance is a common strategy in urban decision making:

Public officials delay decisions interminably, attempting to appraise the balance of power pro and con. They may defer decision indefinitely if the balance is approximately equal, and will reach decisions only when there is clearly preponderant support for one position. . . . Frequently decisions may be referred to experts or to other levels of government so that local public officials can evade responsibility or place it elsewhere.[79]

We return to the problems of decision making in Chapters 6 and 7. There, in the context of the policy process and budgetary politics, we illustrate some techniques for making choices where pure rationality is not feasible.

Summary

In this chapter we have explored a number of subjects, ranging from the structure of community power to the process of decision making under conditions of limited resources. There is a certain discontinuity between research on formal decision makers and informal power structures. One of our working assumptions, however, is that no power structure is so nearly monolithic and completely controlling that the roles of mayors, council, managers, and bureaucrats become insignificant. In some cities, small and informal groups outside the formal government structures may formulate certain key decisions. It is equally true, however, that few decisions implement themselves. Key decisions made by formal or informal groups are not compelling in practice unless applied systematically by administrative heads and middle- and lower-level bureaucrats. Nor can the decisions of even the lower-level bureaucrats be discounted as insignificant; their cumulative impact may be greater than that of a single major policy decided by a power structure. It is important to understand both the informal and the formal sides of community decision making. Ignorance of either facet will provide only a partial view of the urban political system.

Notes

1. C. Wright Mills, *The Power Elite* (New York: Oxford University Press, 1956).
2. Max Weber, *The Theory of Social and Economic Organization*, ed. by T. Parsons (New York: Free Press, 1957), p. 152.
3. Robert A. Dahl, "The Concept of Power," *Behavioral Science, 2* (July 1957), 202.
4. A similar formulation is suggested by Robert A. Dahl in *Modern Political Analysis* (Englewood Cliffs, N.J.: Prentice-Hall, 1963), p. 47.
5. An excellent overview of these three approaches is found in Charles M. Bonjean and David M. Olson, "Community Leadership: Directions of Research," *Administrative Science Quarterly, 8* (December 1964), 291–300. This article is reprinted, along with other studies of community power, in Willis D. Hawley and Frederick M. Wirt, eds., *The Search for Community Power* (Englewood Cliffs, N.J.: Prentice-Hall, 1968).
6. Samuel A. Stouffer, *Communism, Conformity, and Civil Liberties* (Garden City, N.Y.: Doubleday, 1955), pp. 15–19.
7. Floyd Hunter, *Community Power Structure* (Chapel Hill: University of North Carolina Press, 1953).
8. *Ibid.*, pp. 100–101.
9. Raymond Wolfinger, in his critique of the reputational approach, has argued that this "advantage" of the reputational over the decisional approach is comparable to that of a TV dinner over a home-cooked one—it does not taste very good, but it is quick to fix.

See Raymond Wolfinger, "A Plea for a Decent Burial," *American Sociological Review, 27* (December 1962), 841–847.

10. See, for example, Edward C. Banfield, *Political Influence* (New York: Free Press, 1961).
11. See especially, Robert A. Dahl, *Who Governs?* (New Haven: Yale University Press, 1961); and Nelson Polsby, *Community Power and Political Theory* (New Haven: Yale University Press, 1963).
12. Dahl, *Who Governs?*, p. 183.
13. *Ibid.*, p. 233.
14. See Robert Agger, Daniel Goldrich, and Bert E. Swanson, *The Rulers and the Ruled* (New York: Wiley, 1964), pp. 76–77.
15. Robert A. Dahl, *A Preface to Democratic Theory* (Chicago: University of Chicago Press, 1956), pp. 124–132.
16. John Walton, "Discipline, Method, and Community Power: A Note on the Sociology of Knowledge," *American Sociological Review, 31* (October 1966), 688.
17. Robert L. Crain et al., "The Influence of Reputational, Positional, and Decisional Elites in Northern Cities." Paper presented at the Annual Meeting of the American Sociological Association, Montreal, September 1969.
18. Claire Gilbert, "Trends in Community Politics," *Social Science Quarterly, 48* (December 1967), 378.
19. Agger, Goldrich, and Swanson, *op. cit.*
20. See Crain et al., *op. cit.*; and Terry N. Clark, "Community Structure, Decision-Making, Budget Expenditures, and Urban Renewal in 51 American Communities," *American Sociological Review, 33* (August 1968), 576–594.
21. Agger, Goldrich, and Swanson, pp. 648ff.
22. Peter Bachrach and Morton Baratz, *Power and Poverty* (New York: Oxford University Press, 1970), p. 4.
23. *Ibid.*, p. 6.
24. *Ibid.*, p. 11.
25. Theodore Sorensen, *Decision-Making in the White House* (New York: Columbia University Press, 1963), pp. 22–42.
26. The most extensive and potentially useful ones are found in Agger, Goldrich, and Swanson, pp. 73–93.
27. Bonjean and Olson, *op. cit.*
28. For a more extensive listing of propositions derived from the literature on community power structure, see Terry N. Clark, "Power and Community Structure: Who Governs, Where, and When?" *The Sociological Quarterly, 8* (Summer 1967), 291–316.
29. Clark, "Community Structure, Decision-Making, Budget Expenditures, and Urban Renewal," p. 585.
30. Arthur Vidich and Joseph Bensman, *Small Town in Mass Society* (Princeton, N.J.: Princeton University Press, 1958).
31. For Atlanta, see Hunter, *op. cit.*; for Dallas, see Carol E. Thometz, *The Decision-Makers* (Dallas: Southern Methodist University Press, 1963).
32. John Walton, "Substance and Artifact: The Current Status of Research on Community Power Structure," *American Journal of Sociology, 71* (January 1966), 684–699; Clark, "Community Structure, Decision-Making, Budget Expenditures, and Urban Renewal," p. 586.
33. Note, however, that, as we argued in Chapter 3, labor unions are typically much less active in local politics than in state and national politics.
34. Robert S. Lynd and Helen M. Lynd, *Middletown in Transition* (New York: Harcourt Brace Jovanovich, 1937). Middletown is a pseudonym for Muncie, Indiana.
35. The importance of secondary associations is emphasized by Agger, Goldrich, and Swanson; see especially pp. 272ff.
36. John Walton, "Vertical Axis of Community Organization and the Structure of Power," *Social Science Quarterly, 48* (December 1967), 355–357.

37. Clark, "Community Structure, Decision-Making, Budget Expenditures, and Urban Renewal," p. 586.

38. Agger, Goldrich, and Swanson, pp. 662ff.

39. Joseph A. Schumpeter, *Capitalism, Socialism, and Democracy* (New York: Harper & Row, 1947), pp. 232ff; and Seymour M. Lipset, *Political Man* (Garden City, N.Y.: Doubleday, 1960), chap. 2.

40. Bonjean and Olson, p. 299.

41. For examples of research that attempts to link the structure of community power with public policies, see Clark, "Community Structure, Decision-Making, Budget Expenditures, and Urban Renewal"; Agger, Goldrich, and Swanson, *op. cit.*; and Amos Hawley, "Community Power and Urban Renewal Success," *American Journal of Sociology, 68* (January 1963), 422–432.

42. Bryan T. Downes, "Municipal Social Rank and the Characteristics of Local Political Leaders," *Midwest Journal of Political Science, 12* (November 1968), 514–537.

43. Lee Sloan, "Good Government and the Politics of Race," *Social Problems, 17* (Fall 1969), 161–175.

44. M. Arnold, "John Santucci Is a Man in a Wind Tunnel," *The New York Times Magazine,* April 16, 1967, pp. 56–70.

45. Oliver Williams and Charles Adrian, *Four Cities* (Philadelphia: University of Pennsylvania Press, 1963), p. 264.

46. Arnold, p. 62.

47. Downes, p. 528.

48. *Ibid.*

49. Kenneth Prewitt, "Political Ambitions, Volunteerism, and Electoral Accountability," *American Political Science Review, 64* (March 1970), 5–17.

50. Kenneth Prewitt, *The Recruitment of Political Leaders: A Study of Citizen-Politicians* (Indianapolis: Bobbs-Merrill, 1970), chap. 8.

51. For journalistic portraits of Lindsay and Daley, see the contributions by Larry L. King and David Halberstam, "The New Mayor and the Old," *Harper's* (August 1968), 25–44. See also Mike Royko, *Boss: Richard J. Daley of Chicago* (New York: Signet, 1971).

52. One leading Chicago businessman, the president of a major department store, said of Daley and his organization: "Machine? It's just a word. General Motors runs a good machine. So does my store. It's efficient. Good administration makes sense." *The New York Times,* March 5, 1967, p. 78.

53. Halberstam, p. 32.

54. See Peter Yessne, ed., *Quotations from Mayor Daley* (New York: Bantam Books, 1970), pp. 5, 92, 94.

55. Wallace Sayre and Herbert Kaufman *Governing New York City: Politics in the Metropolis* (New York: Russell Sage, 1960), pp. 711ff.

56. Henry W. Maier, *Challenge to the Cities* (New York: Random House, 1966), p. 114.

57. Duane Lockard, *The Politics of State and Local Government* (New York: Macmillan, 1963), pp. 413–427.

58. Alexander L. George, "Political Leadership and Social Change in American Cities," *Daedalus, 97* (Fall 1968), 1196.

59. Deil S. Wright, "The City Manager as a Development Administrator," in Robert T. Daland, ed., *Comparative Urban Research* (Beverly Hills, Calif.: Sage, 1969), p. 218.

60. *Ibid.*, p. 219.

61. *Ibid.*, p. 236.

62. Karl Bosworth, "The Manager Is a Politician," *Public Administration Review, 18* (Summer 1958), 216–222.

63. Ronald O. Loveridge, *City Managers in Legislative Politics* (Indianapolis: Bobbs-Merrill, 1971), especially chaps. 4 and 8.

64. Edward C. Banfield and James Q. Wilson, *City Politics* (Cambridge, Mass.: Harvard University Press, 1963), pp. 207ff.
65. Sayre and Kaufman, p. 405.
66. *Ibid.*, p. 407.
67. *Ibid.*, p. 421.
68. John A. Gardiner, "Police Enforcement of Traffic Laws: A Comparative Analysis," in James Q. Wilson, ed., *City Politics and Public Policy* (New York: Wiley, 1968), pp. 151–172; and Martha Derthick, "Intercity Differences in Administration of the Public Assistance Program: The Case of Massachusetts," in Wilson, ed., pp. 243–266.
69. Gardiner, p. 161.
70. Michael Lipsky, "Street-Level Bureaucrats and the Analysis of Urban Reform," *Urban Affairs Quarterly, 6* (June 1971), 391–409.
71. James Q. Wilson, *Varieties of Police Behavior* (Cambridge, Mass.: Harvard University Press, 1968).
72. Theodore J. Lowi, "Machine Politics—Old and New," *The Public Interest* (Fall 1967), p. 86.
73. *Ibid.*, p. 87.
74. Sayre and Kaufman, chap. 11.
75. Some of the arguments advanced in this section are treated more fully in Ira Sharkansky, *Public Administration: Policy Making in Government Agencies* (Chicago: Markham, 1972), chap. 3.
76. Anthony Downs, *Inside Bureaucracy* (Boston: Little, Brown, 1967), p. 3.
77. Herbert Simon, *Administrative Behavior* (New York: Macmillan, 1961).
78. Ralph Huitt, "Political Feasibility," in Austin Ranney, ed., *Political Science and Public Policy* (Chicago: Markham, 1968), p. 274.
79. William L. C. Wheaton, "Integration at the Urban Level," in Philip Jacob and James V. Toscano, eds., *The Integration of Political Communities* (Philadelphia: Lippincott, 1964), p. 132.

part three

Public policies
and their impacts

Policy is what politics is all about. For many citizens, it is the target of their willingness to discuss politics, to vote, and to campaign for the candidates of their choice. For candidates, the opportunity to shape policy is a major stimulus for the headaches and family deprivations that their work entails. For political scientists, *policy* is a term for certain activities that constitute much of what is worth studying in the urban system.

We devote Chapter 6 to an introductory discussion of public policy, introducing five basic questions about urban decisions. The next six chapters deal with specific problem areas: Chapter 7 examines the fiscal options and choices of urban governments; Chapter 8 explores educational policy, while Chapter 9 deals with policies of poverty and race. Chapter 10 concerns the problem of urban crime and law-enforcement policies, and Chapter 11 examines transportation and environmental problems. Chapter 12 discusses urban growth and the policies which cities use to manipulate, regulate, and facilitate growth patterns, specifically in the areas of planning, zoning, urban renewal, and housing.

In each of these substantive policy chapters, we deal with several basic issues. We try in each case to discuss the problems with which policy attempts to deal, the politics and structure of policy making, the content of major policies, and, finally, the impact of those policies.

chapter 6

Urban problems and the analysis of public policy

In the preceding chapters we dealt with basic features of the urban environment, the political input process, and decision making. In the following chapters, we turn our attention to the outputs and impacts of the urban political system: the efforts of urban governments to affect their environments. This chapter introduces the concept of public policy as a response to urban problems. All public policies involve hard choices, and all represent opportunity costs: A dollar invested in improving the schools is a dollar that cannot be invested in improving transportation or controlling pollution. Frequently in the city, policies are advocated and adopted with little insight into their impacts. Policy makers often fail to evaluate the impacts and effectiveness of policy choices and ignore the spillover effects of particular policies. Our purpose in this chapter is to elucidate the nature of public policy and to point up the issues involved in the analysis and evaluation of policy.

Urban Problems or Urban Crisis?

Almost no one will deny that there are too many problems in the American city. Any listing can be extended almost *ad nauseam*. To take but a handful of examples,

- *The Crime Problem.* Nearly two major crimes are committed annually for every hundred persons.

- *The Pollution Problem.* Water and air pollution have reached such levels as to make human habitation in the city unpleasant for many and nearly impossible for others.
- *The Racial Problem.* The appearance of 200 instances of collective racial disorders in the period 1963–1969 suggests the severity of the racial problem.
- *The Tax Problem.* Some cities are forced to cut back on traditional services in the face of fiscal constraints, while urban tax rates spiral ever higher.
- *The Housing Problem.* For many Americans, the poor especially, but also the middle classes, housing choices are costly and often unsatisfactory.
- *The Poverty Problem.* Despite a decade of commitment to eradicating poverty, many people remain poor amid a sea of affluence.
- *The Fiscal Inequities Problem.* Some urban citizens enjoy the finest levels of public service which money and administrative know-how can produce, while others suffer the leavings.
- *The Police Problem.* Half of all ghetto dwellers believe—rightly or wrongly—that police brutality occurs in their neighborhoods.

We could extend this list by raising issues in education, transportation, energy, and so on. But in its brief form it is long enough to illustrate the widespread feeling that things in the city have gone awry.

Not all problems, of course, are crises. One may have a problem choosing between a big car and a small one, but the choice hardly constitutes a crisis. Not all urban problems are of crisis proportions. Even a summation of all the individual urban problems may not produce an overarching crisis. A crisis exists when life itself is threatened, or when problems threaten to grow to intolerable proportions. Whether these problems constitute crises is a matter of opinion. One can believe that *any* amount of crime, *any* level of pollution, or *any* incident of poverty is intolerable. However meritorious as goals, it is fair to ask what amount of public resources should be used to eliminate such problems entirely, and whether unacceptable side effects of such policies would be encountered. The elimination of *all* crime might require a policeman in every bar, store, and residence; the elimination of *all* pollution would require, not only vast expenditures, but maybe a dramatic reduction in our standard of living. A policy is never free of costs and can rarely be evaluated in isolation from its effects on other problems. The choices are never simple because sometimes an improvement of one problem may exacerbate another. Decision makers must make—sometimes consciously, more often unconsciously—tradeoffs between policy alternatives.

Many problems of the city involve money. As we have seen in

Chapter 2, the irony of urban wealth puts vast human and economic resources just beyond the reach of municipal officials. In a few areas, cities teeter on the brink of bankruptcy. In Newark, New Jersey, property taxes have risen to staggering levels—almost $2,000 on a house worth $20,000—and further increases work mainly to drive more citizens to the suburbs, leaving behind those most in need of services and least able to pay.[1] A handful of cities, Hamtramck, Michigan, for example, have investigated the possibility of municipal bankruptcy proceedings. Presently, these examples are extreme and fortunately atypical. More common is the city whose financial resources are tolerable, but which seems barely able to maintain traditional police, library, fire, and other services. In such places, it is seldom possible to meet demands for new services. In Chapter 7, we shall investigate the urban public finance system, elucidate its problems, and describe its processes.

But even if cities were to solve their financial problems overnight, many policy dilemmas would persist. More serious than the problem of money are the problems of knowledge and information. The production and distribution of knowledge in the United States has multiplied many times in recent decades, yet policies formulated on the basis of inaccurate information still produce frustration. To adopt a policy and proclaim its virtues is one thing; to assure its success is another. Decision makers have often been more eager to proclaim and adopt policies than to evaluate and analyze their impacts. Lyndon Johnson once observed of the presidency that the problem was not to *do* what was right, but to *know* what was right. The presidency has no monopoly on such problems. Even if there were widespread consensus on eliminating the problem of poverty, for example, the number of alternative strategies is large indeed. Some would advocate giving political power to the poor, arguing that the dilemma of the poor is their lack of political clout. Some advocate a guaranteed annual income, arguing that a financial floor will enable the poor to meet minimal needs. Others advocate investments in education or skills development, others demand improvements in the child-rearing or socialization patterns of poor children. Obviously, if resources are limited—and the nature of politics and economics always limits resources—then one cannot do everything at once. Choices must be made, and it is the nature of these choices with which we are concerned in the remainder of this book.

Our own position on the problem of urban policy is that the problem of knowledge is in the long run more important than the problem of money. Just as money does not buy happiness, neither does it guarantee the solution of an urban problem, unless it is used wisely and well. In the present chapter, we outline a conception of urban policy and introduce some important tools for understanding public policy. In the chapters which follow, we sequentially investigate several policy areas, including education, poverty, urban growth, transportation, environment, and others. We try in each case to offer an overview of the problem, describe the policies which have surrounded the problem, examine the principal policy options in the area, and finally present some evidence about the impacts of those policies.

The Nature of Public Policy

A concern with policy is the common denominator in the writing of the classic political philosophers on the one hand, and the activities of Richard Daley, Tom Bradley, and urban administrators, on the other. As political scientists, we recognize that there are disagreements about the kinds of policies that governments *should* enact; we also recognize that political scientists use the term *public policy* in different ways. A simple definition of policy states that it is "the important missions of government." This, of course, leaves unspecified the meanings of *important* and *missions*. It also leaves out any indication of the varying ways that people may view policies. Just dealing with the problem of describing government expenditures, for example, an economist may focus on the sums allocated to programs described according to how they will affect the economy; economic stabilization activities (e.g., unemployment insurance, industrial promotion); income redistribution activities (e.g., health, welfare); resource allocation activities (e.g., highways, police).[2] An administrator may focus on the allocation of funds to various governmental agencies: highway department, police department, schools, sanitation department, fire department. A political scientist may emphasize the perspectives of the decision makers. One political scientist, Austin Ranney, has described the components of policies as:[3]

1. *A particular object or set of objects*—some designated part of the environment (an aspect of the society or physical world) that is to be affected;
2. *A desired course of events*—a particular sequence of behavior desired in the particular object or set of objects;
3. *A selected line of action*—a particular set of actions chosen to bring about the desired course of events; in other words, not merely whatever the society happens to be doing toward the set of objects at the moment, but a deliberate selection of one line of action from among several possible lines;
4. *A declaration of intent*—some statement by the policy makers, whether broadcast publicly to all who will listen, or communicated secretly to a special few, on what they intend to do, how, and why;
5. *An implementation of intent*—the actions actually undertaken vis-à-vis

the particular set of objects in pursuance of the choices and declaration.

Some policy analysts broaden the term *policy* to include the *effects* that government actions have upon the populations they are designed to serve. Some of these effects are encompassed by the terms *outputs, outcomes, spillover effects, impacts* or *feedbacks* of policy. David Easton, one of the progenitors of systems analysis in political science, draws a distinction between *outputs* (roughly, what governments do) and the *outcomes* of these outputs (roughly, what consequences follow from the outputs).[4] Still others use the term *policy* to refer to broadly interrelated government decisions. When we label officials liberal, moderate, or conservative, we use shorthand forms to denote the ways in which specific decisions coalesce into broad policy directions.

Policy-making institutions and personnel convert inputs from the environment into policies that then produce outputs, impacts, and feedback. The major policy-making actors and processes are found in the formal structures of local government and their occupants (mayors, managers, school boards, the bureaucracy); informal community power structures; the procedures used by officials to make their policy decisions; and the commitments, predispositions, and beliefs that shape these officials' decisions. As we saw in Chapters 3 through 5, these features are not fixed. They include many varieties of behaviors, which differ with the kind of issue that is introduced and the ways in which inputs flow from the environment. Among the features that may be found in the conversion process are conflicts between formal rules of procedures and the practices followed by officials; clashes among various officials from different agencies or branches of local government; clashes between decision makers and representatives of interest groups who make innovative demands; and decision makers' use of routine procedures to simplify complex and numerous demands.

In the description of the policy process we present in this and in the following chapters we treat policy sometimes as a dependent variable and sometimes as an independent variable. In the former instance, we are interested in the *dependence* of policy upon features in its environment; we look for evidence on how variations in educational policies, for example, are influenced by variations in its environment. Likely correlates of educational policy are the social characteristics of the community, the economic resources available to the decision makers, and the policy predispositions of the community elite. When we consider policy as an independent variable, we seek its influence upon the environment. We ignore, for the moment, the influence of environment on policy by abstracting policy elements from their surroundings and considering them independently from other sources. We then assess the impacts that policy has upon its environment by treating certain environmental characteristics as dependent variables.

Five Issues in Policy Analysis

Public policy is the focal point of urban politics. Both masses and elites invest their political resources to achieve changes in policy or to preserve the status quo. Typically, the questions raised about policy choices are deceptively simple: Is policy X good or bad? How much will it cost? Who's going to pay for it? Actually, such questions are not very meaningful by themselves, and without further specification. Policy analysts have attempted recently to develop some basic conceptual tools for the analysis of policy and to bring them to bear on urban policy. In our opinion, policy specialists have raised five basic questions about urban public policy.

What choices are made and why?

The making of public policy involves choices among alternatives. Except in a theoretical and ideal world, one free from political factors and with unlimited resources, all choices involve costs. Costs are not only monetary but social, psychological, and political as well. Economists rightly emphasize the importance of a choice perspective:

> Economics can be said to be no more than the study of the costs and benefits of the choices among alternatives; it remains "the dismal science" because it says again and again that societies and individuals face hard choices among alternatives, and that there are few opportunities that have no costs.[5]

Few choices are *free* choices. Choosing among alternatives is what urban politics is all about. Each choice among policy alternatives is constrained by both macro and micro features of the policy environment. The availability of human and economic resources represents a constraint on any policy; one cannot spend money one does not have. The limits of information are a serious constraint on many policy alternatives.

If for no other reason, a policy alternative is never free because all choices involve *opportunity costs*. A dollar invested in road repairs is a dollar which is *not* invested in education. Land used for a public park cannot be used for residential or industrial development. Money invested in reducing the infant mortality rate cannot also be spent on improved housing. Opportunity costs, in other words, pertain to the courses of action that are foregone in order to undertake some particular public policy. Opportunity costs represent no problem at all if we know that a dollar invested in some policy will bring greater social utility than investing it any other way. Unfortunately, we are rarely in possession of such information. Sometimes, therefore, decision makers must make conscious or unconscious tradeoffs between two policy alternatives. We sacrifice some of goal X in order to maximize goal Y. Faced with scarce resources, we may have to trade off a decrease in police patrols for an increase in aid to the poor. Some ecologists argue that urbanites in the future will have to reduce their standard of living to avoid catastrophic drains on the physical environment. Put in other words, these observers demand a tradeoff between life style and survival.

Students of public policy are interested not only in what policy choices are adopted, that is, in the *content* of policy, but also in *why* one policy was adopted and not another. In a sense, this entire book is concerned with why urban governments pursue certain courses of action. Sometimes mass demands for action compel policy makers to establish policy, and we described some of the sources of demands in Chapter 3. At other times, local governments act because of the pressures from state and federal governments which we discussed in Chapter 4. Or, the elites and administrators examined in Chapter 5 can make certain policy choices with little pressure from masses or supralocal governments. Whatever the explanations for particular policies, all of them represent choices—hopefully reasonably conscious and well informed—between alternative strategies.

Who benefits and who loses?

The burdens and benefits of urban policy fall differentially on the urban landscape. Public policies can make the rich richer and the poor poorer; or they can redress social and economic inequalities by giving advantages to the disadvantaged. For each policy alternative, we can ask: Who benefits and who loses?

A few urban policies are *pure public goods* which cannot, by definition, be differentially distributed. Public goods can be enjoyed by one person without diminishing the consumption of the same good by another person. In principle, a public good reaches everyone in a jurisdiction, at least indirectly. Some theorists reason that the public nature of a good (or a *bad* in the case of things like pollution) provides the major justification for governmental activity rather than leaving its distribution to free-market operation. Yet the definition of a public good is not precise, and economists use the concept even when they insist that local governments produce no public goods in their pure form.[6] A few governmental policies come close to being pure public goods. Pollution control and fluoridation are examples. If citizen A receives cleaner air from pollution control, citizen B will automatically receive it as well.

Many public policies can be delivered differentially to citizens but still have aspects of the pure public good. Some neighborhoods may have good, and others poor, schools even while education in general rebounds to the benefit of the community as a whole. Public health services may go only to certain groups, but everyone benefits from having tuberculosis held in check.

Do urban public policies make the rich richer and the poor poorer? We can think of numerous policies that do line the purses of the well-to-do. Regressive taxation, industrial promotional activities, better-quality schools in wealthier areas, and publicly subsidized airports all favor the rich, sometimes at the expense of the poor. They are *redistributive* policies, taking from one group and giving to another.[7] Yet we can easily think of other policies which aid the poor at the expense of the affluent: public health, compensatory educational programs, subsidized housing, and antipoverty programs. The question is whether, in the aggregate, the benefits and burdens of one group are greater than those of the other. Ideologues of the right ("government is robbing the successful to buy off the undeserving poor") and the left ("a government of the rich, by the rich, and for the rich") have their answers, but hard evidence on the redistributive effect of urban policy is skimpy. A study by the Tax Foundation concluded that the tax structures of state and local governments were regressive, that is, favored the rich, but that their expenditures were sharply progressive, and favored the poor. When the relatively progressive federal tax system was figured in, governmental policies overall were judged reasonably progressive, favoring the lower-income groups over the affluent.[8] Unfortunately, the assumptions needed for such analyses are numerous and tenuous. And for some observers the question is not whether policy is *redistributive*, but whether it is *too redistributive* or *not redistributive enough*.

What difference does money make?

Few public policies, other than purely symbolic expressions of intent, do not involve expenditure of public money. The questions of the total size of the public budget and of desirable tax burdens are among the most critical issues in most urban political systems. Each substantive policy involves the question of finance. Officials pay a great deal of attention to budget making, and expenditures are widely viewed as a common denominator with respect to items that actually produce service. Although spending does not by itself meet popular demands for service, it does buy many of the things that produce service. We shall examine spending and taxing issues in Chapter 7.

Throughout each of these chapters on policy, we must be aware of *the veil of money*, that is, the image that money is the real cost or measure of a public service. As one urban economist puts it, "Money does not really matter, except as a device to facilitate transactions (and measurement); what does matter is the use of human and material resources."[9] Sometimes citizens as well as scholars act as if an increase in spending will purchase a corresponding increase in service or a reduction in an urban problem. This is the *spending-service cliché*.[10] But a generous expenditure of funds may have little relation to the quality or quantity of services actually delivered to the public.

We do not bring up these unpleasant thoughts about the problematic role of governmental spending to argue that public spending is ineffectual. To the contrary, it is clear to all but the most hardened advocate of *laissez faire* that governmental investments in health, education, urban development, and other programs have purchased bounties of blessings. Our argument is more subtle, emphasizing that the expenditure of money does not, in and of itself, guarantee a solution to a problem. The amounts expended may be important to citizens, policy makers, and policy analysts, but the policy analyst is concerned more with the impact and effectiveness of money, that is, with what is purchased rather than the price tag alone.

What is the impact of public policy?

The output of a public policy does not necessarily accomplish its goals. Although the elements of a service may be provided by a local agency, they may not have their intended impact on the problem. Impacts represent the effects that a service has on the target population and on other features of the environment. Impacts may be intended or not. Some impacts are planned and anticipated by policy makers. Others—we call them *spillover effects*—represent the unanticipated products of policy. Unintended impacts arise because the urban system consists of interrelated parts that influence one another and because information about all the potential effects of a policy is unavailable. An elusive hope of policy makers is to design public policies whose major consequences are intended and whose unintended impacts are either minimal or benign.

Spillover effects or externalities affect parties not directly conceived as objects of public policy. An example of a *negative externality* is the traffic congestion spawned by a new housing project or a sports arena. Yet a *positive externality* may come as a result of the public spirit generated by a winning team that has been attracted to town by the construction of a new stadium. Often, it is a negative externality generated by private enterprise (sometimes called a *public bad*)—like industrial pollution—that prompts a local government to formulate new policies. All of the public policies we discuss in Chapters 7 through 12 have spillovers, sometimes benign and sometimes undesirable. Urban renewal (discussed in Chapter 12) is one such example. All citizens may benefit from an improved local tax base spurred by a revitalized downtown, but other externalities of urban renewal, particularly the problem of relocating the families living in an area to be renewed, will burden certain elements of the population. A principal concern of policy analysis is to specify as precisely as possible the spillover effects of policies on urban populations.

There may be no question for the policy maker that is more important than policy impact. Policies may not accomplish the intended impacts. Spillover effects may be negative and reduce the system's capacity to attain other goals; and there may be no way to measure or evaluate their impacts. Policy making is problematic at best. Because research on policy impacts has been limited, the information available to decision makers is scarce. Public policy is at least partially made "in the dark" and based on insufficient information about probable impacts on the environment.

How shall policies be evaluated?

Policies can be evaluated in terms of two principal issues: Are the goals pursued by the policy desirable social ends? Do the policies actually accomplish the stated goals? If one dissents from the goal ostensibly furthered by a policy, the issue is simple. Matters are usually more complex, however, because most policies are advocated in terms of seemingly consensual and even noble goals. Policies are said to eliminate poverty, improve consumer choice, provide jobs, improve opportunities, and so on. The tough question is usually, therefore, whether the policy actually accomplishes its goal—and whether it accomplishes the goal more effectively and at less cost than would alternative policies.

Increasingly, policy evaluation depends upon measurement. The rising status of precise measurement and quantitative analysis is evident, not only in academic studies of the causes and implications of certain policies—what might be called *basic research*—but also in applied studies that attempt to measure various cost-benefit ratios of public policies.

Cost-benefit analysis and planning-programming-budgeting (PPB) are techniques currently being touted by some government management specialists. Cost-benefit analysis attempts to estimate the costs of each policy option, including as many spillover costs as can be identified, and to sum up the benefits of each policy. Decision makers then use the results in the choice of alternatives.[11] PPB was originally developed as an aid to budgeting in the U.S. Department of Defense and, at President Johnson's order, was then applied to all agencies of the federal government. Under the prompting of management analysts—and with the funding of experimental projects by private foundations—PPB is being adopted by numerous state and local agencies. Its elements include

1. Defining the major programs in each area of public service;
2. Defining the principal outputs of each program in ways that can be subjected to precise measurement;
3. Defining the inputs relevant to each program (e.g., various combinations of personnel, facilities, funds, and ways of rendering services);
4. Computing the costs of alternative combinations of inputs and the economic value of the various combinations of outputs likely to be produced by each combination of inputs;

5. Calculating the cost-benefit ratio associated with each combination of inputs and outputs.

This book is not the place to explore the claims that are made by advocates of PPB, the allegations made by its detractors, or the changes made in PPB at the national level by the Nixon administration.[12] Yet the very existence of this technique testifies to the need for careful quantitative evaluation of the policy process.

But techniques for analysis do not solve the complex problems of measuring variables. Among social scientists, economists have claimed some success in surmounting the measurement problem, but then their fundamental unit of analysis, money, readily lends itself to measurement. Other social scientists have found measurement of variables a more difficult problem because such concepts as power, alienation, control, culture, and learning do not lend themselves to precisely measurable formulations that are acceptable to social scientists having different perspectives. In recent years, these social scientists have devoted considerable resources to developing indicators of social phenomena. *Toward a Social Report*, published by the U.S. Department of Health, Education, and Welfare in 1969, represented a major effort to measure and assess the state of American society through the use of social indicators.[13] Because measurement precedes evaluation, developments in the availability and use of social indicators will necessarily precede the full-scale applicability of such techniques as cost-benefit analysis and PPB.[14]

Summary

This chapter serves as a bridge between the *urban politics* and the *public policy* aspects of this book. In it, we have argued that the urban problem is a central concern for citizens, decision makers, and policy analysts. Whether the specific itemization of urban ills adds up to an urban crisis is a matter of opinion. It is clear, however, that the state of the city is not as benign as most residents would hope or as some experts think it could be. Several problems of the city can be traced to financial roots (which we elaborate in Chapter 7). Others, however, are a product of our lack of knowledge about the dynamics of an urban civilization. Spending money does not by itself guarantee the solution to anything, unless money is spent on the basis of sound information and evaluation. The effect of money is one of the basic issues policy analysts raise about public policy. They also are concerned with other issues as well, particularly why some policies are chosen and others are not, the distribution of policy benefits, the impact of policy, and its evaluation. These issues are raised throughout the remainder of this book. In

Chapter 7, we specifically investigate urban finances. In the succeeding chapters, we explore how that money is spent in areas of education, law enforcement, housing, urban renewal, transportation, and environmental control. In each of those areas, we try to do four things: (1) to spell out briefly the contours of the problem which make it an object of public policy; (2) to describe the politics and structure of decision making in the problem area; (3) to identify the policy content of major national, state, and local policies bearing on the problem; and (4) to assess the impact of the policies.

Notes

1. *Washington Post,* December 10, 1972, p. 10.
2. Dick Netzer, *Economics and Urban Problems: Diagnoses and Prescriptions* (New York: Basic Books, 1970), p. 170.
3. Austin Ranney, "The Study of Policy Content: A Framework for Choice," in Austin Ranney, ed., *Political Science and Public Policy* (Chicago: Markham, 1968), p. 7.
4. David Easton, *A Systems Analysis of Political Life* (New York: Wiley, 1965), pp. 351–352.
5. Netzer, p. 5.
6. See Werner Z. Hirsch, *The Economics of State and Local Government* (New York: McGraw-Hill, 1970), p. 1.
7. Theodore Lowi introduces the concept of *redistributive policy* as one of three principal classifications of policy outputs. See his, "American Business, Public Policy, Case Studies, and Political Theory," *World Politics,* 6 (July 1964), 677–715.
8. *Allocating Tax Burdens and Government Benefits by Income Class* (New York: Tax Foundation, 1967).
9. Netzer, p. 7.
10. For further discussion of the spending-service cliché, see Ira Sharkansky, *The Routines of Politics* (New York: Van Nostrand Reinhold, 1970), pp. 106–123.
11. An excellent summary of cost-benefit and PPB techniques can be found in Aaron Wildavsky, "The Political Economy of Efficiency," in Austin Ranney, ed., pp. 55–82.
12. The best single-volume compilation of materials is that of Fremont J. Lyden and Ernest G. Willer, eds., *Planning Programming Budgeting: A Systems Approach to Management,* 2d ed. (Chicago: Markham, 1972).
13. Department of Health, Education, and Welfare, *Toward a Social Report* (Washington, D.C.: Government Printing Office, 1969).
14. See Bertram M. Gross, ed., *Social Intelligence for America's Future* (Boston: Allyn & Bacon, 1969).

chapter 7

Taxing and spending

There is a lot of money at stake in urban politics. In 1970, the total revenues of local governments in the United States were $89 billion. Of this sum, $59.6 billion was raised from local sources, and another $29.5 billion was received from federal, state, and other local governments. These sums are of great interest to the municipal officials who distribute public largesse, to those seeking governmental contracts, and to those of us who must pay the bills. Builders of roads and schools, city employees, and suppliers of equipment and services pay close attention to the decisions of local financial officers. These decisions are never far removed from concern with taxes, for local governments are very close—sometimes perilously close—to their taxpayers. The property tax is the prime source of local revenues, and of all the taxes used by American governments it seems to provoke the sharpest and longest-lasting controversies.

In this chapter we discuss the major choices facing the financial policy makers of local governments. We also identify the kinds and amounts of taxes and expenditures made by different kinds of cities and the features in the environments of these local governments that seem responsible for their choices. Among the principal features we consider are the socioeconomic characteristics of the population, the nature of local governmental institutions, and the procedures by which financial decision makers arrive at their choices. We look for patterns in the types of

taxes and expenditures made by different kinds of communities: large
and small, wealthy and poor, WASP and ethnic, and so on. We also try
to take account of deviant cases: individual governments whose
spending and taxing policies are sharply at odds with the practices of
most local governments with similar characteristics.

An Overview:
National, State, and Local Finances

Among the three levels of government in the United States, the local
units collect the least tax revenue from their own sources, but they are
the biggest spenders on domestic programs. Table 7.1 summarizes the
current position of each government in taxing and spending, and
reveals some prominent changes that have occurred since the early
1960s.

The national government is the greatest tax collector, collecting almost
three times as much revenue as local governments. Yet Washington
spends much of its money on national defense and international affairs.
Much of the national budget for domestic programs goes to states and
localities in the form of grants, loans, and revenue sharing. State
governments are now in second position as raisers of tax revenue. Like
the national government, however, much of its money goes as inter-

Table 7.1 *Revenues and Expenditures, by Level of Government, 1962 and
1970–1971*

	General revenues raised from own sources			
	1962 (hundreds of thousands of dollars)		1970–1971 (hundreds of thousands of dollars)	
National	$ 92,016	64.6%	$156,887	56.9%
State	23,677	16.6	61,290	22.2
Local	26,705	18.8	57,491	20.9
Total	$141,398	100.0%	$275,668	100.0%

	Direct general spending on domestic programs			
National	$ 35,728	37.2%	$ 69,508	31.6%
State	20,375	21.2	56,478	25.7
Local	39,831	41.5	94,196	42.8
Total	$ 85,934	100.0%	$220,182	100.0%

SOURCE: U.S. Bureau of the Census, *Governmental Finances in 1970–71* (Washington, D.C.: Government
Printing Office, 1972). Totals may not equal 100% because of rounding.

governmental transfers. Local governments receive transfers from both Washington and their state capitals. Most of the spending on domestic programs—and thus most of the program implementation—occurs at the local level. It is true that localities have lost some ground to state implementation during the 1962–1971 period. Yet ours is still a system of program administration that rests heavily on the shoulders of local officials.

Local Revenue Patterns

Revenue sources of local governments

Urban governments draw upon four major sources of revenue: locally collected taxes, intergovernmental aid, consumer charges for public services, and borrowing. Within these major categories the following specific choices must be made: Which kinds of taxes should be collected and how much of each? What services should the municipality provide on a charge basis? How high should service charges be? What federal or state aids can the municipality obtain? And how much and what forms of indebtedness should it incur? Revenue policies provide clear examples of policy outputs that have direct feedback to decision makers. Subsequent revenues reflect decisions on tax rates, service charges, and borrowing and the burden taxpayers are willing to bear. The data contained in Table 7.2 provide one way of looking at local government revenues. The revenue sources are broken down into two major categories, general and utility revenues. Although some cities make a profit on utilities, their major income is from general revenues. Local governments are primarily self-supporting. Despite the development of grants-in-aid and the cooperative federal system, local governments provide about 70 percent of their own revenues.

The property tax is clearly the most important source of revenue for American local governments. In 1970, it accounted for $10 billion of *municipal governments'* revenues; this sum represented 32.8 percent of total revenues and about two-thirds of all tax revenues. Among all kinds of local governments, the property tax is even more important. When counties, school districts, and other special districts are considered along with municipalities, the property tax accounts for $33.0 billion, 37 percent of total revenues and 85.1 percent of tax revenues. Almost all local governments draw heavily upon the property tax, and relatively few of them make significant use of sales or income taxes. In 1970, all local governments combined collected only $3.1 billion from sales taxes and less than $1.6 billion from income taxes. In fact, local government's dependence upon the property tax has not changed much throughout the twentieth century. Cities relied on property taxes to about the same degree in the early 1970s that they did in 1900.

Table 7.2   *Revenues of City Governments, 1970–1971*

	Amount (millions of dollars)	Percentage of distribution
Total revenues	$37,367	
General revenues	30,575	100%
Intergovernmental	9,697	31.7
State	7,401	24.2
Federal	1,861	6.1
Other local	435	1.4
From own sources	20,878	68.3
Taxes	15,090	49.4
Property	10,041	32.8
Sales	2,780	9.1
Other	2,270	7.4
Charges and miscellaneous	5,788	18.9

SOURCE: U.S. Bureau of the Census, *City Government Finances 1970–1971* (Washington, D.C.: Government Printing Office, 1972). Excludes utilities revenues.

State aid is the second most important source of local-government revenue. It takes the form of grants for specific functions (schools, roads, welfare payments), grants to support general local government (the use of which may be determined by local officials), and state tax money that is returned to the jurisdictions where it is collected. In 1970–1971, the total resources transferred to municipal governments from state governments amounted to $7.4 billion. This was 24.2 percent of total government revenues and almost half (49 percent) the level of taxes that city governments collected from their own sources. Direct aids from the federal government are paltry in comparison with state aids. They amounted to $1.9 billion in 1970–1971, but they do contribute to significant local programs in education, urban renewal and public housing, planning, airport construction, health and hospitals, and highway construction.

The third and fourth most prominent forms of city-government revenue are service charges and borrowing. In 1970–1971, city governments raised $11.4 billion in charges and utility revenues and another $5.3 billion from long-term debt. The most important sources of charges and fees were utilities, especially water and electric systems. Other sums come from hospital charges, rents from public housing, tolls, license fees, and charges for school lunches.

These figures reflect only the general patterns; they do not take account of the complexity that pervades local revenue policies. The main source of complexity arises from the position of local governments as creatures of the states.

The states and local revenues

The powers of cities to tax are heavily circumscribed by the legal constraints of Dillon's rule (see Chapter 4, pp. 105–106). Cities may tax only for such purposes and in such manners as are specifically allowed by state law.[1] Although state legislatures may require cities to perform a multiplicity of functions, there is no necessary guarantee that tax resources will match legal responsibilities. Cities cannot determine on their own to adopt a sales tax or an income tax if state law has not explicitly authorized the levy of such taxes. Even if they are authorized, their upper limits may be specified. Sometimes the uses of each tax are also specified in detail by the legislature. These restrictions make local governments the poor stepchildren of American federalism.

Few municipalities collect sales or income taxes because most states forbid such levies. The property tax, the only major tax allowed by all state governments, is the mainstay of local governments. Furthermore, state governments limit the total amounts even of these taxes that may be raised. They regulate the levels of property taxes, the kinds of properties that are subject to property taxes, and the amounts that local authorities can borrow.

Tax and debt limits are typically based upon the amount of *assessed valuation* in a community: the total value of property as local officials have established it for purposes of taxation. The constitution of Alabama, for example, forbids local governments to raise more than 1.25 percent of the total assessed valuation within their jurisdictions in taxes; that of Washington limits taxation to 4 percent; the debt limit of Indiana municipalities is 2 percent of assessed value; and that of Pennsylvania (except for Philadelphia) is 7 percent.[2] Local authorities can exercise some discretion in the face of these limits by simply increasing the assessments on property within their jurisdictions when they reach the current limits of taxes or indebtedness imposed on them.[3] However, such manipulations usually do not escape the notice of tax-wary citizens' groups, and there are high political costs in manipulating assessments in order to increase taxes. State governments also require tax exemptions and deductions for certain kinds of property. Several states give concessions to veterans, the aged, certain kinds of industrial plants, and *homesteads* (single-family homes occupied by their owners). States also exclude from the local tax base or require special tax rates for farm properties, automobiles, and other forms of personal property.[4] Certain properties of churches and nonprofit organizations, as well as state and federal properties, are exempt from local taxation. The City of New Haven, the home of Yale University, has only a little more than half the actual property within the city limits on its tax rolls. Tax-exempt properties nevertheless add to the total service burden of the city, for they require transportation arteries, police and fire protection, and other "free" public services. Taxable properties in cities having government, medical, and educational centers thus must bear added burdens.

Equity, politics, and attitudes toward taxation

Tax *equity* is an issue that often figures in local politics. Equity can be defined as fairness, equality, or distribution of appropriate burdens. The issue of equity is complicated by long-standing philosophical disputes about equality, as well as by immediate questions of whose pocketbook is to be tapped. In principle, an equitable tax is one that distributes the costs of public service in a fair manner among economic groups. But equity is not simply resolved by an *equal* assignment of taxes among citizens or business firms. There is debate over the wisdom of *progressive* versus *regressive* taxation. Those who advocate progressive taxes argue that burdens should be equal only among those with equal economic resources and that people with large incomes should pay, not only more taxes than people with small incomes, but also higher percentages of their incomes. Some observers favor progressive taxes on incomes, combined with regressive taxes in other areas, because they think that this combination will spread the burden throughout the community most fairly. Regressive taxes, which take larger percentages of the incomes of the poor than of the rich, are defended on the grounds that they leave more resources in the hands of the wealthy, who are likely to promote economic growth with their investments. Regressivity is also supported by those who claim that the poor reap the greatest benefit from domestic spending and should pay for what they get.

In debates about taxation, the subject of equity cannot be considered apart from the *incidence* and *burdens* of taxation and their subsequent impacts on individuals and the local economy. The incidence of a tax—the ultimate payer—is not apparent in the statute that defines the rates and the items to be taxed. When a property tax is first levied, it falls upon the property owner. If he is a landlord, however, he can shift the tax to his tenants by increasing his rents accordingly. The original justification and still-current defense of property taxes is that higher taxes are placed upon properties of higher value. But, because poor people spend larger than average percentages of their incomes for housing, property taxes take larger shares of the incomes of the poor than of those of the relatively well-to-do. Property taxes generally have a regressive impact, although their regressivity can be modified somewhat if certain low-income groups (e.g., the aged) are given special exemptions.

Urban taxation tends to be regressive. Even those local taxes other than property taxes that are commonly used—income and sales taxes—are not progressive in their application at the local level. Sales taxes are generally regressive because they take larger shares of the incomes of poor men, who must spend most of their incomes buying basic necessities that are subject to the tax. At the federal level, of course, income taxes are moderately progressive. Income taxes at the local level, however, tend to take fixed proportions of incomes, typically 1 percent. Considering the whole system of taxation, in which state and local regressivity works against the progressivity of the federal tax structure, the American taxation system is not so progressive as is sometimes supposed. A study of national, state, and local taxes, done several years ago, concluded that people earning more than $15,000 annually paid about 44 percent of their incomes in taxes, whereas those earning $10,000–$15,000 paid about 31 percent of their incomes to various governments. People making less than $2,000, however, suffered tax burdens nearly equal to those of the middle-income group, paying about 28 percent of their incomes in taxes.[5]

Still, the question of tax burdens cannot be dismissed after examination of only the revenue side of government. Although the classic defense of progressive taxation defines the regressive tax as inequitable, certain regressive taxes seem somewhat more equitable because of the expenditures that they support. Local taxes on property and retail sales are regressive in the burdens they impose, but they also help to support such services as public education, health, recreation, and welfare, which provide important benefits to lower-income citizens. Before final answers about tax equity can be determined, we need an analysis of benefits. One such effort has been made by Walter Heller, former chairman of the President's Council of Economic Advisers. Heller estimated that "the state-local expenditure pattern is strongly [progressive], declining steadily [in the benefits offered] from an estimated 43 percent of income for the poorest families to 6 percent for families with incomes about $10,000." He emphasized that "study after study has confirmed the unmistakable pattern of substantially progressive federal taxes and expenditures, strongly regressive state local taxes, and strongly progressive state-local expenditures."[6] The progressive character of the expenditure patterns of state and local governments operates to counterbalance, at least in part, the regressivity of their tax systems.

The issues of incidence, burdens, and equity are important elements in understanding attitudes toward taxation at the local level. The simplest proposition about such attitudes—that self-interest motivates people to oppose any tax increases—contains some elements of truth. Yet people periodically do vote higher taxes upon themselves in local referenda, partly because they perceive taxes as likely to bring improvements in local services. Self-interest does seem to be a major factor in determining attitudes about what *type* of taxes one prefers. A Michigan study found that (1) low-income people preferred income taxes whereas upper-income people preferred other kinds, (2) property owners preferred less reliance on property taxes, and (3) people who lived in areas of high property taxes preferred shifts to other forms of taxation.[7] But self-interest does not alone motivate preferences for levels of taxation. For some people a sense of public-regardingness supports the belief that taxation may produce collective benefits even if taxes bring no immediate benefits. Upper-income property holders, who bear a disproportionate share of taxes, have sometimes been found to support projects of primary benefit to the poor.[8]

The future of local revenues

Local governments face both a revenue bind and a crush of demands for public expenditures. As we emphasized in Chapter 2, urban areas are the centers of most concentrations of American wealth, yet much of that wealth is inaccessible to local governments. Such factors as legal limitations upon the objects and levels of taxation, the hostility of taxpayers, debt limitations, and the reluctance of local officials to take advantage of their fiscal options contribute to the *revenue incapacity* of local governments.

Any hints that local governments propose to increase revenues are usually followed by veiled threats from local industries to move elsewhere and by sharp warnings from business groups that high-tax communities cannot be expected to attract industry and residents. The fact is that a number of studies indicate that the level of state or local taxes is but one of many factors, and often not the most important one, in determining industrial location.[9] One economist has noted the paradox that

the influence of tax considerations on the location decisions of business is grossly overstated . . . [but] its impact on state and local taxation is not. . . . Fear of losing business to another jurisdiction haunts the mind and stills the pen of the state and local lawmaker, and special pleaders have developed the skill of exploiting this fear to a high art.[10]

It would not, however, be fair to lay at the doorstep of local businessmen the sole responsibility for pressures for low taxes. Also culpable are local electorates, municipal officials reluctant to take political risks, and state legislators unwilling to increase local revenue options. At least in terms of taxing, local governments are close to the people, and the property tax hits—quite literally—very close to home. The property tax has fallen under intense pressure from taxpayer groups, legislators, and officials in recent years, and significant cases have been raised in the courts about its impact on school finance (see pp. 232–234).

Now that we have federal revenue sharing, the cities have a new source of funds, unfettered by the requirements that surround traditional grants-in-aid (see pp. 119–122). Yet the record on revenue sharing is too new for a clear evaluation. So far, however, there is no reliable sign that the fiscal wolf has left the door of urban governments.

Urban Expenditure Patterns

The other side of the fiscal coin is expenditures. They are of interest to political scientists and citizens for several reasons. First, budgets indicate relative priorities among public choices. Charles A. Beard once wrote:

In the purposes for which appropriations are made the policies of the city government are given concrete form—the culture of the city is reflected. Indeed, the history of urban civilization could be written in terms of appropriations, for they show what the citizens think is worth doing and worth paying for.[11]

More recently, Louis H. Masotti and Don R. Bowen have noted that "the community budget can be viewed as public policy spelled out in dollars and cents, and that budget decisions represent the allocations of certain kinds of values."[12]

Second, expenditures are of interest because they purchase certain levels of public services through which the municipality can make an impact upon its environment. Educational expenditures buy teachers, schoolbooks, and classrooms in an effort to raise the educational achievement and community aspirations. Police expenditures purchase policemen, cars, paddy wagons, radios, radar equipment, and laboratory devices, all of which are designed to help apprehend transgressors of the law. Expenditures are therefore important as means of procuring certain kinds of output intended to have impact upon the environment.

Third, local expenditures are of interest because they have considerable influence upon the economic system as a whole. That local governments spend about 9 percent of the GNP makes them a potent influence on levels of inflation or deflation and on economic growth.

Where all that money goes

In 1970–1971, city governments spent a total of $31.9 billion on a wide range of services. Table 7.3 details the distribution of city expenditures by major categories of public function. Municipal governments have a very wide range of expenditure categories. Few separate items require more than 10 percent of the typical city budget. Only education and policing account for as much as 10 percent each of total city expenditures. These major items accounted for $39.71 and $26.29 per capita, respectively.

Table 7.3, however, shows only the aggregate patterns of municipal expenditures. The data suffer from several limitations. First, there is wide variation among states in the division of labor. Some state governments perform functions that in others are operated by city governments. In some states, for example, welfare payments are made entirely from state contributions while elsewhere cities contribute to the welfare

Table 7.3 *City-Government Expenditures, 1970–1971*

Expenditure item	Amount (millions of dollars)	Percentage of total expenditures	Per-capita amount
Total general expenditures	$31,947	100.0	$242.02
Education	5,242	16.4	39.71
Police and law enforcement	3,471	10.9	26.29
Highways	2,664	8.3	20.18
Fire protection	1,996	6.2	15.12
Public welfare	2,668	8.4	20.36
Sewage	1,767	5.5	13.39
Health and hospitals	2,324	7.3	17.60
Parks and recreation	1,439	4.5	10.90
Housing and urban renewal	1,442	4.5	10.92
Sanitation other than sewage	1,243	3.9	9.42
Interest on debt	1,308	4.1	9.91
General control	867	2.7	6.56
Financial administration	515	1.6	3.90
General public buildings	489	1.5	3.70
All other	4,512	14.1	34.12

SOURCE: U.S. Bureau of the Census, *City Government Finances in 1970–71* (Washington, D.C.: Government Printing Office, 1972).

function. There is also wide variation in responsibilities among different kinds of local government. Education is the major variable. In some states, particularly in the East, city governments are responsible for the operation of public schools and sometimes for colleges and universities. New York City's billion-dollar school budget (which alone accounts for about a fifth of all municipal governments' spending on education) constitutes a very large proportion of its total expenditures. But in cities in the Midwest, South, and West school expenditures are typically made by special school districts. What in one state may be performed by municipal governments is thus performed in other states by counties, special districts, or the state governments themselves. The endless variations in distribution of responsibility among and within states make it risky to generalize about typical local expenditure patterns. The expenditure categories listed in Table 7.3 provide only a rough overview of the ways that city governments allocate their budgets.

Urban expenditures and the federal system

It is increasingly impossible to separate programs into neat categories of federal, state, or local sponsorship. There are very few programs relevant to urban America that do not involve the federal system as a whole. Education is predominantly a local matter, but assistance to public and higher education is the largest single item in state budgeting, and federal aid to local schools has increased significantly in recent years. Quiet residential streets are built mostly with local money, but state and federal assistance is significant in building major traffic arteries, particularly those connected to the interstate-highway program. The federal government helps to build local hospitals and airports and to train policemen. The housing and urban-renewal programs receive federal and local funds, as well as state aid in some states. Because most of these programs are funded by more than one level of government, any neat effort to sort them by layers of the federal system will be misleading. The federal system is deeply embedded in the expenditure options of local governments.

Because the federal system exerts a significant influence on local budgets, the expenditure decisions of local governments are far from independent. The availability of federal and state money for certain programs may *distort* the expenditure choices of local decision makers. The distortion is intended by Congress and state legislators, who hope to orient local governments more toward the performance of aided functions. It becomes cheaper for municipalities to engage in aided programs than in unaided ones. To spend $100,000 on an urban-renewal program costs the typical city only $33,333 because the federal contribution is two-thirds of the project cost. But to spend $100,000 on upgrading salaries in the fire department will cost close to $100,000, for there are fewer sources of federal assistance.

Grants-in-aid and restrictions on expenditures mean that local governments are not entirely free to make any set of decisions that suit their fancies. State governments require local authorities to perform certain functions in specified ways. Except for general revenue-sharing, federal aid comes with strings attached. Grants are provided for specific purposes, and local governments that do not conform to requirements find their grants terminated. The rules and legislation of state and federal governments thus establish numerous constraints upon local policy.

Communities and Budgets:
A Macro Perspective

Some cities spend more money than do others. In one sense, this difference results merely from financial decision makers' consciously choosing to spend and tax at certain levels. But, in a broader sense, the level of spending is shaped by the socioeconomic, political, governmental, and legal structures of the community and its environment. In this section, we describe some of the community characteristics most commonly associated with variations in expenditures.

Perhaps the most obvious reason why some city budgets are larger than others is the factor of city size. It surprises no one to learn that New York City spends more money than does Kokomo, Oshkosh, or Ogden. Robert C. Wood, in his study of the New York metropolitan region, discovered that population size accounted for the overwhelming proportion of variation in local expenditures.[13] Because of the obvious influence of size, most students of public expenditures *control* their measurements for population size and analyze them in per capita terms.

Socioeconomic factors and spending levels

Table 7.4 provides a summary statement of the relations between seven key socioeconomic characteristics of cities and the expenditure levels of those cities. Each of these relations will be discussed in the following section.

INCOME   As with families, the richer a community, the more money it can afford to spend. For local governments, income and availability of

Table 7.4 *Summary of Relations Between Socioeconomic Variables and Municipal Spending Levels*[a]

Variable	Relation with municipal spending
Income	
High	+
Low	−
Economic base	
Manufacturing	+
Other	−
Density	
High	?
Low	?
Growth rate	
High	?
Low	?
Owner occupancy	
High	−
Low	+
Ethnic character	
Heavy	+
Nonethnic	−
Metropolitan type	
Central city	+
Outside central city	−

[a] A + sign indicates a relationship generally identified as positive. A − sign indicates a relationship generally identified as negative. A "?" indicates a variable about which findings are incomplete or mixed.

resources are very important in determining the level of public expenditures.[14] The city with a poor economic base, a large proportion of poor people, or other economic disabilities possesses serious disadvantages in any effort to provide a high level of public services. In Meridian, Mississippi, only 7 percent of the population has incomes of $10,000 or more; in Edina, Minnesota, more than 60 percent of the families earn $10,000 a year.

In some states, state assistance compensates for income gaps among cities, but the deeper problem is that states like Alabama, Mississippi, New Mexico, and West Virginia do not themselves have the revenues to raise expenditures in their cities to levels of minimum support in other states. Dedication, imagination, and political "savvy" of local officials cannot substitute entirely for missing resources.

ECONOMIC BASE   An economic system based upon manufacturing tends to be associated with higher levels of municipal expenditures. In Wood's analysis of New Jersey communities, industrialization accounted for more of the explainable variation in municipal expenditures than did any other factor except population size. In a study of suburban fiscal policy in the Philadelphia region, Williams and his associates discovered that the largest spenders among communities were suburbs with heavy industrial and commercial activity.[15] Industrialization brings heavy service demands for police and fire protection, roads, and public utilities. Also, as even the most obtuse tax assessor knows, industrial properties provide a lucrative tax base and thus more money for the municipality to spend. In the Detroit area, for example, as much as 95 percent of tax revenues in the industrial suburbs comes from taxes on industrial properties.[16]

DENSITY   Density is commonly measured by number of people per square mile. There are wide variations in this factor, not only within cities (ranging from tightly packed ghettos to quarter-acre single-family dwelling units in fringe areas), but also among cities. The mean number of people per square mile in Boston is 13,936, whereas the comparable figure for Houston is 3,841. The impact of population density on city expenditures seems to vary with the particular expenditures being examined.[17] Where population density is high there tend to be low expenditures per capita on streets and highways, which suggests that economies of scale operate in the transportation field. In other fields, however, high densities operate to increase service needs and tend to increase per capita expenditures. Density adds to problems like traffic control, law enforcement, public health, and fire hazards, and it requires high per capita rates of expenditure for police protection, fire fighting, and sanitation.

GROWTH RATES   On strictly a priori grounds, one expects clear and unambiguous positive relationship between spending levels and growth rates: As a community grows it should spend more to meet new service demands. Richard Spangler's careful analysis of growth rates and spending at the state level found strong associations between population growth and higher expenditures.[18] On the other hand, the spending and debt limits imposed on state governments, the hostility of taxpayers, and the reluctance of politicians to increase taxes suggest that some cities may prefer to "spread themselves thin" and "make do" financially rather than investing substantial resources in coping with urban growth. In contrast to Spangler's findings, other research has revealed that growth rates bear little relation to increases in urban public spending.[19]

OWNER OCCUPANCY   The greater the degree of home ownership in a community, the lower municipal expenditures usually are. Lineberry and Fowler have offered two principal explanations for this:

1. Owner occupancy is correlated (almost by definition) with lower urban population density. High density, bringing all manner of men together in the classic urban mosaic, may itself be correlated with factors which produce demands for higher expenditures—slums, increased need for fire and police protection, and so on.
2. No doubt self-interest (perhaps "private-regardingness") on the part of the home owner, whose property is intimately related to the tax structure of most local government, may account for part of this relationship.[20]

Whatever the underlying explanation, the incidence of home ownership in a community is one of the major negative correlates of municipal expenditures.

ETHNICITY AND RELIGIOUS COMPOSITION   Several studies indicate a strong positive relationship between the ethnicity or the religious composition of a community and its spending levels.[21] This relationship may be direct or spurious. For example, it may be that ethnic groups and Roman Catholics prefer high levels of municipal expenditures and support candidates and referenda that increase spending levels. There is some evidence that Roman Catholics are more sympathetic toward increased governmental activity, particularly welfare-state activities, than are other religious groups.[22] But, on the other hand, the relationship may be better explained by factors that are coincidentally associated with the religious composition and the size of the public budget. Ethnic groups and Roman Catholics may be concentrated in areas of high density or low-owner occupancy; these other factors may explain the relationship between ethnicity and spending.

CC-OCC LOCATION   We saw in Chapter 2 that the location of a city within the metropolitan area may influence the level of its public spending.

Central cities are faced with a greater proportion of the burdens—traffic, poverty, poor housing, crime, decay—necessitating public expenditures. Suburban governments, on the other hand, are mercifully free of many of these problems and can keep public budgets lower. OCCs, however, do contain larger proportions of school-age children and thus have higher educational expenditures than do CCs.

OTHER SOCIOECONOMIC FACTORS   There are countless other socioeconomic factors—incidence of poverty in a community, type of industrial activity, general age of buildings, whether the climate necessitates snow removal, and so forth—that may affect expenditures of city governments. Any attempt to catalogue all the possible elements that impinge upon the level of spending would stretch the boundaries of an introductory text too far. We have discussed a few of the socioeconomic factors on which the most research has been done. Our listing does not imply lesser significance of an array of unmentioned factors that might influence spending levels.

Governmental and political factors and spending

As public officials write budgets, authorize city appropriations, and collect taxes, it might be possible to claim that only governmental and political factors affect local budgeting. This view is, however, a narrow one that denies the significant relations between community characteristics and municipal spending levels. Numerous community characteristics, from the resource base to the amount of snowfall, may affect public expenditures. But it is inappropriate to attribute all intermunicipal variations in spending levels to socioeconomic forces. There are important factors in the political process and the structure of government that bear upon the level of local spending. Some of these relations are summarized in Table 7.5.

STATE-LOCAL EXPENDITURES   Different states use different divisions of labor among governments. Some states spend very large proportions of total state and local revenues and have broad responsibilities for provision of public services. In other states, local governments are assigned many of these responsibilities. West Virginia, Delaware, and Kentucky are highly centralized states, making 62, 53, and 58 percent of total state and local expenditures respectively. At the other extreme, New York and Minnesota are highly decentralized states; the local governments account for 77 and 70 percent of state and local expenditures respectively. The greater the responsibilities assigned to the local governments, the more cities will spend. Alan Campbell and Seymour Sacks found such arrangements between state and local governments to be the most significant predictor of the level of local expenditures.[23]

Table 7.5 *Summary of Relations Between Government Variables and Municipal Spending Levels*[a]

Variable	Relation with municipal spending
State-local centralization	
State responsibilities greater	−
Local responsibilities greater	+
Intergovernmental aid	
High	+
Low	−
State debt and expenditure limits	
Restrictive	−
Unrestrictive	+
Previous expenditures	
High	+
Low	−
Degree of government reformism	
High	?
Low	?
Participation in local politics	
High	?
Low	?
Party competition	
High	?
Low	?

[a] A + sign indicates a relationship generally identified as positive. A − sign indicates a relationship generally identified as negative. A ? indicates a variable about which findings are either incomplete or mixed.

INTERGOVERNMENTAL AID   Because resources determine the amounts of money available to local governments, the amounts of intergovernmental aid received are positively correlated with expenditures. The most significant question about state and federal assistance is its *substitution effect* on local efforts. Opponents of intergovernmental assistance frequently claim that aid simply reduces local governments' dedication to raising money within their own communities and that the net effects of intergovernmental assistance are few. Evidence is, however, that much state and federal aid has a *stimulating effect* on local revenues. Many grant-in-aid programs seem to stimulate local governments to spend more than they otherwise would.

TAX, DEBT, AND EXPENDITURE LIMITS   Although, to our knowledge, no study has ever directly confronted the question and satisfactorily resolved it, it seems reasonable to expect that cities whose fiscal capacities are under stringent state limitations spend less than do cities in states where such restrictions are looser.

PREVIOUS EXPENDITURE LEVELS AND BUDGET EXPERIENCE   Studies of state
expenditure levels have identified the level of previous expenditures as
the most significant single predictor of state budgets. Ira Sharkansky
found correlations between previous and current expenditure levels for
different categories of state-government expenditures ranging from .70
to .96.[24] A similar stable pattern probably prevails in cities. Relevant
data for Houston, Texas, appear in Table 7.6. The correlations of expenditures in several budget categories over time suggest that stable
incrementalism is characteristic of local expenditures. Such findings also
suggest "a conservative element in the political systems of American
states and cities. The conservatism may reflect the influence of habit and
routine, the practices of incremental budgeting, the problems involved
in program expansion and/or the processes of an administration's
maturation."[25] We shall have more to say later in this chapter about the
importance of incremental budgeting.

GOVERNMENTAL REFORMISM   Much of the rhetorical thunder in support
of municipal reforms (manager governments, nonpartisan elections,
and at-large constituencies) claims that lower taxes—and by implication
lower expenditures—will follow their adoption. Lineberry and Fowler's
study of taxes and expenditures in cities of over 50,000 population

Table 7.6   *Correlations Between Per-Capita Budget Categories and Equivalent
Items in Previous Years, Houston, Texas, 1947–1962*

Budget category	Correlation
General revenues	.97
Taxes	.95
Property taxes	.95
Intergovernmental revenues	.84
Charges and miscellaneous	.94
General expenditures	.78
Capital outlay	.27
Police	.91
Fire	.90
Highways	.85
Sanitation	.83
Hospitals	.95
Interest on debt	.97
Utility revenues	.95
Utility expenditures	.20
Current expenditures	.92
Capital outlay	.19
Interest on debt	.90

SOURCE: Adapted from Bernard Brown, "Municipal Finances and Annexation: A Case Study of Post-War Houston," *Social Science Quarterly,* 48 (December 1967), 341, Table 1.

found only slight differences in the expenditure levels of reformed and unreformed cities.[26] Yet, Clark found lower spending in reformed cities.[27] Bernard Booms found that manager cities in Ohio and Michigan had significantly lower expenditures than did mayor-council cities.[28]

LOCAL PARTICIPATION AND PARTY COMPETITION   A well-known hypothesis in political science holds that more vigorous interparty competition and more participation by working-class groups will produce public policies more attuned to working-class interests.[29] The argument is that single-party systems with low voting turnouts probably tend to favor status quo politics beneficial to upper-income interests. The more competition there is, the more parties seek support among wider circles of the electorate. Participation by lower-income groups increases, and their representatives obtain more benefits for them. Yet there are two difficulties with this argument. First, some careful studies of state spending have concluded that neither the level of voter participation nor the degree of interparty competition makes much difference in state expenditure levels.[30] Voter participation and turnout levels in local elections bear little relationship to tax or expenditure levels.[31] Although competition may have a bearing on local finance, the proposition can hardly be assumed out of hand. Second, it is not at all clear that more effective working-class representation operates to raise or lower public expenditures. Higher government expenditures may aid working-class groups who benefit from numerous local government programs. The evidence suggests, however, that lower-income people are the most dissatisfied with governments and their policies.[32] Some research also suggests that numerous working-class voters are alienated and tend to vote against both public expenditures and candidates who advocate increases in public expenditures.[33] Without any direct evidence, we cannot assess the impact of turnout, participation, and party competition on local spending levels.

OTHER POLITICAL VARIABLES   The seven governmental and political factors that we have described do not, of course, exhaust the wide range of political variables that may influence a community's budget decisions. Besides, all the relations that we have identified are only *tendencies*, which mask numbers of deviant cases. Among other political factors of likely significance are the attitudes of community residents, the nature of the local power structure, and the risk-taking propensities of the local officials called upon to propose budget and tax increases. A community dominated by public-regarding people may spend more than one dominated by private-regarding people. A monolithic power structure, ruling in the interests of the upper class, may be less supportive of tax and expenditure increases than would a pluralistic structure.

Community characteristics, political factors, and spending

In principle, it should be possible to examine any particular city, note its relative standings on scales of the major determinants of municipal spending levels, and make some educated guesses about its level of expenditures. Two caveats are necessary, however. First, as already noted, we have so far discussed a collection of mere *tendencies*. Factors unique to a particular community or its political system may account for marked deviation from the patterns predicted by larger studies of numerous communities. Cities may expand or contract their budgets in response to sudden changes in local economic conditions; they may respond to the urgings of strong and powerful political leaders to whittle down or drastically increase local budgets; or they may face particular service problems during single budget periods. A sudden change from a tight-fisted conservative administration to a free-spending liberal one may increase a city's budget expenditures significantly.

Second, we have described factors in isolation from one another. Conceivably, of course, a community could be found to score high on all the factors contributing to higher municipal expenditures. More likely, however, any single community will be characterized by some factors that impel it toward lower budgets and others that impel it toward higher ones. In some communities, one factor might take on greater importance than the same factor would in other communities. The particular mix of influences on spending may be more important than the mere presence or absence of individual elements.

These caveats are important, but they should not obscure the general findings that local budgets respond to community socioeconomic and political characteristics. Budget makers do not simply enter the "fiscal restaurant" and order what they want. The macroeconomic structure of the community provides them with certain kinds of resources and denies them others, and the political structure furnishes additional opportunities and constraints. No amount of zeal on the part of urban officials can eliminate all the strictures imposed by limited resources, political opposition to property taxes, and state spending and taxing limitations. Imagination can be only a partial substitute for resources. Given the macro context of financial decision making that we have described, we can now examine the micro context of budgeting: the process, the actors, and their strategies in the budgeting game.

The Budgetary Process in Urban Government: A Micro Perspective

A budget may be viewed from several angles. "In its most literal sense," according to Aaron Wildavsky, "a budget is a document, containing words and figures, which proposes expenditures for certain items and purposes." From a larger social perspective, budgeting is "the translation of financial resources into human purposes . . . [or] a series of

Table 7.7   *Mayor's Budget Recommendations for Animal Regulation Department,[a] Los Angeles, California, Fiscal 1969–1970*

		EXPENDITURES AND APPROPRIATIONS	
Expenditures 1967–1968	Estimated expenditures 1968–1969		Budget appropriation 1969–1970
Salaries			
$1,198,181	$1,261,964	General	$1,340,524
5,081	7,355	Overtime	5,300
$1,203,262	$1,269,319	Total salaries	$1,345,824
Expense			
$ 9,411	$ 10,950	Printing and binding	$ 10,999
426	548	Traveling expense	1,008
—	8,500	Contractual services	—
21,031	23,000	Transportation expense	24,000
15	100	Governmental meetings	100
9,117	2,055	Uniforms	2,375
2,984	2,966	Office and administrative expense	4,167
21,256	24,035	Operating supplies and expense	27,300
$ 64,240	$ 72,154	Total expense	$ 69,949
Equipment			
$ 3,658	$ 5,098	Furniture, office and technical equipment	$ 2,046
2,580	13,810	Other operating equipment	1,905
$ 6,238	$ 18,908	Total equipment	$ 3,951
$1,273,740	$1,360,381	*Total animal regulation*	$1,419,724
		SOURCE OF FUNDS	
Actual 1967–1968	Estimated 1968–1969		
$1,273,740	$1,360,381	General fund	$1,419,724
$1,273,740	$1,360,381	*Total funds*	$1,419,724

[a]This department enforces laws and ordinances regulating the care, custody, control, and prevention of cruelty to all animals within the City. It operates and maintains animal shelters, and issues permits for the operation of animal establishments and makes inspections thereof. The department issues dog licenses and collects dog license fees, and participates in the County's rabies control program. The department enforces the Leash Law, inspects medical research laboratories, and accepts unwanted animals.

goals with price tags attached."[34] Budgets itemize public revenues and divide public expenditures into categories by programs or expenditure items. National, state, and local budgets are imposing to behold. Some municipal budgets rival the local telephone directories in sheer bulk (and unreadability).

As an example of budgetary detail, Table 7.7 reproduces the mayor's budget recommendations for a single agency, the Animal Regulation Department of the City of Los Angeles. The Los Angeles council considers requests from thirty-three agencies, most of whose budgets are far more complex than this one. This level of specificity is common among national, state, and local budgets. How can such an array of expenditure claims and decisions be handled by local governments? What strategies are employed by actors in the budgetary process? What rules govern their behavior and expectations? How do budget makers cope with the enormous complexity of the budget? What implications does the budgeting process have for the larger policy process in urban government? These questions are addressed in this section.

Decision makers, rules, strategies

There is such a wide variety of organization in local governments that it is difficult to describe a typical budgetary process, but the general patterns and major actors identified in studies of national and state budgeting[35] also seem to hold at local levels. The major actors include *agencies, chief executives* (in local governments, either mayors or managers), and *legislative bodies*. Some cities employ such variations as legislative budget systems, special budgeting boards, or joint committees. In a legislative budget system, the review of agency requests occurs within a committee of the city council before the full council votes on the appropriations. When there is a city budget board, a group of administrative officers, which may include the treasurer and controller, as well as the mayor or manager, reviews agency requests. A joint-committee budget is reviewed by a group that includes both legislators and administrators. But, for purposes of simplicity and because the patterns we describe seem to prevail generally, we shall assume that agencies, chief executives, and municipal councils are the major decision makers.

A fairly typical sequence of steps in the budgetary process is presented graphically in Figure 7.1. Although this diagram is only an aid to understanding a complex process, it identifies the major steps and their interrelations. Of enormous importance for actual outcomes is the fact that *revenue decisions are made before expenditure decisions*. One way to construct a public budget might be to identify all the public needs on which money could be spent, add up their probable costs to the government, draw up a budget, and then establish tax rates. But governments do not work this way any more than families decide their needs first and

Figure 7.1   An Overview of the Municipal Bugetary Process

SOME MAJOR CONSIDERATIONS   STEPS

State-federal-local rules, grants-in-aid, future and past commitments

Local economic circumstances, growth, decline, and so on

Prevailing wages, salaries, equipment, maintenance costs in private sector

Previous expenditures

Balanced-budget requirement (spending must not exceed revenue)

Revenue estimates prepared for chief executive

Chief executive's instructions to agencies

Agency heads' prepared requests

Review and balancing budget by chief executive

Review by council

Budget

——▶ = influences

then arrange for their incomes to meet their needs. Rather, revenue estimates for the coming year are made first, and, to a large degree, they determine the expenditure decisions that are made.[36] Estimates of anticipated revenues are submitted to the office of the chief executive and constitute the first significant input in the budgetary process.

In most large cities it is the legal responsibility of the chief executives to present budgets to the municipal councils. In weak-mayor cities, the councils may themselves play more direct roles, or other officials or even the agencies themselves may be charged with budget preparation. In strong-mayor and manager cities, however, the responsibility normally belongs to the chief executives, either mayors or managers. According to John P. Crecine, the problem confronting the executive is

largely one of recommending a budget which (1) is balanced, (2) at least maintains existing service levels, (3) provides for increases in city employees' wages if at all possible, and (4) avoids tax increases (especially property-tax increases in the belief that increased property taxes cause business and industry to move from the city, reducing its tax base).[37]

Of these four requirements, the most stringent is that of a balanced budget. The constitutions of most states do not permit local governments to engage in deficit spending. Revenues and expenditures must match.

Upon receipt of revenue estimates the mayor or manager issues to his department heads a set of budget instructions. He may include guidelines on service increases, levels of salary and wage increments he proposes to grant, and other matters. His instructions are shaped by the revenue estimates, and they guide actions by agency heads.

One of the most significant items included in the mayor's fiscal program and his budgetary instructions is wages and salaries. In an inflationary economy, municipal employees expect wage and salary increases that help them keep up with the cost of living; over the long run, they also expect to better their relative positions. Moreover, the public sector competes with the private sector for skilled personnel. The municipal government cannot afford to lose large numbers of employees to the private sector as wages become more attractive in business and industry. Thus, the prevailing wage rates in the private sector, plus any inflation that has occurred since the last budget, will almost certainly force increases in the budget.

It is common to expect that public (and private) bureaucracies will seek to expand their own programs by means of increased appropriations. But acquisitive strategies can be pushed too far and backfire. Agencies that consistently ask for much—or for more than their fair shares—will come to be viewed by executives and the council as too aggressive or irresponsible. Such agencies may find their appropriations cut to levels below what they would have received if they had been more reasonable. Many agency heads walk a delicate line between expansion and political feasibility. Their major question, How much shall we ask for? is answered in part by the question, How much are we likely to get?[38]

Agency requests are returned to the chief executive, who then prepares the budget proposal. At this point, "the decision process in the (chief executive's) office can usefully be thought of as a search for a solution to the balanced-budget problem."[39] The mayor's or manager's office is not likely to inquire very deeply into an agency's budget if no increase is requested and if the total city budget is close to being in balance. When cuts or increases are necessary, however, there is a well-defined list of priorities:[40]

1. Administrative salaries;
2. Nonadministrative salaries and wages;
3. Operating expenses, supplies, and materials;
4. Equipment;
5. Maintenance.

Budget reviewers will cut agencies' requests in maintenance and equipment before cutting supplies and salaries, and they will distribute surplus funds to salaries and wages ahead of other categories. It is only after all other categories have been cut that reductions of salaries and wages are ordered, and it is only after all higher categories have received their rewards that any surplus is spent on equipment and supplies. Part of the reasoning behind this hierarchy of priorities is, no doubt, that supplies and equipment do not vote, whereas municipal employees do. The result of all this juggling, adding, subtracting, and dividing is a balanced budget, which is mimeographed or printed and forwarded to the council. The latter has—within the limits of state law—the legal power either to approve, to disapprove, or to change any allocation of municipal funds or the tax rate.

At the federal level, Congress is generally a budget cutter.[41] The House Appropriations Committee in particular views its major role as "guardian of the public treasury" and takes a jaundiced view of most requests for increased appropriations.[42] The typical city council, on the other hand, operates more as a rubber stamp for decisions made by the executive.[43] Councils usually make few changes in the budgets submitted by mayors or managers. The budget is a very complex document, the product of a network of delicate compromises, and to intervene at the final stage would certainly upset this delicate financial balance, for a change in one item would require a compensating change in another, and so on. Moreover, the city council, in contrast to a congressional committee, lacks a staff to assist it in its budgetary review. There are exceptions to the rule of minimum interference, and an unpopular chief executive or one from an opposing political party may find the council in a mood to tinker. Most of the time, however, the executive's budget emerges from the council unscathed.

Incremental budgeting

One way of constructing a municipal budget would be to follow the tenets of rational problem solving that we described in Chapter 5 (pp.

168–169). Each possible goal of an agency's program might be identified, the goals ranked in a preference hierarchy, and then a series of comparisons made among budget alternatives. The end product would, at some level of abstraction, account for all policy goals served by the government and represent a weighing of every possible budgetary strategy to meet these goals. But, for reasons that we explained in Chapter 5—and for additional reasons that we shall discuss shortly—rational budgeting is virtually impossible to achieve. The more common budgeting model is *incremental*: Past experience—and especially past expenditures—is used as a guide to future spending. The nineteenth-century Irish student of public finance, Bastable, wrote:

Fortunately the question of expenditure in all its forms does not present itself as a single problem. It would be quite hopeless to prepare a budget of outlay for any country without the aid of the material collected during previous experience. The great mass of expenditure is taken as settled, and it is only the particular changes that have to be anxiously weighed in order to estimate their probable advantage. This method of treatment simplifies issues very much.[44]

Because "the great mass of expenditure is taken as settled," incrementalism focuses attention mainly on deviations from past behavior. Each agency has an expenditure base below which it is not likely to be cut.[45] It is the increments that are subject to close examination. Agency expenditures, as well as total city expenditures, will be very highly correlated with previous expenditures (see Table 7.6). The tendency toward incremental decisions is not the only factor that produces high correlations between present and past expenditures. The stability of local revenue sources and the availability of continuing grants-in-aid for specific programs are two additional factors.

Incrementalism does not, in a strict sense, lead to rational budget making. It rarely raises the broad questions implied by the rational model. Few alternatives are considered, programs are infrequently subjected to rigorous comparisons among themselves, and little evidence is presented to indicate whether they are accomplishing their ostensible goals. On the other hand, in a system under severe time pressures ("end poverty now"; "mass transit is essential for the immediate future"; "stop discrimination") and with only fragmentary information, incrementalism is not altogether irrational. It rests upon the fundamental proposition that past experience is the best guide to future policy.

The reasons for incremental budgeting are similar to the reasons why rational models do not adequately describe urban decision making. But there also are several factors specific to the budgetary process that promote incrementalism and retard programmatic decision making.

COMPLEXITY As we have emphasized, budgets are complex and detailed documents, and past decisions are the most reliable and handiest tools for grappling with complexity. It is a psychological truism that the human mind tends to respond to similar stimuli in similar ways. That even the largest cities have tiny budget staffs, compared to those of private industry and the federal government, means that there is very little opportunity for close scrutiny of budgets. The Pittsburgh mayor's office, responsible for a budget of more than $75 million, covering scores of accounts and thousands of separate items, has a budget staff of four people.[46]

IMPERFECT INFORMATION AND INCOMMENSURABLE GOALS   Programmatic, or rational, budgeting, in which alternatives are successively compared until an *optimal* complex of expenditures is arrived at, requires measurements that are seldom available. A programmatic budgeting process would weigh the marginal utility of a dollar invested in public health versus that of one invested in education, free school lunches, street repairs, sewer systems, or the like, but there is no scale of measurement upon which all these categories of public investment can be evaluated.

THE "UNCONTROLLABLE" BUDGET   A very large proportion of any budget is quite literally uncontrollable. Support of most local programs is required by law (maintenance of public safety, education, public health), and others receive state or federal grants for which the community has undertaken long-term commitments (urban renewal, public housing, highway construction). Most of the remaining programs have sufficient public support to make reduction politically unwise (libraries, parks, snow removal). Most of the costs of municipal government are absorbed by wages, salaries, and equipment or materials. Changes in the cost of these items is as much a function of the price system as they are conscious choices of decision makers. Wages and salaries must keep pace with the cost of living and with competition from the private sector. Inflation determines the price of labor and materials to the city government. Viewed in this perspective, most items in the municipal budget are simply beyond the reach of decision makers' control.[47]

CONSTRAINTS OF REVENUES   Because most municipal budgets must be balanced and because the revenue options of local governments are resistant to change, revenues operate as a severe constraint on the total size of the municipal budget. Last year's revenues will be highly correlated with this year's revenues, with perhaps a small increment. The simplest way to parcel out the additional revenue is to give agencies whatever new funds may be available as increments over last year's expenditures.

Decisional shortcuts

Because a set of relatively simple rules for decision is followed, it is possible to describe the budgetary process with a limited number of postulates. Although studies of municipal budgeting have been conducted in widely different types of municipalities and in different parts of the country, the findings are sufficiently similar and show sufficient correspondence to studies of government budget making at other levels to suggest a high degree of reliability. Barber's analysis of local boards of finance in twelve Connecticut towns yielded the following rules:[48]

1. Accept many items as uncontrollable because of previous commitments or the feeling that they support essential programs and therefore do not require careful consideration.
2. Focus on the large budget items, and minimize their growth from one period to the next.
3. Base decisions on concrete aspects of a program familiar to some members of the board, even if they constitute only a small portion of the large budget items.
4. Focus on short-range expectations rather than long-range developments that may occur within each field of service.
5. Focus on the dollars and cents of budget requests, rather than on the elements of programs that the funds will purchase.

Crecine's study of budget making in three large cities found similar procedures focused on only limited aspects of each agency's budget, seeking to minimize budget growth and concentrating on dollars requested, rather than on programs promised. The primary concern was to keep each agency's budget close to its previous appropriation and to keep the total municipal budget in balance between revenues and expenditures.[49]

Although the incremental model dominates the decision-making process, the future is never a carbon copy of the past, even in an incremental system. Any complete description of the municipal budgetary process must take account of *deviations* from current expenditure patterns. Indeed, the cumulative effect of these deviations over a period of time constitutes a trend that may itself become part of a base for some particular expenditure item. The sources of deviations are many, and they vary from city to city and time to time. The most nearly universal source of deviation from previous expenditure patterns is the addition of new revenues, especially through grants-in-aid from the state or federal government. Spurts of expenditures can also be explained by factors like a change in administration, a catastrophic event or emergency, and reorganization of functions within the city administration or between the city government and some other unit.[50]

Budgeting and the policy process

Students of budgeting have generally used one of three basic perspectives. Crecine has described them as (1) the "optimizing process," (2) "budgeting as an externally determined event," and (3) "budgeting as an internal bureaucratic process."[51] The notion that budgets *optimize* community values reflects the idea that public budgets are a function of public needs and represent decision-makers' efforts to bring public resources into line with overall community goals. The *externally determined* view is that budgets result from economic and political forces. Citizens' demands for service, the power of community elites, the demands of various groups, and responses to economic pressures are some explanations for a budget's final shape. Business groups are said to seek lower taxes; proponents of law and order demand more money for law enforcement; and PTAs want more money for schools. These demands or requests for services and expenditures are channeled through mayors, councils, and agencies, and the sum of these pressures determines the level of public expenditures. In the third model, that of budgeting as an internal bureaucratic process, external forces are viewed as unimportant, and instead the budget is explained as the outcome of rules and strategies for decision-making employed by agencies, chief executives, and legislative bodies.

The data presented by Crecine suggest that neither optimization of community values nor externally determined events offer realistic explanations of the budgetary outcomes. "It is quite clear (from interviews) that the decision-makers *do not* see the problem as one of optimally balancing community resources, allocating funds among functions to achieve overall community goals, and the like."[52] Nor was there much evidence that decision makers perceived great pressures for higher or lower expenditures from groups. When pressures did occur, the common response was, "We just have so much money and we can't do everything."[53]

According to Crecine's findings, budgeting is primarily a bureaucratic process, operating—once revenue estimates are made—as a relatively closed system. The dominant decision-making method is incrementalism. As we have seen above, however, the local budget maker operates in a context that is determined partly by the macro-level factors of the community's economic resources, social composition, and local government structure, and the constraints imposed upon the city by its state government.

Incrementalism and innovation
In a nutshell, incremental budgeting permits the human mind to manage complexity. Local authorities limit their discretion over budgeting by the ways in which they make budget decisions. Their procedures facilitate speedy, relatively uncontroversial decisions. These decision-making procedures are highly mechanical in nature, and they narrow the choices available to financial officials. Because they are so widely accepted as proper ways for government officials to make their

budget decisions, they serve to inhibit individual officials who would depart from custom in order to innovate. Budget-making procedures thus tend to keep policies of local governments conservative. The budget is a resistant instrument that discourages local policy makers from seeking large amounts of money for new programs.

The simplistic criteria of decisions that are used by local budget makers may help them to cope with complexities of political and economic issues, as well as of fragmented institutions, but they provide little encouragement to those who would use the budget process as the vehicle for program planning or those expecting innovations in the use of public money. The budgetary process tends to project past choices into the future. The programmatic reformer, like the proponent of PPB, must be optimistic to approach the budget maker with a vision of change. The budget system is operated not by officials with compelling sympathies for the program but by officials who use their own past decisions as principal criteria for current decisions and who devise non-programmatic decision-making rules in order to reduce deficits or to distribute surpluses.

Summary

In this chapter we have identified the fiscal-policy options available to local governmental officials and have explained the choices that officials make. Our subject has been one of the most vital resources in urban politics: money. We have identified the major revenue sources of local governments and the major elements of local expenditures. We have found that most revenues come from property taxes, state aids, service charges, and borrowing. The single most important category of local expenditure is education; public utilities, highways, welfare, health, hospitals, police, interest on debt, and other such items take what is left.

We have tried to do more than simply to identify fiscal intake and outgo. We have examined critical differences in the expenditure and revenue patterns of local governments and traced these differences to community social, economic, and political characteristics. From macro perspective, these patterns suggest a lack of individuality or innovation in budgeting. Our discussion of budget-making procedures reinforces this conclusion. Officials do not make budget policy after a thorough review of all the relevant conditions. They rely instead upon mechanical procedures that boil down the potential criteria to very few. Although this tendency is not so strong as to preclude all possibility of innovation, budgeting is a conservative force that militates against introduction of new programs through the local government financial system. Innovations must first be accepted by other officials and must be presented to budget makers only after they have achieved such wide acceptance as to be considered commitments to be honored by the financial officers.

This treatment of revenues and expenditures does not exhaust our interest in local-government policies. Although it is tempting to assume that levels of spending reflect—or produce—the levels of service that residents of a municipality enjoy, this assumption is not valid. Spending is only one ingredient in determining the level of service provided. After budget makers have provided an "adequate" amount of money, other officials must allocate their funds to purchase the right mixture of skilled personnel, suitable facilities, and supplies and equipment. Some determinants of public-service levels are not subject to the control of local officials. They include the sources and severity of problems in the client population, as well as the attraction of the local community for technical and professional people who must be recruited if certain programs are to succeed.[54] The policies financed by local expenditures are the subjects of the chapters which follow.

Notes

1. One exception to this rule is Pennsylvania's so-called tax anything law, in which cities may, in general, tax anything not already taxed by the state.
2. James A. Maxwell, *Financing State and Local Government* (Washington, D.C.: Brookings Institution, 1965), p. 143.
3. Rarely, if ever, are local property assessments actually based on market value. Properties are typically undervalued, and the limited staffs of assessment offices often permit valuations to remain unchanged over decades. Properties in areas with rapidly rising land values thus may still be assessed at much less than their true values. It may also be noted that in local governments not characterized by pristine integrity, assessments have sometimes been manipulated by local officials.
4. Real property most commonly subject to property taxes includes land, dwelling units, office buildings, factories, and the like.
5. *Allocating Tax Burdens and Government Benefits by Income Class* (New York: Tax Foundation, 1967), p. 7.
6. Walter Heller, *New Dimensions of Political Economy* (New York: Norton, 1967), p. 153.
7. Elizabeth Likert David, "Public Preferences and State-Local Taxes," in Harvey Brazer, ed., *Essays in State and Local Finance* (Ann Arbor: University of Michigan Institute of Public Administration, 1967), pp. 74–106.
8. James Q. Wilson and Edward C. Banfield, "Public Regardingness as a Value Premise in Voting Behavior," *American Political Science Review*, 58 (December 1964), 876–887.
9. See, for example, John F. Due, "Studies of State-Local Tax Influences on Industrial Location," *National Tax Journal*, 14 (1961), 163–173.
10. L. L. Ecker-Racz, quoted in Heller, p. 126.
11. Charles A. Beard, *American Government and Politics*, 4th ed. (New York: Macmillan, 1924), p. 727.
12. Louis H. Masotti and Don R. Bowen, "Communities and Budgets: The Sociology of Municipal Expenditures," *Urban Affairs Quarterly*, 1 (1965), 39.
13. Robert C. Wood, *1400 Governments* (Garden City, N.Y.: Doubleday, 1964), pp. 39–40.
14. For supporting evidence, see Solomon Fabricant, *The Trend of Government Activity in the United States Since 1900* (New York: National Bureau of Economic Research, 1952),

pp. 112–129; Harvey Brazer, *City Expenditures in the United States* (New York: National Bureau of Economic Research, 1959), p. 29; and Otto Davis and George H. Harris, Jr., "A Political Approach to a Theory of Public Expenditures: The Case of Municipalities," *National Tax Journal, 19* (September 1966), 259–275.

15. Oliver P. Williams et al., *Suburban Differences and Metropolitan Policies* (Philadelphia: University of Pennsylvania Press, 1965), p. 111.
16. David, *op. cit.*, p. 86.
17. See the mixed findings in Brazer, *op. cit.*; and Davis and Harris, *op. cit.*
18. Richard Spangler, "The Effect of Population Growth on State and Local Government Expenditures," *National Tax Journal, 16* (June 1963), 193–196.
19. Amos H. Hawley, "Metropolitan Population and Municipal Government Expenditures in Central Cities," *Journal of Social Issues, 7* (1951), 100–108; Robert L. Lineberry and Edmund P. Fowler, "Reformism and Public Policies in American Cities," *American Political Science Review, 61* (September 1967), 701–716; Brazer, *op. cit.*; and Wood, *op. cit.*
20. Lineberry and Fowler, p. 712.
21. See *ibid.*; and Terry N. Clark, "Community Structure, Decision-Making, Budget Expenditures and Urban Renewal in 51 American Communities," *American Sociological Review, 33* (August 1968), 576–593.
22. Gerhard Lenski, *The Religious Factor* (Garden City, N.Y.: Doubleday, 1961), pp. 152ff.
23. Alan Campbell and Seymour Sacks, *Metropolitan America* (New York: Free Press, 1967), chap. 2.
24. Ira Sharkansky, "Economic and Political Correlates of State Government Expenditures: General Tendencies and Deviant Cases," *Midwest Journal of Political Science, 11* (May 1967), 173–192.
25. *Ibid.*, p. 191.
26. Lineberry and Fowler, pp. 707–708.
27. Clark, *op. cit.*, p. 588.
28. Bernard Booms, "City Governmental Form and Public Expenditure Levels," *National Tax Journal, 19* (June 1966), 187–199.
29. V. O. Key, Jr., *Southern Politics* (New York: Knopf, 1951), pp. 298–314; and Duane Lockard, *New England State Politics* (Princeton, N.J.: Princeton University Press, 1959), pp. 320–340.
30. Ira Sharkansky, *Spending in the American States* (Skokie, Ill.: Rand McNally, 1968).
31. Edmund P. Fowler and Robert L. Lineberry, "The Comparative Analysis of Urban Policy: Canada and the United States," in Harlan Hahn, ed., *People and Politics in Urban Society* (Beverly Hills, Calif.: Sage, 1972), pp. 345–368.
32. John C. Bollens et al., *Exploring the Metropolitan Community* (Berkeley: University of California Press, 1961), pp. 258–268.
33. John E. Horton and Wayne E. Thompson, "Powerlessness and Political Negativism," *American Journal of Sociology 67* (March 1962), 485–493.
34. Aaron Wildavsky, *The Politics of the Budgetary Process* (Boston: Little, Brown, 1964), pp. 1–3.
35. On national budgetary politics, see *ibid.* Studies of budget making at the state level include Thomas Anton, *The Politics of State Expenditure in Illinois* (Urbana: University of Illinois Press, 1966); and Ira Sharkansky, *The Politics of Taxing and Spending* (Indianapolis: Bobbs-Merrill, 1969), chap. 4. The most sophisticated study of budgetary policy making in urban government is John P. Crecine, *Governmental Problem Solving: A Computer Simulation of Municipal Budgeting* (Skokie, Ill.: Rand McNally, 1969). Our discussion of the process of determining municipal expenditures has benefited from Crecine's penetrating treatments of Detroit, Pittsburgh, and Cleveland.
36. Crecine, pp. 32–34, 192.
37. *Ibid.*, p. 39.
38. Wildavsky, pp. 18–31.

39. Crecine, p. 67.
40. *Ibid.,* p. 74.
41. Wildavsky, pp. 47–48.
42. Richard Fenno, "The House Appropriations Committee as a Political System: The Problem of Integration," *American Political Science Review,* 56 (June 1962), 310–324.
43. Crecine, *op. cit.,* p. 207.
44. Charles Francis Bastable, quoted in Mabel Walker, *Municipal Expenditures* (Baltimore: Johns Hopkins, 1930), p. 37.
45. Wildavsky, pp. 16–18.
46. Crecine, p. 52.
47. The uncontrollability of municipal budgeting (specifically in school districts) is emphasized as a major perception of decision makers in James David Barber, *Government by Committee* (Skokie, Ill.: Rand McNally, 1966).
48. *Ibid.*
49. See Crecine, *op. cit.*
50. *Ibid.,* chap. 9.
51. *Ibid.,* pp. 9ff.
52. *Ibid.,* p. 38.
53. *Ibid.,* p. 189.
54. For an assessment of some factors that limit the capacity of expenditures to ensure the desired level of service, see Ira Sharkansky, ed., *Policy Analysis in Political Science* (Chicago: Markham, 1970), chap. 4.

chapter 8

Education and public policy

By whatever standard we employ, the largest economic enterprise in the United States is the Department of Defense. But next in size and scope is the business of educating an urban population. Defending the nation against its enemies, real, potential, or (according to some critics) imaginary, consumed approximately $78.3 billion in fiscal 1972. Public schooling was easily the second most expensive public investment, accounting for $48.7 billion of state, local, and national expenditures. But, whereas the Department of Defense is highly centralized administratively, and is even housed in the continent's largest single office building, the American educational system is the responsibility of the fifty states and 22,000 school districts. Although each district is regulated by state government, it has considerable autonomy buttressed by American insistence upon local control of schools. The decentralization of the public school system parallels the decentralization and fragmentation of municipal governments themselves. In the Chicago SMSA, for example, there are 327 school districts, in Houston 48, and in Providence 35.

Education has come a long way since Sir William Berkeley, governor of the Virginia colony, observed in 1677 that "Thank God there are no free schools or printing; . . . for learning has brought disobedience and heresy into the world, and printing has divulged them. . . . God keep us from both." Today education is an integral part of the American dream. Education contributes significantly to the nation's economic growth, providing millions of people with training for occupational roles. Americans have a high regard for their public school system. Almost 90 percent of the residents of six metropolitan areas studied by Basil G. Zimmer and Amos H. Hawley reported that they were satisfied with their schools.[1] The major exception to the glowing reviews of the public schools is found in the racial ghettos. There ancient facilities, overworked teachers, and crime and drugs often combine to produce a joyless environment.

Schools and Politics

The contours of conflict

The apolitical and nonpartisan character of American education is a fundamental part of the national credo. But the notion of citizen control of schools, an equally pervasive precept, makes education an object of citizen concern and, inevitably, of political conflict.[2] The structure and organization of local school districts reflect the tensions between the conflicting goals of citizen accountability and educational autonomy. In important respects, the organization of school districts parallels the council-manager system of municipal government. A lay school board has the responsibility to make policy, establish budgets, and hire and fire the superintendent. Like the city manager, the superintendent is thought of as a professional, mobile, and nonpolitical administrator.

About a quarter of the nation's school boards are appointed, but the great majority are elected. The kinds of people who sit on the boards has been the subject of frequent research. The earliest such study is the now classic report by George S. Counts, who published the results of his survey of 6400 board members in 1927.[3] He found that three-fourths of American school-board members were businessmen or professionals and that only a handful (about 3 percent) were members of the working class. Over the years, Counts' study has been repeated many times, with similar results. Businessmen still dominate and the working class has little representation. Most recently, Robert L. Crain, who studied school desegregation in eight northern cities, found that all but ten of the sixty-nine board members in those cities came from business or professional positions.[4]

Board members face, not only the tensions between *citizen control* and the *freeing of education from politics,* but also a conflict between their own legal responsibility for educational policy and the professional credos of educators. Most professional educators believe that education is too important to be left to amateurs like parents and school-board members. Board members find themselves caught between their statutory obligations to govern the schools, and educators' demands for noninterference. Given their limited time and lack of expertise in educational questions, boards typically defer to the superintendent on all matters not plainly political. Educators like it that way. The school superintendent has the same kinds of political resources as does the city manager: time, control of technical information, training, experience, and a near-monopoly of administrative routine.

Citizens, like school boards, ordinarily defer to the professional judgment of school administrators. But because education accounts for the largest single portion of the local tax dollar and because the educational system is believed to be a potent force for molding a new generation, the schools cannot be immune from political controversy. Educational conflict tends to center around three principal issues—taxes and spending, the content of the curriculum, and race—although the quality of the athletic program sometimes overshadows all other issues.

As a general rule, there is less conflict over education in upper-status communities, where there is broad consensus that education is the avenue to an attractive future. Such communities spend generously on school plants and teachers' salaries. In heterogeneous central cities, riddled as they are with racial, class, and ethnic strife, the schools may become the battlegrounds. Youngstown, Ohio, is a case in point: After the defeat of six successive bond referenda and the depletion of operating funds, the schools closed for four months in the fall of 1968. Finally, on May 7, 1969, Youngstown voters passed a school bond referendum by a less-than-overwhelming majority of 57.2 percent. The school year 1971 marked the record low point in the voters' tolerance for school bond issues: Only 46.7 percent survived their referenda. Americans may still value education, but find themselves increasingly annoyed by the property tax and its inequities.

Conflicts over curriculum seem less intense than financial or racial conflicts. In recent years, citizen protests over football programs and their suspicions that socialism was being taught in the schools have abated somewhat, but the issue of sex education may have taken their place. Some parents have pressured boards not to allow or to eliminate already existing sex-education programs from the schools, while others have urged the superiority of classroom programs to the more casual sort of sex education. The issue of race is a pervasive one in the schools, and will be discussed later in this chapter.

Bureaucrats and teachers

In some interesting ways, the public-school teacher and the policeman share common role orientations and occupational frustrations. Both perform important public functions, and both see themselves as receiving little pay and relatively little public esteem. Although the political value system stresses the public accountability of both groups, teachers and policemen consider themselves the experts on their own jobs and resent public interference. Both teachers and policemen tend to be concerned with status and authority, and both are bound by intricate rules and regulations, yet faced with actual situations in which their discretion and autonomy are maximal. And, for both, there are wide gulfs between the idealism of the training period and the realities of practice. Just as the patrolman is graduated from the academy filled with the most up-to-date theories of police science, the teacher emerges from the university steeped in the latest theories of curriculum construction. Prepared to forge the best possible teaching program, the teacher discovers that curriculum policy is made higher up in an aged and entrenched educational bureaucracy. In New York City, for example, individual teachers play almost no role whatever in the formulation of curriculum policy, a task undertaken by a vast corps of bureaucrats in the city school administration at 110 Livingston Street.[5]

The most obvious differences between policemen and teachers are, first, that teachers are more commonly recruited from the middle class and, second, that teachers are overwhelmingly female. Several occupational strains of teachers can be traced to these class and sex characteristics. Teachers suffer some inconsistency in class and status. Although they consider themselves and are considered by the public to belong to a middle-class occupation, their salaries commonly run below the wages of union members. Although a 1963 study of occupational prestige found that the public ranked teachers twenty-ninth of ninety occupations listed,[6] median salaries for the equally prestigious occupations of "accountant for a large business" and "owner of a factory that employs about a hundred people," range from two to five times higher than that for teachers' salaries. Teachers thus suffer from what sociologists call *status inconsistency*.[7]

The social-class position of American teachers is complicated by the high proportion of women in the profession, even though now a much larger proportion of teachers are men than in years past. Today almost one-third of all teachers and a majority of secondary-school teachers are male. Most women who enter teaching are from middle-class origins, but most men are from working-class origins and seek upward mobility. Men who enter the formerly feminine domain of teaching, however, do not expect to make long-term careers of it. Most want to use teaching as a stepping-stone to higher positions, particularly in school administration. Few men, however, ever advance beyond the classroom. Most male teachers, Zeigler found, are thus unhappy with their vocational choices, and their unhappiness intensifies with the years. The frustration level of male teachers is high: Their mobility aspirations are unfulfilled, and they feel they are doing "women's work"—and receiving "women's wages" for it. The male teacher is thus, in Zeigler's words, "the underclass of the teaching profession, a rebel in a female system."[8]

Male or female, most teachers' political expressions are implicitly conservative. In the classroom, the teacher rarely addresses controversial subjects. More precisely, controversial subjects are handled, if at all, noncontroversially. To the degree that teachers cultivate points of view about the American political system, they emphasize a faith in it that borders on chauvinism. In Zeigler's words:

> The classroom operates basically to reinforce a belief in the desirability of maintaining the status quo. It is very doubtful that the classroom experiences of students encourage them toward radical politics. If there is brain washing in the high schools, it is clearly not for indoctrination in socialism; rather, it appears aimed at the production of optimistic, uncritical citizens.[9]

Almost all American teachers are organized in political-interest groups, the largest of which is the National Education Association. The state affiliates of the NEA are among the most active and, according to legislators, the most influential legislative lobbies in the state houses. The NEA is an organization that emphasizes a professional image of teachers paralleling the professional orientations of such groups as the American Institute of Architects, the American Bar Association, and the American Medical Association. The NEA, however, includes in its ranks—and frequently in its leadership—superintendents, principals, and other administrators. According to its chief rival, the American Federation of Teachers, this inclusion makes the NEA a "company union." The AFT, an affiliate of the AFL–CIO, admits only teachers and emulates labor unions in its tactics. This teachers' union makes many upwardly mobile teachers uncomfortable, for union membership is ordinarily incompatible with middle-class status. The AFT thus appeals mainly to urban, male secondary-school teachers, whose frustration levels and status inconsistencies are most marked and whose working-class backgrounds make them most sympathetic to trade unionism.

Although the AFT has been active in many northern cities, nearly one-third of its national membership is drawn from the New York system. There, the 35,000 AFT members constitute the majority of the city's 45,000 teachers. The New York affiliate has been willing to use the strike as a bargaining weapon. Its most bitter and widely publicized dispute was that with the city school board over the latter's plan to decentralize New York schools. After the central school board had given neighborhood boards some autonomy in operating community schools, some black and Puerto Rican boards attempted to rid themselves of certain white teachers. The AFT, insisting, as do unions everywhere, that members have a right not to be summarily dismissed from their positions, opposed the local boards. Leaders of the minority groups, particularly in the Ocean Hill-Brownsville area of Brooklyn, insisted upon the right to control their own schools and claimed that many white teachers discriminated against black students. The conflict was long and bitter and resulted in a strike that lasted for many weeks.

Race and the Schools

The segregation problem

Robert Dentler has argued that "the most urgent urban educational challenge of the day is not curriculum or instruction. It is the challenge of changing race relations."[10] From Washington to the local community, race is the most controversial of all educational issues. The problem has numerous dimensions, including (1) the demands for *community control* of ghetto schools; (2) the great debate, associated with Berkeley psychologist Arthur Jensen, about racial differences in learning capacity; (3) differences in school quality from black to white neighborhoods; and (4) the old school desegregation issue and its contemporary manifestation—busing. For other minority groups, these as well as other issues—the problem of bilingualism in the education of Spanish-heritage children, for example—are also crucial.

Segregation by race in public schools is of two types: *de jure* (required by law) and *de facto* (resulting from socioeconomic circumstances). *De jure* segregation was declared a violation of the "equal protection" clause of the Fourteenth Amendment in the Supreme Court's 1954 decision in *Brown* v. *Board of Education of Topeka,* which theoretically put an end to legally sanctioned segregation in seventeen southern and border states. The Court ordered school systems in those states to desegregate their schools with "all deliberate speed." But seven years after the *Brown* decision the percentage of southern black children in schools with Whites ranged from zero in Mississippi, Alabama, and South Carolina, to 1.5 in Texas. Observers calculated that at the rate of integration in 1954–1961, it would take 3180 years to desegregate southern schools.[11] The pace quickened, however, with the passage of the Civil Rights Act of 1964. This required the U.S. Office of Education to cut off funds to schools that failed to establish and execute desegregation plans. It also authorized the U.S. Attorney General to initiate legal proceedings to hasten desegregation. A few of these plans involved the mandatory busing of black children to previously white schools (and, infrequently, vice versa). Quickly, *forced busing* became the hottest political issue on the domestic scene. The outcry against busing extended from one end of Pennsylvania Avenue to the other, and from Washington to the local school board. The Supreme Court upheld the busing alternative in *Swann* v. *Charlotte-Mecklenburg County Schools* (1971) as a remedy for the vestiges of *de jure* segregation. The school bus, after all, is a familiar

American institution. Two-fifths of the nation's school children were bused to school before *Swann,* including countless black children transported miles past white schools to attend a segregated one.

De facto segregation is a straightforward function of neighborhood segregation in housing and of geographical attendance zones. *Neighborhood schools* means that students living in black neighborhoods go to black schools and students living in white neighborhoods go to white schools. As we shall see in Chapter 12, residential segregation has continued unchanged in cities since Blacks first arrived in the city. Although *de facto* segregation is not technically a product of public policy, local boards have often intensified school segregation by deliberate manipulation of policy. Careful drawing of attendance zones, teacher assignments, construction of new schools in the heart of segregated neighborhoods rather than on the periphery, and other subtle practices reinforced black-and-white school patterns. If segregation has negative effects on pupils, *de facto* segregation is no less serious than *de jure* segregation. According to the Civil Rights Commission, "racial isolation, whether or not sanctioned by law, damages Negro students by adversely affecting both their attitudes and achievement."[12] Nonetheless, both Congress and the courts have been reluctant to hold *de facto* segregation based on the neighborhood-school concept in violation of the Constitution.

Today, the South—the historic bastion of *de jure* segregation—is considerably more desegregated than the North, where *de facto* patterns prevail. After a decade of vigorous legal and political pressure, states like Mississippi and Alabama have taken the lead in the percentages of black children in formerly all-white schools. Table 8.1 provides the evidence. In 1970 Philadelphia had only 8.2 percent of its black children in majority-white schools, and the figures for such places as Cleveland (4.0 percent) and Chicago (2.8 percent) were even lower.

Table 8.1 *School Desegregation, 1971*

	Percentage of black students attending		
Region	All-black schools	80–100 percent black schools	Majority white schools
North	11.2%	57.1%	27.8%
Border	24.2	60.9	30.5
South	9.2	32.2	43.9

SOURCE: United States Bureau of the Census, *Statistical Abstract, 1972* (Washington, D.C.: Government Printing Office, 1972), p. 119.

The policy alternatives and the policy impacts: What, if anything, works?

Barring deliberate alteration via public policy (e.g., massive school busing), school segregation follows inevitably from two factors: neighborhood housing segregation and the neighborhood school. One long-run solution to the segregated school, of course, is housing desegregation. But progress on this front, as we will show (pp. 000–000) has been nil. Short-run policy alternatives for equalizing educational opportunity to minority children are of two kinds, *desegregation* and *compensatory education*. Only Massachusetts has enacted legislation specifically limiting the proportion of black students in any school (50 percent), although other states have undertaken policies to discourage racial concentration.[13] Because of slow progress on the desegregation front, some have sworn off that battle in favor of a program of compensatory education for minority children. Compensatory programs accept the reality of segregated schools, but demand enrichment and special services to disadvantaged children. A coalition of "strange bedfellows" —antiintegration Whites, many educators, President Nixon, and some black activists—have led the battle for compensation instead of integration. Stokeley Carmichael and Charles V. Hamilton, two articulate proponents of Black Power, have argued that "the real need at present is not integration but quality education."[14] Title I of the 1965 Elementary and Secondary Education Act was designed to pour compensatory funds into schools serving poor areas.

Unfortunately, the evidence on the policy impact of both compensatory education and integration via busing is very mixed. Let us consider each in turn. Compensatory programs, it appears, have fallen short of uplifting the motivation and achievement of minority children. The most highly touted compensatory program of them all was designed to give disadvantaged children a "Head Start" with intensive preschool nurturing. Evidence on the impact of the Head Start program, however, indicates some short-term, but few long-term, effects in motivating disadvantaged children.[15]

The evidence on integration is also mixed. It is a canon of integrationist belief that minority children placed in integrated environments will evidence improved motivation and achievement. Some research suggests these results. The Coleman report, commissioned by the Civil Rights Act of 1964 and representing the most thorough study of school performance ever conducted, found that performance of minority children in integrated schools was better than those in segregated schools, and that integration did not adversely affect middle-class children. If correct, this represents the optimal solution to racial equality, with minority performance elevated without diminution of middle-class performance. On the other hand, Harvard sociologist

David Armor, himself a strong advocate of integrated education, reviewed "The Evidence on Busing,"[16] and found it mostly negative. Minority children who were bused showed no appreciable improvement on five dimensions of educational performance (achievement, aspiration, self-concept, race relations, and educational attainment). Control groups of unbused children did as well as bused groups on each dimension. Armor's evidence on busing, however, has been vigorously attacked as biased and selective. His own mentor and fellow Harvard sociologist Thomas Pettigrew, in a rebuttal to Armor's "Evidence on Busing," contended that Armor's evidence ignored studies which showed busing successful, failed to meet scholarly standards for documentation, and established unrealistic standards for success.[17] The evidence must, therefore, be read as inconclusive.

What, then, if anything, works? The evidence is clear on one point at least: no one should expect spectacular changes from a little cross-town transportation or from extra dollars dumped into ghetto schools. Overcoming the disabilities of generations of racial inequality does not yield easily to educational reforms. As with many policy issues, the problem is as much one of goal identification than goal attainment. If an integrated society is a policy goal, then integrated schools are to be preferred in their own right, regardless of the educational consequences. If segregation is either desired or unalterable, then a policy of compensatory education, mixed perhaps with a strong dose of community control, might be preferred. Schools are not autonomous institutions, but are part of society itself. Outside the family, they are the dominant social institutions for millions of children and teachers. Schools are important not only for what they *produce* in learning, but for what they *are*.

Inequality in Education

Americans have always thought of public education as the great equalizer. The tradition of education as a guarantor of social mobility is as old as Horace Mann's establishment of common schools in Massachusetts and as contemporary as the demand for equal educational opportunity for minority children. The road from rags to riches almost always leads through the schoolhouse. Some suspect, however, that the schools do not equalize opportunity but rather perpetuate existing social inequality. If middle-class communities generally provide the best schools and the best teachers, schools cannot do much equalizing. Educational inequality can be seen at both macro and micro levels. At the macro level, there are inequalities of resources among the states, among districts within states, and among schools within particular districts. Micro-level inequality appears as differences in the backgrounds and intellects of individual students and the impact of education on equalizing those inequalities.

Inequality of resources

Some schools, especially those in affluent suburbs, contain superior teachers, working in modern educational "modules," operating fully equipped science and language laboratories, well-stocked libraries, and diverse extracurricular programs. Other schools, especially those in rural and core-city areas, operate in ramshackle facilities with harassed and overworked teachers, where every special program hangs by a fiscal thread. In the Detroit metropolitan area, for example, twenty-five suburban school districts spend an average of $500 per pupil per year more than does the city of Detroit. In the core city of Detroit, almost one-third of the school buildings in use today were constructed during the administration of President Ulysses S. Grant. James B. Conant, former president of Harvard University and a long-time observer of the public schools, notes that "the contrast in money available to the schools in a wealthy suburb and to the schools in a large city jolt one's notion of the meaning of educational opportunity."[18]

One explanation of resource inequality lies in state-to-state differences in wealth. Substantial inequalities also exist among districts within states and within particular districts. These differences are often associated with resource and income differences of states, districts, and neighborhoods. If one believes that high expenditures produce quality education, then one should, if at all possible, locate one's family in an affluent area of an affluent district in an affluent state, and then take care that his fellow citizens support school taxes and bond referenda. Only a handful of families, of course, can make such decisions.

DIFFERENCES AMONG STATES   Of the $48.7 billion spent on elementary and secondary public education in 1972, the federal government contributed less than 10 percent. In the average state, per-pupil expenditures for education was $930, but expenditure for education was $1466 in New York while per-pupil outlays in Alabama and Arkansas were only $543 and $601 respectively. The wealth of a state is commonly used to explain these differences in spending. Although there are exceptions, poor states typically rank at the bottom of the spending heap with wealthy states at the top. This remains true, even though poor states tax their residents heavily for education. Heavy tax burdens and low tax yields are the chronic plight of poor states and poor districts. Although almost all states have equalization programs to even out differences between their poor and rich districts, very few such programs actually equalize educational finance. A typical equalization formula will weigh state aid to poorer districts and districts which make greater tax effort, but many formulas are riddled with exceptions and confusions. The result is that wealthy districts typically outspend their poorer counterparts within the state, and state aid sometimes favors the already favored.

DIFFERENCES AMONG DISTRICTS   On December 23, 1971, a federal court in Texas handed the Texas legislature a novel Christmas present by declaring the state's educational finance system unconstitutional. It ordered the legislature to develop a new scheme which did not discriminate against children in poor school districts. The decision in *Rodriguez* v. *San Antonio Independent School District* paralleled an earlier decision by the California Supreme Court in the case of *Serrano* v. *Priest* (1971). Dimitrio Rodriguez, a parent in San Antonio's impoverished Edgewood district, contended that his tax rates were higher than those of taxpayers in affluent districts, and that Edgewood's per-pupil expenditures were still shockingly inferior to those in affluent districts. Table 8.2 presents some data submitted in behalf of Rodriguez's position. The pattern of poor district-high tax burdens-low tax yields versus rich district-low tax burden-high tax yields is readily apparent in the San Antonio area. Such variations in taxable wealth from district to district make education a function of wealth. As the *Wall Street Journal* observed:

In America, "free" public education is for sale. You buy a good or bad school for your child when you buy a house. You pay the bill when you pay the annual property taxes on your home.

Table 8.2   *Relationship Among Market Value of Taxable Property, Tax Rates, and Tax Yield in Texas School Districts, 1970*

Market value of taxable property per pupil	Tax rate per $100	Tax yield per pupil
Above $100,000 (10 districts)	$0.31	$585
$100,000–$50,000 (26 districts)	0.38	262
$50,000–$30,000 (30 districts)	0.55	213
$30,000–$10,000 (40 districts)	0.72	162
Below $10,000 (4 districts)	0.70	60

SOURCE: Joel Berke, affidavit submitted in behalf of plaintiff, *Rodriguez* v. *San Antonio Independent School District*, United States District Court, Western District of Texas, San Antonio Division, October 1, 1971, p. 13.

Not only is public schooling for sale. It is also priced more erratically than perhaps any other product. You may pay a lot and get an inferior school. Or, you may pay relatively little and come away with a first-class institution. Generally, the poor pay more and get less.[19]

The issue raised by Dimitrio Rodriguez, John Anthony Serrano, and plaintiffs in several other states is whether the states, forbidden by the Fourteenth Amendment of the U.S. Constitution to deny "equal protection of the laws," can permit educational resources to be a function of the wealth of parents and their neighbors. In recent years, state and lower federal courts have rejected finance systems based upon the local property tax and ordered new systems that did not discriminate against lower income school districts. Yet the cases raised as many questions as they solved: Did per-pupil expenditures have to be equalized from the neighborhood to the state line? Must states assume the entire burden of school finance? Would impoverished big-city districts or impoverished rural districts be the beneficiaries? Did money have anything to do with the quality of education, in any case? In March 1973, the United States Supreme Court overturned by the narrowest of margins (a 5 to 4 decision) the lower court decision in *Rodriguez*, arguing that the decision on school finance belonged to legislatures rather than the courts. The narrowness of the decision as well as the political activities of educational interest groups at the state level suggest, however, that the issue of interdistrict inequality has not been laid to rest.

DIFFERENCES WITHIN DISTRICTS   Within a school district itself, there are often marked differences among schools, programs, and teachers serving various neighborhoods. Patricia Cayo Sexton examined elementary and secondary schools in Detroit and discovered strong correlations between income levels of neighborhoods and the quality of their schools. She measured educational quality in several ways, including class size, teacher training, availability of extracurricular programs, and age and nature of facilities. Schools in upper-income neighborhoods had (1) newer buildings, (2) more libraries, labs, and other special facilities, (3) smaller classes, (4) better-trained teachers, (5) more extensive extracurricular offerings, and, incredibly enough, (6) more frequent provision of free lunch and free milk programs.[20] These differences were more closely related to the social class than to the racial characteristics of various neighborhoods. Such patterns of intradistrict inequalities are repeated in city after city, although they are not so universal and seldom so extreme as interstate and interdistrict differences.

The issue of intradistrict differences in school quality has become a lively legal topic, most notably in the District of Columbia. Even though 90 percent of the school population of the nation's capital is Black, white neighborhoods still received the lion's share of school services. Julius Hobson, a black parent and member of the D.C. Board of Education challenged this racially imbalanced pattern in the courts. In *Hobson* v. *Hansen* (1967), Judge Skelly Wright ordered an equalization of instructional expenditures in the District's schools to insure that white and well-off schools were not so favored.

THE PROBLEMATIC IMPACT OF MONEY   Even a brief review of educational finance should convince the reader that school taxation and expenditures are riddled with inequalities. The total picture resembles the biblical dictum that "To every one who has, more will be given, and he will have abundance, but from him who has not, even what he has will be taken away."[21] If the pattern of resource inequality is as commonplace as it appears, and *if school resources are translated into learning differences*, then educational inequalities would parallel and reinforce socioeconomic inequalities. The problem, however, is contained in the *if* clause. The link between the amount of money spent on schools and their educational effectiveness has never been established. The controversial "Coleman Report" (which we discuss in the next section) found that per pupil expenditures, facilities, and even teacher quality were far less important in explaining pupil achievement and motivation than were characteristics of the students themselves and their family backgrounds. Christopher Jencks and his associates summed up the impact of expenditures by bluntly arguing that "the evidence we have examined does not suggest that doubling expenditures would raise students' performance on standardized tests."[22] To be sure, improving test scores is not the only goal of the public schools, but it may be the only measure of educational output comparable from school to school.

The evidence on school resources is not yet conclusive. It does not prove that expenditures make *no* difference in learning, but neither does it prove that they make any appreciable difference. The level of school spending may be a trivial influence on school quality when compared with other considerations. One whose goal is to improve the schools is better advised to concern himself with the content of school services rather than the amount of money spent on them. This view, of course, does not make inequities in school finance equitable. Indeed, one view of school spending holds that low-income students deserve *higher* than average spending in order to buy the services and facilities which compensate for the advantages that middle- and upper-income children receive in their homes. Or, as John Coons, the legal eagle of school-finance cases, observed, "if money is inadequate to improve education, the residents of poor districts should at least have an equal opportunity to be disappointed by it."[23]

Micro inequalities

The macro sources of inequalities in the schools—financial variations among states, districts, and neighborhoods—look abstract and remote when compared to differences among individual students. The explanation of individual performance and achievement is as confused and unresolved as the debates over finance. The discussion about individual performance concerns *innate differences, cognitive abilities,* and *environmental differences* derived from the family.

THE IQ ISSUE   Although millions of IQ tests are given yearly around the world, and thousands of scholarly articles have described, attacked, and defended them, very little about IQ is settled, except perhaps that the tests are a good predictor of "making it" in white, middle-class society. Their controversiality is typified by Berkeley psychologist Arthur Jensen's lengthy report in the *Harvard Educational Review.* He finds that 80 percent of the variation in IQ is hereditary and also hinted at the possibility of racial differences in intelligence.[24] Jensen found himself roundly attacked by some fellow psychologists and had to meet his classes clandestinely as a consequence. Insofar as a large measure (estimates range from 45 up to Jensen's 80 percent) of IQ is inherited, and IQ is related to school performance, then at least some aspects of pupil performance do not yield to educational policy.

FAMILY, RACE, AND CLASS   By the time children enter grade school, they have already had important experiences. Attitudes toward authority and toward the political system—even their political party affiliations— are products of their family environment. Research on political socialization points to the family as the "foremost" or "dominant" agency of political learning.[25] The family's major role in socialization results from its near-monopoly of two critical resources—time and emotional attachment—during the formative years.

The role of the family in student achievement and motivation has been documented by the most extensive analysis of American education ever undertaken. This is the equal educational opportunity survey, usually called the Coleman report after its principal author, Professor James S. Coleman of Johns Hopkins University.[26] The study was commissioned by Congress under the Civil Rights Act of 1964 and was designed to investigate educational opportunities and race. The level of achievement, as Coleman discovered, differs markedly according to race. As Table 8.3 shows, Whites generally scored higher on achievement tests in both the first and twelfth grades. In addition to differences between races in educational achievement, there were also regional differences. Pupils in the metropolitan North were the highest achievers, whereas pupils in the nonmetropolitan South were the lowest achievers, regardless of race.

The single most important factor that Coleman found to explain educational achievement and motivation was the family background of the student. Whatever the school's impact, therefore, it is constrained by family circumstances. Coleman also investigated the effects of several

Table 8.3 *Median Test Scores for Pupils in First and Twelfth Grades, Fall 1965*

	Racial or ethnic group					
Grade	Puerto Ricans	American Indian	Mexican-American	Oriental-American	Black	White
First grade						
Verbal	45.8	53.0	50.0	56.6	43.4	54.1
Nonverbal	44.9	47.8	46.5	51.6	45.4	53.2
Twelfth grade						
Average of five						
tests	43.1	45.1	44.4	50.1	41.1	52.0

SOURCE: James S. Coleman et al., *Equality of Educational Opportunity* (Washington, D.C.: Government Printing Office, 1966), p. 20.

other factors. Consistent with most other evidence, he found that differences in facilities, finances, and curriculum were of scant importance, although teacher competence was not insignificant. Other than family background, however, the most important single predictor of pupil performance was the *composition of the student body*. Particularly for students from minority groups, accomplishment is stimulated by being in school with motivated and able peers. In the words of the report, "attributes of other students account for far more variation in the achievement of minority group children than do any attributes of school facilities and slightly more than do attributes of staff."[27] Elsewhere, Coleman summarized his results by concluding that "the educational resources provided by a child's fellow students are more important for his achievement than are the resources provided by the school board."[28]

Assessing the Impact of Education

Assessing the impact of the schools is an old, tricky, and controversial business. As far back as 1895, Dr. Joseph Mayer Rice, a pediatrician with an interest in the budding field of psychology, attempted to gauge the impact of the schools on spelling competence. He persuaded school officials to administer a spelling test he concocted to sixteen thousand students. The depressing results showed no relationship between the amount of time spent on spelling lessons and scores on Rice's tests. Dr. Rice soon became *persona non grata* in educational circles.[29] As with all measures of policy impact, the effectiveness of schools depends jointly upon the goals specified and the measures selected. (See our discussion of the measurement of policy impact on pp. 187–188.) People differ, of course, about both goals and measures. One Boston administrator viewed it this way: "How does one know whether a school is effective? Any teacher can tell just by walking through the halls. He sees whether the students are wearing coats and ties, whether they are orderly in the corridors, whether they are respectful of authority."[30] Others prefer standards more closely related to learning than orderliness.

The conventional wisdom about the impact of schools has received serious challenges in recent years. The controversy comes from three sources: (1) the discovery that resources are not very consistently related to pupil performance; (2) the emphasis on family background and IQ as the primary determinants of achievement; and (3) the uncertainty attached to both compensatory education and mandatory busing as agents of racial integration. Some of the most sobering conclusions of all regarding the impact of the schools are those of Christopher Jencks and his associates. Their findings about equality, family background, cognitive traits, and the schools may be summarized as follows:[31]

1. Family background and IQ are the most important determinants of school achievement, although they are not sufficient by themselves to explain differences in performance.
2. However measured (by teacher quality, money, facilities, programs, etc.) the equality of schools is far from a reality.
3. But, regardless of inequalities in the schools, school-related factors are trivial in accounting for differential pupil achievement.
4. And, whatever minor effects schools have on pupils are further vitiated by the miniscule correlations between education and later success, measured by occupational status, income, and job satisfaction.[31]

To the degree that equality is a desirable social goal, Jencks argues that there are more direct and effective ways of achieving it than through school reform. In the last analysis, though, all hitherto existing studies bear only on the schools as they are, not as they might be.[32] Whether some dramatic changes in them will make schools the equalizers some think they should be, can only be speculative. The challenge to educational policy is to establish (or reestablish) a link between the quality of the schools and the quality of life in an urban society.

Notes

1. Basil G. Zimmer and Amos H. Hawley, *Metropolitan Area Schools* (Beverly Hills, Calif: Sage, 1968), p. 86.
2. An excellent overview of educational politics is contained in Frederick M. Wirt and Michael Kirst, *The Political Web of American Schools* (Boston: Little-Brown, 1972).
3. George S. Counts, *The Social Composition of Boards of Education* (Chicago: University of Chicago, 1927).
4. Robert L. Crain, *The Politics of School Desegregation* (Chicago: Aldine, 1968), p. 180.
5. David Rogers, *110 Livingston Street* (New York: Random House, 1968); and Marilyn Gittell, *Participants and Participation: A Study of School Policy in New York City* (New York: Center for Urban Education, n.d.).

6. Robert W. Hodge et al., "Occupational Prestige in the United States: 1925–1963," in Reinhard Bendix and Seymour M. Lipset, eds., *Class, Status, and Power* (New York: Free Press, 1966), p. 324, Table 1.

7. Harmon Zeigler, *The Political Life of American Teachers* (Englewood Cliffs, N.J.: Prentice-Hall, 1967), p. 20.

8. *Ibid.*, p. 30; Patricia Cayo Sexton, *The Feminized Male: Classrooms, White Collars, and the Decline of Manliness* (New York: Vintage, 1969).

9. Zeigler, p. 119.

10. Robert A. Dentler et al., eds., *The Urban R's* (New York: Praeger, 1967), p. x.

11. Donald R. Matthews and James W. Prothro, "Stateways vs. Folkways: Critical Factors in Southern Reactions to *Brown* v. *Board of Education*," in G. Dietze, ed., *Essays on the American Constitution* (Englewood Cliffs, N.J.: Prentice-Hall, 1964), p. 144.

12. U.S. Commission on Civil Rights, *Racial Isolation in the Public Schools*, vol. 1 (Washington, D.C.: Government Printing Office, 1967), p. 190.

13. For a discussion of the Massachusetts Racial Imbalance Act, see Frank Levy, *Northern Schools and Civil Rights* (Chicago: Markham, 1971).

14. Stokeley Carmichael and Charles V. Hamilton, *Black Power* (New York: Vintage Books, 1967), p. 157.

15. Christopher Jencks et al., *Inequality: A Reassessment of the Effect of Family and Schooling in America* (New York: Basic Books, 1972), p. 88.

16. David Armor, "The Evidence on Busing," *The Public Interest*, no. 28 (Summer 1972), 90–126.

17. Thomas F. Pettigrew et al., "Busing: A Review of 'The Evidence,' " *The Public Interest*, no. 30 (Winter 1973), 88–118.

18. James B. Conant, *Slums and Suburbs* (New York: McGraw-Hill, 1961), p. 3.

19. *Wall Street Journal*, March 2, 1972, p. 1. Some of the best scholarly material on the inequality of resources problem can be found in Arthur Wise, *Rich Schools, Poor Schools* (Chicago: University of Chicago Press, 1967) and John E. Coons et al., *Private Wealth and Public Education* (Cambridge, Mass.: Harvard University Press, 1970).

20. Patricia Cayo Sexton, *Education and Income* (New York: Viking, 1961), pp. 16–17. See also Martin T. Katzman, *The Political Economy of Urban Schools* (Cambridge: Harvard University Press, 1971), chap. 3; Richard A. Berk and Alice Hartman, "Race and District Differences in Per Pupil Staffing Expenditures in Chicago Elementary Schools, 1970–1971," Center for Urban Affairs, Northwestern University, 1971; and James W. Guthrie, et al., "Educational Inequality, School Finance, and a Plan for the '70's," in Senate Select Committee on Equal Educational Opportunity, *Hearings*, vol. 7 (Washington, D.C.: Government Printing Office, 1970), pp. 3457–3458.

21. Matthew 28:29 (RSV).

22. Jencks, p. 93.

23. Quoted in *Wall Street Journal, op. cit.*

24. Arthur Jensen, "How Much Can We Boost IQ and Scholastic Achievement?" *Harvard Educational Review, 39* (1969), 1–123. Jensen's answer to his own question was, in brief, "very little." On the IQ debate, see also Richard Herrnstein, "IQ," *Atlantic* (September 1971), 43–64; William Labov, "Academic Ignorance and Black Intelligence," *Atlantic* (June 1972), 59–67; Hans Eysenck, *The IQ Argument* (New York: The Library Press, 1971); and Jencks, chap. 3.

25. These descriptions are used, respectively, by Herbert Hyman, *Political Socialization* (New York: Free Press, 1958), p. 69; and Richard E. Dawson and Kenneth Prewitt, *Political Socialization* (Boston: Little, Brown, 1969), p. 122.

26. James S. Coleman et al., *Equality of Educational Opportunity* (Washington, D.C.: Government Printing Office, 1966). For some commentary on the Coleman report by other social scientists, see Frederick Mosteller and Daniel P. Moynihan, eds., *On Equality of Educational Opportunity* (Cambridge, Mass.: Harvard University Press, 1972).

27. Coleman, p. 302.

28. James S. Coleman, "Toward Open Schools," *The Public Interest*, no. 9 (Fall 1967), 21.
29. Dr. Rice's story is told by Edward Wynne, *The Politics of School Accountability* (Berkeley, Calif.: McCutchan, 1972), p. 33.
30. Cited in Katzman, p. 19.
31. Jencks, *op. cit.*
32. For some critiques of the schools as they are, see Ivan Illich, *De-Schooling Society* (New York: Harper & Row, 1971); Mario Fantini et al., *Community Control and the Urban School* (New York: Praeger, 1970); and Charles E. Silberman, *Crisis in the Classroom* (New York: Random House, 1970).

chapter 9

Poverty, race,
and public policy

Disregarding the biblical warning that "the poor
shall never cease out of this land," President Lyndon
Baines Johnson, on August 20, 1964, signed the
Economic Opportunity Act. Speaking at the signing
ceremony in the White House Rose Garden, the
President declared this nation's commitment to
"eradicate poverty among its people." Armed with
the metaphor, if not the money, of the military, the
government inaugurated the War on Poverty. The
enemy, poverty, would prove to be as elusive and
difficult to define as the Vietcong, and the debate
over strategies would be only slightly less furious
than that over Southeast Asia. In the same year President Johnson signed the Civil Rights Act of 1964,
widely regarded as the most significant step ever
taken toward realization of the Fourteenth Amendment guarantee of "equal protection of the laws."
Both civil-rights and poverty policies had thus been
initiated in Washington, D.C., but both, especially
the latter, have deeply implicated urban governments
all over the nation.

The Problem of Poverty

Defining and discovering poverty

Poverty, of course, is a matter of definition. If the
relative approach is adopted, and the American poor
are compared to average Haitians or Ethiopians, then

Table 9.1 *Changes in the Number of Poor Persons, 1967–1971*

	Number of poor	Change from previous year
1967	27.8 million	*down* 741,000
1968	25.4 million	*down* 2.4 million
1969	24.3 million	*down* 1.1 million
1970	25.5 million	*up* 1.2 million
1971	25.6 million	*up* 100,000

Classified as poor in 1971

13 percent of all Americans
10 percent of all Whites
32 percent of all non-Whites

SOURCE: United States Bureau of the Census. Note that the Census Bureau definition varies according to number in family and place of residence. For example, in 1971, a nonfarm family of four with annual income of less than $4137 was considered poor.

one can virtually eradicate poverty in America with a flip of the definitional wrist. If, on the other hand, one emphasizes a standard of relative deprivation, or inequality of income, then there is plenty of poverty in the United States. Whether poverty is increasing or decreasing is a matter of the initial definition. The Census Bureau has developed a standard of living for an urban family of four and used it as a means to establish a *poverty level*. Using the Census Bureau standard, Table 9.1 provides data on poverty in the United States from 1967 to 1971. While the proportion of Americans poor by constant standards has been declining throughout the decade of the 1960s, the early years of the 1970s saw a reversal of this trend.

It is an interesting question in the sociology of knowledge to ask when exactly Americans began to discover their poor. During the 1950s, both popular and scholarly writers discussed the *affluent society* and a *people of plenty* and debated the meaning of leisure time. Although economists like John Kenneth Galbraith emphasized the presence of pockets of poverty in an otherwise well-off society, their emphasis on affluence captured more attention in that comfortable Republican decade. In many ways, it was the 1963 publication of Michael Harrington's *The Other America* that brought home the persistence of poverty in the affluent society. President John F. Kennedy himself was influenced by Harrington's account of how the other America lived—the day after the assassination, an adviser found a dog-eared copy of the book in the White House Oval Office—and had proposed a major legislative program addressed to poverty just before his death. President Johnson made the program a major ingredient in his Great Society package of legislation, adopted by the Eighty-Sixth Congress. But before we embark upon a discussion of the war on poverty and urban policy, it may be useful to describe the nature and structure of American poverty, from both community and individual perspectives.

Macro and micro distribution of poverty

Sometimes we think of the poor as concentrated mainly in the racial ghettos of our biggest cities or in the most rural backwoods of Appalachia. The pattern, however, is somewhat more complex. Statistically speaking, there is *proportionately* more poverty in rural areas than in metropolitan areas, but, *in absolute terms*, there is more poverty in metropolitan than in rural areas, simply because such a large proportion of the nation's population (about two-thirds) lives in metropolitan areas. Moreover, there is proportionately less poverty in the largest than in the smallest cities. The percentage of poor people is, for example, twice as high in Bryan, Texas, as in Dallas; in East St. Louis, Illinois, as in Chicago; and in Newburgh, New York, as in New York City. But again, because so many more people live in cities like Chicago, New York, and Dallas than in smaller ones, the absolute number—and the concentration—of poor people in major metropolitan areas is greater and offers greater challenges.

Within the metropolitan area itself, there are also important differences in the distribution of poverty. It is common to view metropolitan CCs as the havens of the poor and downtrodden and the suburbs as the homes of the white well-to-do. This image is, however, so oversimplified as to be seriously misleading. The size of the metropolitan area is a crucial variable in understanding the distribution of poverty within the metropolis. In the largest metropolitan areas, there is indeed a clear tendency for poorer people to reside in the CCs and wealthier ones to live in the suburbs, but this pattern reverses itself in the smaller metropolitan areas. In those with populations of less than 250,000, there are proportionately more poor people in the fringe areas than in the CCs. Within each CC, of course, there is a marked tendency for the poor to live in the oldest parts of town, where housing is cheapest. But the poor are not always separated by great physical distances from the wealthy. Some of the poorest neighborhoods in Washington, D.C., are within a short walk of affluent Georgetown. The socioeconomic distance between New York's Park Avenue and its slum dwellers is great, but the physical distance is surprisingly short.

Just as poverty is distributed on a macro scale, that is, among and within communities, it is also distributed on a micro scale. The probability of being poor varies from group to group and person to person. Certain types of families and individuals are especially likely to fall below this poverty line. Poverty is particularly concentrated among the aged, families headed by females, members of minority groups, and those with mental, emotional, physical, or occupational handicaps. In 1971 approximately 13 percent of all family units in the United States were classified by the government as poor, but, among the aged, the figure was twice as great. Among other groups about 10 percent of white families lived below the poverty line, but a third of the nonwhite families were poor. The differences in the proportions of poor and others are greater between races than between the old and not old, suggesting that being Black may be a more significant cause of poverty than being old. These disadvantages appear to be cumulative, so that being both old and Black significantly increases one's chances of being poor.

Myths and realities

American public opinion is riddled with myths and misunderstandings about poverty and the poor. Among them, we would surely have to include these:

1. *Most of the poor are unemployed.* Because most of the poor are, of course, either aged or under eighteen years of age, this myth is literally true. But the overwhelming proportion of employable poor are in fact employed, though at wages so low as to keep them below the poverty line. Among nonaged families with male heads, nearly all the men work. The poor are no exception. Among the poor, 87 percent of white and 91 percent of black male family heads work.
2. *Most of the poor are on welfare.* While the numbers of persons receiving welfare payments has increased rapidly, an estimated one-half to two-thirds of persons legally eligible for welfare receive none.[1]
3. *Poverty is a black problem.* Although a much larger proportion of Blacks than Whites (one-third versus 10 percent) are poor, a much larger *number* of Whites are poor. In fact, two-thirds of the poor are white.
4. *Most of the poor live in large CCs.* Among Blacks, most poverty is concentrated in big cities. Among Whites, however, there is more poverty in OCC areas. And, among both groups, a larger proportion of rural than urban dwellers are poor.

If myths about the *facts* of poverty are commonplace, then myths about its *causes* are even more widespread. Poverty is obviously a multicausal phenomenon, its sources ranging from physical and mental problems, to age, to inadequate opportunity, to the state of the national economy. Yet, most Americans cherish a simplistic view of poverty. Joe R. Feagin studied American attitudes toward poverty and concluded that "Americans still believe that God helps those who help themselves."[2] He asked a sample of the American population to list the major reasons why "there are poor people in this country." Their explanations, ranked by frequency of mention, included:

1. Lack of thrift and proper money management;
2. Lack of effort by the poor themselves;
3. Lack of ability and talent among poor people;
4. Loose morals and drunkenness;
5. Sickness and physical handicaps;
6. Low wages in some businesses and industries;
7. Failure of society to provide good schools for many Americans;
8. Prejudice and discrimination against Negroes;
9. Failure of private industry to provide enough jobs;
10. Being taken advantage of by rich people;
11. Just bad luck.

Clearly, Americans adhere to an individualistic, micro-level, explanation for poverty. Loose morals, drunkenness, laziness, and improper management, constitute the dominant explanations. Some social scientists share this individualistic perspective. Edward C. Banfield, for example, maintains that poverty is a function of the *present-orientedness* of the lower classes, who are congenitally incapable of foreseeing and planning for the future.[3]

Individualistic explanations, however, overlook some significant structural or macro-level explanations for poverty. For the poor who are concentrated on the farms, the mechanization of agriculture has helped to create their plight, even forcing some to flee to cities, where they are scarcely equipped for urban existence.[4] For those in the core cities, a deteriorating economy reduces economic opportunities even for the most energetic and well educated of the poor. To the degree that there are limited housing opportunities outside the CC for persons of low income, the poor suffer the worst schools and services in the metropolitan area and face the most stagnant economic circumstances. It is also true that practices of many businessmen add to the poverty of the poor. David Caplovitz, for example, studied consumer practices in poor neighborhoods and uncovered a consistent pattern of high prices, poor quality, high interest rates, and unethical merchandising.[5] Finally, as both liberals and conservatives alike concede, the welfare system works to perpetuate poverty through a series of selected disincentives (see our discussion below). As these considerations indicate, structural explanations for poverty should compete with individualistic explanations.

Being poor
So far poverty has been treated as if it were entirely a matter of having a low income. Being poor, however, means much more than having too little money to buy what others consider essential. During the summer of 1969, several U.S. senators and their families simulated poverty for a week by living on a welfare-budget diet. The results, dutifully reported to the press, were persistent hunger, constant exhaustion, chronic irritability, and general malaise. However much this noble experiment

dramatizes and personalizes poverty, it still fails to capture the multi-dimensional nature of being poor, especially because the poor cannot look forward to the weekend.

Research has identified numerous variables on which the poor differ from the rest of the population.[6] Although a mere catalogue cannot do justice to the interrelated characteristics of the culture of poverty, it may illustrate the life style of the poor. They are more likely to be victims of crime. They also are more likely to be victims of disease, mental illness, and malnutrition. The psychological costs of being poor are indicated by the much larger proportions of poor people who report being generally unhappy, by the higher incidence of mental illness among them, and by their feelings that they can do little to manipulate their own environment. This last feeling of social ineffectiveness is paralleled by a low sense of political efficacy and a high sense of political futility. The poor see the political world as alien, complicated, distant, and impervious to them. Poor neighborhoods have very weak systems of social ties and organizations; most socializing takes place within the extended families and immediate neighborhoods. Very few poor neighborhoods have produced indigenous community or group leaders, which makes all efforts to organize the poor very difficult. Leaders claiming to represent the poor have usually gained their status by reference to race, rather than to poverty alone. Family life among the poor often tends toward instability, sometimes fostered by welfare dependency. Family instability in turn produces higher levels of insecurity and occasionally deviant behavior among youth.[7]

Nonetheless, we should avoid the image of a nearly complete homogeneity of attitudes and behavior among the poor. No more than we would assume that every person whose income is over $10,000 thinks and behaves as does every other should we assume that all the poor are stamped from the same mold. Perhaps the most significant factor dividing the poor is race; conflict between Whites and Blacks overshadows whatever common interests are engendered by economic circumstances. The variety of belief and behavior patterns among the poor is particularly evident in political life. Political alienation, for example, is found more often among low-income groups than among the more affluent, but not all the poor are alienated. Even among the alienated, some express their hostility and isolation by withdrawal and nonparticipation, whereas others actively participate in ways that sedate members of the middle class would call deviant. The intensity of this *negative participation* may be expressed by voting against both incumbent office holders and referenda propositions. For some black Americans, participating in racial disorders is protest against the system. Authoritarian political attitudes, characterized by intolerance of dissenting views and hostility toward out-groups, also characterize many lower-class people, although the better educated among the poor are no more authoritarian than are other Americans. These observations on the political life of lower-class Americans suggest that, though some clear tendencies can be identified, the poor are certainly not a monolithic mass whose behavior can be perfectly predicted by their low incomes alone. But, even recognizing the variations among the poor, we may still agree with Harrington's political assessment:

> . . . The poor are politically invisible. It is one of the cruelest ironies of social life in advanced countries that the dispossessed at the bottom of society are unable to speak for themselves. The people of the other America do not, by far and large, belong to unions, to fraternal organizations, or to political parties. They are without lobbies of their own; they put forward no legislative program. As a group, they are atomized. They have no face; they have no voice.[8]

Fighting Poverty: Two Strategies

The welfare system

The traditional method for dealing with urban and rural poverty in the United States has been the public-welfare system. Public welfare is an administratively complex, even labyrinthine, set of specific programs, including (but not limited to):

1. Old-age, survivors', disability, and health insurance;
2. Aid to the blind, to the permanently and totally disabled, and to the aged;
3. Aid to families of dependent children;
4. Workmen's compensation;
5. Child-health and maternal services;
6. Unemployment compensation;
7. Mental-health services;
8. General relief.

Speaking broadly, welfare services may be classified as programs based on the social-insurance principle, for example, old-age, survivors', disability, and health insurance (commonly called *social security*); and those that provide such categorical assistance to the deserving poor as aid to families with dependent children. Welfare programs are a prototypical part of the cooperative federal system. They operate according to a maze of rules and regulations laid down by different governments, use multiple systems of support, and are administered by federal, state, and local agencies. About half the money for welfare programs comes from the federal government. The remainder is made up by combinations of state and local support that vary widely from state to state. But the day-to-day administration of the welfare system is usually decentralized among agencies of counties and other local governments, which employ thousands of social workers.

The public-welfare system has never been popular in America. To the public, welfare symbolizes social support for the indolent, paid for by taxing the hard-working. To the social workers charged with day-to-day operation of the system, it is riddled with red tape, complex rules and regulation, and it often fails to deal with the most pressing cases. Recipients feel the degradation attached to the "dole," dislike the surveillance of the system, and deplore the built-in disincentives to work. Among the public, the social workers, and even the recipients themselves, there remains the nagging suspicion that many people who prefer doles to work are being subsidized by the welfare system. Feagin asked his respondents for their attitudes about welfare recipients. Some of his results are indicated in Table 9.2. To say that welfare recipients are not popular with their fellow citizens would be an understatement. Most pointedly, overwhelming majorities of Americans suspect that hordes of able-bodied men are mooching out of the welfare trough instead of working. In fact, only about 1 percent of the nation's welfare recipients are able-bodied males, and state laws universally require that such persons actively seek work.[9] The actual breakdown of welfare recipients indicates that most of the other 99 percent are children without fathers, elderly, or physically and emotionally disabled. Very little evidence indicates that vast numbers of recipients are cheating the states and cities. Occasional purges of the welfare rolls usually reveal only 3 to 5 percent of ineligible recipients, and the costs of such investigations are often greater than the payments saved. The small proportion of ineligible recipients actually receiving aid is offset by the finding that at least twice as many people are eligible for aid as actually receive it.

The 1960s witnessed a *welfare explosion* of truly incredible proportions. Even though the number of poor persons actually declined from 1960–1970, the number of persons receiving welfare aid doubled! In 1971, the proportion of citizens receiving aid was 1 in 10 in Atlanta, 1 in 5 in Boston, 1 in 8 in Detroit, 1 in 7 in New York City, and 1 in 12 in Memphis. What accounts for the welfare explosion? Francis Fox Piven and Richard Cloward, in their provocative challenge to the welfare system,[10] argue that welfare rolls always rise in a period of civil disorder (such as the racial disorders of the 1960s), and represent the government's effort to ameliorate the crisis. Welfare payments permit the government to regulate the behavior of the poor, by denying payments to those with unacceptable behavior. Most of the welfare explosion of the 1960s took place in the aftermath of the riots of the period, and large proportions of the new recipients were black. Court rulings also expanded eligibility and reduced agency capriciousness in cutting off assistance. In 1969, for example, the Supreme Court struck down residency requirements as a condition for aid; in 1970, it held that residents were entitled to a trial-like hearing before an agency could terminate their assistance. In addition, the emergence of legal assistance programs through the war on poverty provided both information and legal aid for the poor in doing battle with welfare agencies. The National Welfare Rights Organization pressured local and state agencies to process applications expeditiously and to treat claimants more civilly.

Despite such expansions in the number of welfare recipients, the program has remained as unpopular with liberals and conservatives, masses and elites, experts and laymen. Some of the bluntest charges have been leveled by the National Advisory Committee on Civil Disorders:

> The Commission believes that our present system of public assistance contributes materially to the tensions and social disorganization that have led to civil disorders. The failures of the system alienate the taxpayers who support it, the social workers who administer it, and the poor who depend upon it. As one critic told the Commission, "The welfare system is designed to save money instead of people and tragically ends up doing neither."[11]

Among specific criticisms of the welfare strategy of attacking poverty are, first, that it contains built-in discouragement to advancement. Until recently all payments received from work were deducted from welfare payments that the individual or family could otherwise receive. If the mother of dependent children undertook to improve her economic lot by working part time, she would thus lose an amount of welfare aid equal to her wages. Under recent amendments, earnings of up to $30 a month will not be charged against welfare payments, but the discouragement is still apparent.

Table 9.2 *Public Perceptions of Welfare Programs*

	Agree	Disagree	Uncertain	Total
There are too many people receiving welfare money who should be working.	84	11	5	100
Many people getting welfare are *not* honest about their need.	71	17	12	100
A lot of people are moving to this state from other states just to get welfare money here.	41	31	28	100

SOURCE: Joe R. Feagin, "America's Welfare Stereotypes," *Social Science Quarterly,* 52 (March 1972), Table 1, p. 923.

Second, the coverage of the system is limited both in terms of money provided and of people included. Only five states provide payments high enough to lift poor persons above the Census Bureau's poverty level and many states pay less to recipients than their own law requires. Most poor persons, of course, do not receive welfare at all.

Third, there is wide variation both among and within states. In 1972 the monthly payments under the Aid to Dependent Children (ADC) program varied from $86.51 in Hawaii to $14.69 in Mississippi. The most important explanation for such variations is the variations in states' economic resources, and the poor in poor states are thus supported at low levels. That is, "the greater the need [for welfare], the less effort put out by the state to meet the need."[12] Moreover, local program administrators seem to have wide discretion in determining eligibility and payment levels, especially in the general relief program: People eligible in one jurisdiction may not be so in another.

Fourth, the public-welfare system is institutionalized charity and has the usual social stigma attached to such doles. Because eligibility requirements are complex and usually rigid, there is considerable personal investigation and long-term surveillance of recipients. The most extreme form is the *midnight raid,* in which a welfare agent checks to see if there is a man around the house of a mother receiving aid to dependent children, an agency practice the Supreme Court recently outlawed.

Fifth, the relations between social-welfare workers and clients are commonly "abrasive" and "brittle," in the Kerner Commission's words. The caseworker is forced into antagonistic relations with clients he is supposed to be assisting. Although the worker is expected to establish a high level of personal rapport so that he may be able to influence client behavior, he also plays the antagonistic role of investigator and "snoop." Like the policeman, the welfare worker is a symbol of society and its authority, a society in which the clients have so visibly not "made it." And, in the client-caseworker relationship there is an element of paternalism, which is not lost on the welfare recipient.

Although we oversimplify somewhat, the common thread linking most of the criticisms of the welfare system is the assumption that poverty is primarily an individual phenomenon, the solution to which lies in the distribution of some cash and material benefits to families and individuals, and scrutiny against undesirable behavior. The caseworker deals with individuals and families. His professional training—if he has had any—impels him toward individual uplift. But, if the poor as a group lack the political and economic resources to demand what they need, critics say, a philosophy of individual change represents, at best, only a holding action against poverty. Many critics argue that the welfare system is based upon the theory that *defects in socialization* are the cause of poverty but that, in fact, the cause lies in the social system. This shift from a micro to a macro perspective on poverty characterized the intellectual underpinnings of the war on poverty.

Warring on poverty—and city governments

If Harrington is right in claiming that the poor are invisible and political-ly powerless, why then did the national government declare an uncon-ditional war on poverty in 1964? The answer, of course, is that it was not the poor, but the experts—Daniel P. Moynihan calls them "professional reformers"—who launched the war on poverty. As Moynihan says, "the war on poverty was not declared at the behest of the poor: it was declared in their interest by persons confident of their own judgment in such matters."[13]

During the Kennedy administration, a group of Washington, D.C., bureaucrats, mostly in sub-Cabinet positions, came together informally to prepare legislation aimed at the problem of poverty in the United States. Although members of the group were divided among themselves on specific strategies, they universally held to a structural, as opposed to an individualistic, view of the causes of poverty. Such a perspective con-tained within it the seeds of a critique of traditional welfare policies, which they viewed as aimed at amelioration of individual problems rather than at institutional change. In the eyes of some members of the inner circle of poverty planners, public-welfare bureaucracies actually impeded antipoverty action, for they are more concerned with maintenance of their own organization than with major social change. In June 1963, President Kennedy gave Walter Heller, who as chairman of the Council of Economic Advisers had been a major figure in the planning, his support for the antipoverty legislation. Those plans were nearly complete when Kennedy's death placed Lyndon Johnson in the White House.

Despite some planners' fears, Johnson evinced immediate interest in the legislation then being prepared for Congress: "That's my kind of program. It will help people. I want you to move full speed ahead," he told Heller. Once the commitment to do something had been made, jockeying for support among elements of the federal bureaucracy followed. The Labor Department favored a major program of job re-training under its own administration. The Department of Health, Education, and Welfare favored major educational and health programs, though it was willing to provide some money to Labor for summer work programs. The Commerce Department favored loans to small entre-preneurs among the poor, whereas the Agriculture Department argued that there were surely as many poor farming entrepreneurs as there were poor businessmen. The Interior Department mentioned poverty among the Indians but did not formulate a program. These conflicts among the departments, as well as between the departments collectively and the Bureau of the Budget, became severe enough to threaten a delay in the legislative program. President Johnson appointed Sargent Shriver chairman of a task force to come up with a presentable program. After eight weeks of balancing, negotiating, and compromising, the task force drafted the legislation.

The result was a hastily forged compromise. The task force's most important contribution to the legislative package was the idea of an independent agency in the Executive Office of the President to administer the program. The Office of Economic Opportunity (OEO) thus became the nation's antipoverty agency. In both draft and final legislation the OEO was given the responsibility for administering several specific components of the war on poverty. The Job Corps was designed to provide education, vocational training, and work experience for youth. The Volunteers in Service to America (VISTA) program was envisioned as the domestic analogue of the Peace Corps, a group of volunteers who were to work in public projects or with community-action programs. The Head Start program, the least controversial of the programs, was to provide preschool training for disadvantaged youngsters. The Neighborhood Youth Corps would provide work experience and vocational training for youths living at home. The OEO was also charged with administrative responsibility for community-action programs.

There was a general belief among the poverty planners that local choice and flexibility should be maximal. As the circumstances of poverty varied from community to community, it was necessary to include a *decentralizing element* in the legislation. The planners differed in their views about the Community Action Agency, but most favored its inclusion. The local agencies would be directed by boards broadly representative of the communities and would tailor specific projects to meet local needs, even though they would be funded mainly by the federal government.

Three little words, however—"maximum feasible participation"—threw the whole community-action concept into intense controversy once the warriors headed for the battlefield. The phrase appeared, innocently enough, in the definition of a community-action project in Title II, Section 202(b) of the Economic Opportunity Act. Specifically, a CAP was defined as an agency that (1) would mobilize community resources for an attack on poverty, (2) provide services to eliminate poverty by improving human performance and the like, and (3) would be "developed, conducted, and administered with the maximum feasible participation of residents of the areas and members of the groups served." Even participants in the original planning disagree about the source of the phrase, for at first no one paid much attention to it. In congressional hearings on the bill, only Robert F. Kennedy made even incidental reference to maximum feasible participation. Moynihan has claimed that the intent of the framers was merely to ensure that the poor were, in fact, the beneficiaries of the programs. If the poor, particularly Blacks in the South, were "not sharing—that is, participating—in the benefits of the new program, Washington could intervene on the grounds that the requirements of the legislation were not being met."[14] In any event, no one, not even the most radical of the planners, intended the phrase to mean that the poor should be given control of the local programs. That some people, especially militant poverty workers, interpreted maximum feasible participation to mean policy control by the poor came to be the major political albatross of the war on poverty.

The draft legislation, maximum feasible participation and all, sailed through Congress with the minimum imaginable debate. Only a handful of changes were made in committee, and the bill passed both houses of Congress with comfortable majorities. Most of the opposition rhetoric was ideological, but even conservatives were cautious in their criticisms for fear of appearing to support poverty in an election year. Nearly all Democrats outside the South supported the legislation, and they were joined by most liberal Republicans. Opposition came mainly from southern Democrats and conservative Republicans, not an uncommon lineup against domestic social-welfare legislation.

The controversial cornerstone of the war on poverty was the local Community Action Agencies. The governing boards of the CAAs were to consist of representatives of three groups: public agencies, including the city government, school systems, and social-welfare agencies; private groups, including business, labor, and religious groups, and leaders of established minority groups like the NAACP; and representatives of the neighborhoods to be served by the programs. Local agencies could choose among a variety of programs authorized by the Economic Opportunity Act, including: (1) remedial or supplementary educational programs such as preschool day-care centers; (2) employment development, job training, and counseling; (3) health and vocational-rehabilitation programs, like health examinations and family-planning advice; (4) home management and improvement; (5) improving welfare services; (6) consumer-information projects; (7) legal aid; (8) creation of neighborhood centers and organizations; (9) VISTA and Job Corps activities; and (10) encouraging resident participation in the policy making of both the CAA itself and of such other public and private institutions as the traditional welfare programs.

For the most part, these CAAs were dominated by establishment forces within local communities, typically operated *for* the poor (at least some of the time), but rarely *by* the poor. Some local agencies, however, were soon engulfed in conflict over the implementation of the "maximum feasible participation" requirement. Spokesmen for the poor emphasized the need for *maximum* participation; city officials countered with emphasis on *feasible* participation. In San Francisco, for example, "the fight for maximum feasible participation evolved from a contest between the mayor and minority group spokesmen for control of the program into a succession of power struggles within the target areas and between them and the central administration."[15] The overwhelming proportions of the budgets and energies of the OEO nationally and the CAAs locally went to such programs as child development, Head Start, health services, and social services, but OEO activities in legal aid and neighborhood organization made the headlines. Many observers, including some congressmen, a few journalists, a number of mayors, and former Vice-President Agnew, were certain that the OEO was dominated by radicals intent on redistributing political power from elected officials to self-appointed spokesmen for the poor. The subsequent trials and tribulations of the war on poverty could fill (and have filled) volumes.[16]

The impact of the war on poverty: was it a failure?

The second Nixon inaugural was followed immediately by administration plans to dismantle the Office of Economic Opportunity. Howard Phillips, newly appointed as director of the agency, announced on February 3, 1973, that the program was a "failure." Was it? The answer depends, as in all questions of policy evaluation, on one's perceptions of program measurement and policy goals. The simplest indicator—counting the number of poor in the United States before the inception of the program and after several years of its operation—is grossly misleading, particularly because the proportion of the poor had been declining long before the dawn of antipoverty programs. Any thorough evaluation of the impact of the war on poverty would have to take account of both short-range, ameliorative goals and long-range goals like reduction in the probability of poverty over several generations. Against such benefits to be attributed to antipoverty efforts certain costs would have to be tallied. Perhaps, as some critics have feared, the class and racial antagonisms fostered by the antipoverty program constitute costs whose total cannot yet be measured. No public policy is devoid of spillover effects, and no discussion of policy impact can be complete without taking account of them. As measurement of those effects is difficult, if not impossible, we must emphasize that studies of the impact of the poverty program are both tentative and incomplete.

An exacting cost-benefit analysis of the decentralized and multifaceted war on poverty very likely will never be available. A few studies indicate, however, that the program's effectiveness varied enormously from community to community. Clark and Hopkins evaluated a dozen CAAs and classified them into three categories of effectiveness. Five were relatively effective (New Haven, Syracuse, Newark, Paterson, and

Minneapolis), four were mixed (New York, Washington, San Francisco, and Los Angeles) and three were relatively ineffective (Chicago, Cleveland, and Boston).[17] The more effective programs were relatively autonomous and free from political intervention by local officials; they were program, rather than patronage, oriented; and they were led by sophisticated boards with real political power. James Vanecko studied fifty local antipoverty programs and concluded that the most effective ones emphasized community organization and mobilization of the poor.[18] Both of these studies indicate that politically independent and activist-oriented boards coexist with the most effective kinds of local agencies. Obviously, these are also the most controversial politically.

New directions in fighting poverty
The decade of the 1960s was marked by the transition from a micro to a macro strategy of fighting poverty. By the beginning of the 1970s the traditional welfare system was under fire from numerous quarters. A number of economists were proposing a *negative income tax* or a *guaranteed annual income.*[19] The OEO experimented with a guaranteed annual income for 1359 families in New Jersey and Pennsylvania. Despite the fears of critics, virtually all the families with guaranteed incomes worked hard and even improved their employment circumstances. Earnings increased for 53 percent of the families receiving assistance and for 43 percent of a control group receiving no aid.[20] Whether or not the implications of such experiments will lay the foundation for public policy in the 1970s, however, time alone can tell.

Support among both masses and elites for some form of guaranteed annual income has increased from miniscule levels in the early 1960s to significant pluralities by the 1970s. One study of public opinion found that a plurality of Americans (42 percent) preferred an income-maintenance program to the traditional welfare system (37 percent) and to the option of cutting off all assistance to the poor (9 percent).[21] President Nixon proposed a *family assistance program* (FAP) which would overhaul the welfare system and establish a small (about $1600) minimum income for each family, provided that family heads accept "suitable" jobs when offered them or enroll in job training programs. The Family Assistance Plan passed the House of Representatives but met repeated defeats in the Senate, and early in 1973 President Nixon withdrew his own support from continued legislative efforts in its behalf.

Race, Poverty, and the "Culture of Poverty"
Novelists like John Steinbeck, anthropologists like Elliot Liebow and Oscar Lewis, and social critics like Michael Harrington have all emphasized the *culture of poverty*, which tends to perpetuate poverty from

generation to generation. The President's Council of Economic Advisers put this argument in the following terms:

> Poverty breeds poverty. A poor individual or family has a high probability of staying poor. Low incomes carry with them high risks of illness; limitations on mobility; limited access to education, information, and training. Poor parents cannot give their children the opportunity for better health and education needed to improve their lot. Lack of motivation, hope, and incentive is a more subtle but not less powerful barrier than lack of financial means. Thus the cruel legacy of poverty is passed from parents to children.[22]

Just as a child inherits his religious affiliation, his party identification, and his place of residence from his parents, so he inherits a predisposition toward being poor or being rich. Stated simply, the culture-of-poverty theory holds that people stay poor because they are born that way.

One blunt fact is that a near-majority of non-Whites are poor, whereas a majority of Whites are not. Non-Whites may be predominantly poor, not because they inherit a predisposition toward poverty, but because they inherit a genetic, but socially conspicuous, characteristic of skin color. The inheritance-of-poverty theory is that being born poor keeps people poor, whereas the inheritance-of-race theory is that being born black keeps Blacks poor. The satisfactory resolution of this conflict between theories would be most significant in prescribing the content of any policy designed to eliminate poverty among nonwhite groups. If the inheritance-of-poverty theory is correct, then antipoverty strategy should not differ according to the race of the clientele. But if the inheritance-of-race theory better explains poverty among nonwhite groups, a strategy intended to eliminate discrimination might seem more likely to be effective than would one designed merely to break the poverty cycle.

The most imaginative research into the issue of inheritance of race versus inheritance of poverty has been conducted by Otis Dudley Duncan.[23] In a national random sample of working Americans, Duncan identified an annual income differential between Whites and Blacks of $3790. What explains this income gap? Using statistical techniques that permit apportionment of variation among specific factors, Duncan concluded that $1010 of the differential can be explained by family characteristics (for example, father's education and occupation and number of siblings in the family). The rest, however, is attributable to differences in educational attainment ($520), to occupational discrimination resulting from racial factors ($830), and to a residual category that Duncan has called *income discrimination*. Even when family backgrounds and educational and occupational disadvantages suffered by Blacks are accounted for, black men thus still receive considerably lower wages than do white men of comparable backgrounds, educations, and occupations. Although family-background factors are important, they are not nearly as important as are the collective effects of disadvantages of educational, job, and income discrimination. In Duncan's words, "Negroes (that is, disproportionate numbers of them) are poor mainly because they are Negroes and are defined and treated as such by our society. . . . Their poverty stems largely not from the legacy of poverty, but from the legacy of race."[24] This conclusion does not deny the existence of a poverty cycle, but it does suggest that for nonwhite Americans race is a more significant barrier to social mobility than are backgrounds of poverty. It directs our attention to public policies designed to eliminate racial discrimination.

Civil Rights and Urban Policy

Most of the initiative for civil-rights legislation and policy has come from the federal government, and most of the federal initiative has been that of the Supreme Court or the executive rather than of Congress. The policies are not those of urban governments, although they affect urbanites. Many of these federal efforts are discussed in other chapters and need be only briefly mentioned here:

1. The 1954 Supreme Court decision (*Brown* v. *Board of Education of Topeka*) requiring desegregation of all public schools;
2. A succession of court decisions requiring equal access to public facilities like swimming pools;
3. The 1957 and 1960 Civil Rights Acts, which established a civil-rights section in the Department of Justice and authorized the U.S. Attorney General to sue to enjoin interference with voting rights in federal elections;
4. The Civil Rights Act of 1964, which forbade discrimination in public accommodations and in programs or facilities supported by federal funds, like public schools;
5. The Voting Rights Act of 1965, which sent federal registrars into several southern states to register voters;
6. The 1968 open-housing legislation, which forbade discrimination in the sale or rental of housing and, by January 1, 1970, covered nearly 80 percent of all housing units;
7. The U.S. Supreme Court decision (*Jones* v. *Mayer*) in 1968 that held all discrimination in the sale or rental of public housing to violate section 1982, Title 42, of the U.S. Civil Code.

Relatively few initiatives in civil-rights policy have come from the states, although New York, New Jersey, and Connecticut were early innovators in housing, employment, and public-accommodations legislation. Even fewer initiatives have come from local governments.

Summary

We have described in this chapter two related policy areas involving expansion of citizens' opportunities—the war on poverty, designed to broaden economic opportunities; and civil-rights legislation, designed to expand political and legal opportunities. Of the two, the poverty program has been fought out mostly in the terrain of local politics. Poverty, of course, is a multifaceted problem, with economic, racial, psychological, political, and social dimensions. Poverty questions are especially intertwined with issues of race. Although there may be a *culture of poverty* that perpetuates poverty over generations, a major barrier to Blacks is not this legacy alone but the effects of past and present racial discrimination.

Still, one of the principal myths about poverty is that it is mainly a problem of minority groups packed in racial ghettos. Although poverty is disproportionately concentrated in minority groups, a majority of the poor are White. Another myth is that most of the poor are now being served by conventional welfare systems. The inadequacies of the welfare apparatus were one of many reasons for the inauguration of the war on poverty. If poverty were a matter only of having too little money, it could be eliminated (at least statistically) with comparative ease. But the complexity of the problem makes it resistant to solution by public policy. Whether the war on poverty has made a significant impact on the lives of the poor is a question that—though we have offered some fragmentary evidence—cannot now be determined.

Notes

1. Joe R. Feagin, "America's Welfare Stereotypes," *Social Science Quarterly*, 52 (March 1972), 929.
2. Joe R. Feagin, "Poverty: We Still Believe That God Helps Those Who Help Themselves," *Psychology Today* (November 1972), 101–110ff.
3. Edward C. Banfield, *The Unheavenly City* (Boston: Little, Brown, 1968), chaps. 3, 6, 10.
4. Niles Hansen, *Rural Poverty and the Urban Crisis* (Bloomington, Ind.: Indiana University Press, 1970).
5. David Caplovitz, *The Poor Pay More* (New York: Free Press, 1963); see also, Frederick Sturdivant and Walter T. Wilhelm, "Poverty, Minorities, and Consumer Exploitation," *Social Science Quarterly*, 49 (December 1968), 643–650.
6. An excellent summary of this research is contained in the bibliographical essay by Zahava D. Blum and Peter Rossi, "Social Class Research and Images of the Poor: A Bibliographical Review," in Daniel P. Moynihan, ed., *On Understanding Poverty* (New York: Basic Books, 1969), pp. 343–398.
7. Notable for its emphasis on the importance of family structure, especially among Blacks, is the "Moynihan Report," reprinted in Lee Rainwater and William Yancey, eds., *The Moynihan Report and the Politics of Controversy* (Cambridge, Mass.: The MIT Press, 1967).
8. Michael Harrington, *The Other America* (New York: Macmillan, 1963), p. 14.
9. Feagin, "America's Welfare Stereotypes," p. 924.

10. *Regulating the Poor: The Functions of Public Welfare* (New York: Pantheon, 1971).
11. National Advisory Commission on Civil Disorders, *Report* (Washington, D.C.: Government Printing Office, 1968), p. 252.
12. Richard E. Dawson and James A. Robinson, "The Politics of Welfare," in Herbert Jacob and Kenneth N. Vines, eds., *Politics in the American States* (Boston: Little, Brown, 1965), p. 403.
13. Daniel P. Moynihan, *Maximum Feasible Misunderstanding* (New York: The Free Press, 1969), pp. 23, 25. For accounts of the origin of the Economic Opportunity Act, see Richard Blumenthal, "Antipoverty and the Community Action Program," in Allan P. Sindler, ed., *American Political Institutions and Public Policy* (Boston: Little, Brown, 1969), pp. 180–229; John C. Donovan, *The Politics of Poverty* (New York: Pegasus, 1967); and Sar A. Levitan, *The Great Society's Poor Law* (Baltimore: Johns Hopkins Press, 1969).
14. Moynihan, p. 87.
15. Richard Kraemer, *Participation of the Poor* (Englewood Cliffs, N.J.: Prentice-Hall, 1969), p. 66.
16. See, for example, Moynihan, *op. cit.*; Kraemer, *ibid.*; and Levitan, *op. cit.*
17. Kenneth B. Clark and Jeanette Hopkins, *A Relevant War on Poverty* (New York: Harper & Row, 1968), chap. 5.
18. James Vanecko, "Community Mobilization and Institutional Change: The Influence of the Community Action Program in Large Cities," *Social Science Quarterly, 50* (December 1969), 609–630.
19. See, for example, the President's Commission on Income Maintenance, *Poverty Amid Plenty* (Washington, D.C.: Government Printing Office, 1969).
20. See the report on this experiment in Fred J. Cook, "When You Just Give Money to the Poor," *The New York Times Magazine*, May 3, 1970, pp. 23ff. On the Nixon administration's efforts to pass a Family Assistance Plan, see Daniel P. Moynihan, *The Politics of a Guaranteed Income* (New York: Random House, 1973).
21. William Watts and Lloyd A. Free, *State of the Nation* (New York: Universe, 1973), pp. 173–174.
22. *1964 Economic Report of the President* (Washington, D.C.: Government Printing Office, 1964), pp. 69–70. For a critique of the culture-of-poverty concept, see Charles A. Valentine, *Culture and Poverty* (Chicago: University of Chicago Press, 1968).
23. Otis Dudley Duncan, "Inheritance of Race or Inheritance of Poverty?" in Daniel P. Moynihan, ed., *On Understanding Poverty*, pp. 85–110.
24. *Ibid.*, p. 87.

chapter 10

Crime and law enforcement

Crime is a perennial growth stock in any listing of urban problems. Political campaigns from mayor to the presidency are fought over law and order issues; the number and variety of devices for home security now threaten to literalize the cliché that "a man's home is his castle"; the growth of private security forces has been so rapid that private policemen now outnumber the public police by a 2 to 1 ratio. A national survey of Americans' hopes and fears conducted in 1972 lists violence, drug addiction, and crime as the first-rank problem of public concern.[1] Evidence from population surveys shows that about half the women and a fifth of the men hesitate to walk in public places at night for fear of muggings, stabbings, and other acts of violence. Even the high and mighty (like Senator John Stennis) are not immune from street violence. In the schools, some fear that the latest version of the "three R's" has become rape, robbery, and rebellion. Americans' fears that the crime rate is increasing seem to be verified annually by the Federal Bureau of Investigation's *Uniform Crime Reports*. The 1972 figures on the crime rate indicated a slight dip in the crime *rate* but a continued increase nonetheless occurred in some major types of crime.

Crime in Urban Society

How much crime?

The President's Commission on Law Enforcement and the Administration of Justice divided crimes into two categories: *crimes against the person* and *crimes against property*. It discovered that reported instances of both types had increased markedly since the first national crime statistics were assembled in 1933.[2] Crimes against property (burglary, motor-vehicle theft, and larceny of more than $50) had multiplied much more rapidly, however, than crimes against the person (homicide, forcible rape, robbery, and aggravated assault). There is also evidence to suggest that white-collar crime—for example, frauds, stock manipulations, antitrust violations, and similar transgressions by middle-class businessmen —is also rising. Political corruption appears in countless indictments against mayors, former governors, state legislators, and national party officials. The Watergate affair suggests that crime and corruption can be found in high places.

Actually it is pretty clear that FBI statistics, which are based entirely upon offenses known to or reported to the police, considerably understate the actual incidence of crime. Studies undertaken for the President's Commission used population surveys to uncover actual rates of criminal activity and revealed that the number of crimes against the person reported to interviewers was almost twice as great as FBI reports indicated. The amount of crime against property was more than twice as large. In some areas, the amount of unreported crime was nearly ten times greater than reported crime.

The problem of unreported crime suggests some of the difficulties in determining precisely how much crime there is in the contemporary United States. It is also difficult to ascertain whether there has been an increase in the crime *rate* in the last few years. Statistics have sometimes been used to demonstrate that American society has experienced an increase in *criminality*. Several objections can be leveled at this use of crime statistics, however. First, valid comparison of crime rates over time requires a constant relation between reported and unreported crime. Even if the amount of crime were the same today as it was in 1933 and if twice as many crimes were reported today, a purely statistical crime wave could be said to have occurred. There is reason to suspect, however, that more crime is being reported today, partly because of improved police efficiency and reporting practices. American police forces have never ben particularly good at statistics. For some cities, crime reporting to the FBI has been wildly unrealistic. Chicago for many years reported twice as much robbery as New York, a city twice its size.

At one point in the late 1940s, the FBI discontinued reporting New York City's crime statistics because it no longer believed them. Newark and Jersey City, quite comparable in many respects, reported differences as large as 17 to 1 in certain categories of offenses. Crime reporting in New York and elsewhere has improved in recent years. Citizens also seem to be reporting more crime to the police, partly because more people have insurance, and payment of claims requires reports to the police.

In addition to the nature of crime statistics themselves, there are several other reasons for doubting arguments that criminality is increasing. They involve changes in the social and economic structure of society. Youth, the most crime-prone age group (more fifteen-year-olds are arrested than are people of any other age, and sixteen-year-olds are close behind), constitutes a larger proportion of the population now than ever before, making an increase in the rate of crime partly an artifact of an increasingly youthful population. One out of every six males under the age of 18 will be hauled into court at some point. A crime rate is also a function of the activities that society proscribes. In one sense, there are more criminals simply because there are more laws to be broken today. The police officer in Michigan, for example, must uphold an estimated 50,000 laws! Urbanization itself is associated with high crime rates, and Americans are increasingly an urban people. Finally, an affluent society provides more temptations to prospective criminals. In the long run, the question of how much crime there is in American society is, in our view, largely unanswerable. It is safe to say that *reported* crime rates have increased faster than the population. But beyond that generalization, we are reluctant to go.

We do think that the available evidence offers good reason for discounting some near-hysterical fears about "crime in the streets." Although urbanites seem to fear most the possibility of danger from a stranger or group of strangers on the streets, in fact, the most serious crimes involving personal violence (aggravated assault, forcible rape, and homicide) are far more likely to be committed by acquaintances, "best friends," or spouses than by strangers. One's chances of falling victim to a homicide are slim in any case (about 5 per 100,000 population, approximately the same probability as for death from fire or drowning and about half as likely as death from a fall), but the chances are *eight times as great* that one will be done in by a "friend," relative, or spouse than by a perfect stranger. (In a sense, the individual is his own worst enemy, for suicides are twice as common as homicides.)

The causes of crime

Arguing about the causes of any social phenomenon is tricky in any case, but criminology involves so many complexities and competing perspectives that it is especially susceptible to wrangling. Certainly one confusing factor is the legal definition of crime. Presumably, few would disagree that homicide is a crime, but many disagree about whether possession of narcotics, for example, should be classified as a crime. It strikes some as incongruous that selling marijuana is a crime, whereas selling tobacco is not.

The explanations for crime most commonly offered tend to be either a micro type (related to the individual) or a macro type (related to the society). The micro, or individual, explanation rests upon the assumption of moral accountability. Each man is considered sufficiently rational and responsible so that a criminal act can be viewed as a moral dereliction: essentially a "bad-man" explanation of criminality. The rise and acceptance of psychology and psychiatry, however, have spread recognition of the psychodynamic aspects of criminal behavior. In this view, crime is considered a function of psychological disturbances, rather than a function of character defects. More recently, some social and biological scientists have unearthed evidence that proneness to crime may be related to genetic characteristics.[3]

Macro-level explanations of crime stress socioeconomic circumstances like poverty, deprivation, discrimination, and defects in the socialization process as factors contributing to criminal behavior. Such explanations are buttressed by the fact that there is more crime among the poor than among the wealthy; victimization rates are also eight to ten times higher for ghetto dwellers than for the more affluent. (Interestingly, surveys by Louis Harris and others have consistently revealed that *fear* of crime is inversely related to the *probability* of criminal victimization; middle-class people are thus more anxious about crime than are lower-class people.)

These competing explanations of crime have important implications both for the impact of law-enforcement policy and for the choice of an appropriate societal response to crime. If crime is interpreted as the result of moral irresponsibility or as a function of biopsychological forces, the response to crime should be directed at the individual. Depending upon one's assessment of the cause, punishment, reform, or rehabilitation will seem the most appropriate response. This individualistic orientation toward crime will encourage selection from among a range of responses, including incarceration (if the individual criminal is held morally culpable) to psychiatric treatment or even, conceivably, genetic manipulation—an issue that may open up a legal and moral quagmire in time to come. If, on the other hand, criminal behavior is viewed as a function of macro factors, caused by problems in the larger social system, responses to crime will take very different forms. One aspect of this view is that society itself is partly responsible for crime, either because it tolerates conditions that engender crime or because it has failed to prevent crime.

Crime and heroin

One of the newest and most controversial aspects of the crime problem is the link between criminal behavior and the use of hard drugs. The drug problem ranges from the local school to international diplomacy, even to charges that the CIA masterminded a "connection" to supply drugs from Southeast Asia.[4] Yet hard evidence on hard drugs and crime is hard to come by. Little is known for sure about (1) the numbers of heroin users; (2) the proportion of crimes committed by users; (3) whether these users would be prone to crime even in the absence of their addictions; and (4) the actual causes of the apparent increases in use. Fragmentary evidence from several studies indicates that usage is growing and that it is associated with crime. Between 1967 and 1971, for example, Los Angeles authorities reported a threefold increase in the number of deaths from addiction. In Boston, there may have been a tenfold increase in usage during the 1960s. Estimates of the proportion of crimes against property committed by addicts ranges from 25 to 67 percent.[5]

The policy alternatives advocated to remedy the heroin-crime connection have been controversial and fraught with uncertainty about their impacts. Generally, three alternatives are debated: *cutting off the sources, conventional law enforcement,* and *decriminalization.* As with policy alternatives in many areas, each of these shades at some point into the others. Moreover, none promises complete effectiveness and each entails certain spillover effects. Eliminating sources falls largely in the domain of international politics and worldwide law enforcement. If someone would defoliate Turkish and Asian opium fields, supplies to domestic users should dry up. But unless the strategy is foolproof, what heroin remains in circulation could become vastly more expensive, and addicts might redouble their efforts to pay the higher prices. Conventional law enforcement has been directed at both addicts and pushers. But enforcement against pushers may also drive up the price by eliminating sources. On the other hand, enforcement against addicts may reduce demand and hence lower the price, making heroin within the reach of more novice users. Recognizing these difficulties, some have despaired of all legal strategies and advocated instead decriminalization of heroin, coupled with either government-supplied heroin or a methadone-maintenance program. Aside from its political unpopularity, there is no assurance that decriminalization schemes would be free of negative spillovers. Wider availability might increase the incidence of addiction. Moreover, addicts will not necessarily eschew crime and join the economic mainstream even if heroin or methadone is provided free of cost. Crime committed *by* addicts is not necessarily crime committed *because of* addiction. Moreover, the criminal organizations that now sell drugs might turn to some other illegal business if their present market disappears.

The Police

Police and their roles

We begin our discussion of the police by reproducing a description, recorded by the President's Commission on Law Enforcement and the Administration of Justice, of an actual tour of duty by two officers, whom the commission called Jones and Smith:

After receiving routine instructions . . . Officers Jones and Smith located the car to which they were assigned and started out for the area in which they would spend their tour of duty. While en route, they received instructions from the dispatcher to handle a fight in an alley. Upon arrival, they found a group of young men surrounded by their parents, wives, and children.

The mother of B was the complainant. She claimed that C had attacked her son with a knife and she demanded that C be arrested and jailed. C readily admitted that he had been fighting with B, but he claimed that he had just tried to protect A. C had been drinking and was very belligerent. He indicated a readiness to take on anyone and everyone, including the police. . . .

A attempted to explain the situation. . . . A's mother-in-law interrupted at this time to explain that A was innocent; that the fight was B's fault. B's mother did not stand for this accusation and entered the fray.

The confusion spread . . . Officers Jones and Smith decided to take the participants to the station where conditions would make possible a more orderly inquiry. [Finally, at the station] C was formally arrested and charged with disorderly conduct. By charging C with disorderly conduct rather than a more serious crime, the officers felt that they were saving themselves some paperwork. They felt that their action in letting the mother sign a complaint against the "loudmouthed" C had served to pacify her.

[After filling out arrest reports on C, Jones and Smith were dispatched to two successive domestic quarrels, in which wives complained that their husbands had beaten them up and then left the houses. After advising each to obtain a warrant or peace bond, they were then dispatched to two noisy parties, advised each host to "hold it down," and stopped for cokes before placing themselves back in service. After breaking up a rowdy crowd at a hotdog stand, arresting a drunk, and warning instead of ticketing a Vietnam veteran for a traffic violation, the officers requested permission from the dispatcher to eat. Instead, he sent them back to the first party they had quieted. Again denying their request to eat, the dispatcher sent them to a public pool, the scene of a stabbing.]

There were three persons present—two lifeguards and a watchman. One of the lifeguards had been knifed. He was placed in a police car and the officers started off to the nearest hospital. . . . [They] later returned to the scene but found no additional information. . . . The reports were turned in for attention by the detectives.

The officers then, without asking, took their meal break, after which they reported that they had completed their work on the stabbing. They were dispatched to a party disturbance. . . .[6]

Without knowing whether Jones' and Smith's tour is typical, we can nonetheless deduce from it some useful generalizations, particularly the degree of *ambiguity* and the amount of *discretion* involved in performing the police function. Ambiguity and discretion are mutually reinforcing. Both situations and legal codes (e.g., those dealing with disturbing the peace) are ambiguous, and the more ambiguous the law and the immediate situation are, the greater are the discretion and judgment required of the police officer.[7]

POLICE ROLES   Social scientists and experienced policemen seem to agree that the police play three important roles in urban society. Joe Fink, commander of New York City's Ninth Precinct has enumerated them: "One [role] is law enforcement. Another is keeping the peace. The third is furnishing services."[8] Wilson, one of the leading academic

Table 10.1   *Citizen Complaints Radioed to Police Vehicles, Syracuse Police Department, June 3–9, 1966[a]*

Calls[b]	Number in sample	Percentage
Information gathering	69	22.1
Book and check	2	
Get a report	67	
Service	117	37.5
Accidents, illnesses,		
ambulance calls	42	
Animals	8	
Assist a person	1	
Drunk person	8	
Escort vehicle	3	
Fire, power line or		
tree down	26	
Lost or found person		
or property	23	
Property damage	6	
Maintenance of order	94	30.1
Gang disturbance	50	
Family trouble	23	
Assault, fight	9	
Investigation	8	
Neighbor trouble	4	
Law enforcement	32	10.3
Burglary in progress	9	
Check a car	5	
Open door or window	8	
Prowler	6	
Make an arrest	4	
Totals	312	100.0%

[a]Based upon a one-fifth sample of the week's calls.
[b]Not included are internal calls: those originating with other police officers or purely administrative calls.
SOURCE: James Q. Wilson, *Varieties of Police Behavior* (Cambridge, Mass.: Harvard University Press, 1968), p. 18.

observers of policemen and their departments, has emphasized the same three functions and has provided some systematic data on the relative frequency with which they are performed.[9]

The most common public image of the policeman is that of law enforcer, but, as the Syracuse data in Table 10.1 indicate, only about 10 percent of police calls require exercise of the law-enforcement function. Very few of the calls appear to represent opportunities for officers to make dramatic "pinches" of hardened criminals, and, in fact, the International Association of Chiefs of Police estimates that only about 10 percent of total police work is related to the traditional enforcement of criminal law.[10]

The role of providing service is far more common. Some police departments, according to Wilson, even emphasize service. For example, those in Nassau County, New York, and Brighton, Massachusetts, provide courteous and efficient, though perhaps low-keyed, law enforcement but also spend enormous amounts of energy and money on community relations. The Nassau County Police Department stands ready to provide articulate speakers at civic or school affairs and maintains a full-time staff of twenty-four officers to operate the department's boys' club program. Departments emphasizing services recruit well-educated men, pay them well, and demand scrupulous honesty from them. This emphasis is most common in homogeneous, upper-middle-class suburban communities. But, regardless of whether the department emphasizes service, a considerable part of any policeman's time and energy is devoted to providing it to citizens.

The police role that Wilson has called "order maintenance" and Fink has called "keeping the peace" is both the least recognized and the most controversial. Situations requiring maintenance of order sometimes involve transgressions of the law—especially if the law is sufficiently ambiguous—but more often they involve breaches of public serenity. In most such situations, at least two parties (bickering spouses, feuding neighbors, and people in and outside bars) are involved in disputes in which the fault is not self-evident and is possibly shared equally. (The confrontation of A, B, and C by officers Jones and Smith is a classic example of the exercise of this function, one that happened to lead to an arrest.) These cases involve maximum ambiguity and therefore maximum discretion on the part of the officer. According to Wilson, the policeman "approaches incidents that threaten order *not in terms of enforcing the law but in terms of 'handling the situation.'*"[11] Although it might be possible to turn every such case into a law-enforcement case, strong reasons militate against it: Tempers cool quickly, participants are reluctant to file charges, blame is difficult to determine, and law enforcement involves detailed reports and tedious court appearances. Officers thus tend to handle such incidents informally. When a clear violation of written law occurs—burglary, vandalism, or dope pushing—the police have little discretion, especially if they regard it as a "serious" crime. But the discretion that officers have in maintaining public peace is their greatest opportunity both to inject a personal element into the abstract business of law enforcement *and* to exert their personal idiosyncracies, whims, and prejudices. In Wilson's words, maintenance of order involves "sub-professionals, working alone, [exercising] wide discretion in matters of utmost importance (life and death, honor and dishonor) in an environment that is apprehensive and hostile."[12]

BACKGROUND AND ATTITUDES   After the John Birch Society introduced the "Support Your Local Police" bumper sticker (the phrase appeared recently on Alabama's state license plates), New Left critics countered with a bumper sticker of their own, reading "Control Your Local Pigs." A hero to conservatives, who view him as the last bastion of law and order, the policeman is depicted as bent on violence, authoritarian, and bigoted by the Left and by many Blacks. Perhaps the police self-image is equally stereotyped: Most police officers see themselves as performing tough, poorly paid, and unpleasant jobs, risking their lives and receiving either hostility or, at best, grudging tolerance from the public at large. Wilson found from surveys of Chicago police sergeants that policemen believed that (1) most Chicagoans did not respect them or their work, (2) most people gave only minimum cooperation, (3) most people obeyed the law only for fear of getting caught, and (4) even their civilian friends were likely to criticize the department.[13] This image is, however, contradicted by countless studies of public attitudes toward the police indicating that overwhelming proportions of Americans (especially white Americans) think that the police in their communities are doing "excellent" or "pretty good" jobs. Although police see themselves as downwardly mobile in the occupational structure, studies of occupational prestige indicate that their relative position has improved over the years.[14] There is, therefore, a wide gap between *actual* public acclaim for the police and *perceived* public support by the police.

Why, when the general public so widely supports police work, do policemen sense hostility? Part of the answer is provided by Wilson, who has observed that "most police contacts are not with the general public and thus general public opinion is not most relevant."[15] Rather than interacting with a random cross section of the public, the police see much of the worst kind of people and the best people only at their worst. Police work involves antagonistic contact with a very atypical segment of the public in situations of maximum hostility. The policeman's lot—the necessity for physical violence, personal danger, low pay, verbal abuse from self-proclaimed good citizens—is hardly conducive to an optimistic, tender-minded view of human nature. Most policemen, moreover, are recruited from working-class backgrounds; only a handful come from the middle class. "Working class background, high school education or less, average intelligence, cautious personality —these are the typical features of the modern police recruit," Nieder-hoffer has observed.[16] It thus happens that policemen are recruited from that segment of the population most inclined toward intolerance of unpopular views, racial prejudice, and authoritarian conceptions of family life and public policy.

Recruits bring with them the attitudes and behavior patterns of their backgrounds, including a preference for things physical rather than intellectual, a predisposition toward toughness, and high regard for established authority and ways. But there is little evidence to suggest that police recruits are any more authoritarian than are other members of the working class.[17] It seems to be the occupational milieu of the force that engenders extremes of authoritarianism, cynicism, and political conservatism among experienced officers. Although police authoritarianism has probably been overemphasized, the police system itself tends to heighten this image by promoting the better-educated and least-authoritarian officers, leaving behind for patrol work and public contact those with the strongest predisposition toward authoritarianism.

Cynicism about both life in general and the department in particular appears shortly after the rookie has left the police academy, with its social-scientific emphasis on professionalism and has entered the grimy world of the precinct station. General cynicism was expressed by the late Chief William H. Parker of Los Angeles, who claimed that "this civilization will destroy itself, as others have before it." Cynicism about the force itself is indicated by the widespread belief that getting ahead is a result of whom you know rather than what you do. Political conservatism is also a typical police attitude. Chief Parker described the political ideology of the nation's peace officers as "conservative, ultra-conservative, and very right-wing." The dominant political philosophy on the police force is a Goldwater-type conservatism, and such organizations as the John Birch Society harbor generous sprinklings of the "men in blue."[18]

Police and minority groups

In some respects, the police themselves may be viewed as a minority group—they are physically distinguished from the rest of us by uniforms, they exhibit high in-group loyalty, they view the outside world as hostile, and they interact heavily among themselves. Conflict among minority groups is a commonplace in American political annals. Moreover, as the police in some cities are recruited primarily from ethnic groups (e.g., the Irish), existing ethnic hostilities spill over into police-citizen relations. In any event, the National Advisory Commission on Civil Disorders' report on ghetto violence in the 1960s observed that "the policeman in the ghetto is the most visible symbol of a society from which many ghetto dwellers are increasingly alienated."[19] It has not been demonstrated that the police are more prejudiced against Blacks than are other Whites.[20] Yet the commission's surveys indicated that police relations were the leading grievance of ghetto residents, even more significant than housing deficiencies, inadequate schools, and unemployment. Incidents involving the police precipitated most of the major race riots of the 1960s, including those in Los Angeles, Detroit, and Newark.

Three major ingredients characterize the hostility between the police and ghetto residents. First is the familiar charge of *police brutality.* Whether or not and how much brutality exists depends, of course, upon definitions. But fully half the residents of Watts in Los Angeles believed that some brutality had occurred there. Perhaps more important, more than four-fifths complained of instances not of overt physical force but of *harassment,* including "insulting language," "stop and search for no good reason," and the like. In Denver, similar proportions of both police and minority-group members (about one-fourth in each case) claimed to have witnessed either harassment or excessive use of police force. The problem of harassment appears to be far more common than that of brutality. The President's Commission on Law Enforcement and the Administration of Justice investigated 5339 police-citizen contacts and found that only a minuscule proportion had involved excessive force, but that a much larger proportion had involved rude, discriminatory, or abusive verbal behavior.[21] Even though the proportion of police-citizen contacts involving roughness or rudeness may be small, the continual nature of police work enhances the probability that an individual ghetto dweller will at some time experience a hostile confrontation with the police.

The second source of police-ghetto tensions lies in what the ghetto sees as *inadequate police protection.* Regardless of class or income level, Blacks are far more likely than are Whites to see the police as ineffectual law enforcers. Ghetto leaders and residents are painfully aware of the crime and delinquency in the ghetto: Black men are six times and black women eight times as likely to be victims of crime as are white men and women respectively. The third ghetto complaint involves the *inadequacy of grievance mechanisms.* Disputes over civilian review boards, supported by Blacks and white liberals and bitterly opposed by the police, reflect tensions over grievance procedures. Most citizens' complaints against policemen have been handled internally by the departments, in which high "in-group loyalty" and "out-group hostility" have often meant perfunctory treatment of the grievances.

Needless to say, all these police-ghetto tensions have been intensified by racial disorders and police responses. From the police perspective, racial disturbances are clear examples of insurrection against lawful authority; from the black perspective, they are protests aginst white institutions, including the police themselves. Partly because the police have found it difficult to find a successful response to disorders, they have sometimes vacillated between over- and under-reacting to ghetto violence.[22]

Short of eliminating the ghetto and the conditions associated with it, society is not likely to lessen police-ghetto tensions. The ghetto is a high-crime area, and police are likely to resort to what few techniques they have to reduce the crime rate there: techniques that the police call "aggressive enforcement" and the residents call "harassment." Movement toward centralization of police authority and concurrent reduction of discretion at the patrol level, as well as higher employment standards and salaries may improve the situation marginally. But Wilson is not optimistic about the impact of changes in personnel on the numerous other factors that influence police-citizen relations: ". . . If all big-city police departments were filled tomorrow with Negro college graduates and placed under the control of the neighborhoods they are supposed to control, most of the problems that exist today would continue to exist and some in fact might get worse."[23]

Police and the "rule of law"

Through all the policeman's activities—law enforcement, maintenance of order, dealing with minorities, and so forth—he is expected to exhibit respect for individual rights and to provide nonarbitrary treatment for all. In recent years, the U.S. Supreme Court has attempted to spell out the rights of the accused that must be preserved under constitutional guarantees. Beginning in 1957 with the *Mallory* case, in which the Court held that a suspect must be taken before a magistrate for arraignment immediately following his arrest, the Supreme Court has acted to narrow police discretion in the performance of its law-enforcement function. In *Mapp* v. *Ohio* (1961) the Court established the principle that evidence collected in an "unreasonable search and seizure" cannot be used as evidence in either state or federal courts. The most far-reaching decision on suspects' and defendants' rights, that in *Miranda* v. *Arizona* (1966), laid down five principles governing pretrial conduct by law-enforcement officers:

1. A suspect must be informed of his right to remain silent and of his right to have counsel present during interrogation and must be warned that anything he says may be used in evidence against him.
2. Defense counsel must be provided if the suspect desires, but cannot afford, counsel.
3. The prosecution must demonstrate that the suspect knowingly waived his rights if he confessed without benefit of counsel.

4. Prolonged interrogation may be construed as a lack of such waiver.
5. If a suspect indicates "in any manner" that he wishes to remain silent, even after starting to talk, questioning must end.

To be sure, the Burger court has backed off somewhat from the stringency of the *Miranda* decision, but the recent impact of the courts is unquestionably to increase—at least theoretically—the rights of the accused. But what the Supreme Court orders does not necessarily become station-house practice. Well-represented and well-publicized defendants like Angela Davis may enjoy the fruits of court decisions that elude others' cases. Overcrowded dockets, ignorance and disregard by arresting officers of the rule of law, the injustices of the plea-bargaining system,[24] and other factors leave the typical defendant to enjoy fewer rights in practice than he does in legal theory.

The Impact of Law-Enforcement Policy

Cops, crimes, and convictions

Figure 10.1, though it does not directly assess the impact of law-enforcement policy, does provide us with some useful perspectives on the system of criminal justice and the rather narrow role of the police in it. These figures show more than 2.75 million crimes committed and listed in the FBI's index of serious crimes. (Our earlier discussion of underreporting of crime suggests that this figure is lower than the real incidence of crime.) Only 727,000 arrests followed. This figure suggests that the *clearance rate* by arrest is about 25 percent. About one-third of those cleared by arrest were juvenile offenses, and about 40 percent of those arrested were released or given reduced charges. Of the remaining 177,000, the overwhelming majority (160,000) either pleaded guilty or were convicted and jailed, fined, imprisoned, or paroled. The most-significant facts seem to be, first, that there is an enormous gap between the crime rate and the clearance rate by arrest and, second, that of 727,000 arrests only a fraction (160,000) resulted in guilty pleas or convictions in adult courts. Superficially at least, the sort of data presented in Figure 10.1 inspires pessimism about the impact of police law-enforcement policies. If only a quarter of crimes are cleared by arrest and only a fraction of those arrests result in convictions, law enforcement cannot be entirely successful in affecting the crime rate.

Crime and punishment

One of the most commanding questions about law enforcement is one of the most difficult to answer: Does the swiftness or severity of punishment have anything to do with reducing crime rates? A study by the prestigious International Association of Chiefs of Police, for example,

Figure 10.1 Flow of People Through the Criminal Justice System, 1965

SOURCE: Simplified from the President's Commission on Law Enforcement and the Administration of Justice, *The Challenge of Crime in a Free Society* (Washington, D.C.: Government Printing Office, 1967), pp. 262–263.

shows that traffic enforcement rates have little or no connection with highway deaths.[25] A quasi-experimental study by Campbell and Ross of a crackdown on speeding in Connecticut showed that the redoubled efforts of police were indecisive.[26] The research firm of Arthur D. Little was cautious in its conclusions but it too was dubious about the effects of traffic enforcement: "At present there is no firm evidence to indicate the degree to which enforcement contributes to traffic accident reduction."[27]

Even more uncertain is the evidence on the impact of enforcement on major crimes like rape, robbery, homicide, and assault. Some evidence suggests a clear linkage between the swiftness and severity of punishment and a lower crime rate in states.[28] But whether prisons have a deterrent effect on future crime or serve merely as schools and laboratories for crime is not yet known. The national recidivism rate (i.e., the probability that a convict will later commit another crime) is now about 60 percent. And if the conditions in state prisons are not comforting to one's humanitarian and rehabilitative impulses, the conditions of local jails are even more depressing.

Constraints on law enforcement

All the evidence presented here is best described as *indirect. Direct* evidence on police impacts is even most difficult to accumulate, partly because of the *displacement problem.* When a vigorous law-enforcement policy is adopted, it may be quite effective in *displacing* crime to other locales but not in reducing the total amount of crime. The displacement problem is a spillover effect of vigorous law enforcement in a single community or a single neighborhood. In any event, the displacement problem means that any convincing evidence on the impact of better, more professional, or more vigorous law-enforcement policies is nearly impossible to obtain.

If we expect law enforcement to result in actual reduction of crime rates, we may be setting unreasonably high standards for our police departments. The President's Commission on Law Enforcement and the Administration of Justice put the argument this way:

The fact is, of course, that even under the most favorable circumstances the ability of the police to act against crime is limited. The police did not create and cannot resolve the social conditions that stimulate crime. They did not start and cannot stop the convulsive social changes that are taking place in America. They do not enact the laws that they are trying to enforce, nor do they dispose of the criminals they arrest. The police are only one part of the criminal justice system; the criminal justice system is only one part of the government; and the government is only one part of society. Insofar as crime is a social phenomenon, crime prevention is the responsibility of every part of society. . . . Some "handcuffs" on the police are irremovable.[29]

Summary

Whether or not crime is on the increase in American cities, there is at least consensus that there is too much of it. Developing public policies which have the intended impact on crime, however, involves first understanding the nature of crime itself. Explanations for crime are diverse, but we suggest two broad classes of these explanations, macro (holding social conditions responsible for crime) and micro (holding individual attributes responsible). One's choice of appropriate crime-reduction policies will differ according to the preferred explanation. Whatever the causes, it is clear that the law enforcement goal of crime reduction is not as easily attained in practice as in theory. Police are not only crime fighters, but also service and order-maintenance personnel. Occupationally, their role conflicts and clientele problems make their jobs difficult. There is, unfortunately, little hard evidence about the impact of law enforcement on criminal activities. Not only is such evidence difficult to gather, but law-enforcement policy also faces numerous constraints upon its effectiveness.

Notes

1. William Watts and Lloyd A. Free, *The State of the Nation* (New York: Universe, 1973), p. 35.
2. President's Commission on Law Enforcement and the Administration of Justice, *The Challenge of Crime in a Free Society* (Washington, D.C.: Government Printing Office, 1967), pp. 18–27.
3. See, for example, Ashley Montagu, "Chromosomes and Crime," *Psychology Today*, 2 (October 1968), 43–49; and Kennedy McWhirter, "XYY Chromosomes and Criminal Acts," *Science*, 164 (June 1969), 1117.
4. James McCoy, *The Politics of Heroin in Southeast Asia* (New York: Harper & Row, 1972).
5. These data are drawn from James Q. Wilson et al., "The Problem of Heroin," *The Public Interest*, no. 29 (Fall 1972), 3–28. Our discussion of the crime and heroin linkage has benefited heavily from this penetrating analysis.
6. President's Commission on Law Enforcement and the Administration of Justice, *Task Force Report: The Police* (Washington, D.C.: Government Printing Office, 1967), pp. 14–16.
7. Police discretion is discussed in James Q. Wilson, *Varieties of Police Behavior* (Cambridge, Mass.: Harvard University Press, 1968), chap. 4; and in Albert J. Reiss, Jr., *The Police and the Public* (New Haven, Conn.: Yale University Press, 1971).
8. Saul Braun, "The Cop as Social Scientist," *The New York Times Magazine*, August 24, 1969, p. 69.
9. Wilson, *Varieties, op. cit.*
10. Cited by Arthur Niederhoffer, *Behind the Shield* (Garden City, N.Y.: Doubleday, 1967), p. 71.
11. Wilson, *Varieties*, p. 31.
12. *Ibid.*, p. 30.
13. James Q. Wilson, "Police Morale, Reform, and Citizen Respect: The Chicago Case," in David Bordua, ed., *The Police* (New York: Wiley, 1967), pp. 137–162.

14. Among ninety occupational groups, the ranking of policemen by the general public went from fifty-fifth in 1947 to forty-seventh (just a notch below the median) in 1963. If anything, the police are upwardly mobile. See Robert W. Hodge et al., "Occupational Prestige in the United States, 1925–1963," in Reinhard Bendix and Seymour Martin Lipset, eds., *Class, Status and Power* (New York: Free Press, 1966), p. 324, Table 1.

15. Wilson, *Varieties*, p. 28.

16. Niederhoffer, p. 38.

17. A Denver survey found that policemen were no more "authoritarian" on the "F scale," a common measure of authoritarian attitudes, than were the rest of the working class. See David H. Bayley and Harold Mendelsohn, *Minorities and the Police* (New York: Free Press, 1969), pp. 17–18.

18. Jerome Skolnick, *Justice Without Trial* (New York: Wiley, 1966), p. 61.

19. National Advisory Commission on Civil Disorders, *Report* (Washington, D.C.: Government Printing Office, 1968), p. 157.

20. Evidence on police prejudice varies. Skolnick (pp. 80–88) has argued that prejudice is commonplace on the police force. But the Denver data reported in Bayley and Mendelsohn, (p. 144) found police no more prejudiced than the rest of the white population.

21. President's Commission, *Task Force Report*, p. 147.

22. With tongue in cheek, Edward C. Banfield listed some "guidelines" for handling riots, in "Dos and Don'ts of Riots," *Harvard Review*, 4 (1968), 41–44:

DO	DON'T
1. Assign black officers to cope with black crowds.	1. Don't assign black officers to riot duty, as they are particularly resented by blacks.
2. Keep uniformed police out of the ghetto as much as possible in order to avoid provocation.	2. Don't deprive ghetto dwellers of police protection; this is a major grievance of the ghetto.
3. Close all bars at once.	3. Don't close the bars as this will put scores or even hundreds of half-drunk men on the streets.

23. James Q. Wilson, "Dilemmas of Police Administration," *Public Administration Review*, 28 (September–October 1968), 409.

24. Plea bargaining is a system under which a defendant's attorney bargains with the prosecutor for a reduced sentence in exchange for a guilty plea.

25. Robert L. Shumate, *The Long-range Effect of Enforcement on Driving Speeds* (Washington, D.C.: International Association of Chiefs of Police, 1960), cited in John A. Gardiner, "Police Enforcement of Traffic Laws," in James Q. Wilson, ed., *City Politics and Public Policy* (New York: Wiley, 1968), p. 171.

26. Donald T. Campbell and H. Lawrence Ross, "The Connecticut Crackdown on Speeding: Time Series Data in Quasi-Experimental Analysis," *Law and Society Review*, 3 (August 1968), 33–53.

27. Cited in Wilson, *Varieties*, p. 77.

28. Jack Gibbs, "Crime, Punishment, and Deterrence," *Social Science Quarterly*, 48 (March 1968), 515–530.

29. President's Commission, *Task Force Report*, p. 1.

chapter 11

Cities, cars, energy, and environment

The linkage between cars, energy, and environment is closer than one might think at first glance. The automobile is a symbol of industrialized, urbanized America. Indeed, one out of every seven persons in the labor force is directly or indirectly associated with automobile production, maintenance, or distribution. The car is also closely related to two other urban problems currently receiving attention. These are the issues of energy and environment. The petroleum which fuels the car also fuels the city. The waste products from automobiles are the major source of air pollution in the city. In this chapter, we examine problems, policy, and impact in the areas of transportation, energy, and environment. In each policy area, we first describe the problem, then discuss the politics and policies which have surrounded the problem, and in conclusion survey some evidence on policy impact.

Urban Transportation Policy
Cars and cities

That a few Americans orbit the globe in less time than it takes others to get to work illustrates the urban transportation problem. The provision of a transportation network ranks just after education and policing as a major item of urban public expenditure. More than any other municipal policy, decisions about transportation are characterized by their permanence. Transportation facilities, whether roads or rails, are costly and long lasting. This fact is even more significant because the transportation web influences the location of homes, commerce, and industry. Decisions about transportation have an impact upon the shape of the city that extends over generations.

Among other appellations, the twentieth century has been described as the "age of the automobile." Eighty percent of American families—all but a few of the very rich and a number of the very poor—own cars. Many a family owns two, and increasing numbers own three.

If Detroit is the city of the automobile from the point of view of production, Los Angeles is the city of the automobile in consumption terms. In Los Angeles, one-third of the total land area—two-thirds of the downtown area—is devoted to uses related to motor vehicles: principally streets, freeways, parking lots, and facilities to sell, service, and destroy automobiles. In Los Angeles and elsewhere, there is a reciprocal relationship between the decentralization of the metropolitan population and the ubiquity of the car. (*Reciprocal relationship* is a social scientist's term for what laymen might describe as a chicken-and-egg problem.) The automobile has made metropolitan deconcentration possible; deconcentration has made the car essential. Of course, the automobile alone did not cause the suburbanization of the American urban population. Other factors such as central-city land values and deterioration, affluence, and the sheer demand for space abetted population decentralization. Ownership of automobiles by urbanites may not be a *sufficient* condition for suburbanization, but it is almost surely a *necessary* one.

The most frequent use of the automobile is for commuting between residence and job. A significant proportion of such commuting takes place between central cities and their suburbs. Although most urban workers live and work in the same sectors of the city, millions of others commute daily from the suburbs to the CCs, and smaller numbers commute from CCs to the urban fringes. Although a few American cities have systems of mass transportation that are as convenient as private cars, the overwhelming proportion of commuting is by automobile.

To be sure, the deconcentration of the urban population is not the sole explanation for the dominance of the automobile. Its importance depends upon a number of interrelated phenomena, including (1) the increasing affluence of American workers, (2) the role of the automobile as a status symbol, (3) technological innovations that put automobiles within reach even of families with modest means, (4) the deterioration of urban mass-transit systems, (5) the attraction of jobs in the suburbs, and (6) state and federal policies favoring automobiles over mass-transit systems.

The structure of transportation policy making

Transportation policies, like most other policies affecting urban America, are intertwined with the federal system. At the federal level, the first assistance-to-highways program was inaugurated in 1916, but it was not until 1944 that the present direction of federal highway policy was made clear. In that year Congress created the skeleton of the now-familiar interstate transportation system, authorizing 41,000 miles of federally assisted interstate highways; no significant funding appeared in the federal budget until the mid-1950s, however. In 1956, Congress (1) established the dominance of the federal government in interstate road financing by providing federal funding for 90 percent of the cost, (2) reoriented the interstate system from a principally rural pattern of roads to an interurban system, (3) gave the Bureau of Public Roads effective power to determine the routes to be taken by the interstate system. When the system is complete, 41,000 miles of highways will link the nation's major cities.

Along with education and welfare, the highway program has long been one of the "big three" items in state finance. But for many years states have tended to use highway-financing formulas that favor rural over urban areas. This pattern has been common among the states, regardless of the equity of their legislative apportionments. Urban governments have thus been compelled to undertake a larger share of the burden of providing traffic arteries than have their rural counterparts. Within metropolitan areas, the fragmentation of local governments has further complicated the planning of balanced transportation systems to serve the needs of both suburbanites and central-city interests. CCs have often made heavy expenditures for transportation facilities used by suburbanites, who, in most cases, pay no taxes to the CCs.

Road versus rail

At all levels—national, state, and local—transportation politics has centered on the conflict between advocates of roads and equally ardent advocates of rail, or mass-transit, systems.[1] At least in the larger metropolitan areas, the essential elements of the *road coalition* have been officials of state and federal highway departments, truckers, automobile associations, construction and materials companies, petroleum interests, bus companies, and a number of business interests that would benefit from the expansion of the road network. Their commitment of political resources has been high.

In contrast to the politically potent road coalition, the *rail coalition* is a shaky alliance at best. Central-city commercial, political, and newspaper interests; commuters; and the railroads themselves have been the main spokesmen for balanced transportation, but there is considerable disharmony among them. The railroads themselves have often been eager to divest themselves of unprofitable commuter runs, and commuters are often at odds with the railroads over inadequate service.

So far, at least, the policies of national, state, and local governments have clearly favored roads over rails. The amount of federal aid for mass transportation is minuscule compared to that for the interstate highway system, and local governments, faced with a crush of demands for expansion of other services, have been reluctant to invest millions or hundreds of millions of dollars in developing rail transportation. Local governments have stood pat on the status quo—and the status quo means the automobile.

In an effort to persuade Congress to pass a long-term $10 billion mass-transportation-assistance act in 1969, President Nixon recognized that "man does not travel by road alone." Nevertheless, the very reason that the President found it necessary to shore up the rails is that urbanites are traveling more and more in private cars. According to the President, the number of transit passengers has declined to one-third the 1945 level; transit-company profits have declined from $313 million in 1945 to $25 million in 1967; and, in recent years, 235 bus and subway companies have gone out of business. "The remaining transit companies," he concluded, "have progressively deteriorated. Today they give their riders fewer runs, older cars, and less service,"[2] a fact that riders of most commuter lines knew long before the President told them about it. Although rail-commuting facilities have been developed or modernized in Toronto, Montreal, and Mexico City recently, the only American area developing a new mass-transit system has been San Francisco, which introduced its Bay Area Rapid Transit System (BART) early in 1971.

Highways and politics: a case study

Few large American cities have been free from controversy over the location and construction of highways. In Boston, antiroads forces combined to battle a loop of I-95 around the city.[3] Elsewhere, opponents of highways have argued that the economic, human, and environmental cost of continued highway building is simply too high and have pressed for a moratorium on freeway construction. The San Antonio, Texas, North Expressway controversy offers a useful insight into the politics of highways. San Antonio environmentalists waged a long and complicated battle with the City of San Antonio and the Texas State Highway Department to prevent construction of the North Expressway which would have sent—in order to dodge some expensive homes in the suburb of Olmos Park—the highway through the center of a college campus, within a stone's throw of the bear pits at the city zoo, and through the city's historic Brackenridge Park.[4] Although planning for the expressway began in 1956, it was not until 1959 that the State Highway Department and city officials picked a route which would have taken the highway through the zoo and park. Subsequently, the San Antonio Conservation Society got wind of the routing and opposed the passage of a 1960 bond election financing the project. By the slimmest of margins (331 votes) the money to finance the local share of the North Expressway's costs was disapproved. Following the defeat, however, City Hall and the San Antonio civic leadership mobilized all their resources. The city council constituted itself as the Parks and Expressways Committee and determined to "wake the public up" to the need for the road. The second bond election held on January 10, 1961, passed decisively.

Conservationists took the issue to the courts and were joined by Incarnate Word College, whose campus would be severed by the routing. While the issue bounced around state and federal courts, the Highway Department proceeded with planning, negotiation of rights-of-way, and contract awarding. After several years of contesting, the City of San Antonio finally offered the Sisters of Incarnate Word $1.2 million, which placated their objections sufficiently so that they settled out of court. The conservationists persisted in their legal and political battles and were rewarded with a partial victory when Congress in 1966 passed legislation forbidding construction of highways through public parks unless there was no other feasible alternative. The Department of Transportation in Washington tentatively approved the state's plans for the North Expressway, pending revisions to preserve the park. The state responded by splitting the expressway project into three sections. Since it could not secure federal approval for the middle one, it wanted to proceed with the two noncontroversial parts. By 1970, the environmentalists' suit had worked its way up to the U.S. Supreme Court, which rejected their demand for injunctions against the construction by a narrow decision. But on March 2, 1971, the Supreme Court upheld a conservationist suit challenging a federal highway project through Overton Park in Memphis. While environmentalists led a protest march of 800 people along the proposed route of the North Expressway, the San Antonio controversy went back to federal court, this time armed by the precedent of *Citizens to Preserve Overton Park, Inc.* v. *Volpe*. A series of court decisions in 1971 appeared to kill off the project once and for all. But there was still life in the proponents. The state announced in 1972 that it had withdrawn its request for federal funds (thus putting it outside the control of the 1966 congressional legislation against destroying parks) and would go it alone. The issue went back to the courts, where it had been for much of its life.

The impact of transportation policy
American transportation policies, especially favoritism for the automobile over mass transit, have literally reshaped the landscape of the American city. Some small towns withered when the highway passed them by; other areas within and outside the metropolis have become modern boom towns with the appearance of a new freeway. The automobile has also affected the living patterns of urbanites. Cities which developed primarily after the proliferation of the car (like Los Angeles and Houston) have much lower densities than those which predated auto-

mobiles (like Boston and Buffalo). The emergence of the car has hastened the deconcentration and suburbanization of families and firms. Industrial operations which were once tied to waterfront or rail facilities can now locate almost anywhere within the metropolis. For both persons and production, the motor vehicle has disaggregated transportation decisions, adding to consumer choice and urban mobility.

The public policies favoring the automobile have exhibited, however, some serious spillover effects. The car and its highways have eaten up vast quantities of urban land at a very high cost. Part of this cost is financial. A mile of freeway constructed within a metropolitan area costs many millions of dollars, destroys tax-producing enterprises, and requires expensive maintenance, repair, and police patrol. But another part of the spillover costs of the car is human. Most major freeways have been routed through low-income neighborhoods because these neighborhoods are closest to the central business district and because property values are lower. Moreover, low-income neighborhoods are often ineffectual politically in comparison to upper-income areas. Highway planners have thus followed "the geographic path of least political resistance. Until recently, that path has often run directly through the lowest-income neighborhoods."[5] Persons displaced by highway programs exhibit many of the same problems as those displaced from urban renewal. (See our discussion of urban renewal in Chapter 12, pp. 308–319.) The burdens of the highway often fall disproportionately on the poor.

The final spillover effect of the automobile is probably the best known: its impact on pollution. In the United States, the automobile is the major air pollutor, accounting in some cities for more than 80 percent of pollution content of sampled air. The automobile is also an enormous consumer of natural resources and energy. Coal, steel, chromium, and other resources are consumed in the production of automobiles, and petroleum is burned for their operation. This seems, therefore, an appropriate point to raise the urban problems of energy and environment.

Environment, Energy, and Public Policy

The two faces of the environmental problem

Architect Percival Goodman once observed that "the time has been reached when society's basic institution, capitalism, has begun to consume irreplaceably its basic resource, the environment."[6] The environmental problem has two faces, both inextricably linked to growth. One derives from the *exploitation* of natural resources faster than resources are discovered or replenished. The other stems from the *despoilation* of the environment by ever-present effluents from the affluent society. To be sure, the twin problems began when primitive man slew his first meal and dumped the bones into a river. No one was much troubled, however, until population growth reached such a point as to threaten the exhaustion and intolerable degradation of the natural bounty. In this sense, exploitation and despoilation are the inevitable by-products of population and economic growth. An M.I.T. team of scientists have dramatically and forcefully emphasized the linkage among population, resource usage, pollution, and economic growth in a controversial book, *The Limits to Growth.* [7] In the absence of limits on growth, the inexorable march of the other elements in their model lead to dire global consequences.

In the American city, the environmental problems range from minor annoyances like temporary brownouts and blackouts to serious challenges such as those arising from dangerous concentrations of lead, carbon monoxide, and other pollutants in the atmosphere. Because municipal (and state) governments either operate or regulate the major energy-producing utilities, the increasing consumption—and shortages —of fuels is a major concern of urban decision makers. Years of technological advances in home appliances, the development of bigger and faster cars, and the affluence needed to purchase them have combined to skyrocket the urbanite's consumption of energy. Americans, who constitute 6 percent of the world's population, consume a third of its resources, and consumption patterns are increasing faster than the population. [8]

Air, water, land, and pollution

The resources of the natural environment—land, air, and water—constitute the raw materials for our affluent society. Yet the natural environment is also the receptacle of our economy's waste materials. What engineers call the *law of materials balance* holds that the total weight of materials taken from nature will equal the total weight of wastes discharged into the environment plus any materials recycled. [9] The air, land, and water from which the resources to build a civilization are extracted become the repository for that civilization's solid, liquid, and gaseous waste products. Viewed from the perspective of material balance, pollutants are the inevitable by-products of the economic system, but to most specialists in public health and environmental engineering, the problem of waste and pollution has become grim indeed.

Air pollution consists primarily of carbon monoxide, hydrocarbons, nitrogen oxides from automobiles and industrial uses, and sulphur dioxide from the burning of oil and coal. Also contained in city air are fragments of solid materials like lead, zinc, and asbestos. Automobiles are responsible for the largest proportion of air pollution—approximately 60 percent nationally but 88 percent in Los Angeles. In fact, the role of the automobile in producing pollution is one of the major arguments for developing mass-transit systems and a viable alternative to the gasoline-powered engine. It is now acknowledged that air pollution has become a serious health hazard. Roger Revelle, a specialist on pollution and public health, notes, however, that the effects are not fully understood: ". . . common sense suggests that pollutants capable of darkening house paint, disintegrating stone statues, corroding metals, dissolving nylon stockings, and embrittling rubber must also be injurious to delicate bronchial and lung tissues; but there is little hard evidence at present."[10]

It is clear that air pollution is a very serious problem in areas where thermal inversions occur regularly. Such meteorological phenomena, in which layers of warm air settle over layers of cool air and prevent the dispersion of pollutants, are said to have produced 4000 deaths in London in 1952 and 200 in New York in 1953. Although there is some disagreement about the causal connection between pollution and various respiratory and pulmonary diseases, few, if any, scientists doubt that there is a threshold beyond which air pollution becomes a serious public-health problem. The difficulty has been in specifying that threshold.

Like air, water is also used as a receptacle for waste. Lake Erie, the main source of water for 10 million Americans from Detroit to Buffalo, is virtually closed to swimming and fishing; were it not for massive investments in treatment facilities, it would be undrinkable too. The Cuyahoga, Delaware, Potomac, and other rivers are at times unsafe even for boating. In fact, the Cuyahoga has caught fire several times. Although industrial pollution may be more serious than municipal pollution, municipalities have often dumped minimally treated sewage into rivers that are used as water sources by communities farther downstream.

Land is also both a source of raw materials for the economy and a receptacle for waste products. Americans now produce over 200 million tons of solid waste annually, about 1 ton per capita, and all of it must either be recycled or disposed of. According to Revelle, "solid wastes can be burned, buried, flushed, reused, or simply thrown away in more or less open country in the hope that they won't be noticed."[11] But each of these options implies certain costs. The first three methods produce air, land, and water pollution respectively. Reusing wastes has so far not been found economical. Simply throwing trash away is a popular, but aesthetically unpleasant and increasingly expensive, method. In many areas, sanitary land fills are exhausted, and refuse must be either barged out to sea (in coastal areas) or hauled to rural areas, at ever-higher costs. Technological changes have complicated the problem of disposal of solid refuse. The aluminum can, for example, is much more difficult to get rid of than tin cans were, and some plastics are nearly indestructible; others create noxious gases when they are burned, thus adding to air pollution.

The politics of pollution

Americans exhibit a high degree of abstract concern for the environmental plight. Urbanites, not surprisingly, are more worried than their rural counterparts, and better-educated citizens are more concerned than less well-educated ones.[12] Regardless of such differences, concern is general and not unique to particular population groupings. But, as we noted in Chapter 3 when we discussed environmental interest groups, abstract commitment is often coupled with behavioral malaise. A fifth of the population, for example, is unwilling to pay any additional taxes for water-pollution abatement or for cars with emission-control devices. A majority is unwilling to pay more than an extra $50 for such improvements. When the fundamental issues are broached—such as the possibility of sharply curtailing economic growth or government-imposed curbs on population increases—the public is sharply divided.

Matthew Crenson has written a penetrating study about the politics of pollution in the city. He studied the issue (or nonissue) in 51 American communities.[13] The simplest hypothesis suggests that pollution-control policy reflects a serious need for the policy, as measured by the dirtiness of the air. It was true that there was a positive relationship between seriousness of the problem and the likelihood of antipollution activities, but the correlations were only modest. We must consider factors other than the degree of need to explain why some communities invoke pollution controls and others do not. Crenson relies heavily on the concept of *nondecision* (see our discussion in Chapter 5, pp. 139–140) to explain pollution politics. Once the issue was raised and placed on the council's agenda, its chances of passage were almost perfect. Thirty of the fifty health commissioners Crenson interviewed reported that antipollution ordinances had been introduced in their cities, and *not one ordinance was defeated by council vote.* No local politician, presumably, wants to get a reputation of being *for* pollution. If the pollution-control ordinance is to be countered, the only way "is to prevent the issue from coming up in the first place."[14] Opponents require a nondecision. Because support for the pollution-control policy is diffuse and opposition is concentrated in industrial corporations, it is sometimes easy for proponents to be deterred by the power they see in the corporations. In such cases, the *reputation for power* may be effective in deterring proponents of control, even if the power is never exercised. Whatever the particulars of local pollution politics, however, it is almost always elite politics. The issue rarely energizes the masses, as school busing, fluoridation, or taxes sometimes do. The battle is usually fought by a limited number of protagonists, with the principal supporters of air pollution control being the city bureaucracies and its principal opponents being the corporations. Citizens, for the most part, are bystanders.

Costs, benefits, spillovers, and tradeoffs

In no area of public policy are costs, benefits, spillover effects, and tradeoffs so complex as in the energy-environment domain. Issues as basic as whether society should encourage or discourage population and economic growth have become entangled in the pollution problem. Tradeoffs and spillover effects pose painfully difficult choices for decision makers. In an effort to reduce pollution levels, it is sometimes necessary to increase resource exploitation. One example concerns federal air-pollution regulations which require emission controls on automobiles. Such devices, however, increase gasoline consumption (1973 cars used 20 percent more gasoline than cars built before the regulations) and thus hasten exploitation of petroleum reserves. Sometimes tradeoffs must be made between different types of pollution. The banning of garbage burning reduces air pollution but it increases the need for refuse dumps and aggravates land pollution. At other times, there are tradeoffs between economic growth and pollution. A few states and cities have adopted growth-limitation policies in an effort to reduce despoilation of their environments ("Oregon is a nice place to visit but we wouldn't want you to live here"). Yet the benefits of limiting growth do not come without painful costs. Growth means jobs, profits, and the money to pay for increasing urban service demands. Limiting economic growth also may hurt the poor more than anyone else, because they are the last hired and first fired in time of economic constriction.

Pollution policy and its impact

The most significant constraint on public officials who deal with the pollution problem is that, quite literally, pollution cannot be eliminated. At best, public policy can only reduce the most serious forms of pollution and then select among several alternatives for distributing the remainder among land, water, and air. The dominance of a market economy with weak central direction means that most decisions about pollution are often really nondecisions, the product of accumulated individual decisions of families and firms. As with many urban policies, much of the original impetus for pollution control came from supralocal sources, particularly from a few states and the federal government. California passed the first air pollution-control law in 1947, but even as recently as 1961 only seventeen states spent as much as $5000 annually to fight air pollution. The more significant initiatives have come from the federal government. The federal water pollution-control acts of 1954, 1962, and 1965 expanded federal jurisdiction to include all interstate waterways. Administered by the Secretary of the Interior, these acts permit the federal government, as a last resort, to institute legal action against major water polluters. The laws, however, may be more stringent on paper than in practice and are probably more effective in regulating the major polluters than the myriad small polluters of lakes and rivers. In 1972, Congress passed a powerful (and costly) water pollution-control law, but it was vetoed by President Nixon.

The control of air pollution has been directed mainly at controlling automobile emissions, but the Clean Air Acts of 1963 and 1970 also deal with stationary sources. The Environmental Protection Agency is required under the statutes to approve or disapprove state plans for air-quality control, in order to guarantee *acceptable* standards of pollution by 1975. The Department of Transportation, required to regulate automobile production to minimize pollutants from engines, has engaged in a long battle with Detroit over their stringency. The Department's staged standards took effect with 1972 models, with full implementation required by 1975, and now postponed by administrative action until 1976. Automobile manufacturers fought the regulations in the courts, but in 1972 the Supreme Court upheld the government's right to impose emission standards.

The overall impact of pollution control is difficult to gauge. Stringent controls are so new that their effects have not been fully felt. There is some evidence that air- and water-pollution rates have leveled off, but little evidence that the trend has reversed. The Environmental Protection Agency has maintained that the benefits derived from pollution control will exceed the costs. In 1972, for example, it estimated that the five-year cost of air-quality standards would represent only a 1-percent increase in consumer prices, with economic benefits of $14.2 billion exceeding costs of $12.3 billion.[15] Presumably the noneconomic benefits in improved health would be—if measurable—even greater. Whether, in the long run, such advances in pollution control will be sufficient in an urbanizing world of accelerating population, industrialization, and resource exploitation, only time will tell.

Summary

In this chapter, we have investigated problems, policies, and impacts in the fields of transportation and environment. The decentralization of the urban population and the widespread ownership of automobiles are factors in both transportation and pollution-control policies. Most transportation policy has emphasized roads over rails. This emphasis has had significant spillover effects in the arena of pollution control because automobiles are the major source of air pollution. More generally, however, pollution is a product of economic life itself. The *law of materials balance* holds that output into the environment equals intake from the environment, minus whatever materials are recycled. There are a number of ways that an urban society can dispose of its wastes, and cities, individuals, and factories have tried many of them. Only recently have significant efforts—and some doubt their significance and sincerity—been made to reduce the problem of pollution in urban America.

Notes

1. See the discussion of road-versus-rail interests in Jameson W. Doig, *Metropolitan Transportation Politics in the New York Region* (New York: Columbia University Press, 1966), chap. 2; and Frank C. Colcord, Jr., "Decision-making and Transportation Policies: A Comparative Analysis," *Social Science Quarterly,* 48 (December 1967), 383–398.
2. *The New York Times,* August 8, 1969, p. 13.
3. Alan Lupo, Frank C. Colcord, and Edmund P. Fowler, *Rites of Way: The Politics of Transportation in Boston and the American City* (Boston: Little, Brown, 1971).
4. Our account of the North Expressway controversy is based on Susan Knight, "The North Expressway" (unpublished manuscript, Lyndon B. Johnson School of Public Affairs, University of Texas, 1972).
5. Anthony Downs, *Urban Problems and Prospects* (Chicago: Markham, 1970), p. 218.
6. "Prologue," *Georgetown Law Journal,* 58 (March–May 1970), 671. Goodman's view is misleading, however, if it attributes environmental problems to capitalism. Marshall I. Goldman has described the serious environmental problems of the Soviet Union in his *Spoils of Progress: Environmental Pollution in the Soviet Union* (Cambridge, Mass.: M.I.T. Press, 1972).
7. Donella H. Meadows et al., *The Limits to Growth* (New York: Universe Books, 1971).
8. Gerald Garvey, *Energy, Ecology, Economy* (New York: Norton, 1972), contains a useful discussion of the energy problem.
9. Allen V. Kneese, Robert U. Ayres, and Ralph C. d'Arge, *Economics and the Environment: A Materials Balance Approach* (Baltimore: Johns Hopkins University Press, 1971).
10. Roger Revelle, "Pollution and Cities," in James Q. Wilson, ed., *The Metropolitan Enigma* (Washington, D.C.: U.S. Chamber of Commerce, 1967), p. 84.
11. *Ibid.,* p. 103.
12. William Watts and Lloyd A. Free, *State of the Nation* (New York: Universe Books, 1972), pp. 147–154.
13. Matthew A. Crenson, *The Un-Politics of Air Pollution* (Baltimore: Johns Hopkins University Press, 1971).
14. *Ibid.,* p. 90.
15. Environmental Protection Agency, *The Economics of Cleaner Air* (Washington, D.C.: Government Printing Office, 1972).

chapter 12

Managing urban growth

As almost all population growth in the United States is concentrated in urban areas, there are some good reasons for keeping them habitable. Twenty years ago E. B. White concluded that "it's a miracle that New York works at all. The whole thing is implausible." There is, he said, "reason enough to abandon the island to the gods and the weevils."[1] There is perhaps something to be said for the idea, but few have seriously espoused it. Two-thirds of the American population live in metropolitan areas, and the proportion is likely to increase further. The character and consequences of urban growth are the subjects of this chapter. Here we examine the nature of the growth process, the consequences it has for policy, and the ways in which urban governors attempt to contain, modify, or adjust to it. Planning and zoning are the principal ways decision makers try to channel the growth process. Decay and deterioration are by-products of the growth process which decision makers confront through housing and urban renewal policies.

The Nature of Urban Growth

Except for a few cities that were actually *planned* by farsighted founding fathers, most American cities have simply *grown*. Populations have swelled because of immigration, industrialization, and rural decline. The number of persons living in SMSAs increased to almost 70 percent of the population according to the 1970 Census, and the number of farm folk declined by an incredible one-third in the 10-year period from 1960 to 1970. More important than the growth *of* metropolitan areas is the pattern of growth and decline *within* metropolitan areas. Urban densities increased and, then, with the rise of the automobile, decreased again. The centrifugal movement of persons and production to the periphery of the city, the decay of older sections and central business districts, and the differential clustering of classes and races in the metropolitan area constitute the driving forces behind much of the plight of the contemporary city.

Edward C. Banfield has described the "logic of metropolitan growth" as follows:

Much of what has happened—as well as what is happening—in the typical city or metropolitan area can be understood in terms of three imperatives. The first is demographic: if the population of a city increases, the city must expand in one direction or another—up, down, or from the center outward. The second is technological: if it is feasible to transport large numbers of people outward (by train, bus, and automobile) but not upward or downward (by elevator), the city must expand outward. The third is economic: if the distribution of wealth and income is such that some can afford new housing and the time and money to commute considerable distances to work while others cannot, the expanding periphery of the city must be occupied by the first group (the "well-off") while the older, inner parts of the city, where most of the jobs are, must be occupied by the second group (the "not well-off").[2]

While true enough as *tendencies*, these fall short of being *imperatives*. Banfield's view understates the importance of government and public policy in shaping urban growth. Demographic changes are not merely the accidental by-products of market forces, but are intentionally manipulated by public policy. Zoning policy is the most notable way in which local government attempts to shape its social and economic environment, but it is not the only way. The selection of highway sites, the use of urban renewal and housing, the quality and quantity of urban public services, and a myriad of other factors affect the location choices of persons and production.[3]

Decentralization of production and population is the fundamental feature of metropolitan America. Millions of urbanites have moved to the suburbs. As most young suburbanites have never lived in any other kind of community, it is becoming dated to speak of the *suburban migration*. Industries, department stores, and commercial establishments have also found their places in the suburbs. On almost every indicator of economic activity, CCs have experienced a relative decline in comparison with fringe areas, and some CCs have experienced absolute declines as well. The cost of relocation within the CC may be many times greater than a move to the suburbs. The same economic patterns appear to affect both families and firms: The most prosperous of both are the most mobile, with the result that the poor, whether firms or families, are left behind to add to the human and economic problems in the CC. At the very time when the greatest demands are being placed upon city governments, those best able to pay for services have departed for the hinterlands. The flight of economic resources is paralleled by an intensification of service needs in the CC. This is another example of the irony of urban wealth (see pp. 19–31).

Logically, three alternatives are available to deal with the deterioration of American CCs: Accelerate it, ignore it, or impede it. Whatever alternative is preferred, the basic socioeconomic forces—the cost of land, the transportation revolution, the impact of technology, and the immigration from rural areas—may be beyond the reach of public policy in a democracy. But decisions to accelerate or ignore these forces are not lightly undertaken, for then at least three considerations must be dismissed:

1. Millions of Americans live now in those CCs, and more will arrive because of the low cost of deteriorated housing.
2. Minority groups, particularly Blacks and Spanish-speaking Americans, whose fate is a matter of policy concern, are heavily concentrated in central cities.
3. The CC continues to perform important social and economic functions, particularly with respect to the production of culture and the financial and commercial operations of the economic system.

Urban Planning

Planners and their activities

If we take *planning* to mean identifying goals and the resources and constraints involved in attaining them, then it is clear that we all plan to some degree all the time. Most such planning, however, covers only some of the available alternatives. The same is true of city politics, in which all actors (voters, mayors, agency heads, party leaders) attempt to match scarce resources to general goals. More narrowly, though somewhat tautologically, the term *city planning* refers to the activities undertaken by the city planning department and its professional staff. Like city managers, planners are professional employees of the municipal government; in principle they are hired on the basis of their professional competence, rather than because of their personal contacts. Organizationally, the planning staff is a part either of a quasi-independent agency, usually called the planning commission, or of a staff agency assisting the mayor or city manager. Directors of most planning agencies are appointed by the chief executives, although a minority is still appointed by city councils or by the planning commissions themselves.[4]

Regardless of the professional backgrounds or organizational milieus of planning agencies, several activities form a common denominator for almost all such staffs. All necessarily must *gather information* and *process data*. Although all municipal agencies gather and analyze data, cities with large and effective planning staffs are increasingly centralizing some of these activities in their planning departments. The information available to the planner is his most important resource. One of the most visible products of planning activities is the *land-use plan*, which reflects technical studies of existing land use, trends and projections of economic growth, municipal policies toward economic development, and planners' conceptions of community goals. Whatever the plan, once it is formulated the planner is usually involved in its implementation.

Zoning, the principal tool for enforcing use of private property as prescribed by the municipality, is designed to restrict what planners call "nonconforming uses," use of land in contradiction to the plans proposed by the professionals and adopted by the council. Ordinarily, after the adoption of a plan, nonconforming uses (e.g., building a service station on a quiet residential street) may not be undertaken, and already existing ones may not be expanded. Land-use plans also include rules and regulations for subdivisions, specifying such details as sizes of lots, setbacks from streets, and sidewalk and street construction. Building codes containing standards for industrial, commercial, and residential construction are usually included in plans formulated and implemented by the planning office.

Planners and their orientations

Their education, their occupational milieu, and the intellectual origins of the planning movement itself incline planners toward the view that physical and spatial relations strongly determine social interaction. David C. Ranney has described this attitude as a philosophy of "environmental determinism."[5] For planners, land and its uses, spatial relations, and aesthetics are critical components in any formula for the good life.

Environmental determinism is rooted in the origins of the planning movement. One of the founding fathers of city planning was Ebenezer Howard, whose book *Tomorrow*[6] stressed that most urban problems arise from the sheer size and density of the urban population. Howard argued that smaller, less dense settlements would solve the social and economic ills of the cities and advocated the creation of new towns of limited size (32,000) and severely limited density. Altering people's spatial relations, he argued, could eliminate the social and economic problems attributable to high densities. Although new towns have been developed extensively in Great Britain and the rest of Europe and advocated vigorously in the United States, there are few important examples on this side of the Atlantic. Reston, Virginia, and Greenbelt and Columbia, Maryland, are perhaps the most important.

The urban-planning movement began with the reformism of the Progressive era, with which it shares an important affinity. Like the reformers, planners are interested in the community as a whole, which they believe transcends narrow and private-regarding interests of community segments. Accordingly, the public interest appears to them both different from and morally superior to transitory individual and group interests. "The view," according to Alan Altshuler, "that clashes of interest are only apparent has always appealed to one element of the American intellect. It is assumed by most conservative defenders of the status quo no less than by progressive attackers of 'politics.' "[7]

Many planners share with both the Progressives and the contemporary reform groups a bias against things political. Ranney has suggested that "planners have traditionally distrusted local government, viewing it as the pawn of special interest groups. This distrust is at least partly the result of the relationship between the planning movement and the municipal reform movement."[8] Rightly or wrongly, many planners see the municipal political process as sacrificing community-regarding goals in favor of rewards to self-seeking individuals and groups. Politicians, as we saw in Chapter 5, cannot often claim to behave rationally because of the myriad constraints upon rational choice. Planners, however, are likely to believe that rational choice, though never easy, is in principle an attainable goal.

The master plan

The most ambitious activity undertaken by planners in city government is what is called *master planning* or *comprehensive planning*. A master plan, according to Banfield and Wilson, "is a set of maps and policy statements that describe in general terms the present intention of the authorities respecting actions they may take over the long run and that may affect the physical development of the city."[9] The emphasis is on physical, rather than social, phenomena. An ideal master plan would guide specific land-use decisions in both the public and private sectors. A question of use for any parcel of land could be determined simply by matching up the plan's prescriptions with the proposed use. Just as the late Justice Owen Roberts once defined the task of the Supreme Court as putting the particular law in one hand and the relevant part of the Constitution in the other and seeing that they are squared, so the planning agency would need only to evaluate each proposed change in land use as it conformed with the master plan. Indeed, Charles M. Haar, a specialist in planning law, once called the master plan the "impermanent constitution" of a city.

The layman may think that the formulation of a realistic master plan for a city of thousands of people, a complex social and economic structure, and infinitely varied preferences about the role of government would be impossible to achieve—and he would not be all wrong, for few master plans can be both comprehensive and detailed enough to guide decisions. Nearly every city has developed, under the spur of federal legislation, some type of master plan, and many of these plans have been condemned as "ninety-day wonders." Because master planning is in principle a rational process—general goals are stated, and the most efficient means to attain those goals are incorporated—we can gain some insights into the constraints upon master planners by reformulating our discussion of rational decision making (see pp. 168–172) in terms of planning.

When the planner attempts to identify the abstract goals of a city before formulating them in a specific master plan, he is inevitably struck by their abstractness and their contradictions. Various groups in the community have different stakes and interests in public and private policy, and the common denominator of agreement may permit the planner to state his goals only in terms so abstract as to be vacuous. The goal of the St. Paul land-use plan, for example, was stated as the "evolution of St. Paul as a better place to live and work." Surely only a misanthrope would dissent from such a goal!

A second barrier to comprehensive planning is the sheer complexity of predicting changes in the environment. The urban system is an open one, with both external and internal forces shaping changes. Predicting changes within the community is difficult enough, but predicting changes in external forces is nearly impossible. Although planners have developed sophisticated models of systems analysis, cost-benefit theories, and computerized simulations of urban change, prediction accurate enough to use in prescribing policy for future decades remains an ephemeral goal. The impossibility of accurate prediction has led some advocates of master planning to call for *plasticity*, or *flexibility*, in plans, in order to permit adaptation to environmental change. (This call is reminiscent of the late Senator Everett Dirkson's dictum that "I am a man of principle and my first principle is flexibility.") Flexibility, however, undercuts a strictly rational approach to planning and is, moreover, difficult to use as an operational guide.

A third barrier to rational planning lies in the nature of politics. In Banfield's blunt words,

The important questions are settled ultimately by elected officials (politicians) whose decisions are normally mere by-products of their competitive struggle to get and keep office. No competent politician will sacrifice votes that may be needed in the next election for gains, however large, that may accrue to the public 10, 20, or 30 years hence.[10]

Given the limited information available to most voters, the immediate costs of any proposal must be weighted more heavily than the long-term gains. Politics, according to Lowi, "works in the short run," but comprehensive planning emphasizes the long run. (John Maynard Keynes' observation that "in the long run we are all dead" strikes a deeper chord in the politician and the public than in the planner.) Given all these constraints upon comprehensive planning, we might expect it to be most successful when (1) planners' information is at a maximum, (2) articulated goals are congruent with those of politically influential groups in the community, and (3) politicians and voters are willing to sacrifice short-term for long-term satisfactions. This set of requirements for successful comprehensive planning is stringent indeed.

Zoning and Urban Growth

Zoning as public policy

Probably the greatest single impact of planning upon the socio-economic environment of American cities has been through zoning policy. The typical regulations, which consist of the zoning ordinance itself, subdivision regulations, and building codes, divide the city's space into various categories. The most common classifications are industrial, commercial, and residential, although each may contain gradations within. The residential category, for example, may be further divided into land for single-family dwellings and multiple-family dwellings. In the industrial classification distinctions may be made between areas for industries with noxious effects (smoke, noise, congestion) and those without. Requests to alter the zoning classification of a particular piece of property are usually considered by the municipal planning commission, whose decisions are ordinarily subject to review by the city council. Some planning commissions take a jaundiced view of any modifications in a zoning classification laid down in the ordinance and reject all requests for change. Others are sometimes eager to permit numerous exceptions in the form of *spot zoning*, granting exceptions for a few pieces of property in a larger area of homogeneous land use. Zoning ordinances, housing codes, and subdivision regulations typically prescribe land use and other matters as well. For residential areas, minimum lot sizes, the buildings' distance from streets, and certain other regulations may be invoked. Requirements also may be established for commercial and industrial property. The latter may also be regulated to minimize smoke, pollution, and noise.

As zoning represents a government's efforts to control the uses of private property, the rights of municipalities to enact and enforce zoning have been repeatedly challenged in the courts. But, despite arguments that zoning is socialistic and an infringement on private property rights, the late Justice George Sutherland, usually considered a very conservative member of the Supreme Court, wrote a crucial opinion supporting zoning, in *Village of Euclid* v. *Ambler Realty Co.* [11]

Zoning as public policy accomplishes a number of purposes. It contributes to the aesthetic appeal of neighborhoods and communities, rids residential areas of noxious commercial enterprises, and secures property values from deterioration by forces beyond the homeowner's control. Yet, it also has significant policy impacts in shaping metropolitan growth, in determining where children go to school, where families can purchase homes, what tax bases communities and school districts possess, and the quality of services which can be provided. Zoning is important because it has economic and social impacts. We call these two functions of zoning *fiscal* and *social* zoning.

FISCAL ZONING AND PROMOTION   Zoning alone does not lead to the kind of economic development that residents desire. It merely classifies land for use. If industry is wanted, a hospitable zoning policy must be combined with the willingness of city planners to gather data for prospective firms, with special promotional efforts, and, in many communities, with tax incentives. Where the desire to keep taxes low is a major objective, communities usually try to attract industry. Industries, it is widely believed, are generous taxpayers. Moreover, their operations spill over into the macro and micro sectors of the local economy. Yet industries are not only taxpayers but also very heavy service consumers. In the Philadelphia region, for example, the highest municipal expenditures were found in the industrial suburbs, largely because of service consumption by industries.[12] Industries also bring workers and managers who consume municipal services, particularly education. Some industries impose higher service costs than they contribute in taxes to the public coffers. The trick is thus to secure industries whose input into the public and private sectors is high and whose outtake from the public sector is low. Firms specializing in research and development employ highly trained and well-paid personnel and are preferred to noisy, sooty factories that contribute to congestion. The problem is that there are not enough such firms and their equivalents to go around.

Municipalities are thus compelled to play a fiscal zoning game in an effort to attract—or pirate from other communities—industries that pay more in taxes than they consume in municipal services.[13] The nature of communities will restrict strategies in the fiscal zoning game. Although some residents may settle for any industry that pays its way, others draw the line at noisy ones, smoky ones, or ones that bring congestion. Whatever the limitations, most communities, large and small, play the game through promotional policies, free or inexpensive services to new business, and favorable land-use policies.

SOCIAL ZONING   Some communities want no part of zoning and related policies to attract industry. These communities are typically high-income, upper-class residential suburbs, which prefer to accept the increasing costs of local government in order to retain the pristine character of a residential greenbelt. These cities play the game of social zoning rather than fiscal zoning. Zoning industry out is easy enough; all land can be reserved for residential and retail development. It is more challenging to manipulate land-use regulation to secure a particular class (and, by accident or design, racial) composition. It may be accomplished by requiring, for example, minimum lot sizes from half an acre to four acres or by establishing such stringent building-code requirements that housing costs become prohibitive except for the wealthy. Greenwich, Connecticut, and Scarsdale, New York, and other upper-middle-class communities have used tight zoning restrictions to maintain homogeneous residential communities amid creeping industrialization. Such practices, when carried to extremes, produce what Whitney Young called "gilded ghettos." *Restrictive covenants*, devices by which deed restrictions are used to prevent the sale of housing to members of minority groups, were declared unenforceable by the Supreme Court in 1948,[14] and Congress has forbidden racial discrimination in the sale or rental of housing since 1968. But zoning policies that substitute class for racial premises may have consequences similar to racial ones.

Planning, Zoning, and the Battle of the Suburbs

Zoning is both more popular and more effective in newer suburbs than in older CCs. The reasons are not obscure. As the physical development of older cities took place before zoning had been developed to a fine art, land use there has been determined by the often-haphazard decisions of the marketplace. Today nearly all large cities have zoning ordinances (Houston, Texas, is the only significant exception). In most, however, zoning affects choices only at the margins. Most land-use decisions are already "given" by earlier market considerations. But many suburbs, whose development has postdated the zoning revolution, began their growth with rigid land-use restrictions already in force. Zoning has quite literally shaped those communities. One disgruntled property owner in Greenwich, Connecticut, has grumbled that "in Greenwich, no one can get elected unless he swears on the Bible, under a tree at midnight, and with a blood oath, to uphold zoning."[15]

It is not difficult for a suburban community, if it passes an effective zoning ordinance before land development is really under way, to guarantee a simon-pure residential haven. To the affluent suburb, an influx of lower-income neighbors means larger school enrollments, more service demands, higher tax rates, and—to many residents—a deterioration in the "quality" of the community. There are ample techniques of social zoning available to insure a quality community. Building codes can be designated for half-acre or larger lots, or multifamily structures can be prohibited. These practices, variously called *snob zoning* or *Cadillac zoning*, have the effect of inflating housing costs. This can put suburban housing in attractive areas well beyond the financial reach of younger, larger, or middle-income families. Zoning and land-use policy thus constitutes an effort to manipulate the social and economic environment of a community. Robert Wood, in his study of the New York metropolitan region, noted that, "planning, zoning, and promotion . . . represent ways by which [local governments] can keep 'undesirables' out and encourage 'desirables' to come in, if they choose. And, of course, the definition of desirables and undesirables varies from place to place."[16]

The racial, social, and economic impacts of snob zoning are significant. Upward residential mobility out of the CC and older suburbs is retarded by the high cost of much suburban housing. The groups left behind are condemned to deteriorating housing, poorer schools, excessive tax rates, and declining service levels. Moreover, because virtually all economic growth within the metropolis is concentrated in OCC areas (see our discussion in Chapter 2, pp. 23–31), persons in the core city area may live far from job opportunities. Many suburban communities have zoned parcels of land for industry—thus securing an industrial tax base—but little or no land for working-class residences. Workers may work there, but at night must return to older—and often poorer—cities. In such cases, the fiscal and social zoning games merge into a single zoning game. The object is to secure the blessings of urban development (e.g., tax bases) for one's own community, but to consign the problems (e.g., crime, higher school enrollments, and service demands) to another community. The Advisory Commission on Intergovernmental Relations has argued that "under present zoning law, the affluent suburbs are able to exclude low income families and minimize tax burdens which are then transferred to the overburdened central city."[17] Robert Wood calls such strategies "beggar thy neighbor" policies.[18]

The battle of the suburbs has been waged by spokesmen for poor and minority groups, intent on breaking down the barriers of suburban exclusivity.[19] To them, zoning is like Jehovah's advice to Ezekiel, to "put seigeworks against it, and build up a seige wall against it, and cast up a mound against it; set camps also against it, and plant battering rams against it round about. And take an iron plate, and place it as an iron wall between you and the city (Ezekiel 4:2–3)." The "iron plates" of suburban zoning have been under legal attack in Blackjack, Missouri, New Canaan, Connecticut, Troy, Michigan, Mahwah, New Jersey, and elsewhere. In an alliance of "strange bedfellows," developers and contractors have often found it in their self-interest to press for curbs on zoning authority. A few skirmishes have been won in the courts, and New York and Massachusetts have passed antisnob zoning laws. But the battle of the suburbs is just getting under way. It serves to demonstrate that urban zoning and land-use policies have significant policy impacts in shaping urban growth.

Housing and Urban Growth

Housing is important, not only in its own right, but also because it insures or deters access to public and private advantages. One may live in a rapidly developing area, where jobs are plentiful, or in an economically stagnant area where even low-skilled work is scarce. Where one lives affects his taxes, schools, and the quality of other urban services. Of all the public policies we discuss in this book, housing policy probably has more implications for more people than any other. No personal choice (except perhaps marriage and divorce) is more carefully weighed than housing, at least among persons whose income permits them a choice. Public policy, principally through federal resources, has had a significant impact on housing choices for Americans of all income levels. Almost all housing programs have their roots in the New Deal. Not only is the federal government (through local authorities) the nation's largest landlord for poor families, it is also the impetus for millions of middle-income families' housing investments.

Housing and the poor

That poverty and substandard housing are related is a truism, but whether this fact means any more than that poor people live in the poorest housing is not clear. Plainly, people are not poor merely because they live in inadequate houses. But still it is possible that the quality of housing itself has something to do with the behavioral, economic, and psychological syndrome we call poverty. One view, that poverty has little to do with housing, is argued cogently by the sociologist John Dean, in a somewhat dated, but still excellent, critique of the traditional notion of slums and poverty. The simple-minded implication of many housing reformers, he has argued, is " 'Remove the slums and you remove the social ills!' . . . but it would be just as illogical to say that the ills of slum areas are caused not by substandard housing conditions, but by the absence of telephone service, which also correlates with indexes of social disorder."[20]

Dean has emphasized that a correlation between slum housing and the incidence of social problems must not be interpreted as establishing a causal relation. Alvin Schorr, on the other hand, thinks that such a causal link between poor housing and poverty can be demonstrated. Poor housing may lead, he has argued, to:

. . . a perception of one's self that leads to pessimism and passivity, stress to which the individual cannot adapt, poor health, and a state of dissatisfaction; pleasure in company but not in solitude, cynicism about people and organizations, a high degree of sexual stimulation without legitimate outlet, and difficulty in household management and child rearing; and relationships that tend to spread out into the neighborhood rather than deeply into the family.[21]

According to Schorr, the effects of inadequate housing are no less significant for their obviousness. Inadequate space for sleeping means that less sleeping is done; the lack of privacy for schoolwork means that schoolwork is done in the midst of turmoil or not at all; excessive cold or heat means discomfort; cramped quarters send children into the streets, which means that they escape parental supervision younger than do well-housed children. Dean and Schorr do not agree fully about the precise effects of housing conditions, but both acknowledge that poor housing creates real problems.

There is ample evidence to suggest that the American housing situation has improved significantly since Franklin D. Roosevelt announced that "one-third of a nation [is] . . . ill-housed, ill-clad, ill-nourished" in his 1937 inaugural address. The data in Table 12.1 detail the current housing picture in the United States and clearly suggest that the overwhelming majority of housing units are structurally sound and sanitary. Most of the inadequate housing is found in rural areas, rather than in cities. At least half the substandard housing units in the United States are in rural areas, and fewer than a quarter are in large cities. Still, most middle-class Americans would not consider only such facilities as hot and cold running water and private baths to be very reliable criteria of creature comforts. The higher one's standards for good housing, the larger is the number of units that must be described as substandard.

Were inadequate housing units scattered about the city randomly, they would probably be of little moment for politics and policy, but substandard housing is not randomly distributed. It tends, rather, to cluster in certain areas. There are five significant consequences of this clustering of substandard housing (slums).

First, such housing tends to be occupied by the poor and minority groups because of economy and the tendency to associate with peers. People select houses for numerous reasons, but their incomes limit their choices: Their home sites are near their places of work, their information on alternatives is limited, and racial discrimination limits the alternatives themselves. Lower-class groups face common constraints and end up living next to one another. An important social consequence is that *they reinforce one another's behavior and value patterns.* This reinforcement may, of course, be good or bad, depending upon one's evaluations of the patterns, but it does reduce the exposure of one class to another's beliefs, behavior, and preferences.

Second, because schools in America have historically been tied to neighborhoods for reasons originally related to transportation technol-

Table 12.1 *Housing Conditions, 1960 and 1970*

	1960	1970
Total occupied units	53,024,000	63,417,000
Percentage with all plumbing facilities	84	95
Percentage lacking some facilities	16	5

SOURCE: *Statistical Abstract of the United States* (Washington, D.C.: Government Printing Office, 1972), p. 690.

ogy, the poor tend to attend the same schools, which produces a high degree of class and racial segregation. A child's peers in school are thus other poor children, who reinforce the common set of norms and behaviors. Teachers in such schools commonly tend to be the least experienced or the least dedicated of the city's teachers.

Third, because there is so much mutual reinforcement of lower-class value and behavior patterns in slums—and because the concentration reinforces the middle-class stereotype of slum dwellers—upward mobility is more difficult than it would otherwise be.

The fourth and fifth consequences of residential segregation by race and class are political. In cities that use ward elections, the poor are likely to have at least one councilman of their own, unless gerrymandering chops up the slum area. Finally, the fact that the poor are concentrated in specific areas tends to enhance their effectiveness as an organized group. Communication is facilitated, leadership is easier to exercise, and a sense of community can be developed. Residential dispersion of the poor, without other changes in their condition, would condemn the poor to being a permanent minority throughout the city. A concentration of the poor in a few areas at least guarantees them majorities in those areas. These last two consequences of the concentration of substandard housing and of the poor suggest that neighborhood segregation is a mixed blessing. The social and economic disadvantages of neighborhood concentration are thus to some degree offset by the political advantages. Black Power advocates have increasingly come to recognize that, *for political purposes*, the ghetto may be preferable to integration.

Housing and race
The overwhelming majority of Whites, regardless of income, live in white neighborhoods, and the overwhelming majority of Blacks live in black neighborhoods—in CCs and suburbs, small cities and large ones, the North and the South. Moreover, black areas are almost universally poor, whereas white areas are usually not poor. In 1960, only 12 percent of Whites with incomes above the poverty level were living in poverty areas, but fully two-thirds of Blacks with comparable incomes were living in poor neighborhoods. By far the most extensive research on race

Table 12.2   *Average Values of Indexes of Residential Segregation for Regions, 1940, 1950, 1960*

Region	1940	1950	1960
Northeast	83.2	83.6	78.9
North Central	88.4	89.9	88.4
West	82.7	82.9	76.4
South	84.9	88.5	90.7
Total	85.2	87.3	86.1

SOURCE: Reprinted from Karl E. and Alma F. Taeuber, *Negroes in Cities* (Chicago: Aldine, 1965); copyright © 1965 by Karl E. and Alma F. Taeuber.

and residential segregation has been undertaken by Karl and Alma Taeuber.[22] They have developed a "segregation index," which varies from 100 (complete segregation with no Whites in black areas and no Blacks in white areas) to 0 (random distribution by race). Table 12.2 demonstrates the average segregation scores for 109 American cities in 1940, 1950, and 1960. The national pattern, reflecting only slight regional variations, is compellingly simple: The overwhelming majority of American cities are very highly residentially segregated by race. Although no one has yet updated Taeuber and Taeuber's study with data from the 1970 Census, evidence from special censuses taken between the regular 1960 and 1970 periods confirms the pattern of high segregation. We doubt that dramatic changes would be revealed by 1970 data.[23]

What are the causes of this residential segregation? Karl Taeuber has cited Gunnar Myrdal, the distinguished Swedish economist and student of the American race problem, who has offered three hypotheses to explain housing segregation. First, it may result from deliberate preference for living among members of one's own race. Second, it may result from poverty. Because the income levels of Whites and Blacks differ markedly, Blacks may simply be unable to afford homes anywhere but in the poorest neighborhoods. Housing segregation would thus be a matter of class, rather than of race. Third, it may be the result of discrimination.

There is no doubt some merit in each of these explanations. Surely deliberate choice is involved in residential location, but Myrdal and the

---

Figure 12.1   Residential Segregation Indexes for Fifteen Cities.
Actual and expected segregation indexes are shown for these cities on the basis of 1960 census-tract data. The comparison relates to the argument that the poverty of Blacks is the sole cause of residential segregation. The "expected" indexes (lower bars) show how much racial segregation there would be if the amount paid for housing were the only cause of segregation. Actual segregation indexes (upper bars) are much higher, indicating that factors other than poverty are involved in the determination of black housing patterns.

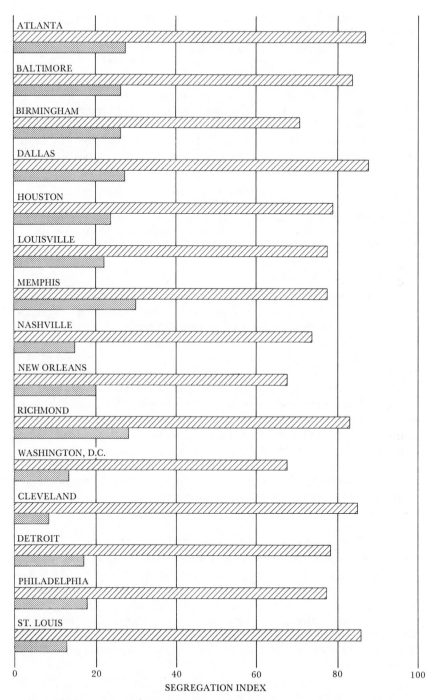

SEGREGATION INDEX

SOURCE: Reprinted by permission from Karl E. Taeuber, "Residential Segregation," *Scientific American*, 213 (August 1965), 18.

Taeubers all have noted that choice is not altogether *free* when made in a society in which racial discrimination and prejudice are widespread. The more probable explanations for segregated housing patterns are thus the income and discrimination theories.

Some data on the relative validity of these two theories are contained in Figure 12.1. Statistically, the figure demonstrates the degree of *expected segregation* there would be if the amount paid for housing were the only factor in housing choice and compares this figure with the actual amount of segregation for each city. It is apparent from the graph that the economic factor explains only a small fraction of existing segregation. Karl Taeuber has concluded that:

Negroes are excluded from many residential areas in which their economic status could allow them to live. . . . Discrimination is the principal cause of Negro residential segregation, and there is no basis for anticipating major changes in the segregated character of American cities until patterns of housing discrimination can be altered.[24]

Housing and public policy

There are at least four possible governmental responses to the housing problem of the poor. First, government can do nothing at all. It can assume that the private sector will handle the problem,[25] that its own efforts would be ineffective, or that the spillover costs would outweigh the benefits. Second, government can adopt an indirect strategy of general assistance to the poor but not for housing per se. The underlying premise of this strategy is that poor housing is merely symptomatic of deeper and more pervasive poverty, which should be attacked through welfare payments or a form of guaranteed annual income. Third, the government can, in Lawrence Friedman's words, "attempt to get rid of bad housing by forbidding it."[26] This approach includes enforcing housing codes for new construction and maintenance codes to which landlords must conform. Fourth, the government can try to provide good housing. In practice, of course, these four strategies are not mutually exclusive, and federal and city governments actually use combinations of them.

The problem of inadequate housing did not begin with the Depression of the 1930s, but the first significant housing legislation was the National Housing Act of 1934, which recognized housing as a subject of national concern and created the still-thriving Federal Housing Administration. The FHA's principal activity through the years has been to guarantee home mortgages. In the third of a century of its existence, it has insured billions of dollars of single-family housing. The FHA, however, has consistently benefited families with medium incomes, rather than the poor.

Another Depression agency, the Public Works Administration, undertook some slum clearance during the 1930s and constructed a few units of public housing, but it was the Housing Act of 1937 that laid the real basis for public housing, slum clearance, and later urban renewal. That act created the U.S. Housing Agency, funded it with a half-billion dollars, and authorized it to lend money to local public-housing authorities to clear slum land and provide public housing. Once minimum federal standards had been met and the loan provided, a local public agency (LPA) was responsible for land acquisition, clearance, planning, construction, and operation.

The Housing Act of 1937 was the first in a series of laws tying public housing to slum clearance, but with the Housing Act of 1949, and especially its 1954 amendments, public housing began to take a back seat to *urban renewal*. Title I of the 1949 act authorized the purchase of slum land by local public authorities. The land would then be sold to private developers, who in turn were required to use the land for "predominantly residential" construction. Local housing or redevelopment authorities could use the power of eminent domain to acquire land and sell it to private development corporations.[27] The difference between the high price paid for the land and the lower price received for it would be made up largely by federal grants. The federal government would absorb two-thirds (in certain cases, three-fourths) of the "net project cost," that is, the difference between purchase and sale prices. The local government was required to make up the other one-third (or one-fourth) in cash, kind, or services. Not surprisingly, some groups, real-estate interests, for example, which had vocally opposed public-housing legislation gave wholehearted support to Title I.

The 1949 act linked the concept of urban redevelopment to public housing. The public-housing provisions of the act were not popular with either Congress or business interests, but federal subsidizing of land transfers was attractive to city officials and commercial interests. Cities could shore up sagging tax bases with revenues from more-valuable property, and developers could enjoy federal subsidies instead of small profits and possible losses. Urban renewal thus became a popular vehicle for redressing the urban financial imbalance, while public housing continued to eke out narrow victories or heavy losses.

Some of the sluggish growth of public housing has resulted from the rude facts of political power. Such housing has its proponents, but it also has a formidable array of opponents, including the National Association of Real Estate Boards, the construction industry, banks, and savings-and-loan institutions.[28] Public housing has also challenged some fundamental precepts of American ideology, including laissez faire and faith in private ownership. To conservatives, the program smacks of socialism because it rewards those who are least "deserving." One congressman, in debate on New Deal housing legislation, declared that "the poor are living in shacks and hovels because God made them unable to earn more."[29] Recently, public housing has suffered a further challenge, which Friedman has called the *"disillusionment* of the experts." "The cause of public housing," he has written, "has been psychologically abandoned by many of its former supporters. In the past ten years, assessment of public housing has been more and more negative."[30]

As with other urban problems, public housing has been complicated by the dilemma of race. Housing projects can be located either in the heart of the ghetto, thus promoting segregation, or in white neighborhoods, thus facilitating integration. The former is objectionable to civil-rights leaders, and the latter upsets Whites because of what they regard as encroachments upon their life styles or property values. Even sympathetic councilmen are reluctant to locate black housing projects in their wards.[31] In Chicago and perhaps in other cities councilmen seek to punish their enemies by voting to locate housing projects in their constituencies.[32]

Much of the disillusionment among the experts results from the sterility of the projects themselves. Cost of land in the central city makes high-rises imperative, and housing projects of twenty stories are not uncommon in the larger cities. The interiors of the buildings are often drab; social interaction is minimal; crime in hallways and elevators is high; racial conflict is sometimes intense; the stigma of charity is pervasive; and parental supervision is simply impossible from ten stories up. There is little encouragement for either community or individuality. Many of the residents have been relocated from neighborhoods bulldozed for highways or urban renewal. They exhibit sustained grief and frustration.[33]

Public housing suffers the further disability of aiding only a limited segment of the poor. It aids neither the poorest nor those just below the poverty line. Projects must be financially self-sustaining. A local agency must cover operating costs from rents, and it cannot, therefore, accommodate many of those who can afford only token payments. At the other extreme, there are income limits upon eligibility. A family that earns more may be evicted to make room for the more deserving. The policy also operates to discourage people from seeking better jobs because the price of a wage increase may be the need to seek housing in the private market, where rents are often much higher. Moreover,

[the departure of those] who did increase their incomes and who went out into the private housing market. . . represented a serious loss to the quality of life in the projects, for they tended to be the more energetic, ambitious, and "responsible" tenants. . . . Those left behind were, to a large extent, families who would never be successful by the usual tests of achievement in America.[34]

No one is better aware of the dilemmas and spillover effects of housing policy than are housing administrators. But they are locked into dilemmas by the compelling realities of financial necessity, political considerations, and the ingrained American suspicion of "socialism."

New priorities and old problems

Widespread dissatisfaction with public housing augured the demise of the federal government as landlord. A series of court decisions in the early 1970s seemed to seal its fate. A federal court in Chicago held that federally subsidized housing projects could not be built in the ghetto, the effects of which would be to accentuate racial segregation. If the federal government was to build and operate housing, it would have to be in white or mixed neighborhoods; however, public housing has not been greeted with open arms in such areas. The Supreme Court, in *James* v. *Valtierra*, upheld the rights of local communities to hold a referendum on proposed public housing projects. Public housing projects thus became squeezed on both sides: It was difficult to locate them in core-city areas where they would perpetuate segregation, but it was not likely that they would be dispersed to the suburbs where voters would not approve them. Nor were public housing programs especially popular with the Nixon administration.

The Johnson administration inaugurated several programs to improve housing opportunities for low-income Americans. Among them were schemes to subsidize rents of the poor and to pay private lessors a supplement for renting to the poor.[35] The Housing Act of 1968 set a 10-year goal of housing starts to eliminate substandard housing for all Americans and assure sufficient housing for established and newly created families. Figure 12.2 shows, however, that the targets were not met, even in the initial years. When housing opportunities are constricted, it is typically the poor who feel the pinch most seriously. In fact, federal

Figure 12.2 Housing Goals and Actual Production

SOURCE: The National Urban Coalition, *Counterbudget: A Blueprint for Changing National Priorities* (New York: Praeger, 1971), p. 148. Reprinted by permission of the publisher.

housing assistance has probably provided more benefits to the middle-income family than to the poor. Two principal policies have benefited the middle class: FHA mortgage insurance and tax writeoffs on home loans. Over 4 million families since 1950 have had their homes insured by the Federal Housing Administration and almost all of these have been middle- or higher-income families (less than 10 percent of FHA borrowers have incomes under $7000).[36] Deductions from federal income taxes on home interest constitute a form of *tax expenditure* by the government, subsidizing home purchasers. Over $4.5 billion is thus allocated annually to subsidize home owners. In 1972, only $750.2 million was spent on all the public housing assistance programs of the federal government.

Urban Renewal

Origins

Urban renewal, as we have seen, was originally tied to public housing in the 1949 and 1954 Housing Acts.[37] The 1949 legislation established the principle of federal subsidies for land sold to private developers through the slum-clearance program. Between 1934 and 1954, slum clearance in its various forms eliminated an estimated 400,000 substandard housing units, but they constituted only 7 percent of the 5.6 million substandard units counted in the 1950 Census. There was no net increase in the availability of low-cost housing; in fact, more slum dwellings were demolished than public-housing units were constructed. Moreover, there was an inevitable lag between demolition and construction, and, as long as the program continued to expand, more units were taken out of the market than were replaced. The 1954 Housing Act was partly designed to rectify these flaws, by providing what some called "an alternative to the bulldozer." The 1954 provisions, which added the term "urban renewal" to our vocabulary, emphasized rehabilitation rather than demolition and wholesale reconstruction of an area. Structures that are deteriorating but salvageable can be renewed rather than demolished. The act also broke earlier precedents that had insisted upon the predominantly residential requirement for all new construction. It permitted 10 percent of federal grants to be used for nonresidential construction, a figure that was increased to 20 percent in 1959 and to 30 percent in 1961. Urban renewal became, through a series of incremental changes, more and more remote from the notion of impoved housing. Increasingly, it became a program to revitalize the private marketplace and the city treasury. To city officials faced with crushing demands for services and limited resources, urban renewal was a blessing in disguise. The disguise was public housing.

Urban renewal in operation

Like the social-security system and the interstate-highway program, urban renewal is an example of cooperative federalism. The key ingredients are congressional definition of standards and sharing of costs and administrative responsibilities by federal and local agencies. The program is administered through the Department of Housing and Urban Development, while operation at the local level is the responsibility of local public authorities.

The national administration of the housing and urban-renewal programs has undergone a series of reorganizations, and today programs are headed by the Assistant Secretary of Housing and Urban Development for Renewal and Housing Assistance. Under him are two deputy assistant secretaries, one running the Housing Assistance Administration and the other the Renewal Assistance Administration. These agencies are responsible for carrying out the intent of the housing acts by laying down standards for local programs, approving or rejecting local applications, and disbursing grants and loans. Participation by local governments in both housing and urban renewal must be authorized by state enabling legislation, which specifies the form and structure of the "local public authority."

As of December 31, 1971, the Renewal Assistance Administration had approved 2697 urban-renewal projects in 1093 communities. A total of $8.2 billion was authorized for these projects, although only .622 projects had actually been completed.[38] The financial picture, or budget, of a fairly typical urban-renewal project is given in Table 12.3. The figures in this table do not represent average costs but are used rather for simplicity of calculation and presentation. Assuming that total or gross cost

Table 12.3 *A Sample Urban-Renewal Project: The Financial Structure*

Gross project cost	
Land acquisition	$ 8 million
Demolition, relocation	1 million
Provision of public facilities by city	1 million
Total	$10 million
Proceeds from sale of land	$ 4 million
Net project cost: Gross cost less proceeds from land	$ 6 million
Grants	
Federal grant for two-thirds (sometimes three-quarters) net project cost	$ 4 million
Local grant of cash, kind, or services	2 million
Total	$ 6 million

of the project is $10 million and that proceeds from the sale of land are $4 million, there is a deficit, or "net project cost," of $6 million. Two-thirds (or three-fourths) of this sum is supplied by federal grants and one-third (or one-fourth) by local contributions in cash, kind, or services.

Variation in housing and urban-renewal expenditures

The urban-renewal and public-housing programs have received varying support from American cities. Several scholars have examined the correlates of community commitment to the two programs.[39] Among the major variables associated with per-capita support for the two programs are the following:

1. Communities with high incidences of poverty spend more heavily upon both programs.
2. The more pluralistic and decentralized the decision-making structure, the higher is the level of spending.[40]
3. Larger and older cities spend more money on both programs.
4. Governmental reformism is not strongly related to urban-renewal and housing commitments, but the direction of the relationship is negative; that is, cities with manager governments, nonpartisan elections, and elections at large have smaller urban-renewal and housing programs.
5. Although the evidence is mixed, some studies have concluded that heavily ethnic or Roman Catholic cities have higher per-capita urban-renewal expenditures.

None of these correlations or even their combined effect is so strongly associated with variations in urban-renewal and public-housing expenditures that spending levels can safely be predicted from macro characteristics alone. There are a number of micro characteristics in each community that explain its commitment to both programs. The dedication of a mayor, the effectiveness of an urban-renewal entrepreneur, the political clout of a city's congressman, and other unique factors cannot be discounted. To gain additional perspective on these features, we shall now move from a macro to a micro level of analysis, examining urban-renewal policy in two cities, Newark and New York.

Case study: the NHA

Two communities whose commitments to urban renewal are rarely exceeded are Newark, New Jersey, and New York City. New York City alone has accounted for almost one-third of all new construction under urban renewal.

Newark is an extreme example of the physical deterioration of large American cities, the suburbanization of the middle class, and the residual human and economic problems. Newark's class and racial structure was "inverted" during the 1960s, as a result of long-term population shifts. From 1960 to 1967, the city lost a total of 70,000 white residents, mostly to nearby suburbs. The composition of the population changed from 65 percent white to 52 percent black and 10 percent Cuban and Puerto Rican.

The emigration of commerce and industry and massive social problems were a constant drain on the city's treasury. Property taxes soared to such staggering heights—$2,000 on a $20,000 house in 1972—that those who were able moved to the suburbs. One-third of the land within the city was occupied by the Newark airport and thus unavailable for taxation. In Harold Kaplan's view, "the single most significant characteristic of Newark's politics in the last quarter-century has been the alienation of the city's business and professional groups. Throughout the 1940s the city's corporation executives, lawyers, realtors, and educators fled Newark for suburban residence."[41] The economic, social, and political milieu of Newark made it a tinderbox, and on June 20, 1967, a race riot erupted during which twenty-three people were killed. One of the major background issues in that disorder, incidentally, was the urban-renewal project in the Central Ward, which involved a proposal to devote 150 acres of ghetto land to a state medical college.

Newark's renewal program was one of the first to be authorized and funded. Its first project was announced less than eighteen months after the passage of the Housing Act of 1949. Much of the credit for the brisk start belongs to Louis Danzig, the executive director of the Newark Housing Authority. The NHA had been established in 1938 to provide low-rent public housing under the provisions of the Housing Act of 1937. Danzig, who had taken over direction of the NHA in 1948, was as far removed from the image of the pencil-chewing, paper-pushing bureaucrat as could be imagined. Like Edward Logue of New Haven and Boston and Robert Moses of New York, Danzig was an urban-renewal entrepreneur. Jewell Bellush and Murray Hausknecht have described the three interlocking elements of the entrepreneurial role, comparing the public entrepreneur to the early capitalist.[42] First, the entrepreneur supplies money—not his own, of course; he is a master of applying for grants. Second, he is a manager and a technocrat, whose efficiency is measured quantitatively—in number of acres cleared, value of construction completed, and number of families relocated. Third, the modern entrepreneur is a major link between the public and private sectors. The urban-renewal program provides the opportunity for the public sector to alter the physical character of the private sector, and the renewal entrepreneur's goal is maximum impact. Danzig was such an entrepreneur.

The effectiveness of Danzig's entrepreneurial skills was maximized by the decentralized and permissive character of Newark politics. In urban-renewal and housing decisions, the NHA was very nearly autonomous. Its unchallenged power was apparent in both its relations with the successive mayors and councils of the city and its dealings with grassroots groups. At the outset, Danzig secured a commitment of noninterference in his program from city hall. The NHA never informed the council or the mayor of its plans until a public announcement was being prepared, and the council and mayor never failed to assent. They trusted Danzig as an efficient administrator to have already considered all possible problems. One way in which he retained the support of successive council majorities was to permit councilmen some intervention in selection of tenants for public housing. Such matters were unimportant to the bricks and mortar of the project, but they were of political interest to councilmen.

Nor did the NHA ever encounter much resistance from neighborhood groups in areas to be renewed. Neighborhood committees of incensed owners or renters in areas scheduled for the bulldozers and the cranes sometimes organized but never obtained many concessions from NHA. Other actors did not lack the power to thwart the NHA—councilmen and mayors could have balked at appropriating funds, neighborhood groups could have protested seriously, as did New York's Greenwich Villagers, the NHA directors could have examined instead of merely accepting Danzig's proposals. But none of these potential obstacles developed.

The urban-renewal system in Newark was quite unlike the model of the monolithic power structure that we described in Chapter 5. No covert, behind-the-scenes group made Newark's urban-renewal policy. But, on the other hand, renewal decision making did not reflect the pluralist model either. In Kaplan's words, "the model of alert interests, strongly committed to their goals and prepared to press these goals at every occasion, does not apply to Newark renewal."[43] This permitted the NHA to exercise considerable influence over renewal policies. Urban renewal in Newark is a good example of the bureaucratic dominance in urban power (see pp. 151–153).

Case study: the West Villagers

It is just a short distance across the Hudson River from Newark to Greenwich Village in New York City. Over the years the Village has developed a reputation as a habitat for Bohemians, beatniks, and itinerant artists and intellectuals, but actually it is an enormously heterogeneous neighborhood, a microcosm of New York City. Many middle-class professionals live in the Village, as do many Italians, Puerto Ricans, and other recent immigrants. Although opinions differed on whether the neighborhood was blighted or simply old, the 1960 Census had identified 42 percent of the housing units in the area as deteriorating or dilapidated.

In November 1960, sensing both a need for and neighborhood sentiment favoring additional housing in the Village, the city's Housing and

Redevelopment Board selected a site in the West Village to study as a renewal and middle-income housing area.[44] In February 1961, the board announced its plan and submitted a request for planning funds to the New York City Board of Estimate, the budgeting unit of the New York City Council. The Housing and Redevelopment Board took pains to indicate that it was not proposing a "bulldozer approach" to urban renewal and favored instead a program emphasizing preservation and rehabilitation. The city council took the proposal under advisement.

Then Villager Jane Jacobs, mother of three and assistant editor of *Architectural Forum*, entered the scene. Mrs. Jacobs is also the author of *The Death and Life of Great American Cities*,[45] a scathing critique of contemporary planners and urban renewers and, particularly, their knack of destroying socially integrated neighborhoods and building homogenized, ultramodern, antiseptic and high-rise neighborhoods. In her view, Greenwich Village was the quintessence of the desirable neighborhood and did not need urban renewal. The city had assumed that neighborhood sentiment in the Village favored new housing, but it had not taken into account Mrs. Jacobs and her Committee to Save the West Village (CSWV), a group of residents and sympathizers devoted to killing the entire renewal project. The committee, a masterpiece of political organization, had a solid base for support, not only among the upper-middle class professionals, but also among the Italian, Irish, and Puerto Rican minorities.

Complicating the conflict over the Village proposal was a broader political conflict related to the New York City elections of 1961. The incumbent mayor, Robert F. Wagner, was renouncing his long allegiance to Tammany Hall, the Democratic organization, and was trying to build support among the Reform Democrats. The mayor and his loyal Borough President of Manhattan, Edward Dudley, tended to favor renewal projects in principle, but they hesitated to antagonize constituents in an election year. Pressuring the mayor thus became an important tactic in the Villagers' campaign to avert renewal. Finally, on April 27, 1961, the Board of Estimate met and faced a hostile assortment of residents from the CSWV. Following a bitter exchange between Deputy Mayor Paul R. Screvane and the Villagers, the Board of Estimate decided to avoid conflict by sending the proposal back to the City Planning Commission for further study. On June 7, in a meeting that lasted from 4:00 P.M. to 4:00 A.M., the planning board heard testimony from the Villagers, who had a solidly crafted political strategy: Three lawyers discussed the illegality of the city's moves, an acoustical engineer presented data to demonstrate that the Village was quieter than the rest of the city, a resident provided statistics from the city's air-pollution department to show that the air was cleaner in the Village, and a Puerto Rican resident argued that the area was happily integrated. In another demonstration of conflict avoidance, the City Planning Commission delayed its decision on the project.

This delay gave Mrs. Jacobs and her committee even more time to drum up support through press releases, meetings, and letters to politicians.

On October 18, the Planning Commission met and declared the West Village area "blighted," an official designation required before planning for a renewal project could proceed. Some Villagers responded with a sit-in at the commission's meeting room and were ejected by the police. Finally, a week later, the Housing and Redevelopment Board announced that it was scrapping the West Village project. The Villagers remained adamant, however, in their efforts to have the blighted label removed from their area. Upon his reelection, Mayor Wagner prevailed upon the Planning Commission to remove the blighted designation from the West Village. The Villagers had routed the redevelopers.

One difference between the unusually successful Newark program and the defeat of the Housing and Redevelopment Board over the West Village project was the characteristics of the neighborhoods in question. Both cases suggest that the most significant opposition to urban-renewal programs comes not from the hard-core slums but from those neighborhoods composed of relatively stable populations with middle-class components.[46] The Village is an extreme example of the kind of neighborhood where citizen protest is both most intense and most likely to be successful. Most of the areas chosen for renewal in Newark, on the other hand, were lower-class neighborhoods, where social organizations that might provide the basis for opposition to renewal were minimal. Urban-renewal legislation requires that a "workable program" for renewal include citizen participation. Yet Wilson has noted that this requirement usually means that "middle-class persons who are beneficiaries of rehabilitation will be planned with; lower-class persons who are disadvantaged by rehabilitation are likely to be planned *without*."[47]

The impact of urban renewal

We tread on difficult terrain when we attempt to assess the impact of urban-renewal programs. Many of their most-important dimensions are not susceptible to measurement. Although several excellent studies have attempted to apply cost-benefit analysis to urban renewal, many variables have had to be either measured indirectly or ignored altogether.[48] The costs and benefits of a project, from the perspective of the municipal budget, are relatively easy to measure but the costs and benefits to those relocated cannot be measured without making some capricious assumptions.

THE ECONOMIC AND FISCAL IMPACT   The most universally accepted claim for urban renewal, and probably the most valid one, is that it has expanded the tax base and improved the economic vitality of the city. The Urban Renewal Administration likes to emphasize the "before" and "after" tax effects of renewal.⁴⁹ For 768 projects on which land acquisition had been completed by 1971 the estimated increase in property values was from $464 million to $1.7 billion; from this increase the cities could reap generous tax revenues. In economic terms, each of these projects also had a potential *multiplier effect*, stimulating more jobs and production in service industries. Given evidence of this sort, it is small wonder that some city officials have considered renewal a godsend. Nevertheless, Martin Anderson has cautioned that such lavish assessments of the economic productivity of renewal projects should be discounted somewhat.⁵⁰ He has noted that (1) some of the new construction would have been undertaken in any case; (2) cities lose tax revenues between the times when structures are demolished and new construction is completed—often a period of five to ten years; and (3) even without renewal projects, land would increase somewhat in value over the years. Anderson investigated the tax gains from Boston's West End project and concluded that it would not begin to "break even" and make up the revenues lost after demolition until 1980 or later, even though the city had taken title to the land as early as 1958. Although Anderson's case may be overstated,⁵¹ it is a useful corrective to unqualified enthusiasm over renewal's contribution to city tax coffers. On balance, and despite Anderson's reservations, most of the evidence from specific cities indicates that both direct and multiplier effects enhance municipal revenues and stimulate economic growth.

The success of renewal in raising municipal tax receipts has led to the somewhat paradoxical pattern of a public project that must turn a *profit* in order to be successful. The necessity for profit from urban renewal is registered in two ways. In the private sector each project must be profitable enough to attract private developers to whom land can be sold. In the public sector, the city government seeks profit for its own treasury from increased tax receipts. The former requirement is obvious enough. The first renewal project undertaken by the NHA in the North Ward was stalled for several years while the agency tried to find a private redeveloper to purchase the site. The NHA soon remodeled its redevelopment schemes on the principle "Find a redeveloper first, and then see what interests him."⁵² The responsibility for site selection, planning, and decisions about land reuse is thus defined in terms of profit for the redeveloper, as well as of professional criteria.

Renewal must also be attractive to city government. Its net effect should be to produce, rather than to consume, tax revenues. What kinds of projects are likely to be profitable to both developers and city governments?

A negative answer is easiest. The least-profitable use of cleared land is for public housing, simply because the latter yields neither city taxes nor private profit. Perhaps the next least profitable use is low-cost private housing, for it produces relatively little in taxes and attracts people with low incomes, who have minimum "multiplier effects" upon the economy. The most productive residential use, of course, is for middle- or high-income housing. Equally productive—sometimes more productive, depending upon the kind of business attracted—is commercial or industrial use. In some respects, the net effect of urban renewal is thus to *redistribute land to higher- and higher-cost enterprises.* Newark is again a case in point. As one Newark redevelopment official said, NHA's goal was "middle income housing on cleared slum sites."[53] Because of the profit incentive in urban renewal, the initial choice of land for clearance is important. The key questions become whether the private developer can make a profit from middle-income housing (or other justifiable use under the law) and whether the city can improve its fiscal situation. The local renewal authorities and prospective redevelopers thus "tend to pick the best possible area that could still be justified as a slum to meet the requirements of the Title I law."[54] In Newark, at least, there appeared to be "an inverse correlation between the degree of blight in the area and its acceptability to [federal renewal officials] and the redevelopers."[55] The upshot of the public and private profit requirements is that few of the very worst slums are renewed.

One of the more significant consequences of renewal legislation has been to shift land use from residential to nonresidential purposes. As such, it has taken a toll of housing opportunities available to lower-income families. The 1949 renewal law required that renewal land was to be used for *predominantly residential* purposes. The term *predominantly* was usually interpreted to mean that *over half* of the new land use would be residential. In a succession of amendments, however, the requirement for reuse in residential purposes has been relaxed. The effect of such amendments is to reduce the pressure on local authorities to replace the

Table 12.4 *Housing Stock Changes Associated with Urban Renewal*

Fiscal year	Housing units razed	New housing units planned Total	New housing units planned Public, low and moderate income	New housing units completed Total	New housing units completed Public, low and moderate income
1967	383,449	195,999	76,363	106,961	42,601
1968	422,817	226,031	97,573	124,781	52,399
1969	460,482	256,978	113,485	144,317	63,021
1970	499,407	286,707	133,199	169,224	80,696
1971	538,044	324,615	162,587	200,687	101,461

NOTE: All data are cumulative.
SOURCE: John A. Weicher, *Urban Renewal: National Program for Local Problems* (Washington, D.C.: American Enterprise Institute, 1972), p. 6.

housing stock razed by the federal bulldozer. The data in Table 12.4 indicates the pattern of changes in housing stock. Between 1967 and 1971, 538,000 housing units were razed, but only 201,000 replaced.[56] This gap represents about 0.3 percent of the nation's housing stock. The burdens of the housing gap associated with urban renewal have typically fallen hardest on the poor.

The economic effects of urban renewal are not limited to land use and financial gains to real-estate interests and municipal governments. Charles Abrams has described "some blessings of urban renewal":

1. Increased capacity of cities to attract and maintain industries and commercial establishments;
2. Ability of universities, hospitals, and other public institutions to expand facilities;
3. Impetus to cultural improvements like New York City's Lincoln Center;
4. Expanded middle-income housing;
5. Revitalization of downtown and central-city areas;
6. Greater aesthetic appeal.[57]

The spillover effects

We have emphasized that all public policies have *spillover effects,* or *latent impacts,* the unintended by-products of the manifest (or intended) impacts of the policies. Perhaps the spillover effects of no other public policy have been so much investigated as have those of urban renewal; perhaps these impacts have been decried by critics more loudly than have those of any other policy. Many, though not all, of the spillover effects of urban renewal are related to relocation and displacement of people.

Since the passage of the New Deal public-housing acts and the urban-renewal provisions of the 1949 and 1954 acts, hundreds of thousands of Americans have received letters similar to the following:

The building in which you now live is located in an area which has been taken by the Boston Redevelopment Authority according to law as part of the Government Center Project. The buildings will be demolished after the families have been relocated and the land will be sold to developers for public and commercial uses, according to the Land Assembly and Redevelopment plan presently being prepared.[58]

A congressional study estimated that, between 1964 and 1972, no fewer than 825,000 families and 136,000 businesses would be required to vacate their present structures because of urban-renewal and federal highway programs.[59] If we estimate that each of these families has three people (possibly an underestimation), then in eight years about 2.5 million people, equivalent to the population of Los Angeles, would be displaced. Some people have moved into areas slated for later clearance, thus becoming "two-time losers."

Needless to say, the vast majority of families and individuals who have to relocate are the poor and the nearly poor. More than 60 percent of the displaced are nonwhite, leading to charges that the urban-renewal program is really Black removal. Many families and unrelated individuals in renewal areas are elderly, both white and black.

The Renewal Assistance Administration has estimated that 54 percent of the families displaced are eligible for public housing, in which they are given priority. According to the RAA, however, only 20 percent of the dislocated families actually move into public housing. There are four principal reasons:

1. Public housing is simply unavailable for many who would take it. The urban-renewal program, as we have explained, has been more dedicated to construction of middle-income units than public housing. Moreover, as long as the urban-renewal program continues to expand, more housing units are being taken out of the market than are being made available for families.
2. For many families, public housing has a social stigma attached to it.
3. Many uprooted families have incomes *too low* for public housing. As housing authorities must meet fixed costs (paying off bonds, operation, maintenance, salaries), they can accept only a certain proportion of very low-income tenants, whose payments on the sliding scale of rents will be too low to cover the costs of their own housing.
4. Finally, many people find the sterile, tightly regulated, spartan accommodations of the high-rise public-housing project distinctly distasteful.

Urban-renewal legislation requires authorities to establish that adequate housing is available for all people to be displaced by renewal projects. They are also required to assist in relocation and to provide relocation payments, but the average relocation payment per family is less than $100, principally for moving expenses. Most critics and many supporters of urban renewal consider the relocation problem its most serious defect. The critics doubt that local authorities can in practice guarantee suitable accommodations at reasonable costs to the displaced. They argue, reasonably enough, that, if suitable housing were available at rents that the relocated could afford, they would be living there already, instead of in slums. Urban-renewal officials claim that more than 90 percent of relocated families have moved to standard housing, but most private studies dispute such claims.[60] Not only do these urban displaced persons often move into substandard housing, but their rents typically increase as well. John Weicher concluded that "all things considered, the typical relocatee is probably worse off. To claim that he is 'really' better off is to substitute the judgment of the government for a person's own judgment of what is best for himself."[61]

Small businessmen are especially vulnerable to relocation. Most businesses in renewal areas are small, employing only handsful of people and depending upon carefully nurtured neighborhood clienteles. A Boston study indicated that almost 40 percent of the businessmen who were forced to evacuate renewal areas went out of business,[62] and the Renewal Assistance Administration's own national studies indicate that about a third of dislocated businesses have discontinued operations altogether.[63] The disappearance of the small businessman, partly because he seems an anachronism in our age of mass production and mass marketing, is particularly likely to be a spillover effect of urban renewal.

Finally, relocation has exacted a psychological cost as well. People's reactions differ, of course, when they are displaced from their homes and forced to seek other habitation, but for a good many, according to Marc Fried, "it seems quite precise to speak of their reactions as grief."[64] Some of the relocated from Boston's West End, whom Fried studied, expressed intense emotion at separation from the old neighborhood social patterns: "I felt like my heart was taken out of me"; "What's the use of thinking about it?"; "Even now I feel like crying when I pass by." To middle-class Americans, these strong emotional responses may be surprising. But the social networks and spatial relations within a neighborhood are much more salient to lower-class than to middle- and upper-class people because almost all the socializing of lower-class Americans takes place in the immediate neighborhood, whereas middle-class contacts and interactions are much wider. For this reason, the disruption of neighborhood social ties can foster deep feelings of alienation and frustration among low-income residents.

Summing up the impact

The multidimensional impact of a public policy involving a dozen legislative acts, years of development, and billions of dollars does not lend itself to hasty summary. Although significant public resources have been provided to cities, the overwhelming majority of decisions about land use, housing, and industrial location are still made in the private sector. The $9.4 billion previously committed to urban renewal by the federal government represents only a fraction of the estimated $43 billion spent in 1971 on residential construction alone. The major constraint upon the renewal program's goal of restructuring the urban environment is the hundreds of thousands of private decisions made by families, commercial establishments, and industrial corporations. Similarly, the public-housing units constructed since the Depression represent only a fraction of the total number of existing housing units. Decay, obsolescence, and mobility may have been slowed by renewal and housing programs, but they have not been halted. And, as with all public policies, even the gains have not been won without spillover costs.

Model Cities

The model-cities program is the latest in the arsenal of weapons to restructure the urban environment. This highly touted program was created by the Demonstration Cities and Metropolitan Development Act of

1966. (For fear that the title might imply a reward to demonstrations by rioters, the program came to be called *model* rather than *demonstration* cities.) The city applying for a grant must develop a comprehensive program to improve the quality of life in a given neighborhood, through education, housing, municipal services, crime and delinquency control, health services, economic development, and transportation plans. Model-cities grants take three principal forms. A planning grant covers a year of planning, during which time governmental officials, private groups, and neighborhood residents establish priorities and prepare a request for additional funds, which are available to those cities whose plans are approved. They can be used for various purposes consonant with the approved plans but are directed primarily at those parts of the program for which conventional grants are not available. Urban-renewal grants cover redevelopment activities within the "model neighborhoods."

Local officials have been enthusiastic about the model-cities program. From their perspective, it introduces considerable flexibility into federal aid to urban areas. In principle, everything from sewers to schools may be included in the program. Moreover, model cities, though not guaranteed assistance under related federal programs, are given priority. The program also appeals to local officials because they have the final say about each component of the total package. In model-city plans, city hall has a veto over any particular item, in contrast to both the urban-renewal and antipoverty programs, where quasi-governmental agencies have had considerable autonomy. City councils are also comforted by the predominantly bricks-and-mortar orientation of this program. In contrast to the war on poverty and its Community-Action Agencies, model neighborhoods are to be improved mainly through upgrading facilities and services, in contrast to the poverty program, which often sought to improve the lot of the poor by "politicizing" them.

Yet the enabling legislation for model cities does require "widespread citizen participation" in both planning and execution. (Note that this phrase is milder than the "maximum feasible participation" of the Economic Opportunity Act.) Neighborhood groups, often through organizations developed under the poverty programs, have, in many cities, succeeded in winning concessions from city hall. In the final analysis, neighborhood groups will have difficulty defending themselves against the charge of ignoring neighborhood sentiments. The planning stage in some model cities has been marked by continual skirmishing between neighborhoods and city halls, whereas the traditional public and private bureaucracies (for urban renewal, social welfare, and school systems) have played relatively small roles.[65]

The model-cities program is designed to provide *models* for comprehensive and coordinated development of *disadvantaged* neighborhoods.

Such models were to be major social experiments, which could then be adopted by other cities. The degree to which this goal could be met depends, of course, on financing. Under the original proposal, a handful of cities (a commonly mentioned figure was six) were to receive generous aid for major innovations. Programs providing benefits to few constituencies, however, are not popular in Congress, and the number was later increased, first to 63, then to 150, and still later to any city which could meet the grant requirements. The philosophy of social experimentation behind the model-cities legislation may be less significant than its funding of basic social services to poor neighborhoods. Streets have been paved, consumer-education centers established, crime-prevention programs inaugurated, and a host of other services provided in poor neighborhoods.

But model cities, like urban renewal and public housing, has not been popular with the second Nixon administration. Model cities suffered heavier proposed cuts than any other agency except the war-on-poverty agencies. The availability of general revenue-sharing funds meant that cities could continue to support model cities at previous levels, if they chose to do so. But whether many cities—pressed by myriad demands from their more established bureaucracies and more influential citizens —will do so we cannot predict.

Summary

Planning, zoning, urban renewal, housing policies, and model cities are all designed to manage urban growth. Changes in the urban environment—weathering, deterioration, population and production mobility—all produce a dynamic metropolis. Many of the forces of metropolitan growth operate beyond the control of public policy. The vast majority of location decisions of persons and firms are made independent of any governmental influences. But while market forces are important, the role of government in manipulating urban growth is not insignificant.

Using planning, zoning, and related policies, urban governments can attempt to secure particular kinds of environment. Through sophisticated use of planning and zoning, it may be possible to create an environment uniquely satisfying to the community or to important groups within it. These strategies, however, typically involve spillover costs to other communities within the metropolis.

Redevelopment and public-housing policies are also intended to have impacts on the urban physical environment. Although the two were originally coupled, urban renewal has been effectively divorced from public housing and has been more favored by municipal officials—partly because it can compensate somewhat for the loss of tax revenues resulting from commercial and personal emigration. Renewal programs also have significant unintended impacts, particularly those arising from the dislocation of families and businesses in areas slated for the bulldozer. Public housing has not been able to accommodate more than a fraction of those displaced by urban renewal; indeed, over the years, public housing has been a source of consternation to both its friends and its enemies. The former have managed to save the housing program but have expressed some disillusionment over its effects, and its enemies oppose it as a socialistic infringement on the private-enterprise system. Model cities is the latest in the arsenal of redevelopment policies. Although its effects are not yet fully apparent, it is designed to create models for managing urban growth. But, as with the other policies examined here, it suffers significant constraints. The most significant is what Banfield has called the "logic of metropolitan growth": The character of the metropolis is shaped by powerful socioeconomic forces that are not easily deflected by public policy.

Notes

1. Quoted in *Newsweek*, August 18, 1969, p. 51.
2. Edward C. Banfield, *The Unheavenly City* (Boston: Little, Brown, 1970), p. 23.
3. For a provocative treatment of location choice as a crucial factor in local politics, see Oliver P. Williams, *Metropolitan Political Analysis* (New York: Free Press, 1971).
4. Organization of the planning office under the chief executive or an independent commission seems to have little effect, however, on its political power. See Francine Rabinovitz, *City Politics and Planning* (New York: Atherton, 1969).
5. David C. Ranney, *Planning and Politics in the Metropolis* (Columbus: Merrill, 1969), p. 20.
6. Ebenezer Howard, *Garden Cities of Tomorrow* (Cambridge, Mass.: M.I.T. Press, 1965; first published as *Tomorrow* in 1898).
7. Alan Altshuler, *The City Planning Process* (Ithaca, N.Y.: Cornell University Press, 1965), p. 315.
8. Ranney, pp. 28–35.
9. Edward C. Banfield and James Q. Wilson, *City Politics* (Cambridge, Mass.: Harvard University Press, 1963), pp. 188–189.
10. Edward C. Banfield, "The Uses and Limitations of Comprehensive Planning in Massachusetts," in H. Wentworth Eldridge, ed., *Taming Megalopolis* (Garden City, N.Y.: Doubleday, 1967), vol. 2, p. 713.
11. 272 U.S. 36 (1927).
12. Oliver P. Williams et al., *Suburban Differences and Metropolitan Policies* (Philadelphia: University of Pennsylvania Press, 1965), pp. 91ff.
13. Alan K. Campbell and Seymour Sacks, "The Fiscal Zoning Game," *Municipal Finance*, 65 (1964), 140–149.
14. *Shelley* v. *Kraemer*, 334 U.S. 24 (1948).
15. *The New York Times*, May 29, 1967, p. 13.
16. Robert C. Wood, *1400 Governments* (Cambridge, Mass.: Harvard University Press, 1961), p. 79.
17. Advisory Commission on Intergovernmental Relations, *Metropolitan Fiscal Disparities* (Washington, D.C.: Government Printing Office, 1967), p. 44.

18. Wood, p. 85.
19. On the politics of suburban exclusivity, see Richard Babcock, "The Courts Enter the Land Development Marketplace," *City*, January-February 1971, pp. 65–68; *Newsweek*, November 15, 1971, pp. 61–70; Daniel R. Mandelker, *The Zoning Dilemma: A Legal Strategy for Urban Change* (Indianapolis: Bobbs-Merrill, 1971); and Wood, *op. cit.*
20. John P. Dean, "The Myths of Housing Reform," *American Sociological Review*, 14 (April 1949), 283.
21. Alvin Schorr, *Slums and Social Insecurity* (London: Nelson, 1964), pp. 20–21.
22. Karl E. and Alma F. Taeuber, *Negroes in Cities* (Chicago: Aldine, 1965).
23. Reynolds Farley and Karl E. Taeuber, "Population Trends and Residential Segregation since 1960," *Scientific American*, 159 (March 1, 1968), 953–956.
24. Karl E. Taeuber, "Residential Segregation," *Scientific American*, 213 (August 1965), 19.
25. Martin Anderson has argued that "there is not a physical shortage of decent housing units. The real problem is that there is a certain group of people who either cannot or will not spend enough money to rent or buy this housing." Martin Anderson, *The Federal Bulldozer* (Cambridge, Mass.: M.I.T. Press, 1964), p. 200.
26. Lawrence M. Friedman, *Government and Slum Housing* (Skokie, Ill.: Rand McNally, 1968), pp. 22–23.
27. Eminent domain is the power of government to take possession of property for public purposes, paying just compensation to the owner. There was little doubt of the constitutionality of slum clearance in its earlier form, in which property was taken and *retained* by local housing authorities. The constitutionality of the 1949 Title I provisions, which permitted local authorities to use eminent domain to obtain land and then *sell it to private developers* was a more serious question. The Supreme Court, however, upheld Title I in *Berman* v. *Parker*, 348 U.S. 26 (1954).
28. For an analysis of group politics and public housing, see Leonard Freedman, *Public Housing* (New York: Holt, Rinehart & Winston, 1969), chap. 2.
29. Quoted in Jewell Bellush and Murray Hausknecht, "Urban Renewal: A Historical Overview," in Bellush and Hausknecht, eds., *Urban Renewal: People, Politics and Planning* (Garden City, N.Y.: Doubleday, 1967), p. 9.
30. Friedman, p. 141.
31. Although only a minority of the poor are black, a majority of public-housing residents are black. See Freedman, pp. 140–144.
32. Martin Meyerson and Edward C. Banfield, *Politics, Planning, and the Public Interest* (New York: Free Press, 1955), p. 121.
33. Marc Fried, "Grieving for a Lost Home: Psychological Costs of Relocation," in Leonard J. Duhl, ed., *The Urban Condition* (New York: Basic Books, 1965), p. 151.
34. Freedman, p. 108.
35. For a comparative evaluation of these programs with conventional public housing, see Arthur P. Solomon, "Housing and Public Policy Analysis," *Public Policy*, 20 (Summer 1972), 443–471.
36. National Urban Coalition, *Counterbudget: A Blueprint for Changing National Priorities, 1971–1976* (New York: Praeger, 1971), p. 150.
37. The origins of the urban renewal program are detailed in Bellush and Hausknecht, *op. cit.*
38. *HUD Statistical Yearbook* (Washington, D.C.: Government Printing Office, 1971), p. 48.
39. George S. Duggar, "The Relation of Local Government Structure to Urban Renewal," *Law and Contemporary Problems*, 26 (1961), 49–69; Amos H. Hawley, "Community Power and Urban Renewal Success," *American Journal of Sociology*, 68 (January 1963), 422–431; Terry N. Clark, "Community Structure, Decision-making, Budget Expenditures, and Urban Renewal in 51 American Communities," *American Sociological Review*, 33 (August 1968), 576–593; and Michael Aiken and Robert R. Alford, "Community Struc-

ture and Innovation: The Case of Urban Renewal," *American Sociological Review, 35,* (August 1970), 650–664.

40. Hawley, *op. cit.,* found that more centralized power structures had higher urban-renewal activity, but later evidence from both Clark, *op. cit.,* and Aiken and Alford, *op. cit.,* suggests that decentralization is associated with higher urban-renewal expenditures.

41. Harold Kaplan, *Urban Renewal Politics* (New York: Columbia University Press, 1963), p. 61. Our case study of the Newark Housing Authority is based upon Kaplan's excellent treatment of the Newark experience.

42. Jewell Bellush and Murray Hausknecht, "Entrepreneurs and Urban Renewal: The New Men of Power," *Journal of the American Institute of Planners, 32* (September 1966), 289–297.

43. Kaplan, p. 177.

44. James Clarence Davies, III, *Neighborhood Groups and Urban Renewal* (New York: Columbia University Press, 1966). Our discussion of the Villagers and their battle is based upon Davies' chap. 4.

45. Jane Jacobs, *The Death and Life of Great American Cities* (New York: Random House, 1961).

46. Kaplan, p. 136; and Davies, p. 153.

47. James Q. Wilson, "Planning and Politics: Citizen Participation in Urban Renewal," in James Q. Wilson, ed., *Urban Renewal* (Cambridge, Mass.: M.I.T. Press, 1966), p. 418.

48. Stanley Rothenberg, *Economic Evaluation of Urban Renewal* (Washington, D.C.: Brookings Institution, 1967) and John C. Weicher, *Urban Renewal: National Program for Local Problems* (Washington, D.C.: American Enterprise Institute, 1972).

49. *HUD Statistical Yearbook 1971,* p. 55.

50. Anderson, chap. 10.

51. See the critique of Anderson's book in Robert Groberg, "Urban Renewal Realistically Appraised," *Law and Contemporary Problems, 30* (Winter 1965), 212–229.

52. Kaplan, p. 24.

53. *Ibid.,* p. 15.

54. Davies, p. 15.

55. Kaplan, p. 16.

56. Weicher, p. 6.

57. Charles Abrams, *The City is the Frontier* (New York: Harper & Row, 1965), chap. 9.

58. The quotation is from a letter sent on October 25, 1961, to residents of a Boston area slated for renewal cited in Anderson, p. 1.

59. Cited in Advisory Commission on Intergovernmental Relations, *Metropolitan America* (Washington, D.C.: Government Printing Office, 1966), p. 57.

60. One widely quoted study is Chester Hartman, "The Housing of Relocated Families," *Journal of the American Institute of Planners, 30* (November 1964), 266–286.

61. Weicher, p. 47.

62. Basil G. Zimmer, "The Small Businessman and Relocation," in Wilson, ed., *Urban Renewal,* p. 382.

63. Cited in Advisory Commission on Intergovernmental Relations, *Metropolitan America,* p. 69.

64. Fried, p. 151.

65. Roland Warren, "Model Cities First Round: Politics, Planning, and Participation," *Journal of the American Institute of Planners, 34* (July 1969), 245–253.

epilogue

The urban crisis and political science

Local politics is no longer one of the dustbins of political science. Urban affairs present some of the most dynamic and controversial issues in contemporary society, and social scientists are using tools of increasing sophistication in order to comprehend urban phenomena. They are also turning to a wider range of sources as the need to know grows. Political scientists, for example, make use of materials produced by sociologists, psychologists, economists, geographers, and ecologists to comprehend the human and physical dimensions of urban affairs and offer in turn their own insights about the dynamics of urban politics and the policies produced by urban political systems.

In this text we have presented the best of the material about urban politics in a framework emphasizing the policy-making process. We have considered a number of elements that shape the policies of urban areas, the major policies offered in several fields of service, and—as far as possible—the effects of environment and policy feedback on the decisions of public officials. In this epilogue we shall take an overview of urban problems and deal with two evaluations of urban life: one negative, one positive. We shall also reconsider our tools of analysis. By themselves, these tools do not solve any problems of urban life. Yet they can help to define the magnitude of social and economic problems that occur in given communities and may help define a set of policies that are feasible for local conditions.

The Urban Crisis: The Negative View

The urban crisis has many aspects. At the very least, it represents a sharp divergence between aspirations and achievements in personal income, employment opportunity, racial segregation, education, housing, health, crime, and pollution. At worst, it represents failure in all these areas, failure that may—if not remedied—destroy our culture. Some critics see the various components of the urban crisis as fitting together in an interrelated whole. To us, however, the picture is less one of an integrated whole than of various pieces that may or may not be related to one another in various communities.

One element in the urban crisis is economic. The poor in the central cities have little immediate hope of rising out of their poverty. The most visible feature associated with poverty is race. Poor Whites live in cities, but it is the poor Blacks who present the most serious concentrations of poverty and who suffer numerous other social dislocations that seem based upon—and to feed—their poverty. Blacks show the highest rates of unemployment and underemployment; they are segregated in primary and secondary schools that are said to be "holding pens," rather than educational institutions whose graduates are fit for productive lives; their crime and disease rates are the highest in any city; and they have meager opportunities for decent housing and public recreation.

Although Blacks in central cities face an array of obstacles to the good life that seem nearly insurmountable, the parameters defining the crisis affect all city dwellers. Among these parameters the following are the most significant:

1. Growing central-city concentrations of the poor, uneducated, and black;
2. The segregation of Blacks in central-city neighborhood schools;
3. Educational programs and teachers who are unresponsive to the social and linguistic problems of the urban poor and unable to provide the training necessary to maximize their economic potential;
4. Unemployment concentrations among males eighteen to twenty-five years old with little education, which makes them highly visible and susceptible recruits for civil disorder;
5. Periodic social conflagrations far beyond the capacities of local police to control;
6. Dispersion of industrial and commercial jobs to the suburbs, beyond easy commuting range of the central-city labor pool;
7. Failure of mass transit to meet the needs of low-income communities for cheap home-to-job transportation;
8. Poor diets resulting in low stamina for school and job performance;
9. High rates of infant mortality and mental retardation, traceable partly to inadequate prenatal care and infant diets;
10. High rates of venereal disease and illegitimacy, with attendant

problems of fatherless homes and delinquency passing through the generations;

11. Substandard housing, plus social and economic barriers against the dispersion of low-income, especially black, populations to better neighborhoods;

12. High crime rates in poor neighborhoods, which reflect social dislocations and add to the burdens carried by neighborhood residents.

The city dweller's emotional response to these features of the urban crisis is heightened by his view of government as incapable of correcting them. It is said that local governments lack the commitment or ability to deal with such problems and that state and federal governments fail to provide the incentives and resources necessary to deal with them. In fact, some pessimists argue that federal policies serve to aggravate, rather than to alleviate, urban problems.

As we have seen in Chapter 2, urban areas contain the greatest concentrations of wealth in our society, but many governments compete for this wealth. The state and national governments soak up huge amounts of resources through their income and sales taxes, and a plethora of local governments divide the funds available from taxes on real property. The cities are thus left with the least popular and least flexible sources of revenue. Moreover, city governments are most vulnerable to tax competition. Industrial and commercial taxpayers have numerous options among the jurisdictions of a metropolitan area, and local officials are susceptible to the argument that high taxes will keep away—or drive away—property owners who would otherwise make substantial contributions to the local economy.

Large cities also find themselves left with the legacy of their historic wealth in the form of requirements that they contribute to state and federal coffers so that poorer rural areas may receive intergovernmental assistance. Undoubtedly the urban areas will have to continue acting as fiscal crutches for the hinterlands. Yet many anachronistic formulas of state and federal aid provide greater benefits to wealthy suburbs than to struggling central cities. As the cities are caught between the migration of big taxpayers to the suburbs and the competition from state and federal tax systems that do not return fair shares to the cities, their schools and other social services seem totally inadequate in the face of demands from populations beset by problems.

At one time the inequitable representation of central-city residents in state legislatures and Congress was said to be responsible for the meager response to urban needs. Now that we are more than a decade into the era of reapportionment this political reform seems to be less rewarding than had been expected. Suburbs have gained more representation than central cities, and the new urban legislators are frequently unable to agree on policies. Urban representatives reflect the divisions in social backgrounds, political parties, and philosophies that mark the populations living in metropolitan areas, with the result that there may be little change in the benefits coming to central cities. In most states the central cities seem destined for minority status in the electorate. Any "goodies" they extract from the states will have to come on the same old basis of persuasion and not from any newly acquired political clout.[1]

Even recent awareness of environmental pollution presents problems for urban politics. Among middle-class college students, the environment ranks as a unifying issue. They all favor clean air and water. Yet, to one perceptive segment of black urban leadership, the ecology issue represents a diversion of both funds and interest from the Blacks' basic needs for jobs, housing, and education. They regard cutbacks on urban industrial development just when Blacks seem on the verge of getting their share of the "action" as one more instance of the double racial standard in American life.

The Urban Crisis: A Brighter View

Edward Banfield is one of the most vocal proponents of the view that things are not as bad as they seem. In fact, he finds them better than ever before:

> The plain fact is that the overwhelming majority of city dwellers live more comfortably and conveniently than ever before. They have more and better housing, more and better schools, more and better transportation, and so on. By any conceivable measure of material welfare the present generation of urban Americans is, on the whole, better off than any other large group of people has ever been anywhere. What is more, there is every reason to expect that the general level of comfort and convenience will continue to rise at an even more rapid rate through the foreseeable future.[2]

In *The Unheavenly City*, Banfield has not disputed the existence of an urban crisis, but he has defined it in terms of frustrated expectations rather than of objective deprivation. According to him, the problems of poverty, ignorance, disease, poor housing, and crime affect "only a rather small minority of the whole urban population."[3] Moreover, some of the problems are necessary accompaniments of the attractions of urban society. Congestion will not go away as long as many people find great benefits in living close to many other people and the jobs and commercial and cultural opportunities that exist in urban areas. Traffic snarls will remain as long as people resist staggered employment hours.

Banfield has not denied the presence of segregation, inadequate housing, and poverty in urban areas, but he has claimed that conditions are better than in poor rural areas. The vast majority of inadequate housing exists *outside* large cities and metropolitan areas. Education levels are, to be sure, lower in central cities than in the suburbs, but they are lower in rural areas than in central cities. The urban police may be intemperate in their dealings with Blacks and other ethnic minorities, but not to the extent of rural southern sheriffs.

Banfield has found some of the alleged problems in urban areas grossly exaggerated. Population growth in low-income neighborhoods was greater in earlier decades of urban history because of immigration of the European poor, he has said, and to those who argue that vast numbers of poor Blacks will overburden the cities' capacity for economic and social accommodation, he has replied that earlier decades of peasant immigration placed larger numerical strains on urban political systems.

There are urban problems that do concern Banfield. One is the unprecedented concentration in cities of urban Blacks whose psychological alienation from the dominant society may be far greater than suggested by indexes of material deprivation. Young, unemployed black males have especially bleak economic prospects, and, though their condition may be no worse economically—and may even be better—than that of their rural forebears, their concentration in urban ghettos provides the human masses that can explode and threaten our basic social fabric. Second, there is a gap between anticipated social and economic gains and the benefits actually achieved. As long as aspirations rise faster than do accomplishments, this gap will continue to widen; no matter how much social progress is achieved, the tinder for a social revolution will remain. Third, government programs that are unable to solve basic social and personal problems nevertheless sometimes help to increase aspirations and thus pave the way for increased frustrations:

To a large extent. . . our urban problems are like the mechanical rabbit at the racetrack, which is set to keep just ahead of the dogs no matter how fast they may run. Our performance is better and better, but because we set our standards and expectations to keep ahead of performance, the problems are never any nearer to solution. . . .

The effect of too-high standards cannot be to spur us on to reach the prescribed level of performance sooner than we otherwise would, for that level is by definition impossible of attainment. At the same time, these standards may cause us to adopt measures that are wasteful and injurious and, in the long run, to conclude from the inevitable failure of these measures that there is something fundamentally wrong with our society.[4]

There is merit in both the negative view of the urban situation and in Banfield's brighter assessment of it. Banfield seems right in his claim that things have never been better, yet he concedes that achievements have not caught up with aspirations and may even be falling farther behind. Social progress is not measured only by what is but also by what could be.

A Crisis of Ignorance

Any talk of *measurement* with respect to urban problems raises the issue of our capacity to understand and to prescribe. There is much about urban affairs that lies in the realm of speculation. We can cite the variety of urban problems, note the environmental factors that might influence policy makers, list the difficulties in translating policy goals into impacts, and recite unanticipated consequences and spillovers. In few cases, however, can we go beyond qualitative description to a precise measurement of elements and a statistical analysis of their relationships. Any sound knowledge of cause and effect—unlimited by a large component of educated guesswork—lies somewhere over the horizon.

In this book we have tried to cope with the problem of ignorance by offering a framework for analysis (the urban political system), and showing how findings from various studies can be assembled on that framework. The aim is to organize the myriad of information we do have in the hope of understanding the elements that influence urban policy makers, and the capacity of policy makers to shape the urban environment.

Our concern is less to identify and to prescribe cures for urban problems than to introduce a set of analytic techniques that political scientists (and other social scientists) can use to improve our information about the problems and opportunities that face urban policy makers. We offer not solutions but means of understanding. As scholars, we must claim that understanding is the first step toward solution. Yet perfect understanding is not much easier to obtain than are perfect solutions when we are dealing with complex problems that so far have proved intractable. Policy analysts can learn much that is useful but not everything they should know. Policy makers cannot wait until all the information is in before they make decisions. But it is to be hoped that they are always open to new information and will take cognizance of it at some point in the endless cycle of policy formulation, implementation, and reformulation.

Basic Research in the Policy Process

In recent years academic political scientists and economists have shown considerable interest in the analysis of public policy. This interest is wide-ranging and includes oratory in behalf of certain favored policies, case studies designed to flesh out elaborate models of the policy-making process, sophisticated commentaries at high levels of abstraction on the ways policies are chosen, academic adaptations of benefit-cost analysis, and elaborate comparisons of the policies offered by different governments.[5]

Macro-comparative policy analysis

One concern is with macro-comparative studies that pursue a consciously scientific course in measuring policies in several jurisdictions and defining their statistical relations with various features in their environment. Although much of the literature concerns policy processes of state governments, a good deal is also relevant to local political systems.[6] Even what is almost exclusively oriented to the state level suggests modes of analysis that are relevant to local politics.

Some scholars are interested in explaining the policy differences that exist; they look at certain policies as *dependent variables* and consider their relations with the economic, social, or political characteristics that seem likely to have shaped them. Others are interested in explaining the effects of different policies; they look at certain policies as *independent variables* and consider their relations with the economic, social, and political characteristics that may be affected by them.[7]

In order to grasp the possibilities and limitations of macro-comparative policy analysis, it is necessary to look at some representative findings. One line of research that seems especially fruitful in identifying constraints and resources for the policy makers involves the level of economic development within a jurisdiction. The model used to guide this research is simple. It merely posits that macro-economic features of a jurisdiction have something to do with the nature of public policy. This model is used most often as part of a systems framework that treats the economy as providing the inputs of resources, demands, and supports for a conversion process in which other inputs from politics may affect the relations between the economy and policy.[8] Some regard the macro-economic policy model as too simple because it leaves out many specific features of the policy-making process. It does, but its simplicity also offers several benefits: a demonstrated capacity to support empirical research and to produce a series of propositions about the conditions that create more or less powerful relationships between various features of the economy and various features of public policy. The practitioners of macro-comparative policy analysis append various additional aspects of the policy-making process to this basic model and consider several kinds of economic traits as correlates of public policy. By reviewing the findings available to date, we can assess the strength of the economic-policy links and how much latitude for policy innovation is permitted by economic constraints.

According to much of the current literature, the nature of a jurisdiction's economy limits the magnitude and quality of the jurisdiction's *policy outputs*. Limiting the resources available is said to limit an official's capacity for current performance and innovation. It is important to understand which limitations may be placed on the policy maker by economics and under what conditions they are likely to inhibit innovation. The first wave of research into economic-policy links tended to exaggerate the strength of economic influence over policy and to neglect findings that provided clues to policy arenas that are relatively free from economic influence. There is no "iron law" of economics that establishes the level and content of public policy. Rather, the economy varies in its influence over policy. This variation can occur between different levels of government, different periods of time, different kinds of public service, and at different levels of affluence. Some of the comparative findings on state and community policy indicate these kinds of variations in economic influence over policy.

Economic influences appear to be strongest in local policy processes and weakest in those of state and federal governments.[9] Explanations cite differences in economic resources and fiscal opportunities. Most local governments must draw upon limited geographical areas for resources and are confined to one major revenue source (property taxes). State governments, in contrast, can draw upon their larger jurisdictions and can transfer resources from have to have-not communities. State officials also have wider revenue options, including taxes on income and retail sales. State income and sales taxes appear to be less upsetting politically and less vulnerable to economic downturns than do local property taxes. As a result, state officials can escape many of the constraints on policy that seem to originate in the economic sector and that limit the policy discretion of local government officials. Federal officials can also escape economic constraints, partly because of their ability to tax resources of wealthy areas throughout the country and partly because of their power to borrow to meet current deficits in the balance between taxing and spending. Indeed, the federal government operates numerous programs to control levels of employment, interest, and wages and may be as much the master as the subordinate of the economy. Moreover, not all local governments are equally influenced by the nature of local economies. Where the municipality has adopted "reformed" government structures there is less of an economic-policy link than where it has an unreformed structure. The principal features of a reformed local government structure are a professional city manager, nonpartisan elections for local offices, and a council selected at large rather than by wards. These features seem to depoliticize the social and economic cleavages within a community and to permit local officials to make their policy decisions with relatively little concern for the demands of different economic factions.[10]

There are also variations in economic influences on policy over time. There is some evidence that the influence of economic conditions on state and local government policies is diminishing. Alan K. Campbell and Seymour Sacks, for example, found a decreasing correlation (from .920 to .558) between state and local expenditures and income levels in 1903–1965.[11] Although the influence of economic elements still appears quite important, policy makers may now have greater independence from their economic environment. Some of this increased flexibility may reflect changes in federal aid. The federal government is able to tax multiple sources of wealth and to make up for some of the differentials between states. Also state and local governments now have somewhat more flexible tax structures than in the past.

Economic conditions exert less constraint on some kinds of policy than on others. The political salience of a policy is one of the factors that can lessen the influence of economics. To the extent that programs are the subject of prominent disputes among individual candidates and political parties, they can attract the use of substantially more resources than are normally associated with the jurisdiction's level of wealth. Officials try harder under the impetus of public demand. Under other conditions—when public demand runs counter to a program—performance is less than would be expected on the basis of economic conditions. There are also differences between policies supported by earmarked revenues and those that compete in each budget cycle for their share of general funds. Funds for highways and natural resources generally come from taxes or license fees specified for those purposes by state statutes or constitutions. Whatever each year's economic activity produces through those taxes and fees goes to those activities. Only occasionally does a legislature grant a change in such allotments or a special appropriation. In the case of most states' welfare and education programs, however, officials in the executive and legislative branches make funding decisions during each budget cycle. There is a much greater chance for political or program considerations to produce higher—or lower—education and welfare budgets than would be expected on the basis of economic indicators.[12]

Micro policy analysis: incrementalism and innovation

The range of microanalytic studies of urban politics and public policy is enormous—from studies of citizens' attitudes and voting behavior and the varieties of decisions made by city managers and council members to economic, anthropological, and sociological approaches to the study of policy impacts. In various chapters of this book we have reported findings from this work. Few studies have dealt with more than a few components of the urban political system. Most investigations of policy makers, for example, have not dealt with the impacts of the policy makers' decisions; and most studies of impacts have not considered the effects on policies of the economic and political environments in which they are made. Likewise, studies of one policy field (e.g., education) do not consider the similarities or implications of their findings for other policy fields (e.g., transportation or welfare).

The model of the urban political system does not fill in these gaps in our understanding. Yet by providing a common framework for assembling discrete analysis, it suggests a common set of questions for those who would pursue subsequent studies. As we assemble discrete information on the model we may perceive questions that remain unanswered for individual sectors of policy, and findings that appear inconsistent from one policy sector to another. Any sensitive reader of the earlier chapters has found issues that seem to be unexplored, and sometimes, even, inconsistent findings.

We saw earlier in macro-comparative policy-making studies the variable role that economic factors play in shaping public policy. But the variability of the economic-policy relationship does not mean that policy innovation comes easy. Micro-analytic studies of incremental decision making show another significant constraint upon policy change that may stifle innovation. Even in those areas where the economy seems to have little influence over policy making, officials may be bound tightly by the inhibitions of their own decision routines. Studies of national, state, and local budgeting illustrate the pervasiveness of incremental decision making.[13]

Incrementalism points to a feature of the policy-making process that is of primary importance: its conservatism, except under unusual circumstances that provoke rare departures from previous levels of activity. Ralph K. Huitt, commenting on the difficulty of innovation in an incremental system, has written:

> Paradoxically, it is politically attractive to tout a proposal as "new" so long as it is generally recognized that it is not new at all, but a variation on a familiar theme. . . .
>
> It follows that what is most feasible is what is incremental, what can be made to seem a comfortable next step under a program that has already received the good-conduct medal. Nothing is better than an amendment.[14]

Policy Analysis and the Urban Crisis

One source of incremental policy making lies in the information shortages of policy makers. The unavailability or high cost of information, both political and technical, encourages decision makers to rely upon incrementalism. Participation in urban politics is low, and what there is is filtered through input channels that may obscure interests, rather than clarify them. Elections are rarely effective in presenting clear alternatives to the voters, and their results are ambiguous guides to policy. Reformed institutions, including manager governments, nonpartisan elections, and constituencies at large may bring greater efficiency to municipal services, but they may also impede the identification of interests. In light of multiple interests and the limited economic and informational resources available to them, decision makers often take the incremental path of least resistance.

As we have said before, urban governments are short on technical information. Although civil engineering has progressed to remarkable levels, social engineering is still in its infancy and represents—to some —a disquieting idea in any case. Civil-engineering projects usually work. Bridges rarely collapse; highways seldom crumble. But we never know whether social engineering might have its intended impact. Numerous findings of weak correlations between spending levels and actual environmental change suggest the frustration of many policy goals. Comparative policy analysis helps explain why some city governments outspend others, but it has yet to enlighten us on the actual impacts of public policies on the resources of communities and individuals. Moynihan observed of the war on poverty that "the government did not know what it was doing," and we suspect that this observation is equally applicable to other policy areas.[15] The lack of technical knowledge about policy supports the concerted search for the determinants of policy outputs. It also emphasizes the need for greater knowledge of such dimensions of the policy process as performance, use, distribution, and impact.[16] The dearth of information both on human wants and needs and on the impacts of policy on them impedes responsible urban policy making. The blame for imperfect information must be shared alike by citizens, policy makers, and social scientists.

As academic social scientists, we concentrate on the need for more and better information. Yet the practicing policy maker cannot usually afford the luxury of reflection. The academic can decry the imperfect state of our knowledge, but the policy maker must face public pressures for action. Solutions to urban problems do not wait upon the final and tidy theories of the social scientist. Nevertheless, some academic techniques of policy analysis (both macro and micro) will aid the specific concerns of the policy maker. The perspectives of this book provide, we hope, a sense of realism about urban problems and about the range of permissible change.

A Personal Postscript

We wish we could end this book with a definitive statement about the urban future. In this volatile urban age, however, all predictions are hazardous.[17] Whether the urban system is in crisis may be open to debate, but it is irrefutable that the cities do face a massive array of problems. Many of these problems may be ultimately beyond the reach of public policy in a democracy. Some of them—crime, congestion, decay—may be inherent aspects of the urban condition and simply irremediable. Others—pollution, for example—are the almost inevitable by-products of the forces that produce urban wealth. In many cases, a solution to one problem will exacerbate another. The pollution of land, air, and water, for instance, cannot be solved without partially dismantling the economic system, which in turn would make the fight against poverty even more difficult. Moreover, some public policies may, as conservatives and radicals both argue, do more harm than good.

We part company with those conservatives, however, who believe that urban problems are absolutely unyielding to public policy. We also part company with those radicals who deny that real reform of urban government is possible and demand radical or revolutionary change. We believe that urban governments have massive human and economic resources that are available to policy makers in principle but inaccessible in fact, and we believe that this situation is exacerbated by severe service needs, prevailing philosophies of incrementalism rather than innovation, substitution of rhetoric for responsibility, and policies constructed upon fragmentary information.

Notes

1. A. James Reichley, "The Political Containment of the Cities," in Alan K. Campbell, ed., *The States and the Urban Crisis* (Englewood Cliffs, N.J.: Prentice-Hall, 1970), pp. 169–195.
2. Edward C. Banfield, *The Unheavenly City* (Boston: Little, Brown, 1970), pp. 3–4.
3. *Ibid.*, p. 11.
4. *Ibid.*, pp. 21–22.
5. See, for example, Michael Lipsky, *Protest in City Politics: Rent Strikes, Housing and the Power of the Poor* (Skokie, Ill.: Rand McNally, 1970); Graham T. Allison, "Conceptual Models and the Cuban Missile Crisis," *American Political Science Review, 63* (September 1969), 689–718; Yehezkel Dror, *Public Policymaking Reexamined* (San Francisco: Chandler, 1968); Charles E. Lindblom, *The Policy-Making Process* (Englewood Cliffs, N.J.: Prentice-Hall, 1968); Bruce M. Russett, "Who Pays for Defense?" *American Political Science Review, 63* (June 1969), 412–426; and W. Lee Hansen and Burton A. Weisbrod, *Benefits, Costs, and Finance of Public Higher Education* (Chicago: Markham, 1969).
6. Some representative pieces include Thomas R. Dye, *Politics, Economics and the Public: Policy Outcomes in the American States* (Skokie, Ill.: Rand McNally, 1966); Bryan Fry and Richard Winters, "The Politics of Redistribution," *American Political Science Review, 64* (June 1970), 508–522; Robert L. Lineberry and Edmund P. Fowler, "Reformism and Public Policies in American Cities." *American Political Science Review, 61* (September 1967), 701–716; Ira Sharkansky and Richard I. Hofferbert, "Dimensions of State Politics, Economics and Public Policy," *American Political Science Review, 63* (September 1969), 867–879; and Alan K. Campbell and Seymour Sacks, *Metropolitan America* (New York: Free Press, 1967).
7. Strictly speaking, it is inaccurate to say that current research identifies the *influence* of certain elements over policies or the changes that policies *cause* in their economic, social, or political surroundings. The closest approach to causation is the discovery of relations that are consistent with causal patterns. Starting with the hypothesis that element A brings about Policy B we can infer support for that hypothesis if we find element A and policy B typically associated in the same time and place. Of course, we must determine if the coexistence of A and B result from the common trait C. That is, we must "control" the relationship between A and B to discover if it is not simply a product of C. One hypothesis, for example, is that high levels of political participation bring about high levels of public service. If we find that cities with high citizen participation also have high levels of public service, we have superficial support for the hypothesis. But we must check other explanations of the findings. It may be that the general level of economic well-being influences both political participation and the availability of public services. We know that people who are wealthy and well educated show more than the average interest in politics, and we know that wealth has something to do with the resources necessary to support public services. The amount of economic wealth in a city may thus cause both its high (or low) levels

of political participation and public services. On the other hand, it is possible that the political cultures in certain cities lead their citizens to participate more (or less) actively than would be expected on the basis of wealth, or lead their government officials to greater (or lesser) levels or commitment in offering public services. At this point, it appears that participation has an "independent" relationship with certain kinds of state policies: those that are "politicized" and the subjects of intense public dispute. See Sharkansky and Hofferbert, *op. cit.*

8. See Dye, *Politics, Economics and the Public;* Glenn W. Fisher, "Interstate Variation in State and Local Government Expenditures," *National Tax Journal, 17* (March 1964), 57–73; and much of the literature cited there.

9. Ira Sharkansky, *The Politics of Taxing and Spending* (Indianapolis: Bobbs-Merrill, 1969), chaps. 4 and 5.

10. Lineberry and Fowler, *op. cit.*

11. Campbell and Sacks, p. 57.

12. Cnudde and McCrone, *op. cit.*; and Sharkansky and Hofferbert, *op. cit.*

13. Otto Davis, M. A. H. Dempster, and Aaron Wildavsky, "A Theory of the Budgetary Process," *American Political Science Review, 60* (September 1966), 529–547; John P. Crecine, *Government Problem Solving: A Computer Simulation of Municipal Budgeting* (Skokie, Ill.: Rand McNally, 1968); and Ira Sharkansky, *The Politics of Taxing and Spending* (Indianapolis: Bobbs-Merrill, 1969).

14. Ralph K. Huitt, "Political Feasibility," in Austin Ranney, ed., *Political Science and Public Policy* (Chicago: Markham, 1968), p. 274.

15. Daniel P. Moynihan, *Maximum Feasible Misunderstanding* (New York: Free Press, 1969), p. 170.

16. Ira Sharkansky, *Policy Analysis in Political Science* (Chicago: Markham, 1970), chaps. 4 and 6; and Edwin Olson, "Research in the Library Service Process," in Irene A. Braden and Alice S. Clark, eds., *Quantitative Methods in Librarianship: Standards, Research, Management* (Columbus: Ohio State University Press, 1970).

17. For some attempts, however, see the computerized futurism of Herman Kahn and Anthony Wiener, *Toward the Year 2000* (New York: Macmillan, 1967); and of Jay W. Forrester, *Urban Dynamics* (Cambridge, Mass.: M.I.T. Press, 1969); and D. Meadows et al., *The Limits to Growth* (New York: Universe, 1972).

Index